Praise for *The Complete Guide to Service Learning*

"*The Complete Guide to Service Learning* ... share ideas with our partner organizations and with anyone ... information, ideas, and practical suggestions, this g... ...ur youth are and what valuable contributors they can b... ... life."

—*Elaine Leibsohn, America's Promise Alliance*

"How can teachers begin or support a service learning program in their classroom or school? What role does [service learning] play in the curriculum? What are the true benefits to society and to students? . . . Kaye answers these questions and more. Fresh insights, practical guidelines, and useful resources make this book essential."

—*Curriculum Connections*

Praise for the previous edition:

"An informative book for those interested in creating or overseeing service-learning programs."

—*Youth Today*

"A wonderful step-by-step guide with handy tips and practical advice. An outstanding resource, a must-have."

—*Voice of Youth Advocates (VOYA)*

"A rich resource."

—*Library Media Connection*

"Cathryn Berger Kaye's energy, commitment, knowledge, and compassion are an inspiration. *The Complete Guide to Service Learning* captures all of these qualities, along with her practical advice and years of experience in educating the hearts and minds of the young. Putting these ideas into action in your classroom will forever change the lives of your students and just might help change the world."

—*James Howe, author of* Bunnicula *and* The Misfits

"Service learning expert Cathryn Berger Kaye writes a powerful guide to invigorate students, teachers, and youth leaders. The practical service learning strategies and diverse themes will awaken and engage even the most reluctant learners."

—*Denise Clark Pope, lecturer, Stanford University School of Education and author of* Doing School: How We Are Creating a Generation of Stressed-Out, Materialistic, and Miseducated Students

"*The Complete Guide to Service Learning* addresses civic and character education and service learning all in one work, at a time when renewing the civic mission of schools is becoming more urgent."

—*John Minkler, Ph.D., author of* Active Citizenship, Empowering America's Youth, *and* Teacher Tools for Civic Education and Service-Learning, *with Don Hill*

The Complete Guide to

Service Learning

Proven, Practical Ways to Engage Students in Civic Responsibility, Academic Curriculum, & Social Action

Revised & Updated Second Edition

Cathryn Berger Kaye, M.A.

free spirit
PUBLISHING®

Library of Congress Cataloging-in-Publication Data
Kaye, Cathryn Berger.
  The complete guide to service learning : proven, practical ways to engage students in civic responsibility, academic curriculum, & social action / Cathryn Berger Kaye. — Rev. & updated 2nd ed.
      p. cm.
  Includes bibliographical references and index.
  ISBN 978-1-57542-345-6
  1. Service learning—United States—Handbooks, manuals, etc. 2. Civics—Study and teaching—United States—Handbooks, manuals, etc. I. Title.
  LC220.5.K39 2010
  370.11'5—dc22

                                                                    2010000213

ISBN: 978-1-57542-345-6

Free Spirit Publishing does not have control over or assume responsibility for author or third-party websites and their content. At the time of this book's publication, all facts and figures cited within are the most current available. All telephone numbers, addresses, and website URLs are accurate and active; all publications, organizations, websites, and other resources exist as described in this book; and all have been verified as of May 2014. If you find an error or believe that a resource listed here is not as described, please contact Free Spirit Publishing. Parents, teachers, and other adults: We strongly urge you to monitor children's use of the Internet.

Service learning occurs in each of the fifty United States and internationally. Some project descriptions are attributed to specific schools or youth groups and identified by city, state, or region. All efforts have been made to ensure correct attribution. The names of the young people quoted throughout the book have been changed to protect their privacy.

Edited by Jennifer Brannen, Meg Bratsch, and Darsi Dreyer
Cover and interior design by Tasha Kenyon

15 14 13 12 11 10 9 8
Printed in the United States of America

Free Spirit Publishing Inc.
6325 Sandburg Road, Suite 100
Golden Valley, MN 55427-3674
(612) 338-2068
help4kids@freespirit.com
www.freespirit.com

Printed on recycled paper including 30% post-consumer waste

As a member of the Green Press Initiative, Free Spirit Publishing is committed to the three Rs: Reduce, Reuse, Recycle. Whenever possible, we print our books on recycled paper containing a minimum of 30% post-consumer waste. At Free Spirit it's our goal to nurture not only children, but nature too!

green press INITIATIVE

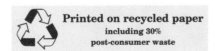

Free Spirit offers competitive pricing.
Contact edsales@freespirit.com for pricing information on multiple quantity purchases.

DEDICATION

With great admiration, to the students and teachers who bring service learning to life every day.
And to my mother who always believed I could.

ACKNOWLEDGMENTS

Just as it takes a village to raise a child, a community has contributed to this book. This has been a journey of commitment and passion influenced by many in the service learning world. The following people made exceptional contributions. Truly, I thank you with a full and grateful heart. With special gratitude to:

- the fantastic authors for their inspiring books and interviews; you are my "rock stars"!

- Joe Follman, Florida Learn & Serve, for his priceless response to my first edition manuscript and his generous contribution of the foreword

- Nan Peterson of The Blake School for encouragement, heartfelt messages, and reminders of why we care so deeply about youth and service learning

- Artemis Brod and Ariel Kaye who participated as research assistants

- Judy Galbraith for her vision and the Free Spirit Publishing staff for wholeheartedly embracing this enterprise, especially my editor Meg Bratsch for great insights

- and my family—my sisters Marsha Rueff and Betty Berger, who remain my cheerleaders, and my wonderful husband Barry and daughters Ariel and Devora for challenging my thinking, showing infinite patience, offering absolute support, and nurturing me daily with love

Many thanks to colleagues across the country who read and recommended some of the new titles added to the theme bookshelves: Julie Rogers Bascom, Betty Berger, Tracy Harkins, Anne Hill, Don Hill, Resa Nikol, Nan Peterson, Laura Rog, Fran Rudoff, Susan Sneller, Veray Wickham, and Artemis Brod (who fell in love with children's and young adult literature from reading so many books!).

Thanks to Toni Plummer and Betty Berger for their assistance with the Planning for Service Learning templates found in the chapters Healthy Lives, Healthy Choices, and Special Needs and Disabilities.

Several students, teachers, and service learning advocates contributed to the Recommendations from the Field book suggestions. Many thanks to the following for this valued contribution: Jill Addison-Jacobson, Betty Berger, Robert Bhaerman, Michael Blankenerg, Nelda Brown, Grace Coffey, David M. Donahue, Denise Dowell, Marty Duckenfield, Christopher Galyean, Carolina Goodman, Barbara Gruener, Don Hill, Ariel Kaye, Devora Kaye, Gail M. Kong, Nan Peterson, Terry Pickeral, Denise Clark Pope, Antoinette C. Rockwell, Omer Rosenblith, Susan Starkweather, Sarah Grimke Taylor, and Susan Vermeer.

I extend my gratitude for the Voices from the Field essays, which appear in full in the digital content. Thanks to contributors Susan Abravanel, Roser Batlle, Anne Thidemann French, Ada Grabowski, Mike Hurewitz, Ron Perry, Nan Peterson, Donna Ritter, Evelyn Robinson, and Jon Schmidt.

And finally, to all the students, educators, community groups, and colleagues too numerous to mention by name whose dedication to service learning excellence inspired the descriptions of service learning success stories in this book—many thanks.

Contents

PART THREE. A Culture of Service

List of Reproducibles

Digital Content

You may download these forms at www.freespirit.com/CG2SL-forms. Use the password 2serve.

Forms from the Book
See List of Reproducibles on page viii.

Bonus Materials (in digital content *only*)

Planning for Service Learning Examples

Elementary, AIDS Education and Awareness

Middle School, AIDS Education and Awareness

High School, AIDS Education and Awareness

Elementary, Animal Protection and Care

Middle School, Animal Protection and Care

High School, Animal Protection and Care

Elementary, Elders

Middle School, Elders

High School, Elders

Elementary, Emergency Readiness

Middle School, Emergency Readiness

High School, Emergency Readiness

Elementary, The Environment *(see Forms from the Book)*

Middle School, The Environment

High School, The Environment

Elementary, Gardening

Middle School, Gardening

High School, Gardening

Elementary; Healthy Lives, Healthy Choices

Middle School; Healthy Lives, Healthy Choices

High School; Healthy Lives, Healthy Choices

Elementary; Hunger, Homelessness, and Poverty

Middle School; Hunger, Homelessness, and Poverty

High School; Hunger, Homelessness, and Poverty

Elementary, Immigrants

Middle School, Immigrants *(see Forms from the Book)*

High School, Immigrants

Elementary, Literacy

Middle School, Literacy

High School, Literacy *(see Forms from the Book)*

Elementary, Safe and Strong Communities

Middle School, Safe and Strong Communities

High School, Safe and Strong Communities

Elementary, Social Change: Issues and Action

Middle School, Social Change: Issues and Action

High School, Social Change: Issues and Action

Elementary, Special Needs and Disabilities

Middle School, Special Needs and Disabilities *(see Forms from the Book)*

High School, Special Needs and Disabilities

Interviews with Authors: The Story Behind the Story

AIDS Education and Awareness
James Cross Giblin
Allan Stratton

Animal Protection and Care
Kathe Koja

Elders
Eve Bunting
Richard Michelson
Eileen Spinelli

Emergency Readiness
Danica Novgorodoff
Dana Reinhardt

The Environment
Laurie David
Don Madden

Gardening
Pat Brisson

Healthy Lives, Healthy Choices
Jordan Sonnenblick

Hunger, Homelessness, and Poverty
Lindsay Lee Johnson
Marion Hess Pomeranc

Immigrants
Francisco Jiménez
Tony Johnston

Literacy
Janet Tashjian
Jake Tashjian
Ann Whitehead Nagda

Safe and Strong Communities
Sharleen Collicott
Phillip Hoose
James Howe
Jerry Spinelli

Social Change: Issues and Action
Deborah Ellis
Sonia Levitin
Diana Cohn

Special Needs and Disabilities
Ellen Senisi
Cynthia Lord

Voices from the Field

(Note: Brief excerpts of these essays are included in the book)

Building the Sustainable Service Learning Partnership *by Susan A. Abravanel*

Creating a Culture of Service Through Collaboration *by Roser Batlle*

Creating and Supporting a Culture of Service Through Professional Development *by Anne Thidemann French*

District-Wide Implementation: Character and Service *by Ada Grabowski*

Getting Started in the Process of Creating a Culture of Service: Developing Service Learning in a Texas School District *by Mike Hurewitz*

A Local Service Learning Association *by Cathryn Berger Kaye and Donna Ritter*

The Legacy Project: From Student Voice Comes a Transformative Model *by Ron Perry*

Mission and Coordination: An Independent School Perspective *by Nan Peterson*

Youth Empowerment to Create a District-Wide Culture of Service *by Evelyn Robinson*

Urban Service learning *by Jon Schmidt*

Additional Bookshelf Titles

(Note: These lists include Recommendations from the Field.)

The AIDS Education and Awareness Bookshelf

The Animal Protection and Care Bookshelf

The Elders Bookshelf

The Environment Bookshelf

The Gardening Bookshelf

The Healthy Lives, Healthy Choices Bookshelf

The Hunger, Homelessness, and Poverty Bookshelf

The Immigrants Bookshelf

The Literacy Bookshelf

The Safe and Strong Communities Bookshelf

The Social Change: Issues and Action Bookshelf

The Special Needs and Disabilities Bookshelf

Foreword

In a world and in schools beset with challenges, service learning is increasingly recognized as an effective solution. How can this be? How can a mere teaching and learning strategy improve education and also address global issues like literacy, war, social justice, climate change, and poverty? The answer lies in what happens during effective service learning and in the impacts the cumulative experiences have on both those who are serving and those who are served.

In school- or community-based service learning, young people investigate issues and then design, implement, reflect on, and tell or teach others about how they have met real-world needs. They help younger children learn reading, math, or science; raise awareness about violence and teen pregnancy prevention; create community gardens to feed people who are homeless; capture important histories and voices that previously have not been heard; design and demonstrate ways to conserve energy; show communities how to prepare for and respond to disasters; and work with officials to improve their schools, towns, nations, and the world.

Through these diverse and meaningful experiences, young people apply knowledge, skills, and behaviors they need to learn, while designing and performing service projects. This confluence of learning and service is the defining characteristic of service learning and what distinguishes it from other types of giving. The secret about service learning is the reciprocity: it is designed to help the server as well as the served.

Research shows that well-designed service learning, in addition to addressing identified needs, results in positive academic, social, civic, and skill development for participating youth. Young people crave opportunities to make a difference. They leap at the chance to use what they are learning in classrooms in ways that help others, to get away from their desks and involved in their communities, to have their voices heard by adults, and to explore careers. They are more likely to come to school and learn when these opportunities are offered. The surprise is that more schools and youth-serving community organizations took so long to make this discovery!

You are a discoverer, and you are on to something big in finding this book, which can help you initiate, expand, or sustain youth service learning. When the first edition of Cathryn's *The Complete Guide to Service Learning* was published in 2004, it instantly became the go-to reference and guidebook in the field, embraced by practitioners across the country as well as internationally. With its clear definitions, examples, reproducible forms, easy-to-use planning suggestions, and ideas for focusing service learning on a wide range of topics and needs, the *Guide* became an indispensable tool. This second edition retains all those practical resources and adds many more. Integrating the new K–12 quality standards for the teaching of service learning, the updated *Guide* has been supplemented with new themes, scenarios, book titles, author interviews, reproducible forms, and ideas for encouraging global literacy and creating a culture of service.

Service learning has evolved far beyond the latest fad to come along in education and youth development. It is not merely one more "thing" that must be added to the countless other "things" educators must contend with. Rather, it is a marvelously flexible strategy for educators to better teach students about themselves and the world, while meeting existing academic objectives. Service learning can be and has been implemented as a teaching methodology in every subject and grade level and is equally effective outside the school context.

Cathryn Berger Kaye has been deeply engaged in all aspects of service learning as a teacher; a local, state, national, and international service learning program developer and advisor; and as one of the nation's leading service learning trainers. She helped shape how service learning is defined and paved the way in helping us recognize the essential roles that literature and demonstration play in effective projects.

The new *Guide* puts all the pieces together for you. This resource can give you what you need to take that first, second, or twentieth step in combining service with learning to help improve children, schools, communities, our nation, and our global society.

Joe Follman
Director, Florida Learn & Serve: A Project of the Florida Department of Education and Florida State University's Center for Leadership and Civic Education

A Word from the Author About This Second Edition

Have you noticed? We are experiencing a global groundswell of service. The issues we face as a planet have now risen to a level that calls more of us to action. Through service learning, we can engage our young people in learning about and addressing critical issues—climate change, population migration, hunger, loss of habitat, illiteracy, and more—while contributing to the betterment of themselves and others. Young people, who are cognizant of the issues and have the problem-solving abilities to address them, matter. Providing them with the skills and knowledge to do this vital work, in their own communities and the larger world, adds relevance to their education. That is why I originally wrote this book and why it's been updated, revised, and expanded.

The first edition reflected my experiences as an educator who spent years integrating service learning in my classroom and assisting others across the United States as a program designer and presenter on the subject. Over decades of working with students, teachers, principals, schools, youth groups, and community leaders, I have continued to develop and refine the practice of this pedagogy. Service learning improves the delivery of knowledge and skills to students, and involves so much more than merely tacking on projects to existing lesson plans. It is a preeminent blend of practical methods that inform, involve, inspire, and move young people to be true students, seekers of knowledge, and active participants in our society.

Teachers confirm that with service learning, their students go beyond required assignments, reveal hidden talents, apply themselves in ways that stretch their intellect, retain what they have learned, and transfer the skills and knowledge to new situations. With academic-rich service learning experiences, students are doing astounding work as they prepare our communities for emergencies, repair our coral reefs, protect animals, construct monuments to honor our veterans, and spend time with otherwise lonely elders.

The field of service learning has evolved since this book's original publication, and I've infused new ideas, new resources, and new possibilities into the second edition. What's new in this edition?

- The K–12 Service-Learning Standards for Quality Practice

- Discussion of the Five Stages of Service Learning and their importance in the service learning process

- Two additional thematic chapters that reflect current issues and describe how young people are responding: Emergency Readiness and Healthy Lives, Healthy Choices

- A chapter entitled Creating a Culture of Service, which provides ideas and resources to advance your service learning practice and increase its viability within your school, district, or organization

- New and updated forms, including Getting Ready for Personal Inventory, Gathering Information About a Community Need, Progress Monitoring, and Literature Circles

- Additional K–12 service learning scenarios for readers to draw upon and be inspired to action

- Updated Web resources for every thematic chapter

- Updated service learning resource listings

- New titles on every thematic bookshelf, including recently published books, to infuse literature and literacy into the service learning process

- New author interviews that demystify the writing process and inspire students to become writers

- Digital content packed with customizable forms, more recommended book listings, author interviews, and "Voices from the Field" essays from service learning professionals providing insights about advancing service learning (see pages 4–5 for more details)

Your engagement in high quality service learning prepares the young people you reach and teach to be the best students they can be, and to be valued contributors to our collective well-being, now and in the future. For all you do, I am most grateful.

Introduction

At a service learning workshop in the mid-1980s, I asked twelve teachers to think back to their earliest memories of service—of giving service, receiving service, or observing service. They willingly shared images of visiting retirement homes with a youth group, collecting money for UNICEF, working in a hospital as a high school student, and tutoring a young neighbor who was struggling with reading. One woman described living in a rural community with few financial resources. Still, her mother prepared food each week that her father loaded onto the back of their pickup to deliver to families whose needs were more urgent than their own. She described watching this and wondering, "Why are they giving away our food?" She paused, reflecting. Then she said, "Maybe that's why I take care of foster children. Maybe that's why I'm a teacher."

I have continued asking this question over the years and I continue to find a connection between people's early personal experiences and memories of service and their later choice to become teachers or otherwise work with children. Teachers—along with others who work in service professions—clearly have a natural affinity with service learning. Part of what draws us into this career is the opportunity to reach children and make a lasting—even profound—difference in their lives. Service learning provides deep and wondrous ways for this to happen.

My own experience with service learning began long before the term was commonly used. I was teaching in a very small school in rural Maine. One morning, a seventh-grade student brought in a newspaper article.

"That's my street," she announced, pointing at the photograph. "See that tree? It's two houses away."

"What's wrong with the tree?" another student asked her.

"Dutch elm disease."

None of us was familiar with the term, but by the end of the day, we had all learned quite a bit about this disease that threatened the magnificent elms in our neighborhoods. The students wanted to get involved. Before long, they were making phone calls to the state and local departments of agriculture and were directed to a science department at the local university. Within a week, they were trained in assessing elm trees. Clipboards in hand, they traveled from street to street diagnosing and reporting on the condition of each tree.

Suddenly, subjects came alive for our middle and high school students. The study of plant cells took on new meaning. In math classes, record-keeping methods, statistics, and percentages gained an importance they had not had before. Students described their excitement and frustrations in journals and stories with feedback from other students and teachers. As a culmination of their work, students submitted their findings to state agencies and made a summary presentation to a college class.

The students couldn't save every tree, of course, however they did help protect some of the majestic elms. Along the way, they learned and practiced scientific reporting methods, became aware of the roles of state officials, and developed partnerships with college students. Motivated by a sense of purpose, our students identified themselves as community activists and came to speak with ease about civic responsibility.

> You should know that the education of the heart is very important. This will distinguish you from others. Educating oneself is easy, but educating ourselves to help other human beings to help the community is much more difficult.
>
> —*César E. Chávez, social activist*

Since my first experience with service learning, I have worked as a classroom teacher, developed programs nationally and internationally, assisted with advancing service learning in teacher preparation and certification efforts, stood before all sizes of groups when presenting a conference keynote or interactive session, and served as a leader of educational workshops for districts and schools. *The Complete Guide to Service Learning* reflects my experiences both as an educator, who presents about service learning and develops and refines its concepts and practices, and as a student, who acquires new ideas from the people I meet.

The desire to incorporate service learning into education is growing exponentially across the globe. Teachers improve their delivery of knowledge and skills and become enlivened by the high level of student engagement that integrated service learning provides. Students make the essential connections that bring forth the best they have to offer and help them create meaningful, relevant experiences. Service learning is truly a win-win for all involved.

Why Is Service Learning Important?

You may approach service learning for many different valid reasons. Perhaps you're drawn to service learning based on experiences you had as a student or due to personal or community values. You may want to introduce service learning to your classroom or school after hearing about the many ways students become motivated and engaged by this hands-on teaching method. You may approach service learning to respond to specific community needs or concerns or to promote involvement with social justice issues. You may have seen the success of a colleague, heard an inspiring speaker, or read a news article that chronicled how kids took what they learned in a classroom and used their knowledge and skills for the benefit of others. Many educators see the direct link between service learning and civic responsibility, literacy, social and emotional development, and improved school culture and climate. Or perhaps you're responding to school or district requirements for incorporating service learning into curriculum and teaching methods, and you want to maximize the benefits for all involved. Regardless of which scenario seems most familiar to you, you'll likely find yourself asking—or answering—the question, "Why is service learning important?"

- Service learning provides meaningful ways for students, teachers, administrators, and community agencies and members to move together with deliberate thought and action toward a common purpose that has reciprocal benefits.

- Students benefit academically, socially, and emotionally; develop skills; explore numerous career options; and may come to appreciate the value of civic responsibility and actively participating in their community.

- Teachers make school and education more relevant for their students, often seeing students blossom and develop previously untapped strengths in the process; collaborate with their colleagues and community partners to develop exciting curriculum; and may find themselves professionally reenergized.

- School administrators may observe a boost in staff and student morale as desired academic outcomes are achieved, and the school's profile is raised in the community.

- Parents find new avenues for conversation with their children, and may help support service learning within the school and create family service experiences.

- Community partners receive much needed help and may find themselves learning from the students as they teach or interact with them.

An entire community benefits by encouraging and supporting its students' thoughtful civic involvement and participation. Young people are acknowledged and see themselves as resourceful, knowledgeable, agents of change who can harness their curiosity, creativity, ideas, energy, and enthusiasm to benefit us all.

The beauty of service learning is that something real and concrete occurs. Learning takes on new and multiple dimensions. When students engage intellectually and emotionally with a topic, they can light up with a revelation or connect two previously separate ideas. What they've learned in school suddenly matters and engages their minds and hearts. Teachers also frequently respond enthusiastically to service learning, finding their students' eagerness and curiosity invigorating. Education becomes relevant, as classroom extends to the larger community. Math, science, social studies, languages, literature, the arts, technology—all are applied, used, and placed in contexts where they really matter.

In addition to the educational benefits, our society depends on active participation of its members to thrive. Our acts of service can shape the society we live in. Even young children marvel at how their thinking and planning and doing makes a difference. Service learning enables a wealth of small and large "differences" to happen. Relationships develop between people with an attendant understanding and appreciation for similarities and differences. Eyes become accustomed to looking for needs in the community and recognizing opportunities for change.

Even though service learning is exciting for teachers as well as students, you may feel daunted by the idea of integrating service learning into an increasingly complicated curricular mix. If so, you're not alone. Often teachers arrive at one of my service learning workshops tired and frustrated by the newest set of mandates to arrive on their desks. Then, as they hear of their colleagues in schools across the country who try service learning and use it again and again, something happens. They see the real possibilities to meet academic standards, improve literacy, increase test scores, and enjoy their profession while they enhance and strengthen their ability as educators.

The Research Is In!

Fortunately for the ever-expanding world of service learning, education researchers are actively exploring how service learning improves education for students and identifying the factors that are most compelling for successful projects and experiences. The Resources section of this book on pages 257–259 includes organizations that are portals for updates on research as service learning continues to thrive around the world.

About This Book

This book is designed to help you successfully use service learning in your classroom, youth group, or teacher education program. You will find ways to sow the seeds for a culture of service learning in your school, district, or community, or plan to initiate professional learning conversations. You will find ideas and strategies to build a strong service learning foundation, advance a well-honed practice, and be positioned as a service learning leader, as well as practical ways to implement service learning with children of all ages. Thematic chapters cover a wide variety of contemporary issues that serve as jumping-off points for service learning. Some thematic ideas are likely familiar, others less so. All of the issues are important and the concepts and suggestions have been used in schools throughout the United States and the world.

How to Use This Book

This guide has three main parts, and it's designed to be used in a specific order. Part One addresses the various elements of service learning, how to get started, and the different ways to use the theme chapters. Part Two is a series of thematic chapters. By reading Part One before moving on to the theme chapters, you will be prepared to apply the principles of service learning. Part Three is about advancing a culture of service within your school, district, or organization; read this chapter when you are ready to expand and grow service learning.

- **Part One: The Service Learning Handbook,** includes three chapters that provide definitions and background information on service learning and describe the necessary components for successful implementation. Chapter 1 discusses the nature of service learning in detail. Chapter 2 gives you a blueprint for how to begin using service learning in your classroom and includes discussion and thumbnails of many reproducible documents and forms to adapt and use as you engage in service learning experiences or share ideas with peers. Keep in mind that the digital content includes all of these forms and more, so you can download them and complete them on your computer. Chapter 3 explains how to use the theme chapters and the service learning bookshelf—annotated bibliographies—included in each theme chapter.

- **Part Two: Service Learning Themes,** is made up of thirteen thematic chapters that will give you ideas for specific areas for action, including themes such as Protecting and Caring for Animals; Safe and Strong Communities; Poverty, Hunger, and Homelessness; Healthy Lives, Healthy Choices; and Special Needs and Disabilities. Each thematic chapter includes preparation activities, a curriculum web to help you make cross-curricular connections, theme-specific resources, examples of actual service learning scenarios, and an extensive bookshelf of nonfiction, picture books, and fiction. Each thematic bookshelf is divided into topics; for example, the topics in the Environment chapter bookshelf are "Learning from History," "Overview of the Environment," "Natural Resources," "Recycling," "Appreciation," and "Activism." Nonfiction and fiction titles are identified by grade level. Books are also cross-referenced where they are applicable to more than one thematic chapter, as noted on an easy-to-reference chart. Every book title is annotated. Author interviews for select titles are included in the companion digital content.

- **Part Three: A Culture of Service,** includes ideas and strategies developed from my years of working within the service learning field and with a community of practitioners. This chapter includes supportive theories, strategies for meeting priorities of schools and districts, and ways to share service learning through professional development and in-service workshops. Suggestions for conversations can also be helpful as you bring other stakeholders into the process. Also included are excerpts of essays contributed by people working "on the ground" to promote service learning; the complete "Voices from the Field" essays are found in the companion digital content.

The book concludes with An Author's Reflection and a general resource list to help you further explore service learning.

About the Bookshelf: The Important Link Between Service Learning and Literature

Books and reading are the basis of all literacy and learning, and I have found they are also essential to the service learning process. Over the years, I have read and gathered many outstanding and memorable books—fiction and nonfiction—that have an authentic connection with service learning themes. A well-chosen book can become the linchpin for an entire

service learning experience or unit, introducing students to relevant issues as they start working on their ideas and plans. Compelling books can keep them thinking about the implications of their endeavors and provoke them to reflection throughout. Both teachers and students gravitate toward a well-told story.

When I travel to lead service learning workshops, books pour out of my suitcases. These traveling companions enliven service learning keynotes and presentations as educators see the relevance and connections between the books, their students, and service that meets genuine community needs. I have included hundreds of my favorite books in the service learning bookshelf sections in the theme chapters of this book. Additional book titles can be found in the companion digital content.

About the Digital Content

The companion digital content to this second edition of *The Complete Guide to Service Learning* has abundant resources well worth exploring. The content can be downloaded at www.freespirit.com/CG2SL-forms. Use the password 2serve. Check out these highlights:

- **Customizable Forms.** All the forms discussed in the book can be filled in on the computer or edited and then saved to use again. This makes it possible to compile a database of completed planning templates and community contacts, and to adapt materials for specific audiences.

- **Planning Templates.** In chapter 2 on page 48, you will find a thumbnail of the Planning for Service Learning template. In the digital content, you will find thirty-nine completed examples—an elementary, middle, and high school example for each of the thirteen theme chapters in the book. These examples provide a guide for new and experienced teachers to make curricular connections, verify community needs, and follow the five stages of service learning.

- **Blank Curriculum Template.** Every thematic chapter has an Across the Curriculum web that models how service learning can deeply connect to and enhance learning objectives in all content areas. A blank curricular web is included in the digital content, which is especially helpful in workshops (see page 249 in Creating a Culture of Service).

- **Additional Book Titles.** As you read the thirteen thematic chapters, you will find a theme-specific bookshelf in each. In the digital content you will find additional titles, including newly published books, old favorites, and books that may be out of print but still worth finding. You will also find the complete "Recommendation from the Field" books and service learning experiences.

- **Author Interviews.** As noted at the end of every thematic chapter, author interviews are included in the digital content. This edition contains eleven wonderful new interviews, plus updates and additions to the previous ones. Altogether, there are twenty-eight interviews, or "stories behind the stories," for you to enjoy and share with your students and other teachers.

Printing a Copy of the Digital Content

To get the most out of the extensive rich material in the digital content, you may choose to print all the PDFs on three-hole-punched paper and add them to a binder with divider pages. In this way the digital content becomes a valuable resource on its own and an indispensable companion to *The Complete Guide to Service Learning*. Do you know a teacher looking for an elementary school service example involving healthy living, a middle school example of interacting with elders, or a high school example of emergency readiness? If so, you have dozens of Planning for Service Learning examples at your fingertips to share. Would you like to send the James Howe author interview to a colleague? Look in the binder. Are you leading a staff development session on curriculum connections? The blank Across the Curriculum template will be easy to find. Expect your digital content binder to be well used, just like this book!

- **Voices from the Field Essays.** Thanks to the growing field of service learning, the knowledge contained in this book includes additional advice contributed by current field leaders. Each essay is briefly excerpted in chapter 17; the full essays are included in the digital content.

Is Service Learning for You?

If you're a teacher, teacher in training, youth worker, group leader, counselor, principal, administrator, or parent who wants to help kids be more engaged and effective learners and take responsibility in their communities, *The Complete Guide to Service Learning* is for you. While this book primarily addresses service learning within a kindergarten through twelfth-grade school setting, service learning also thrives in many colleges and universities. Community organizations, youth groups, and after-school programs also use service learning to enrich their programs. Wherever young people's academic achievement and personal growth is the desired outcome, service learning is increasingly becoming the answer.

Above all, the purpose of this book is to encourage the practice of service learning—to offer a variety of ways you can integrate the service learning methodology of high youth engagement into different curricula so more young people will reap the benefits. Improving how we deliver academic knowledge and skills, while instilling the concept of civic responsibility and enriching educational opportunities for young people of all ages as they become engaged in social action is a gift to your students, your community, and yourself.

In reading this book, you will find that my commitment to service learning is deep. I am part of a dynamic group of countless educators, community members, writers, social activists, artists, and young people of every age who believe we are change agents who can repair, improve, and save this world—I stand with those who believe this is perhaps the finest work to be done. Welcome to the group!

—*Cathryn Berger Kaye*

Part One

The Service Learning Handbook

Chapter 1

What Is Service Learning?

Simply put, service learning connects school-based curriculum with the inherent caring and concern young people have for their world—whether on their school campus, at a local food bank, or in a distant rain forest. The results are memorable, lifelong lessons for students and foster a stronger society for us all.

This is what service learning can look like:

- A teacher reads *Before You Were Mine* aloud to her first graders to prepare for a field trip to the local animal humane society. The trip is a central part of their studies about "our community." After discussing the need to care for pets responsibly, the first graders decide to write and illustrate a booklet called "Taking Care of Your Pet" to hand out to students at their school and a nearby preschool.

- On a visit to a local elementary school, high school students demonstrate garden tool safety and soil preparation as they act out *The Ugly Vegetables* for second graders. During the next visit, the older and younger students work together to plant vegetables in a community garden, using math skills to measure and place the seeds appropriately. Follow-up visits include tending the garden and reading *How Groundhog's Garden Grew*. The students collaboratively design and paint a garden mural to keep the plants "blooming" year-round. The harvested food is gratefully received by a local food pantry.

- Before students from a middle school English class tutor first through third graders in literacy skills, they read *Thank You, Mr. Falker*. Using the book as a springboard, the class discusses the feelings young children may have when they don't read as well as their peers. The students write personal stories in their journals before and following tutoring sessions.

- In a civics class, students read *The Curse of Akkad: Climate Upheavals That Rocked Human History* as they develop a proposal for their school district to reduce the carbon footprint and save much needed dollars. They discuss how populations across the globe are being displaced, the interconnection of our societies, and how being informed creates opportunity for constructive social change. Their resulting proposal to the school board is accepted.

- As part of a school-wide program to eliminate bullying and name-calling, all elementary classes read *Toestomper and the Caterpillars, The Bully Blockers Club,* or *The Misfits.* After various learning activities, students develop peacemaking strategies to create a safe school environment for everyone as part of National No Name-Calling Week.

- A teen youth group decides to learn ballroom dancing and recruits several experienced dancers, men and women who attend a nearby senior activity center. After mastering the basics of the fox trot, waltz, and east coast swing, the young dancers meet with the senior center staff and discuss ways to show their appreciation and gratitude for the lessons. The group plan and host a "Senior Senior Prom" attended by over sixty dancing seniors.

NOTE: Annotated descriptions of all books listed can be found in subsequent theme chapters.

This chapter is designed to give you an overview of service learning from common terms to the criteria that ensure success. An FAQ section will answer key questions to help you get started. You'll be introduced to the process that constitutes the foundation of all service learning activities and how you can maximize student success. You may find that questions in this chapter and their answers help you reflect on what service learning means to you and what forms it can take for the young people you work with. For example, you may find yourself considering the meaning of community and how it will need to be defined to best serve your ideas. Or you might think about what forms of service will be most appealing or effective in your classroom. Of all of these questions, perhaps the most fundamental is: "What exactly is service learning?"

A Definition of Service Learning

Service learning can be defined in part by what it does for your students. When service learning is used in a structured way that connects classroom content, literature, and skills to community needs, students will:

- apply academic, social, and personal skills to improve the community.

- make decisions that have real, not hypothetical, results.

- grow as individuals, gain respect for peers, and increase civic participation.

- experience success no matter what their ability level.

- gain a deeper understanding of themselves, their community, and society.

- develop as leaders who take initiative, solve problems, work as a team, and demonstrate their abilities while and through helping others.

These important and documented academic and social results have helped validate service learning as a valuable, respected, and widely recognized teaching method. They may be why you're using service learning already or looking for ways to introduce it into your classroom, program, or youth group.

Wherever you plan on using service learning, you're going to need a solid definition to guide you in your specific situation. Rather than starting from scratch to create your own definition, you may want or need to tailor a general definition of service learning to reflect the specific needs of your students, curriculum, and community. While the essential structure and process of service learning stays the same, the resulting activities take a great variety of forms. In a school context and in other learning situations, *service learning* **can be defined as a research-based teaching method where guided or classroom learning is applied through action that addresses an authentic community need in a process that allows for youth initiative and provides structured time for reflection on the service experience and demonstration of acquired skills and knowledge.** This definition also works in nontraditional, less formal educational environments such as after-school programs and youth groups. In these settings, staff find meaningful opportunities to infuse the experience of helping in the community with an acknowledgment of what is also being learned.

Before You Start: Frequently Asked Questions

Defining service learning is only the beginning and often leads to other important questions that need to be answered before you can start using or refining service learning. These are some common questions that are asked during my workshops.

Q: How is service learning different from community service or volunteer work?

Service learning differs from other forms of community service or volunteer work because the education of students and young people is always at its core. Students actively participate in the process of understanding, integrating, and applying knowledge from various subject areas as they work to improve their communities. The question "Why am I learning this?" disappears as students help older people, register voters, or work to restore a fragile ecosystem and see what they've learned in action.

Q: Can service learning be used with everyone? Or is it only for older kids? Or gifted kids?

Service learning works with kindergartners and college students as well as every grade in between. Students of all ages and most ability levels can participate successfully, and almost every subject or skill can be enhanced through the practice of service learning. Because service learning can be applied to almost every subject area, this naturally encourages cross-curricular integration, which can help students grow, retain what they have learned, and improve in several areas simultaneously.

Q: How can I interest my students in service learning?

An important aspect of service learning is student participation in the entire process, beginning with identifying the need, researching the underlying issue, and contributing to plans. When students have a voice in choosing and designing a service experience, they are intrinsically more vested emotionally and intellectually. Since the process of service learning often utilizes student strengths and talents that may be less apparent in day-to-day lessons, service learning can motivate students to impressive accomplishments both in and out of the classroom. From primary grades through high school, teachers use this method to do more than meet educational needs and fulfill academic standards. Service learning infuses relevance, purpose, and meaning into whatever content is being taught. Students experience enthusiasm for learning as they build on personal and collective skills and talents, while applying their abilities to the common good.

Real learning gets to the heart of what it means to be human. Through learning we re-create ourselves. Through learning we become able to do something we never were able to do. Through learning we re-perceive the world and our relationship to it. Through learning we extend our capacity to create, to be part of the generative process of life. There is within each of us a deep hunger for this type of learning.

—Peter M. Senge, educator and author

Q: Does service learning mean more work for me?

Initially, as you're learning to use service learning as a teaching method and finding ways to integrate more engaging and youth-driven ideas into your curriculum, you may find that it takes more time than a typical lesson. However, teachers agree that as they become more adept and confident with the practice, curricular connections and possibilities for worthwhile experiences and community partnerships appear much more easily. More than likely, you'll also find your own levels of engagement and enthusiasm reflect that of the young people you work with and guide through service learning. The academic results and accomplishments in the community well reward the effort for everyone involved.

Q: Service learning means reaching out to the community. What is community? How do I define it?

Any discussion of service learning is going to include many references to community. Service learning helps students build and improve community, yet sometimes the who or what of community is unclear. *Community*

can have different meanings in service learning that are influenced by geography, culture, situation, and need, so its definition often depends on the nature of the service learning activity or who's doing the defining.

For some schools, service learning activities may be working toward improving interpersonal relationships or safety on the school campus, establishing cross-age tutoring programs, or beautifying the grounds. *Community* in this case may be defined as the school campus and population, which includes the immediate surrounding area, parents, and any outside agencies assisting with the issues being addressed.

Other schools extend their communities geographically and socially to include the surrounding neighborhood, city, or region. Some communities are international in nature, even if students never leave the school grounds. Examples of off-site locations for service learning include: a local watershed to help with plant restoration, a refugee center where students assist with child care during adult English language classes, or a radio station where students record public service announcements. In these situations, *community* usually includes agency partners.

Whatever is included in your definition of *community*, students engaging in service learning will come to know that community develops and builds through interaction, reciprocal relationships, and knowledge of people, places, organizations, governments, and systems. Through service learning, the often elusive idea of "community" takes shape and has a more tangible meaning for all involved. Recognizing and becoming active in a community builds a true foundation for civic responsibility that lasts well beyond school years.

Q: I understand what service learning means, but what does service mean?

In the context of service learning, "service" is the implementation of a plan, designed or influenced by students, that combines classroom learning with meeting an authentic community need. In some cases, the need is apparent and even urgent—for example, when elementary students rescue duck eggs from a rice field just prior to harvest. In other cases, the students may be supplementing or supporting a larger community effort—for example, by taking dictation of letters for elders in a residential facility or mapping an emergency evacuation route for a rural area. In all cases, service is meant to evoke the spirit of caring in those involved as well as provide a constructive context for their knowledge.

Q: Are there different kinds or categories of service?
Service can take many forms. Usually, though, the "service" in service learning can be classified as direct service, indirect service, advocacy, or research.

- *Direct Service:* Students' service directly affects and involves the recipients. The interactions are person-to-person and face-to-face, such as tutoring younger children or working with refugees. Students engaged in direct service learn about caring for others who are different in age or experience, develop problem-solving skills by following a sequence from beginning to end, and see the "big picture" of a social justice issue. Interacting with animals is also included in direct service, as is on-site environmental work, such as restoring a wetland area or constructing park benches.

- *Indirect Service:* With indirect activities students do not see the recipients, however, their actions benefit the community or environment as a whole. Examples can include stocking a food pantry, donating picture books to a preschool literacy program, collecting clothing for families living in a shelter, or creating a newsletter for a retirement community. Students engaging in indirect service learn about cooperation, working as a team, taking on different roles, organizing, and prioritizing. They also gain specific skills and knowledge that relate to academic content reinforced through application.

- *Advocacy:* The intent of advocacy is to create awareness of or promote action on an issue of public interest. Central to the word is *voc*, which is Latin for *voice*. Through advocacy students provide a voice for an issue, particularly when members of a population may not be able to speak for themselves. Related activities include writing letters, sponsoring a town meeting, performing a play, public speaking. Student advocates learn about perseverance and understanding rules, systems, and processes. They also experience civic engagement and working with adults.

- *Research:* Research activities involve students finding, gathering, and reporting on information in the public interest. For example, students may develop surveys or conduct formal studies, evaluations, experiments, or interviews. They may test water or soil, check the speed of cars passing by their school, or conduct environmental surveys. The students in the Introduction who surveyed local elms for Dutch elm disease are a good example of this kind of service. By participating in research-based service learning, students learn how to gather information, make discriminating judgments, and work systematically. This leads to enhanced skills in organization, assessment, and evaluation.

> We need your service, right now, at this moment in history. I'm not going to tell you what your role should be; that's for you to discover. But I am asking you to stand up and play your part. I am asking you to help change history's course.
>
> —*President Barack Obama, upon signing the Edward M. Kennedy Serve America Act, 2009*

Q: Is one type of service learning better than another?
Each of the service categories offers unique benefits to the community and to the students. When the underlying causes and effects of an issue are investigated and understood, all types of service can provoke questions that continue to engage students in study and learning. Students involved in service continually apply and develop their knowledge in ways that meet and enrich the academic curriculum.

That said, a caution is worth noting related to indirect service. If students who have the ability to experience all four forms of service only have indirect opportunities, a subtle message may be communicated: that we can keep issues and problems distant or at arm's length. Research confirms, particularly with high school students, that direct service and advocacy have the greatest long-term impact on knowledge gained and personal value recognized. Also, younger children are developmentally prone to learning best with concrete involvement.

Q: *What do I do if I've been assigned to coordinate service learning for my grade/school/organization?*

Celebrate! Having a coordinator is advantageous in many ways, particularly since this person (you) can lead the faculty or staff in becoming better informed about service learning through professional development opportunities. You can keep service learning prominent in the minds of administrators and teachers. A coordinator usually provides encouragement, resources, and collegial conversations that support the ongoing efforts of teachers, both new to and experienced with service learning.

This book can be your guidebook in this endeavor. It is designed with numerous activities that can be used to teach the service learning pedagogy in short and long interactive presentations. The questions and responses can be a starting point for ongoing conversations. The blueprint and forms in chapter 2 and chapter 3 provide tools so teachers can more easily concentrate on student engagement, and the process of service learning and youth leadership—the heart of service learning—can be developed. Curricular maps, service learning scenarios, and annotated bibliographies within the thematic chapters all give you, the coordinator, what you need at your fingertips. Part Three, has numerous ideas and suggestions for coordinators (page 238). Additionally, a Resource section offers additional ways to connect with and participate in the growing international service learning community (page 257).

Q: *Does service learning develop youth leadership?*

Absolutely. A well-designed service learning experience affords ample opportunities for students to consider their own ideas and those of others, think critically about what occurs, anticipate possible outcomes, adjust plans, articulate their intentions in both written and verbal forms, and assess the outcomes of their endeavors—all essential leadership skills. Every form of communication is enhanced in the process: listening, speaking, writing, and calculating, as well as using symbolism, body language, and interpretation. Through a series of service learning experiences, the transferable nature of this skill development becomes apparent, and students accumulate expertise. Leadership competencies surface, as well as areas for further improvement and strengthening. At all times,

it is the role of the teacher or adult facilitator to note the areas where students need to develop, and to provide that development. Do students need to learn interviewing skills? Are students prepared to analyze a survey that they are soon to complete? Who in the community can assist youth to prepare a press release or to contact a school board representative or legislator? Service learning is truly leadership in action.

Q: *Does involvement in service learning help students stay in school?*

Research confirms that when asked, a majority of students identified as "dropouts" stated that they would have stayed in school if their classes included the process of service learning or pedagogies like service learning. This makes sense. As students experience the relevance of the learning process, take on roles and responsibilities that contribute to successful collective outcomes, and are depended upon by others, they tend to want to participate. They stay engaged and involved in learning. When the process is further enhanced by students' ability to use their inherent and developing skills and talents, the formula for success is strengthened. Service learning fosters engaging teaching practices, and engagement is how students learn best.

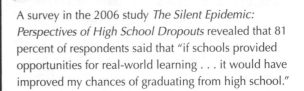

A survey in the 2006 study *The Silent Epidemic: Perspectives of High School Dropouts* revealed that 81 percent of respondents said that "if schools provided opportunities for real-world learning . . . it would have improved my chances of graduating from high school."

Truly engaged learning utilizes analytical thinking, creative thinking, and practical thinking. In his article, "What Is an 'Expert Student'?,"* psychologist Robert Sternberg describes these three components to achieving "successful intelligence": analytical thinking, creative thinking, and practical thinking. Consider how much class time focuses on analytical thinking alone. Adding the creative thinking component draws upon students' talents and skills, while expanding their base

* R. J. Sternberg, "What Is an 'Expert Student'?" *Educational Researcher* Vol. 32, No. 8 (2003): 5–9.

of knowledge. Creativity broadens analytical skills by adding new perspectives and "out of the box" cognitive processes. Practical thinking answers the question, "Why am I learning this?", which illuminates purpose. Practical thinking is also the key to integrating the analytical and the creative, spurring the learner to apply his or her knowledge in fresh or new ways.

A pitcher cries for water to carry
And a person for work that is real.

—*Marge Piercy, from* To Be of Use

Sternberg continues that we can elevate the intent of education by teaching children "not only to think well, but also wisely." Can we move students toward wisdom? As defined by Sternberg, "Wisdom, the opposite of foolishness, is the use of successful intelligence and experience toward the attainment of a common good." What a great encapsulation of what service learning can be!

Q: Can service learning inform students of possible careers?

Students can learn about countless careers through service learning, which adds an exciting dimension for our young people that could otherwise be missed. Most service learning experiences introduce students to community members from varied backgrounds who work in government, business, and nonprofit agencies. Here are some examples: A news reporter meets with students as they prepare to work in a food pantry and explains how the press covers the issue of homelessness. Students who provide tutoring for children with special needs are introduced to careers in speech and art therapy. While building a home with Habitat for Humanity, students work alongside skilled professionals installing plumbing and electricity. Every service learning experience can also connect students with government agencies and expose a range of opportunities for public service, including working with an environmental or agricultural agency or developing policy that protects our aging community.

I've had the great fortune to assist kids in developing leadership skills and exploring career goals through service learning experiences. As one high school participant approached graduation, I asked what he planned to study in college. James responded, "Business." I admit I felt a twinge of disappointment, because I believed he could make such a meaningful contribution to the world of social services. Then he enlightened me by adding, "What's really great is that I've seen directly how many nonprofit organizations lack the ability to create good business plans. As a professional I will be able to contribute my time and help them." What a pursuit! We need service-minded youth approaching every profession to continue contributing their breadth of skills and knowledge to our communities. Service learning connects students with a future rich in meaningful work and civic involvement.

What Makes Service Learning Successful?

To maximize the value and benefits of the service learning process, understanding the K–12 Service-Learning Standards for Quality Practice makes all the difference. Any outstanding recipe calls for the finest ingredients. As you feed and nurture the service learning process with these standards, students are better able to reap the rewards of the experience. Is each standard always a part of a service learning design? Ideally, yes. Research has verified that when all of these elements are present as the base criteria for service learning, the likelihood for significant impact on the students is greater.[*] However, service learning is a process, and every activity and experience is unique. So depending on the particular design and what approach you take, some of these standards may be more evident than others. Still, the more familiar you, your students, and your community partners become with service learning strategies, the more likely that all of these standards will be seamlessly integrated into the process. Keep in mind that the responsibility for infusing these standards in an activity rests primarily on the teachers or other adults, while students focus on progressing through the stages of service learning.

---

[*] S. H. Billig. "Does Quality Really Matter? Testing the New K–12 Service-Learning Standards for Quality Practice." In B. E. Moely, S. H. Billig, and B. A. Holland (Eds.), *Advances in Service-Learning: Vol. 9. Creating Our Identities in Service-Learning and Community Engagement* (pp. 131–157). Charlotte, NC: Information Age, 2009.

K–12 Service-Learning Standards for Quality Practice*

What are the elements that ensure a successful service learning experience? (See form on page 47.)

1. Meaningful Service. Service learning actively engages students in significant and personally relevant service activities. Students identify, investigate, learn about, and articulate a genuine, recognized community need. This need is often verified through the media, surveys, observation, or interviews with informed community partners. With well thought-out plans, students can see their actions having verifiable consequences as they learn and apply academic skills and knowledge. When a service experience has meaning and students see the purpose, engagement and action are sure to follow.

2. Link to Curriculum. When service learning is employed as a teaching method to meet designated content and skills, academics come alive. Knowledge is applied with transparency, allowing students to make explicit connections between subject matter and application within the context of community. This stimulates an intrinsic desire in students to learn the content and skills needed to be effective. While the subject matter and social context may change, the skills learned and practiced by students are transferable. Ideally, the learning and the service weave together and reinforce each other, with the service informing the curriculum and the curriculum informing the service.

3. Reflection. Through service learning, students participate in systemic processes that integrate cognitive thinking—related to social issues and their lives—with empathetic response. This blend of affective and cognitive thought deepens the service learning as students apply and transfer new understandings of themselves, others, and the world around them. If we want to cultivate deep thinkers—young people who are able to personalize what they learn and see, take on a challenge with consideration of self and others, and recognize the need to hit the pause button on a regular basis in this fast-paced world—then reflection is

essential. While all of the standards have importance, "reflection" is a word oft repeated in this book. Many examples of approaches and prompts to reflection are included to show that it is an imperative in all education methods today.

4. Diversity. Imagine all the possible ways service learning can expose young people to the concept of diversity. Whether it involves interfacing with a community partner, an elder in a retirement community, a veteran just returning from war, a recent immigrant, or a government official, participation in service learning provides exposure to a range of backgrounds, perspectives, and ways of thinking and solving problems. Rather than examine the human condition from a textbook, students learn the way they learn best: through experience, which replaces stereotypes with accurate information, opens the mind, and creates memorable events. The term *diversity* takes on a deeper meaning and relevance. Social and cultural boundaries lessen as relationships resonate with mutual respect.

5. Youth Voice. Young people need ample opportunities to express their ideas and opinions, and to make constructive choices and see the results. Service learning enables students to take initiative, make decisions, interact with community representatives, learn about the role of government in social issues, develop critical-thinking skills, put their ideas into action, and assess and evaluate what happened. Students meet significant age-appropriate challenges with tasks that require thinking, initiative, problem solving, and responsibility in an environment safe enough for them to make mistakes and to succeed. Responsibility means being "response-able," or "able to respond" to local and global issues that matter; responsibility is what develops an active populace. When young people recognize their vital role in improving society, working for social justice, and caring for the environment, then they truly understand the concept of democracy. These abilities, when strengthened through repeated service learning experiences, amount to youth leadership. Students recognize how participation and the ability to respond to authentic needs improves the quality of life in the community, which may lead to a lifelong ethic of service and civic participation.

---

* From the K–12 Service-Learning Standards for Quality Practice, National Youth Leadership Council, www.nylc.org.

6. Partnerships. Students participate in the development of partnerships and share responsibility with community members, parents, and other students, as well as with people from organizations, business, and government. These relationships give students opportunities to interact with people of diverse backgrounds in diverse settings. Through these dynamics, students and community members learn about each other and gain mutual respect, understanding, and appreciation. There is an exchange of information, ideas, and skills among all participants in the service learning experience. Reciprocity exists when each person sees the other as having something to share, when roles and responsibilities stay clarified, and when a shared vision moves the group forward.

7. Progress Monitoring. "Did our service learning matter? Did we make a difference?" Even the best service learning intentions can fall flat or require a makeover. Since the service learning experience typically takes place in a youth group or classroom, which are laboratories for learning and efficacy, if something goes awry benefits may still occur. For example, students can learn about the need for perseverance, or find a better strategy to turn a good idea into a city policy. And of course some service learning outcomes appear to be stellar; in fact, everyone may agree. In both circumstances, how are the students to know for certain this outcome? With progress monitoring, students set a baseline of what the status quo is when they begin the process and learn the skill of comparing this with the results. Along the way they observe, report, and calculate to have a sense of where they are headed, allowing for modifications even while in process. When community partners are also engaged in progress monitoring, students can improve their methods as they capture the voices of community.

8. Duration and Intensity. How long should the service learning process last? As long as necessary for a quality experience. A sufficient duration allows the participants to move through the Five Stages of Service Learning—investigation, preparation and planning, action, reflection, and demonstration—with ample time to authenticate and address identified community needs and achieve learning outcomes. The emphasis is on process rather than aiming for a premeditated goal.

Service learning is about moving forward with purpose, while allowing for flexibility, inevitable detours, and unexpected occurrences that are inherent to "real world" participation.

> No one is born a good citizen; no nation is born a democracy. Rather, both are processes that continue to evolve over a lifetime. Young people must be included from birth. A society that cuts itself off from its youth severs its lifeline.
>
> —*Kofi Annan, Former Secretary-General, United Nations*

The Process of Service Learning: The Big Picture

At this point, you've thought about what service learning means, how you may choose to define community, what forms of service might work best for your students, and the standards or ingredients that lead toward impactful experiences. Now it's time to look at the actual process, the sequence the students follow. It is the basis of every service learning activity. If we are keeping in mind that the standards are the ingredients, these Five Stages of Service Learning are the recipe. The essential and interdependent five stages of successful service learning are:

- Investigation
- Preparation and Planning
- Action
- Reflection
- Demonstration

Together these constitute a process that is key to students' effectiveness and critical to their learning transferable skills and content. Even though each stage is examined separately, keep in mind that they're linked together and often experienced simultaneously. Visualize how overlays are used in an anatomy book to reveal what is occurring in the human body system by system. Each stage of service learning in action is like one of these overlays, revealing one part of an interdependent whole. As you read on, you will find elaboration of each of these stages along with repro-ducible documents to use with your students as they progress from ideas to accomplishment.

Investigation

> Nothing has such power to broaden the mind as the ability to investigate systematically and truly all that comes under thy observation in life.
>
> —*Marcus Aurelius, Roman Emperor*

All service learning begins with investigation: 1) inves-tigation of the resources within the student population, called a "Personal Inventory," and 2) investigation of the community need. A personal investigation is of great value, during which students interview each other to identify and consolidate an inventory of each person's interests, skills, and talents. This list, often kept in a visible location in the classroom, is then referenced, employed, and developed while going through all service learning stages. Next, young people identify a community need of interest and begin their research to authenticate this need. During this process, often called "social analysis," they assess the need by designing a survey, conducting interviews, using varied media such as books and the Internet, and drawing from personal experience and observation. Students then document the extent and nature of this need, and establish a baseline for monitoring their progress in meeting it. Community partners are often identified in this stage. If a community partner indentifies the need, students still investigate to authenticate and document this need.

Preparation and Planning

> I cannot predict the wind but I can have my sail ready.
>
> —*E. F. Schumacher, author*

Preparation and planning cover a wide variety of activities, as teacher and students set the stage for learning and social action. Having recognized their interests, skills, and talents, and identified the need

to be addressed, students now learn more about the topic. As this occurs, teachers and students begin to note what skills need to be acquired or improved to have greater effectiveness. Students explore, research, and discuss the topic by using books and the Internet, by interviewing experts—which exposes young people to various careers—and often by going on field trips. They examine primary source materials (such as a school electrical bill if their intent is to reduce the school's carbon footprint). They may enact role plays or more complex simulations (such as turning the classroom into an Ellis Island waiting room in prepa-ration for a focus on immigrants). In this process of active learning and critical thinking, students grow to understand the underlying problem as well as related subject matter. Analysis, creativity, and practicality lead to plans for action. Here again, the class draws upon their personal inventory of skills, talents, and interests to shape the service to come. Students may also find and establish partnerships with other teach-ers and classrooms, local agencies, colleges or universi-ties, or national groups that offer resources.

Action

> If you need a helping hand, you will find one at the end of your arm.
>
> —*Yiddish proverb*

Action is the direct result of preparation and plan-ning. Solid preparation enables students to confi-dently carry out their plan of action, applying what they have learned to benefit the community. Perhaps they plant flowers to beautify school grounds, collect school supplies to send to students in a local shelter and or to an orphanage in Africa, or create a recycling campaign—the possibilities are limitless. Always, this action is intended to have value, purpose, and mean-ing as students continue to acquire academic skills and knowledge. These unique experiences have real conse-quences and offer a safe environment to learn, make mistakes, and succeed.

The plan may be carried out over the course of an academic year, a semester, two weeks, or a single day. The action may move sequentially from initiation to completion, or students may implement the initial stages during a semester in high school, for example, and a new class may resume the process, adding their own ideas. This allows for continuity, which may be necessary to address a complex or time-consuming need. In all cases, the duration of involvement needs to be sufficient for depth of learning and totality of experience. As the students put their plan in motion, they come to recognize vividly how classroom lessons fit into their daily lives and shape the lives of others.

During the action stage, students continue to develop knowledge and skills. In fact, the action stage often illuminates a piece of information or skill that is missing, and the students eagerly work to learn what is needed to be more effective in their community action. Also the idea of "resources" takes shape as students learn about and contact government and community agencies, interact with new people in new ways, and gain a novel perspective on their environment. Over the course of the experience, students raise questions that lead to a deeper understanding of the societal context of their efforts. They witness the real results of their actions and observe their strengths and attributes in relation to those of others, which can give them a new appreciation of their classmates and of people they meet who have varied roles and responsibilities. By taking action, young people identify themselves as community members and stakeholders and, over time, learn how to work within social institutions. Transforming plans into action enables them to use what is inherently theirs—ideas, energy, talents, skills, knowledge, enthusiasm, and concern for others and their natural surroundings—as they contribute to the common good.

Reflection

> To look backward for a while is to refresh the eye, to restore it, and to render it more fit for its prime function of looking forward.
>
> —*Margaret Fairless Barber, author*

Reflection is one of the standards in service learning as well as one of the five stages. It is a vital and ongoing process that integrates learning and experience with personal growth and awareness. Using reflection, students consider how the experience, knowledge, and skills they are acquiring relate to their own lives and communities. The academic program is often so jam-packed that it's easy to miss the meaning behind the details or within the experience. Reflection is a pause button that gives students the time to explore the impact of what they are learning and its effect on their thoughts and future actions.

In the course of reflecting, students put cognitive, social, and emotional aspects of experience into the larger context of self, the community, and the world. This helps them assess their skills, develop empathy for others, and understand the impact of their actions on others and on themselves. To really work, reflection must go beyond students simply reporting or describing what they are doing or have done. When students can compare their initial assumptions with what they have seen and experienced in the real world, reflection can be a transforming experience. They can ask questions and probe deeper into an issue, leading the class to further levels of investigation and understanding. They can use poetry or music to express a change in feelings that occurred or their appreciation of a classmate. They can also consider what they would change or improve about a particular activity.

While reflection in service learning is structured, with the times and activities usually established by the teacher, reflection also occurs spontaneously, stimulated by a student comment or class discussion of a newspaper article. Reflection may occur before, during, and after implementation through the use of different approaches and strategies. Final reflections may include ways to gauge results that further understanding and synthesis. Community partners and others involved in this reciprocal exchange may also share their reflections. In all cases, feedback from adults helps students use reflection to elevate their ability to observe, question, and apply their accumulated knowledge to other situations. To be effective, adults who interact with the students must model reflective behaviors. You'll find that soon, students can devise their own strategies for reflection and lead each other through the reflective process.

Demonstration

> The job of an educator is to teach students to see the vitality in themselves.
>
> —Joseph Campbell, author

The fifth stage of service learning is demonstration, or what I often call "The Big Wow!" During this stage, students make explicit what and how they have learned and what they have accomplished through their community involvement. They exhibit their expertise through public presentations—displays, performances, letters to the editor, photo displays, podcasts, class lessons—that draw on the investigation, preparation, action, and reflection stages of their experience. Presenting what they have learned allows students to teach others while also identifying and acknowledging to themselves what they have learned and how they learned it—a critical aspect of metacognitive development. Students take charge of their own learning as they synthesize and integrate the process through demonstration.

What about celebration and recognition? Descriptions of service learning often list celebration as a key part of the service learning process. Celebrating accomplishments and good work is definitely valuable, but demonstration is more in keeping with the intentions of service learning because students confirm what they have learned and continue the process. It is a significant achievement for students to demonstrate what they've learned clearly and publicly, and celebration can be interwoven within the demonstration. For example, students can invite community members to see their new hiking trail at a nature preserve and also plan a picnic and songfest. Celebration, when planned with thought, can benefit service learning.

The idea is to celebrate in a spirit of shared experience and accomplishment—not to focus on "winning." Infusing a competitive element into the service learning puts the emphasis on an extrinsic reward. This displaces the deep value of service learning as a means to benefit from intrinsic motivation. Students want and need to be taken seriously for their efforts and action. While the emphasis should remain on the intrinsic benefits of learning and the satisfaction of helping to meet community needs, recognizing student accomplishment in a public way may show students that the school and community members understand and appreciate their contribution. For many students, this may be the only time their school success is acknowledged.

An Example of Putting It All Together: Service Learning Meets the Canned Food Drive

So what happens when you put all of the pieces together? A good illustration is to take an activity that you've probably been involved in at some point: a canned food drive. The average canned food drive may be community service, but it isn't service learning.

Typically, the way a canned food drive is run ranges from general public-address announcements, such as "Bring in cans of food and put them in the box by the school office," to a contest in which the class contributing the most cans wins a pizza party. Regardless of the form it takes, the motivation to participate is weak and student learning is negligible. In the end, students are no more informed about the issues of hunger in the community than when they began, and the cans collected often don't meet the needs of the receiving agency or the community members who depend on the food bank.

An elementary teacher, "Mr. Baker," describes how a student made a huge difference in one school canned food drive by accidentally introducing the concept of service learning to his school:

> For years, the same procedure had been followed. An announcement on the loud speaker asked students to bring in their cans and place them in the box by the office. Being new to the school, I was placed in charge of delivering the boxes to a local food bank. Jamal, a student known as a "troublemaker," was asked to help me cart the all too few boxes to my car. Jamal looked inside at the assorted foods: lima beans, pesto sauce, and water chestnuts. Jamal had one comment, "This food stinks." I agreed, and

asked him, "What do you think we should do about it?" Jamal broke into a huge smile and told me his idea. The result? Rather than delivering the boxes, we hosted a luncheon to thank the teachers for helping with the canned food drive. The menu? You guessed it! And Jamal and his friends—the "unlikely" leaders—came and led the teachers in a much-needed conversation. After seeing the poor selection from the food drive offered as a meal, and with impetus from the students, the faculty revamped the canned food drive and considered real learning connections in every classroom. Kids began reading books on hunger, doing research about our community, talking with a representative from the local food bank, and creating all sorts of persuasive written materials that got everybody eager to participate. With ideas and leadership from Jamal and other students, we established our most productive and meaningful canned food drive ever. Communication between students and teachers improved as we talked about what we accomplished and shared our experiences and future plans with parents and community partners. Unexpectedly, we found additional ways to collaborate with the food bank throughout the school year.

The new kind of food drive at "Mr. Baker's" school provided opportunities for learning and applying skills that resulted in significant benefits to the community. During a follow-up discussion, teachers noted that a new group of students had emerged as leaders and that a partnership had been established with a community organization. Student interest in community matters generated classroom conversations about additional local needs and ways in which students could plan and participate. The process of service learning became clear through experience.

What follow are more examples of real-life activities used in effective and meaningful canned food drives. While grade levels are noted, much of the material studied, the resources used, and the actual methods employed are relevant or easily adapted for many grade levels.

First Graders and *Uncle Willie*

While studying "community," first graders read *Uncle Willie and the Soup Kitchen* to identify the many ways people participate in meaningful service. The class takes a field trip and assembles sack lunches for a local agency that delivers meals to people in need. Back at school, the students plan a drive to collect food that will help this agency prepare balanced, healthy meals. With assistance from their fourth-grade buddies, they make posters and flyers, which are given to each class; sort collected food into categories, keeping track of quantities on a large graph; and check cans for expired dates and damage. Together, they write reflective stories with illustrations of their experiences and compile the stories into a book. A copy is presented to the school library at an assembly and one is sent to the partnering agency. Upon receiving it, the food bank requests more. They want to send a copy of the book to every school that donates food to the agency to improve what students learn and what they receive.

Fourth Graders and *The Long March*

A fourth-grade teacher reads aloud *Feed the Children First: Irish Memories of the Great Hunger*, a book describing the potato famine, and *The Long March: The Choctaw's Gift to Irish Famine Relief*. The class learns that in 1847, the Choctaw tribe sent $170 (the equivalent of more than $5,000 today) to help the starving Irish. For homework, students ask an adult to describe how people in need of food were helped in times past. As the students continue their study of American Indians, they examine the parallel of Native Americans' loss of lands and displacement onto reservations with the experience of people who lose their homes today because of poverty. When the school's annual canned food drive occurs, students make a presentation to every class about the Irish and their distant Choctaw friends, including information about the meaningful canned food drive. Students keep journals that become part of their portfolios.

Seventh Graders Learn About Social Services

A middle school social studies teacher reads a newspaper article aloud that describes the increased unemployment in the region and the growing strain on local social service agencies, including food banks. Most students are unfamiliar with social service agencies, and this realization begins their research. Students generate questions regarding what social services are available, what circumstances can lead to the need for assistance, and what organizations help in their community. They want to know: Who receives this food? What foods are the staples of this population? Does this population have supplies to open cans and cook the food, or are prepared foods preferred? What nutritional foods or food groups are in short supply? Teams of students take on specific research tasks, including contacting food banks for lists of foods that are needed to meet current demands. They collaborate with the student council to inform the student body about hunger in their community and what they can do to help. At Back-to-School Night, students create a display and serve as docents showing parents and other guests their full program, from research to deliveries to the food bank. The students sign up the families of students to volunteer directly with the food bank during the summer months.

High School Health

During a ninth-grade health class, students review the foundations of a nutritious diet. They follow up with a guest speaker from the local food bank to learn more about issues of malnutrition, especially how childhood hunger can affect physical growth, learning, and the ability to function. They use online resources to compare the statistics on childhood hunger in their region with other locales, including other countries. Students then develop a school-wide marketing plan to promote participation in the canned food drive and emphasize foods that are healthy for kids. They culminate their activities by creating an original coloring book about fruits and vegetables to give to children through the food bank.

American History Gets *Nickel and Dimed*

An American history class reads *Nickel and Dimed: On (Not) Getting By in America* and draws quotes from the book for discussion. The students are inspired to continue their investigation of poverty in the community through student-designed projects. To learn more, student committees contact local social service agencies to determine their needs and find out about policies that affect low-income and poor people in their community. They discuss the term "food insecurity" and realize that even some people with jobs and homes may not know where their next meal is coming from. At the end of three weeks, building on their interests and talents, students present an original video at a chamber of commerce meeting. The video presents their analysis of local, state, and national policies toward homelessness and hunger, and outlines agency needs and possible community responses. A newspaper runs a student editorial on the class's research and findings. Many letters are printed in response thanking the students for educating the community.

High School Electives Participate

- A drama class responds to an agency request to write a theatrical adaptation of the book *The Can-Do Thanksgiving* for elementary school assemblies to launch a citywide canned food drive.

- Photography students capture images related to the need for food donations. They create a photo display with personal comments that is displayed both at school and at the local public library.

- A choral concert astounds the audience when, in the middle of singing a song about homelessness, students show photographs from their community depicting its needs, and hand out informational brochures about how to become involved.

- In a computer class, students create a pamphlet entitled, "Easy Steps to Improve Your Canned Food Drive," post it on a Web site, and send it to all local schools and many agencies.

What Next?

While you sort through the terms, definitions, and ideas presented here and throughout this book, remember that every teacher has a first experience with service learning. Most begin with practical, manageable efforts that allow them to become familiar with the process. The following chapter offers guidance and a detailed blueprint for launching your efforts. Over time, as teachers, students, and agency partners gain experience with the value and impact of service learning, the efforts and collaborations may expand. If you've used service learning as a teaching method before, then this book will give you new resources and ideas to work with and may help you refine the practice in your classroom or organization. Advanced service learning teachers continually look for creative ideas and resources and seek out new partnerships, collaborations, and ways to encourage student leadership and initiative. And of course, this book can help you coach and teach others how to be part of this growing service learning world. The possibilities and promise of service learning grow with each activity wherever you are in your service learning career.

Chapter 2

A Blueprint for Service Learning

Service learning offers a tremendous array of exciting opportunities, choices, and challenges. If you're considering your first service learning activity, you may ask, "Where do I start?" And even as a seasoned veteran, you may wonder how to improve your service learning strategies and methods. This chapter takes you through each step of the service learning process, providing a blueprint to follow. It will also address issues common to service learning and ways to troubleshoot problems or unexpected situations that may arise both when you're getting started and when you're developing your practice.

In doing we learn.
—*George Herbert, poet*

Getting Started: A Blueprint

Getting started with service learning can seem overwhelming because there are many different concerns that you need to address and balance. However, with planning you can establish a solid foundation for your students to build on in their service learning activities. To help you successfully plan out your approach and curricular ties and prepare for different issues you may encounter, use the step-by-step blueprint of the service learning process featured in this chapter. This blueprint maps out an easy to follow sequence that you can reference as you and your students plan and carry out service learning experiences. The process begins with finding entry points to service learning in your curriculum, with student ideas, or with apparent community needs. The process continues step-by-step toward the important final step of assessing the overall experience. Each step lists the forms provided in this book to help you stay organized and maximize your resources. You'll also find suggestions in these steps for ways to continue developing your service learning practice as you become more experienced.

NOTE: Thumbnails of the forms referred to in the blueprint and throughout the text appear at the end of this chapter, starting on page 47. The full-size forms are included in the digital content.

An Overview of the Service Learning Blueprint

The following steps will guide you through the service learning process. Each step includes a reference to useful forms, with page numbers noted in parentheses. Students can assist with and participate in these steps as is appropriate for their age and ability, taking on more responsibility as they gain experience. Other stakeholders—colleagues, parents, and community members—can be valued partners along the way.

Step One: Points of Entry

Think about what you're teaching. If you're teaching a thematic unit, what are the underlying skills and content you want your students to come away with? All of these are entry points into service learning and can help you make curricular connections. Ongoing school projects, student-identified needs, and community-identified needs are also good ways to find your entry point into service learning activities.

Form: Establishing Curricular Connections: Points of Entry (page 47)

Step Two: Review the K–12 Service Learning Standards

Familiarize yourself with these eight key elements that support best practices for service learning. This list will remind you what will provide the greatest impact for both learning and civic participation.

Form: K–12 Service-Learning Standards for Quality Practice (page 47)

Step Three: Map Out Your Plans

Next get more detailed and start mapping a plan. Identify and record the community needs and your service idea. Include the content and skills that will be taught, the cross-curricular connections you can make, the books the students will read, and the community contacts that would be helpful to find and cultivate. Keep in mind this initial design is a framework to help you meet the academic standards required. Service learning is best when students have an ample voice in shaping the experience, particularly as you initiate the Five Stages of Service Learning: investigation, preparation and planning, action, reflection, and demonstration.

Forms: The Five Stages of Service Learning (page 47), Planning for Service Learning (page 48)

Step Four: Clarify Partnerships

Here is where you seek out partnerships that will support and enhance the service learning. Student participation in this process helps them learn the value of partners and how to identify and secure partnerships. Establish contact with collaborators—teachers, parents, community members, agency representatives, or others—who may want to join. Discuss and clarify specific roles and responsibilities and the reciprocal nature of these relationships for all involved to avoid any confusion once the process is underway.

Form: Community Contact Information (page 53)

Step Five: Review Plans and Gather Resources

Review plans with the students. Determine the kinds of resources needed, and start gathering and organizing them. These may include books, newspaper articles, and reference materials from partner agencies. Also, schedule any visits, guest speakers (see page 24), or field trips; these are good tasks for students to take on as they gain skills and experience.

Step Six: Begin the Process of Service Learning in Action

Now you can begin the process of service learning in your classroom or group. Initiate the five stages of the service learning cycle: investigation, preparation and planning, action, reflection, and demonstration. Encourage youth voice and choice as you move through the service learning process. It's important to be flexible for two reasons: Unexpected things can happen and service learning works best when students are able to see their own ideas in action. Continue to look for opportunities for ongoing reflection.

Forms: Five Stages of Service Learning (page 47), Planning for Service Learning (page 48), Gathering Information About a Community Need (page 51), Personal Inventory (page 51), Taking Action (page 52), Service Learning Proposal (page 52), Progress Monitoring (page 54), Four Square Reflection Tool (page 54)

Step Seven: Assess the Service Learning Experience

Through all stages of the service learning process, students define the current situation and set intentions for making a desired change that is notable and measurable in some form. Once demonstration and closing reflection are complete, review these processes and data to assess the learning accomplished, the impact of the service, the planning process, the reciprocal benefits for all involved, and ways to improve for next time. Debrief with all partners, including the students.

Forms: Progress Monitoring (page 54), Community Response (page 54), Assessment for Service Learning, Parts One and Two (page 55), Student Self-Evaluation (page 55)

Even if you are on the right track, you'll get run over if you just sit there.

—*Will Rogers, humorist*

Success with Speakers—Guaranteed!

A speaker can greatly enhance a service learning experience and inform students about career options especially if the process takes on a town hall format. What could this look like? Rather than a speaker lecturing, let students become active, inquiring citizens who generate and pose questions. To ensure success, the speaker and students should be prepared ahead of time.

Identify the speaker. Discuss with students what information will be helpful as they prepare to take action. Who might provide this information? To identify a speaker, students may ask for referrals from a principal, parents, or other community partners. A newspaper article can provide a lead. The teacher or adult leader can also contribute suggestions.

Make the invitation. Whenever possible, involve students in writing a letter or an email, or making the call with the invitation. Students gain skills by learning how to make effective calls or compose an appropriate written request.

Collect résumés. Ask every speaker to send a copy of his or her résumé at least one week ahead of time. Make copies for all the students. Discuss the résumé format and purpose: to introduce the person to a prospective employer or to provide an introduction of the person to whomever is interested. Ask students what they would like to ask this person about her or his experience related to service learning.

Having a speaker's résumé in advance saves valuable time. Because students already have information about this person, they can learn more about the subject matter before meeting the speaker. Students learn how to construct meaningful questions, participate actively in the interview process, and acquire more of the information they consider important and valuable.

Develop the topics. Write down all the topics you'd like the speaker to address and guide students in forming categories. Usually the range of categories will include personal development leading into the speaker's career, a "day in the life" of this person, theme-related questions, and how students can be involved and contribute to the speaker's field of work. Students then select what group to be in and collaborate within this group to generate questions. Each group presents their preferred questions and receives feedback.

Hold the event. Make sure the speaker knows ahead of time about the "town hall" format, and ask that he or she prepare a short opening statement to be followed by a question and answer exchange.

Debrief the experience. Will students create an article from this experience? Would a storyboard best capture what they learned? Could a series of interviews result in a comic book series about exciting careers in public service? Discuss with students the process they experienced and how their preparation helped. Ask students how they would like to express their gratitude to the speaker. Invite them to extend their creativity beyond a typical thank-you note. For example, a class photo with the speaker could be sent in a hand-made frame along with a note or poem containing a line contributed by each student.

The result? An engaging, informative process that students enjoy and benefit from. Plus, the speaker is usually most impressed!

As you start following the blueprint, questions often arise. Common ones include:

- Is service learning a form of project-based learning?
- How do I come up with ideas for service learning experiences that have strong curricular connections?
- How do I ensure that service learning advances student learning so they meet and exceed academic expectations?

- Where do acts of charity fit within service learning?
- Is competition appropriate as an incentive for service learning?
- How can I plan ahead while leaving room for "youth voice and choice"?
- How can I encourage students to develop a sense of civic responsibility?
- How do I establish partnerships in school and in the community?

What follows are answers to these questions, suggestions on how and where to use the forms in this book, and more detailed exploration of the issues common to embarking on service learning. These will all help you plan your first service activity and provide food for thought for more experienced service learning practitioners.

Is service learning a form of project-based learning?

Service learning has much in common with project-based learning, experiential education, and other methods that strive to engage students in what is often referred to as "real world" interactions. The distinguishing elements of service learning are the students' investigation and authentication of the need addressed, the infusion of reflection throughout the process, and the action that has explicit reciprocal benefits for all involved. Of course, these elements can be found in examples of project-based learning and experiential education. However, these ideas are deeply wedded within service learning pedagogy. Also, the term "project" can be construed to have a beginning, middle, and end. With service learning, the "end" is often another beginning—the investigation of a need and the action taken reveal another situation that compels students to stay involved. While this book occasionally uses the term "service learning project" for convenience, a more accurate term is "service learning experience," which better expresses the growth and continuity that can occur in the process.

How do I come up with ideas for service learning experiences that have strong curricular connections?

First, think about what skills, content, and themes you're already teaching. The five strategies on the Establishing Curricular Connections: Points of Entry form on page 47 may be helpful for generating service learning ideas. The form also provides classroom examples and literature resources. These entry points are examined in more detail in the following pages.

As you consider various ideas to get started, keep in mind that service learning ideas are best developed as a "team sport." Draw others into your planning sessions.

Brainstorming possible activities with students, colleagues, and others guarantees a wealth of options and excitement. This often leads to collaborative service learning activities: a teacher who has contributed a suggestion is more likely to participate, students whose ideas are taken seriously make a stronger commitment, and agencies become more involved partners.

Point of Entry #1: Identify an existing program or activity to transform into authentic service learning. The familiar canned food drive, mentioned in chapter 1, can easily become a service learning experience with visible benefits for the classroom and the recipient agency. It's a simple matter for teachers, students, and community partners to find related learning opportunities, such as studying nutrition, interviewing the receiving agency to identify who is served and what foods are needed, visiting a food bank, and investigating underlying issues of poverty, local housing costs, food security, and unemployment rates. The learning process can include such books as *Soul Moon Soup* and *What the World Eats.* This same mindset can be applied to any large initiative, such as the popular Pennies for Patience or Jump for Heart. Learning about the issues, terms, and needs underlying the cause elevates the idea of service, solidifies its relevance, and provides a reason for participation.

Point of Entry #2: Begin with standard curriculum, content, and skills and find the natural extension into service. What specific content and skill areas need to be addressed in the classroom to meet the academic standards or course outcomes? Fill in those spaces on the Planning for Service Learning form (page 48) first, and consider a service emphasis that extends this classroom learning into a hands-on experience. When students are learning about war in American history, for example, and you want them to improve their verbal communication skills, consider having them interview elders about their military experiences. This works as well for elementary students as it does for high school students. Books such as *Growing Older: What Young People Should Know About Aging* and *Too Young for Yiddish* can elicit a related discussion about the aging process. *Stranger in the Mirror; We Were There, Too! Young People in U.S. History;* and *Eyes of the Emperor* can add depth to the historical aspects while addressing specific academic standards. Books about contemporary events, such as *Sunrise Over Fallujah*, bring a sense of immediacy, sensitivity, and accessibility to situations often difficult to comprehend. Community partners can also provide information that is otherwise missing from classroom lessons.

Point of Entry #3: From a theme or unit of study, identify content and skill connections. Most broad themes or topics, such as "interdependence" or "the rain forest," have service implications. Identify the specific content and skill areas to be addressed, and then, after examining the needs, students select a service application developmentally appropriate for all involved. For example, with the theme "the individual's role in society," younger children can dramatize the lives of people they admire after reading *Amelia to Zora: Twenty-Six Women Who Changed the World,* highlighting their perseverance, imagination, and strength along with their diverse contributions. Sharing this knowledge through performances for other classes, senior citizen groups, or at a community celebration reinforces the learning while educating and inspiring others to action. Older students may read nonfiction stories of exemplary acts such as *A Woman for President: The Story of Victoria Woodhull* and *After Gandhi: One Hundred Years of Nonviolent Resistance.* With this foundation of knowledge about how social change occurs, students would then research agencies that meet community needs and study underlying social issues. After conducting their research, students can produce a series of informative pamphlets on these agencies for young people.

Point of Entry #4: Start with a student-identified need. There are several ways to use student-identified needs as departure points. As a class, identify students' skills, talents, and interests using the Personal Inventory form on page 51. Then have students think about local problems that may be extensions of their interests or talents and conduct research to authenticate a specific need using the Gathering Information About a Community Need form on page 51. Next, students identify the causes of the problems, list who is already helping (perhaps a student in your classroom), brainstorm ways young people can help, conduct research to learn more, and create an action plan. The Taking Action form on page 52 provides a tool for this

process. Next, students can prepare a formal proposal using the Service Learning Proposal form on page 48. Alternatively, students may volunteer ideas and concerns with no prompting. For example, a student may come into class and proclaim that "something has to be done about the empty lot next to the school," and suggest a cleanup or a community garden. Another student might burst into class upset that "the skateboard park is about to be closed" and want to let people know how unfair that is. Or a student could describe how a fire destroyed a neighbor's home and wonder what could be done to help the family. These unpredicted "teachable moments" can initiate the process of clarifying immediate community needs and determining ways to become involved. Each can become rich realms for academic study, whether by reading *Seedfolks* about cleaning a lot and creating a garden, by interviewing a city council member about the use of public spaces, or by becoming proactive about emergency readiness. Integrating academics along the way becomes exciting for both teachers and students.

Point of Entry #5: Start with a community-identified need. Good news travels fast. Once a school has a reputation for providing service or has established community partnerships, agencies or organizations may ask your students for assistance. Stories in the local media are another common way of identifying community needs. A newspaper article or evening news report can also make a need apparent to the students. For example, either method could lead to your students providing a childcare center with one-on-one literacy preparation, perhaps with children who do not speak English. Students can create lessons to introduce basic language skills or lead activities in which the younger children make letter shapes with their bodies. Older and younger pairs can enjoy writing and illustrating bilingual books on themes chosen by the younger children. Children can take copies of the books home, and copies can also be donated to the library, a childcare facility, and other places that need books such as health clinics and family shelters. Again, literature (such as *A Movie in My Pillow—Una película en mi almohada* or *La Mariposa*) can be excellent texts to use in preparation.

NOTE: All of the books mentioned in this chapter can be found in the service learning bookshelves of Part Two. A list of bilingual books referenced in the thematic chapters can be found on page 68.

How do I ensure that service learning advances student learning so they meet and exceed academic expectations?

There are two primary ways. The first involves planning. Service learning advances and enhances student learning when teachers plan ahead to establish authentic curricular connections. The two-page Planning for Service Learning form on page 48 helps you map out a service learning experience and identify opportunities for learning. On this form, you can write down each step, including specific content, skills to be developed, opportunities for youth voice, literature to be used, and community contacts to be made, as well as curricular connections—all in a format that is easy to construct. The second page encourages consideration of elements such as leadership skills, career exposure, global connections, and social and emotional aspects to be addressed. Many teachers have found that this tool serves as a continuing reference and reminder of the stages to be followed and the quality standards to be considered and integrated. As new learning opportunities arise during the service learning process or at the conclusion, you can update this form for documentation and record keeping purposes and to share with others.

To use the form, insert whatever information you have at the onset, for example, the key content, a few skills necessary to develop, and perhaps a way to integrate technology. Then use that information to generate ideas, ideally in collaboration with peers, community partners, and students. If you're a single-subject teacher, you may find opportunities for interdisciplinary collaboration as you identify related areas of study and other teachers who want to venture into a service learning collaboration.

To give you an idea of the various ways this form can be used, four examples of filled-in forms are provided. The elementary example (page 48) began in one classroom and evolved over four years to include many students and teachers. The environmental theme and activities developed as several teachers exchanged ideas. Each teacher made adjustments for grade level, class needs, and personal teaching style. When implementing the plan, each teacher also made changes as students added or modified ideas and community partnerships were identified. The middle school example (page 49) was a natural extension of a classroom study of immigration. Students' enthusiasm and interest compelled the teacher to engage in community outreach, greatly benefiting the academic achievements of his class while meeting an authentic community need. The high school literacy project (page 49) began as a one-time interaction in which older students were going to read books to younger children. With student leadership, the plans evolved into a comprehensive bookmaking activity over three weeks that included extensive preparation and several class visits. Through the fourth example (page 50), children with autism in elementary through middle school grades learned about plants and strengthened community skills while being helpful neighbors.

NOTE: The digital content has thirty-nine filled-in Planning for Service Learning forms—elementary, middle, and high school examples for each of the thirteen thematic chapters found in Part Two of this book.

The second way we can ensure that students advance academically through service learning is to pay particular attention to the skill development that occurs. While the theme of service may change—from hunger to climate change to protecting animals to emergency readiness—the underlying skills remain the same. Service learning is ideal for developing the incremental skills students need to know, skills that transfer to all subjects and classes and truly improve students as learners while building competence and confidence. I often ask teachers during a workshop, "Who does more of the service learning, the teacher or the students?" All too often the candid response is: "The teachers." There needs to be an environment where students develop, revisit, reapply, and integrate skills that move them toward achieving competence and confidence. With service learning, students thrive through active engagement rather than being passive recipients. Complex skills and concepts that typically overwhelm students can be examined, discussed, experienced, and integrated to compose a rich vocabulary for successful learning.

Through service learning, students can have myriad opportunities to:

- ask questions
- listen and retain
- observe
- identify similarities and differences
- work independently, with partners, and in groups
- identify and apply their skills and talents
- acquire assistance as needed
- be resourceful
- gather and manage information
- summarize
- test hypotheses
- solve problems effectively, step-by-step

Where do acts of charity fit within service learning?

Charity is usually associated with the image of contributing money or collecting goods to donate. Some school campuses seem to always have some sort of collection going on, from coins to school supplies to winter coats. Often school staff members and parents appear to be doing most of the organizing work, while kids transport dollars or items from home to school. Typically this operates as community service; however, a growing number of schools are transforming charity to service learning, as authentic academic connections are made. For example, students learn about childhood leukemia and teach others before initiating a penny drive. Or students make recycled tote bags out of juice pouches as part of a study of recycling and develop a plan to market the bags to raise funds for a family in transition. What would having *all* acts of charity filtered through the lens of classroom academic connections look like? Who would do most of the work then? And what could be learned?

Some schools report that charitable acts done by students may even serve some of the students involved in the process. Teachers describe how this allows every student to see themselves as contributors.

Have you heard adults say that young people should be involved in service to "give back"? This tends to imply that kids "should" participate in acts of philanthropy. But perhaps "giving back" applies better to adults than kids who are still growing and developing a sense of themselves through the experiences that shape them. Also, in every community we can identify young people who feel disenfranchised. For them, hearing, "You should give back," may evoke the response, "What have I ever gotten in the first place?" So why should kids participate in service if not to give back? Because they can. Because kids have tremendous talents and ideas that already make significant impacts on communities worldwide. And within schools and youth serving organizations, when charity becomes service learning, more of these talents and ideas can be utilized while academic connections are made.

Is competition appropriate as an incentive for service learning?

In a word: no. A companion to every winner is a loser. For kids involved in service learning, transforming competition into collaboration always improves the dynamic. Everyone wins. This said, there is still a place for the occasional award or recognition for exemplary service, primarily because the stories of young people, made prominent, inspire others to consider taking initiative or joining a cause. This is much different from competition as an incentive to become involved in the first place. Remember that engaging kids through knowing the underlying causes of childhood hunger has much more power to stimulate participation than winning a pizza for bringing in the most food. Kids are compassionate. They want to solve problems and improve how we live. The most powerful incentive is engagement. People have long asked me, "How do you motivate students?" One day I realized I can't motivate anyone; motivation comes from within. What all of us can do is engage a person, and being engaged can lead the person to choose to be motivated. Intrinsic motivation—that's what we are aiming for!

How can I plan ahead while leaving room for "youth voice"?

A well-designed service learning framework provides ample opportunities for student learning to occur. Often this planning occurs in advance of implementation. Standards, textbooks, and mandates from many directions usually means you must have a well-thought-out plan for the upcoming year before the first day of school. The initial framework for service learning as a teaching methodology may be part of this plan. So how can you leave room for genuine decision making by students, for their "voice"—one of the K–12 Service-Learning Standards for Quality Practice? The key is to remain flexible, so that plans can be revised as students and partners introduce new ideas.

Even when the original plan remains intact, opportunities abound for students to make choices:

- A first-grade teacher decides that having her class paint a mural depicting the local community fits into her language arts and social studies curriculum. The students look at three sites and select one at a childcare center where the need for a mural is greatest. After discussing what "community" means, making field trips to fire stations and food markets, and reading many books aloud, students determine the content and design of the mural.

- Middle school students interviewing seniors at a retirement community for a social studies project find that many of the older people have extensive experience gardening. Although gardening was not an original focus of the project, students make a change. The students and their senior friends decide to grow vegetable plants and write an intergenerational gardening guide together. Together they distribute the plants and guide at a community event for healthy living.

- High school biology students conduct research on water quality using a real-world set of water quality testing methods. They must analyze land use, set their sampling sites to take account of a feedlot or construction project, and collect and analyze the data. They must figure out the best way to apply these methods locally, which offers many opportunities for student input and direction.

- Members of a youth group agree to learn how to be docents at a children's museum and are given program materials and a script for greeting and guiding the participants. They are asked to review all documents and make suggestions for improvement. Students recommend both new written text for the museum brochures and ways to make the tours and activity centers more kid-friendly and engaging.

Encouraging youth voice and skill development involves having students take on clearly defined roles and responsibilities that add to project productivity and efficiency and may, over time, reduce your workload. Students can form teams that have assigned tasks such as:

- **Communication Specialists** make and keep a project log of phone calls and write correspondence.

- **Photographers** take pictures that create the visual timeline of memorable moments.

- **Publicists** learn how to write captivating press releases to send to school board members and media outlets.

- **Historians** assemble a scrapbook of artifacts—program materials, photographs, news articles—that tell the complete service learning story.

The teams' success depends upon being prepared for the tasks, which will require lessons and practice activities to hone the required skills. However, once accomplished, the students build on this foundation through practice, ongoing support, and constructive feedback. Students have been known to compose a guidebook to teach other students about their roles and even lead peer workshops to establish teams in other classes. Students can also help determine what the teams are and rotate jobs so they learn and develop multiple skills. When can you start using this approach? The answer is: Any age when you can match age-appropriate skills that fit the project and plan accordingly. First graders at a rural school formed teams called "The Greeters," "The Appreciators" (they write thank-you notes), and "The Scrapbook Keepers" as part of their school's nature trail project. Middle school students who love to chat on the phone learned appropriate phone manners to survey community representatives. High school students were surprised that their affinity to shopping had great value when doing price comparisons for building a playground at a housing development.

The more familiar you become with the service learning process and the unique talents of your students, the earlier you can draw students into the planning process. (For more suggestions on this and other ways to refine this area of your service learning practice, see "Developing Youth Initiative" on page 34.)

Why not go out on a limb? Isn't that where the fruit is?

—Frank Scully, author

How can I encourage students to develop a sense of civic responsibility?

Participation in service learning creates the potential to develop civic knowledge, community awareness, and literacy. Enliven the idea of civic responsibility through activities that promote understanding and knowledge about the different roles that individuals, collaborative efforts, and government all play in a thriving democracy. Consider the following activities as strategies you can use to build a foundation of civic responsibility into your service learning programs.

Personal Impact. Include stories of individuals who have made contributions to the well-being and advancement of society through their initiative and collaborative efforts. Books provide stories such as *Planting the Trees of Kenya: The Story of Wangari Maathai,* about a Kenyan environmentalist and human rights activist and her determination to protect and improve the community's economy, health, education, and land use by planting seven million trees. Use the book *Belva Lockwood: Equal Rights Pioneer* to teach about a woman who fought for social justice for women and all underrepresented people.

At every age, students also benefit from meeting people within their communities who participate as volunteers, service providers, civic leaders, and elected officials. Students can meet and conduct interviews with people they know or read about in local newspapers who make ongoing contributions through their work, such as police officers, council members, and even teachers. Questions may include, "What do 'service' and 'civic responsibility' mean to you?" "How does your work contribute to our community?" This can lead students to discuss the importance of what an individual can contribute and what each of them hopes to accomplish through service learning.

Collaborative Experience. Introduce anthropologist Margaret Mead's quote, "Never doubt that a small group of citizens can change the world. Indeed it is the only thing that ever has." Have students discuss what this means in small groups, and look for evidence that supports or contradicts this statement. Students can draw from the period of history they are studying or from literature (fiction or nonfiction) to substantiate their perspective. Using literature can bring lesser known historical moments to life, such as the book *The Long March: The Choctaw's Gift to Irish Famine Relief,* which documents how an indigenous population in the United States made a significant contribution to a distant population in need despite their own poverty and limited resources.

The Role of Government. Have students identify and contact the government agency associated with their service learning efforts. For younger students, the teacher or a parent may help with this task. For example, there are state agencies that govern the rules and regulations for convalescent facilities. Many states offer free education packets about recycling or toxic waste. City council members or their staff can provide information about services offered for people who are homeless. The role of government becomes more vivid as students gain familiarity with its range of offices, services, and policy. Students can initiate contact through phone calls, the Internet, letters, or visits with city officials. Students can also make presentations at school board meetings, city council meetings, or to the state legislature or attend simply to learn how the meetings work. Knowing that government consists of offices filled with people doing work on behalf of the populace creates an informed citizenry. As students learn how government is influenced by ordinary citizens, they may be inspired to extraordinary acts.

A Thriving Democracy. Discuss the foundations and principles of a democratic society and who maintains this democracy. Service learning activities can be developed based on student-generated ideas that will support these principles. For example, a fourth-grade class initiated a local campaign to "Vote for America," a nonpartisan effort to increase voter registration and turnout. A middle school social studies class planned and led a town meeting on usage of a town park. A high school Spanish class partnered with an adult education citizenship class to improve their Spanish conversation skills and tutor the adult students about the Constitution. As students learn what democracy represents and understand how nonprofit organizations, grassroots efforts (including their own), and service learning play a part in social change, students may become invested caretakers of a thriving democracy.

How do I establish partnerships in school and in the community?

Collaboration can be the lifeblood of service learning. Partners add a variety of perspectives to the process, which can fuel debate and reflection as well as help students gain a better understanding of social issues and generate ideas for civic improvement. Collaboration can provide additional opportunities to acquire knowledge and expertise. Teachers often ask how to set up constructive partnerships with other teachers, community members, and parents.

Partnerships with Teachers

Communicating peer to peer effectively establishes a network of teachers who bring service learning to life within a school. By telling colleagues about the value of service learning, how the basic process works, and any personal experience, you may ignite someone's curiosity or uncover willing partners. Sharing an article from an education journal or an example found on the Internet is another way to stimulate conversation and ideas. Administrative support can also give service learning vital credibility as a teaching method, which can lead to staff development sessions that foster knowledge and faculty interest.

Consider these ideas to bring other teachers on board:

- Even casual discussions often reveal that colleagues are curious about service learning and may be willing to participate. During a lunchtime conversation, for example, one teacher mentions that her second graders want to donate an original picture book to a childcare center. Another teacher suggests that her class could make a companion counting coloring book. A third teacher recommends contacting a friend who teaches Spanish at the local high school. As the result of a simple conversation, the childcare center receives a bilingual picture book, along with a coloring book and, as a bonus, a relationship between three classrooms in two schools is established.

- More formal meetings can also be used to initiate collaborations. During a small group planning session among fourth-grade teachers, a middle school teaching team, or high school English department, request time to develop an idea for a service learning unit for your class. The Planning for Service Learning form on page 48 can provide a road map that the group can help fill in, and it also helps novices understand the different aspects. Some teachers may be willing to participate, others may want to observe and join in later. Be certain to let your colleagues know how their input impacted the process. Also make a point of sharing this information with your students, because they may choose to express appreciation to these teachers verbally or with a written note.

- Are you in search of ideas for cross-curricular collaborations in the middle and high school grades? Brainstorm with students for original ideas. Students can often approach teachers in other subject areas and ask them to help meet specific project needs. Here are some examples: A computer teacher agreed to have her students help a social studies class design a brochure for a local meals on wheels organization; a photography class documents high school science students leading chemistry experiments with fifth graders; and several music students compose background melodies for a family consumer education class's public service announcements on nutrition and exercise.

- Showcase student success! Have students demonstrate their learning and service at a faculty meeting. A creative display of the knowledge acquired, skills developed, and community involvement achieved may encourage other teachers to learn more or to get involved.

If opportunity doesn't knock, build a door.
—Milton Berle, comedian

Establishing Partnerships in the Community

Service learning offers wonderful opportunities to involve partners from outside the traditional school setting. Everyone concerned benefits, especially when the concept and process of service learning is understood and valued uniformly. The degree of need and commitment usually dictates the involvement of the partners. A community partner may simply provide written materials to help a class learn about setting up a recycling program at school. Another partner may be more involved; for example, a convalescent facility sends a staff person to lead a simulation about the aging process with a class preparing for a site visit. Sometimes, community partners actually identify learning opportunities within their organizations that match classroom objectives for content or skill development. Always, partnerships are best developed with an explicit purpose and clearly defined roles, responsibilities, and benefits for all involved.

Who can be a partner? Nonprofit organizations, service clubs, businesses, and government offices are all potential partners in the service learning world. Interacting with kids frequently appeals to members of these groups, especially as they find out about how they enrich student learning and the meaningful contributions being made by young people.

Community colleges and universities also make excellent service learning partners. Across the country, colleges and universities are integrating service learning in various curricular areas with the result being abundant opportunities for collaboration. These might include joint service learning experiences; elementary, middle, or high school students demonstrating their expertise to a college class; programs in which classroom teachers mentor teacher education students in the service (or vice-versa); and cross-age tutoring projects that include service learning as one aspect of the relationship. Many institutions of higher learning have service learning coordinators for general education and are integrating service learning pedagogy, experience, and practice into teacher preparation classes.

Find partners by first identifying the purpose of the relationship: How could the interests of all partners be met and how do they intersect? How will this partnership support and strengthen the learning and service aspects of your project? What are the reciprocal benefits? Teachers and students can come up with lists of potential partners, and students can get additional ideas from their families, by interviewing the school principal, from reading local newspapers and Web sites, or by doing a tour of the area surrounding the school to find out what agencies, organizations, businesses, or other community groups may want to be involved.

Teachers or parents frequently initiate contact with potential partners. However, after learning and practicing effective communication skills, students can become proficient at finding and interacting with potential community partners. Lessons on making phone calls, writing correspondence, and even using telephone or online directories can match with academic standards. These skills are valuable in general and especially helpful as students take more initiative in planning and preparing for service learning. Even very young students can develop such skills, though an adult usually calls ahead to provide a general introduction and lay the groundwork for the child.

As contacts are made, the Community Contact Information form on page 53 helps the class or school maintain an ongoing record of interaction that can be used by all teachers and students from year to year. In some schools, students conduct interviews with numerous agencies to create a notebook, directory, or database of willing partners. The directory serves as a useful reference during a given project and in the future.

Once you've identified and established relationships with your partners, keep them informed and appropriately involved at all stages of your service learning efforts. You can include them in reflection as well—the Community Response form page 54 is designed for just this purpose. The form provides a structure for students to collect feedback and learn more about the impact of their contribution. Often, the community partner also appreciates participating in any public demonstration of the service learning process. Students have made presentations to board of directors of community groups, to local chambers of commerce, at city council meetings, and in other venues with partners in attendance and sometimes participating. When the time comes to express gratitude for the partnership, students can design their own special way of saying, "thank you!" through cards, presentations, skits, songs, or other creative methods.

Parents as Partners

Schools want parents to be involved in the education of their children. In fact, active school-family relationships provide the best educational atmosphere for all children. In terms of service learning, parents can contribute valuable resources, information, and ideas. They can help in the planning and implementation of service learning, identify community partners, assist with group work, join in field trips, collect and prepare supplies, document activities, and help write grants for funding. Even parents who work during the school day may be able to help make phone calls or cut fabric squares for a quilting project. Be certain that parents only fill roles that students are unable to do, so that adults' good intentions do not override what the kids could accomplish. A gathering of parents for an overview of service learning and clarifying roles and responsibilities can help set the stage for a partnership with parents—one that provides kids with the skills and parents play supporting roles and contribute when necessary.

To find a role for every parent, begin by identifying your parent resources and your program needs. Students in grades three through twelve can survey parents and other family members to develop a database of information: when parents are available to help, their personal hobbies and talents, and their community connections and involvement. Some schools even have parent liaisons for service learning. Once parent leaders emerge, they can coordinate parent involvement school-wide, facilitate workshops giving information on service learning and ways to get involved, and even identify opportunities for families to join together outside of school hours to perform service together.

Beyond the Basics: Advancing Your Service Learning Practice

Perhaps you're so familiar with the basic issues of service learning that addressing them has practically become second nature. If you're looking for ways to enhance your approach to service learning, here are some important areas to focus on:

- clarifying your purpose
- developing youth initiative in planning service learning activities
- infusing reflection in preparation, action, and demonstration stages
- assessing student learning and service
- publicizing student activities
- going global

Clarifying Your Purpose: The Underlying Imperative for Service Learning

Understanding what you want to achieve for your students guides you along this worthwhile journey. Before you read further, consider what you most want to accomplish from engaging your students in service learning. Your answer will influence how your students investigate, prepare and plan, take action, reflect, and demonstrate. It may also influence which community partners you seek out, whether students work in large or small groups, and the way you integrate academics into the process. If, for example, you want to improve a sense of community in the class, then varied partners and small groups would be ideal. If one teacher wants her class to see real-life applications of math, and another wants his students to improve their persuasive writing, would this impact the service experience? Of course! Your overarching purpose may or may not have anything to do with the social theme addressed, yet knowing this purpose will influence the unique structure of the process, and will especially impact the process of reflection (discussed in-depth later).

Here are examples of overarching themes teachers have shared:

- To improve observation and analytical skills

- To see modern applications of issues studied in ancient civilizations

- To learn how to write editorials

- To understand the inner workings of state or provincial government as compared to local and federal branches

- To develop manners through interaction with elders

- To examine the impact of global warming on everyday choices

- To clarify misunderstandings, perceptions, and biases about a population

- To replace bullying with respectful relationships

- To examine conflict resolution strategies while studying war

- To improve retention of knowledge through application

Write your overarching purpose on the Planning for Service Learning document (page 48).

Developing Youth Initiative

Why should you work on developing youth initiative in planning service learning activities? Youth initiative means youth involvement. When students play a key role in choosing and defining their service activities, their commitment and satisfaction are intensified. They become more confident in their actions and better able to recognize their impact on the community. If students are truly to grow as individuals and leaders through the service learning experience, they must take this step.

Launching a service learning experience that has evolved through student brainstorming and planning may seem risky. Certainly, it can involve a greater sense of the unknown. Your role is still the same—to remain a steadfast guide and mentor. Sometimes you are providing an overall framework, often setting boundaries, giving encouragement, and making sure that clear academic connections are infused throughout. A key service learning mantra to keep in mind is: skills, skills, skills. Sometimes we take for granted that students have certain skills. For example, they know how to make a phone call, but do they know proper etiquette when contacting a community partner? (Such as beginning a conversation with, "Is this a good time to talk?") And they know how to take on a task, but do they know how to delegate tasks to others to keep from becoming overwhelmed? Would a good dose of time management and prioritization techniques be helpful? Making time for skill development saves time, and students learn transferable lessons and develop the capacity for civic participation and leadership.

Bounce Theory

Once during a school consultation, I visited a first-grade class. While standing in the doorway, a little girl bounced up to me boldly announcing, "I can read! I can dance!" and gleefully bounced away. In this whirlwind, I felt the contagious delight that comes with accomplishment and confidence. I began asking teachers: At what grade do we begin to siphon off "the bounce"? The nearly unanimous agreement was around third or fourth grade. As high stakes testing begins, students often are told to focus on academics and leave personal stories at home. Possibly, this imposed school restraint silences a critical part of the child and removes the "bounce." While not every child expresses enthusiasm with an actual bounce in the step, most kids do have a unique way of being passionately themselves—a metaphorical "bounce." Without a place to identify and express interests and abilities, a child may experience a depressed identity and lack a forum for self-exploration and expression. Engaging students in a Personal Inventory becomes a reconnection with their "bounce." For a book that celebrates a child's enthusiasm, read *Looking Like Me* (page 208).

Helping Youth Define Themselves

Another important aspect of developing youth initiative is related to child development. In a workshop, a teacher stated, "My students only think about themselves." I answered, "That's to be expected—they're kids!" Children and adolescents strive to make sense of their world and their place in it, so they must think about themselves. The beauty in service learning, when implemented with youth initiative, is that kids get to see themselves as people of influence. When students beautify their school grounds, they see their sphere of influence extending to the edges of the school property. When they collaborate with recent refugees to plant and care for a community vegetable garden, they see their sphere of influence extend to locales in their city. When they register adults to vote, their sphere of influence extends throughout their nation. And when they join young people around the globe in sponsoring an

Taking an Inventory of Student Skills and Knowledge

Every student brings skills, talents, and interests to the class. Finding out what they are is one of your first tasks. Create a class database or chart of this useful information to help you get to know your students and to facilitate them getting to know each other. (Older students can help create this database.) They will frequently discover unexpected commonalities and sometimes fascinating differences.

This information can help the class in a variety of ways. A student who enjoys talking on the phone, for example, with a bit of skill development and practice, can become a group asset by contacting and making arrangements for a service outing. Do you have an "expert shopper" in your midst? Harness that talent for getting items donated or finding the best price on a "must purchase" item. Uncovering a "green thumb" will come in handy, too. What about interests? Knowing that some students have an interest in stopping vandalism or helping animals may set your service learning activity in a particular direction.

Using the Personal Inventory form on page 51, have students interview each other in pairs to reveal abilities and interests that will ultimately be helpful to the group. (For language development, it's enlightening to clarify the terms *skill, talent,* and *interest.*) Before the interview process, use the Getting Ready for Personal Inventory document (pages 50–51) to guide students through the steps of active listening, note taking, and asking probing questions so that interviews will yield more detail and useful skills are developed. Note that students record responses on their *partner's* form.

In the section "Questions for Getting Information," review the prompt: "If the person says 'I don't know,' be ready with a response like . . ." This is a critical part of the Personal Inventory process. When asked, "What are your interests, what are you good at?" too many students are quick to reply, "I don't know" or "Nothing." Remind students that each of us is a person of value. Not speaking favorably about one's self is endemic in society and too often enforced in school with the emphasis on "getting down to work" and restraining youth from individual expression. We admonish kids for bragging rather than modeling the importance of letting others know your assets, opinions, and ideas.

Also, as noted on Getting Ready for Personal Inventory, explore probing questions. A student may say he or she is interested in music. The interviewer could then ask, "Do you play an instrument or listen to music? What kinds of music do you like?" Interviewers record their partners' responses on the form.

The activity should also include having students ask their partners about a time when they helped someone and a time when someone helped them. This develops the recognition of personal reciprocity in the big picture of service learning. By honing their interviewing skills and becoming better acquainted, students prepare for the service learning experience and also develop the confidence for future jobs and college interviews.

With young children, especially those who aren't writing yet, you can adapt this activity using art. Have children draw pictures showing their favorite activities and their talents. Alternatively, they can explore skills, talents, and interests through class discussion or with an older student buddy. In either case, you can develop a list of skills, talents, and interests for the class.

For all age groups, post the list and invite students to add new skills and interests as the year progresses. Refer to this list as you continue to shape your service learning plans.

international day of peace, their influence is boundless. By supporting intentional youth initiative, you help kids define themselves as people of service to others.

Gathering Information About a Community Need, Developing an Action Plan, and Writing a Proposal

Students can begin to take initiative with the document Gathering Information About a Community Need (page 51). This process demystifies the often-cryptic concept of research. For many students, the idea of "research" is daunting. Often a teacher hears the same questions when a research assignment is given, "What do you want me to do?" or "What am I supposed to do?" Frequently this is followed with, "When is it due?" "How long does it have to be?" "How much of my grade will this count for?"

Through the service learning process of addressing authentic community needs, learners are engaged in several key ways:

- The idea of "research" is made clear and doable. The mystery is resolved and students learn there are only four ways to conduct research: using media, interviewing an expert, conducting a survey, or drawing upon one's own experience and observation. As students use this language, the framework of research makes sense. When given a research assignment in the future, students will transfer this knowledge and immediately consider, "Which of the four methods will I use this time?"

- When students have a sense of purpose and know someone is depending upon them for the research, the incentive for grades and meeting basic expectations may be replaced with an intrinsic

Gathering Information About a Community Need

How can a person find out about a community need, whether local or global? Ask students to discuss this in pairs for one minute and list responses. Lead students to categorize their ideas into these four research methods:

Media—includes books, Internet, radio, film, magazines, newspapers; informs the public about issues of common interest and educates about what is needed. For example, if a newspaper has a cover story about homelessness three times a month, that's an indicator of need. Ask for examples of what media students are influenced by most often.

Interviews—usually with a person who has expertise in the subject matter through experience or study. Asking questions of a person with information, skills, or resources informs us about what is needed; this can also be done with small groups of people in what is commonly called a "focus group." Ask for examples of where students experienced an interview or might in the near future.

Experience and Observation—experience is usually what we bring from our past and observation is our deliberate noticing. These can be combined into new opportunities, for example, at a food bank or by a polluted stream. Students usually gravitate toward this

form of research quite naturally since it's active and draws on many of the multiple intelligences. Ask them for examples of observing something that revealed a community need.

Survey—gathering responses from groups of people who may have varying degrees of knowledge about the subject. Students create a form with a series of questions to find out collective knowledge or opinion. This information is then compiled and turned into statistics or narratives of what is going on. Ask students for examples of a time they participated in any form of survey or witnessed a survey.

Have students brainstorm a need that affects them directly at school or impacts people in their community. Divide students into four groups—each focused on one of the four research categories on the Gathering Information About a Community Need form (page 51); smaller groups may form within the same category. Allow five to seven minutes for groups to do their work. Conduct reports by category, and have all students take notes on their form about what is recommended and learned.

Survey the students to come to an agreement on which of these strategies to implement. Following the implementation of these methods, have students report their findings. Students use this information as they move toward taking action.

desire to help a person or a cause. This is a huge shift. The question, "When is it due?" may be replaced with, "When can I get started?"

- As students learn the process through the sequence described, they will be practicing how research is developed, the methodology. When the time comes to determine which method to use, allow students to select at least one method themselves. You can determine a second method as you strive to vary their skills. The next time, two other methods can be used.

Through service learning, students become successful with the often-elusive "research" and gain confidence to do outstanding work, both in the class and in the community.

Use the Taking Action form on page 52 to guide students in developing a plan, beginning with summarizing evidence based on Gathering Information About a Community Need. As students move through each step, they clarify what they already know and determine how to find out more, all leading to taking action to help solve or contribute toward improving the situation. When possible, community partners should be involved in the process so students can learn how respectful collaborations are built and maintained.

The Taking Action form provides a guide in the initial planning process; the final description can be recorded on the Service Learning Proposal form on page 52. When writing a proposal, students clearly articulate their ideas to communicate the action they propose to take, the purpose of the action, the roles of various partners, the anticipated results, the budget for supplies or transportation, the ways in which the effects of their effort will be measured and their progress monitored, and even a timeline for the process. Students may work in committees to perform their designated tasks. While the plans described in the proposal may—and usually do—change during implementation, the document provides an overview and direction as students move forward. The complete document can also be submitted to the school administration for approval, to partners to confirm their participation, and to funding sources if monies or supplies are needed. Students can make changes as required and at the end can use the document as part of their reflection and assessment.

How old do students need to be to participate in making an action plan and writing a proposal? With guidance from their teacher, students in third grade have worked with the Taking Action form and a modified proposal form—Our Service Plan, on page 53. Even in the early grades, much can be accomplished through class discussion and by working in small groups. In first and second grades, for example, you can make a chart of ideas for action generated in class discussion. The ideas can lead to concrete plans, to action, and to the rewarding conclusion: We did it!

Seeking Funds for Service Learning?

The Service Learning Proposal form on page 52 is based on a standard grant application form. After writing a few proposals, many students have successfully applied their proposal writing skills to apply for service learning funds. Curious about service learning grant opportunities? Several are included in the Resources section on pages 257–259. Also, investigate your own community—older students can do the detective work, too—for financial support through service organizations, businesses, local foundations, city council offices, and even your school district. You may find that funders respond most favorably when they know that students have been part of the grant writing process.

Identifying Community Resources

With your guidance, middle and high school students can become involved in identifying community resources and related tasks. Using the Promotion—Turning Ideas into Action form on page 53, students start with an agreed-upon service idea and work in small groups to identify possible new alliances, sources for fundraising (if needed), presentation opportunities, media options, and so forth. Existing community partners may join in the activity, giving students practice in collaboration that leads to community networking.

Action and Monitoring Progress

When students first complete the Gathering Information About a Community Need document, they participate in action research: they are setting a baseline of the situation and developing a plan to remediate and improve the situation. Have them use the Capture the Action form on page 53 to collect visuals and highlights—a scrapbook-type montage of the experience. You might collect or copy these student documents and create a display or include them in a report to school officials, participating agencies, and funders. Most importantly: have students continually add to the Progress Monitoring form on page 54. Numerous skills go into capturing observations, statements, and statistics and ultimately drawing conclusions about what has stayed the same, what has changed in the short term, and what might be construed as long-term systemic change.

Reflecting on Reflection

Reflection is indispensable to the entire service learning process and solidifies the intellectual and emotional knowledge for everyone involved. Through reflection, students can integrate both the learning and the service achieved into their personal frameworks of experience. Since reflection is so central, its design and implementation is important. Reflection may begin as "something else we have to do" within the service learning process, but it quickly changes as students start to see the depth and meaning of the connections made and questions asked, and they begin to understand the purpose of their engagement.

Reflection can have an important role in reinforcing academic knowledge. If a service experience involves interviewing veterans as part of a study of World War II, a reflection activity could be writing a letter to Winston Churchill telling him what he might have wanted to hear from people who served in the military. If students are learning graphic design as part of a service experience, for reflection, have them create a visual that captures the essence of the experience using a maximum of eight words. Or you might begin with a quote such as President John Fitzgerald Kennedy's statement, "Leadership and learning are indispensable to each other," and encourage a reflective analytical

essay in which students agree or disagree based on their service experience. Reflection is always meant to move the learning forward and increase the capacity for meaningful service.

Reflection is just as integral for educators as it is for students. You reflect on the process to design meaningful and appropriate reflection activities for your students. Keep these thoughts in mind as you read about weaving reflection into the service learning process, ways to vary your reflection strategies, ideas for using journals, overcoming discussion hazards, the importance of feedback, and opportunities for student leadership. The Sequence for Reflection form on page 54 can help guide your reflection with students, or you can use it as a checklist. Maintaining your own reflection journal throughout the service learning process can be helpful and informative as you move toward assessment.

Opportunities for Reflection

As emphasized earlier, reflection occurs both through activities structured by the teacher and spontaneously during all stages of the service learning process. As you plan your service learning strategy, include opportunities for reflection during the investigation, preparation and planning, action, and demonstration stages in addition to the actual reflection stage. Reflection is meant to reveal aspects of learning that might otherwise be missed and to inform you of how the overarching purpose is being achieved.

Reflection during investigation. This is the time to capture the baseline of where students are regarding the overarching purpose. If your intent is for students to recognize their efficacy in changing or effecting public policy, begin with a writing prompt such as, "Do you think young people can shape public opinion? What feelings arise when you think about adults listening to kids and taking them seriously?" After completing the Personal Inventory and Gathering Information About a Community Need forms, repeat the prompt. A different answer indicates these activities have shifted attitudes and personal perspective.

Reflection during preparation and planning. Find out what beliefs, assumptions, and attitudes are already in place regarding the theme of service. Where and how were they learned? What do students expect will happen as a result of their actions? Students can role-play situations they imagine will occur to practice and prepare and also to uncover anxieties or misconceptions. Students can consider such questions as, "What will you do if the child you're tutoring won't listen to the story?" "How do you think the convalescent home will look, sound, or smell?" Depending on the situation, you may give students a thought or question to take with them into the service experience. This may encourage them to be more observant, heighten their awareness of a particular need or action being taken, or encourage connection to a curricular aspect.

Reflection during action. As students perform their service, be observant. What do you notice the students paying attention to? What comments do you overhear? What behaviors do you see? Make notes and refer to them later during the reflection that follows the service. As service is actually going on, you may have time to draw students together for on-the-scene reflection and response. Conversation can draw upon your observations. Students can also take the initiative by raising concerns, sharing their excitement, or posing questions. Or you might pose a question such as, "Is there a better way to sort the recycling?" During this on-the-spot reflection, students sometimes have insights or make recommendations that improve their experience and the impact of their contributions right then and there.

Reflection following service. Following the service, use a variety of different methods for reflection: art, poetry, music, role playing, journals, mime, sculpture, drama, movement, photographs. Since people naturally reflect in different ways, you are more likely to elicit a range of responses and involve more students by varying the methods you use. Students can write a recipe for developing youth leadership skills or create a skit that shows a dilemma faced and ask others to step in and respond. Each student can write a haiku to contemplate and describe the experience of a morning spent in a garden. Experiment with less traditional reflection methods as well. For example, have students

Knowing the Difference Between Thoughts and Feelings

Thoughts and feelings are commonly confused in society and therefore by students in verbal and written communication. A student's feelings can be inappropriately expressed in essays or analytical writings that are supposed to only include opinions. Opinions can also erroneously masquerade as feelings. Students may lack the vocabulary to respond to, "What are you feeling?" As we assist students in clarifying the difference between thinking and feeling, we help them become more proficient in communication in general and reflection in specific. Here is an easy way to separate the two:

- Thoughts are generally expressions of ideas, opinions, recollections of events, and descriptions. Examples: Let's go to the movie. School should begin at 8:30 in the morning. I went out of town last weekend. It was cold so I wore a jacket.

- Feelings directly express an emotion: "I feel angry (sad, happy, confused, tired, exuberant)" or "I am

glad (interested, joyful, restless, satisfied)." Often we try to pass off thoughts as feelings by saying things like, "I feel that we should get a snack before the game." Is "we should get a snack before the game" a feeling? No, it's a thought. The speaker more accurately should say, "I *think* we should get a snack before the game." Students grasp this concept quickly, especially if you invite them to listen and be attentive to how adults and their peers confuse thoughts and feelings in this manner. Also, having students create a list of feelings can increase their vocabulary and accuracy in self-expression.

Once students understand the difference between expressions of thoughts and feelings, they often become more attentive to how people communicate. Their writing and speaking generally improves, gaining clarity and effectiveness. You will also see a difference in their reflective expression. Using the Four Square Reflection Tool (page 54) with your students will give you feedback on whether they know how to express thoughts and feelings.

enter class after a service experience to find their workspace covered with butcher paper. In silence, students represent their thoughts and feelings of the experience through art. After drawing for ten minutes on the communal mural, each student adds one word. Then each person takes five words from the mural and composes a poem or rap. Afterward, discuss both the process and the product. This method of reflection has been used successfully with groups of all ages.

Reflection during demonstration. As students prepare their public demonstration—perhaps a presentation to another class or an article for a school newspaper—have them draw upon their reflections, and even use the actual word *reflection,* to concretely explain this essential dynamic to others.

Journal Writing

Consider having students write their reflections in a journal. Keeping a journal encourages writing and personal expression that's often more unbridled than the formal structure of an essay-writing lesson. Once young people are introduced to keeping a journal, many continue to do so on their own. As one of the strategies for journal entries, use The Four Square Reflection Tool on page 54. This approach asks students to write their responses in four categories:

- *What happened?* This is the cognitive realm, where students can describe what they thought and what they observed. They report details: We collected 553 cans for the food shelf.

- *How did you feel?* Students' emotional responses may differ in tone from their cognitive responses. Separating the social and emotional from the cognitive helps students create a more complete picture. They express their feelings: What a disaster! The food shelf had many donations of cans that were expired, so we spent most of the time throwing them away. I felt upset that people didn't know any better.

- *What are your ideas?* They may suggest new ways to plan or collaborate with an agency or come up with new service activities that would meet other community needs. All ideas are welcome, such as: A few of us want to go to the food shelf on

Saturday and help design flyers that inform the community exactly what the food shelf needs.

- *What questions do you have?* What do students want to know about as a result of this experience? This question can help guide their own investigation or assist the class in planning the next steps for learning. To create generations of question askers requires adults to offer ample opportunities where students are encouraged to ask questions rather than be judged. For example, students might ask: How can we get a public service announcement on the radio that would get the right items collected for the food shelf?

Students can refer to these filled-out Four Square Reflection Tool forms for discussions, presentations, and other writing assignments based on their service learning experience.

Reflection Prompts

Whether reflection involves writing poetry or prose, taking photographs, or having a discussion, reflection prompts such as the questions that follow may assist in the process. Questions can be simplified for younger children and adapted to fit the activity. They can be used during every stage of service learning. Questions will vary based on intent. Some are more general to capture what students have learned or are in the process of comprehending; others are intended to relate specifically to the service aspect and whether students see the nuances or big picture of their participation. And some questions go to the heart of the overarching purpose.

- What was special about this activity today?

- What did the experience remind you of?

- What did you learn that you didn't know before? (What you learned might relate to yourself, a peer, the people/place we are helping, or an idea you want to investigate further.)

- How did you feel being at the service site? How did your feelings change from when you first arrived to when we left?

- How did you make a difference today?

- Five years from now, what do you think you will remember about this experience?

- Consider the books you read in preparing for this activity. Do you understand the characters better after your personal involvement with service?

- Which scientific terms make better sense now than when we started?

- What quote best captures how you are feeling now?

- What can we all do to make our time and efforts have a bigger impact?

A person's mind stretched to a new idea never goes back to its original dimensions.

—*Oliver Wendell Holmes, jurist and writer*

Beware the "Smelly Elephants"

Have you ever taken a group of young children to the zoo? After the trip, imagine the students reflecting on their trip through a class discussion. The teacher asks, "What was special about today's activity?" The first child answers, "The elephants smelled," and everyone laughs. Before you know what has happened, every child is describing the smelly elephants, and then the smelly monkeys, and so on until the conversation seems to go in a circle. As in general class discussions, this can be a hazard when students reflect on their service learning experience in a discussion format. The remedy? Have students write down responses to prompts in brief notes before the class starts its discussion, so that they can refer to their written thoughts in conversation. (Young children can draw, instead of writing notes.) This simple act preserves the integrity of each student's experience before it can be influenced by others' impressions and assures that everyone has something to contribute. Many teachers have found this "smelly elephant" remedy so effective, they use it frequently in all sorts of classroom discussions.

Closing the Loop: Giving Feedback

The cycle of student reflection is completed with feedback from you. Your nonjudgmental feedback and response to the students' reflections is important to them individually and to the service learning process as a whole. If journals are kept and you may read them,

ask if you can write a response in the journal or on an attached piece of paper. In discussions, listen carefully and ask questions. Either way, it's important that you appreciate what's being revealed and discovered, and that you respond honestly with your own thoughts or with a reflective quote, poem, or passage from a book.

Student Leadership of Reflection

Students can become skilled at creating reflection prompts for their classmates. In some classrooms, pairs of students eagerly accept the assignment of leading reflection. Often, this leads to including music, making links to historical figures the class is studying, creating a game-show interaction, or some other innovative twist. Even second-grade students delight in composing questions for their classmates to think about regarding the value and experience of service. Teachers can always review the plans and give students feedback prior to use.

Assessing Student Learning and Service

For students, demonstration appears to be the conclusion to the service learning process, however "over" and "done" are usually the wrong words to associate with this stage. In addition to spin-off projects and surprises that lead students to continue their commitment to a cause or theme of service, time needs to be allotted to assess the success of the actual activity, what your students learned, and the effectiveness of your planning and partnerships. This is a continual process and may be a little different for every experience. Teachers want to ensure that the service learning process produced appropriate learning for the students and had verifiable value for the community. In terms of student learning, traditional assessment methods—essays, quizzes, research papers—can be used, along with other forms of inquiry and analysis, including review of documents from student portfolios or of products made, pre- and post-service questionnaires for students and others involved, student presentations or reflective writings, discussions with community partners, and comments from any recipients of the service provided. A conversation with colleagues not directly involved also can help teachers review and improve the service learning process and find ways to strengthen the teaching methods used.

Whatever the method used, the assessment can focus on the following questions:

- *Student learning.* Were the defined content and skill objectives met? Were there any unforeseen outcomes? Did students show initiative or develop leadership skills? Were students able to reflect and place their experience in the larger context of community or society in general? Could students identify both their cognitive and affective growth?

- *Impact of the service.* Were students able to clearly state the need for and purpose of their service efforts? What contribution was made? Did the service help or hinder community efforts? What did the students accomplish? Is the partner agency or service recipient satisfied with the interaction? Have new relationships been formed? Were planned service programs, activities, or products completed?

- *The process.* How effective was the planning? Do you have ideas for specific areas you'd like to improve? For overall improvement? In future activities, how can students participate more and take greater ownership? How can you continue to develop community partnerships?

The two-part Assessment for Service Learning form on page 55 provides a basic method for reviewing these issues. Part one covers student learning, the impact of the service, and the service learning process. Part two asks you to identify the methods used in each of the five stages and to assess whether each of the K–12 Service-Learning Standards for Quality Practice was present and in what manner. You can select questions from the form to present to students so that they can participate in assessing their service learning experience.

The Student Self-Evaluation form on page 55 lets students analyze their learning and contribution. Several service learning organizations have developed sophisticated instruments for assessment. For more information on these, see the Resources listing (page 257). If students began using the Progress Monitoring form in the Action stage, they now can review it and discuss with others what they think has been accomplished, highpoints of the process, and what is still needed.

"One can't believe impossible things."

"I daresay you haven't had much practice," said the Queen. "When I was your age, I always did it for half-an-hour a day. Why, sometimes I've believed as many as six impossible things before breakfast."

—*Lewis Carroll,* Alice's Adventures in Wonderland

Telling Your Service Learning Story

Service learning has produced media-worthy stories all across the country. The act of publicizing service learning activities contains valuable learning opportunities. Publicizing service learning can be ongoing; there are many moments throughout the process that provide great stories. Determine your target audience: Other teachers? The school community? The school board? Legislators? The neighborhood? Post an attractive student-made flyer about an upcoming field trip and other teachers may become inspired to get involved. A student article in a school paper may get other kids wanting to take part in similar "cool" activities and interact with the "real world." A summary news story in a local paper informs the public about what's happening within the school walls and about the positive impact students are having in the community. A press release sent to a local city council member may result in an elected official participating, along with a photographer.

Where can you tell your service learning story? Everywhere. Post the story on the Internet through state and national service learning organizations and newsletters (see Resources, page 257). Find opportunities for students to give presentations to other students, to community groups, on cable or local access television, in organization newsletters, or on the radio. Local newspapers often seek good news, and sometimes students actually write the article. *The Kid's Guide to Social Action* (see Social Change Bookshelf—digital content) includes a section called "Power Media Coverage and Advertising" with tips for getting attention and ways students can promote and publicize their service experiences both before and after they occur. Your service learning story can be a source of youth, school, and community pride.

Going Global

Should service learning "go global"? Certainly, in all of our "backyards" there are enough issues and community needs to attend to. Still, the question persists, and I often ask educators: What value would be added by connecting a local issue with a global context? Discussion usually revolves around students expanding their awareness outside the confines of their daily lives toward awareness of others. This has value. Here

It's Time to Play—Know Your Audience

This activity can help upper elementary, middle, and high school students consider the best way to promote their ideas and plans to a particular audience. For example, a tutoring project would be presented very differently to second graders than to a parent group. This activity makes that distinction extremely vivid.

For this role play, select a service idea, preferably one that the students are enthusiastic about. Create small groups, with each one presenting information to a different audience. Students can get started by brainstorming the reasons for addressing each audience. Here are some suggestions for potential audiences:

- elementary children (specify grade)
- middle school students
- high school parents
- faculty meeting
- community agency
- prospective funding source
- chamber of commerce
- news reporters

As students consider why they're addressing their particular audience, they should start thinking about what methods will present their message most effectively. Encourage students to be creative and dynamic in their presentations, and even to involve their audiences. Students may also use visual aids (posters), skits, or songs to enhance their presentations. After each group makes its presentation, allow time for constructive feedback from the class. The ideas that emerge can be put into practice to inform the broader community about service learning in action.

are four more compelling reasons why going global is a necessity in these times.

Going Global Enhances Critical Thinking. Our academic programs intend to increase student ability to think critically; however, are we truly presenting challenging information to think critically about? As students plan a food drive for a local agency, having them discuss how every day one billion people in the world go to bed hungry[*] could provoke serious contemplation and critical thinking about why this dire situation of hunger exists in both developed and developing countries.

Going Global Makes the "Abstract" Concrete. Putting real faces on people in faraway places makes the abstract become concrete. Books are an effective portal into this transformative process. *A Life Like Mine: How Children Live Around the World* is one of three books in a series produced by UNICEF that belongs in every classroom. The photographs and narratives of children in near and distant places bring students back to the pages again and again. *Close Encounters of a Third-World Kind* uses fiction to transport the reader to Nepal with a girl accompanying her father on a medical mission. *The Photographer* brings the Doctors Without Borders program to life through a graphic-novel format. The idea of "those people over there" dissolves and is replaced with knowledge that we are all in this together.

Going Global Helps Develop a World View. With complex global problems and the need for creative and culturally sensitive solutions, students benefit from developing both a micro and macro perspective. Every issue they address through service learning—whether to impact the school community, neighborhood, or nation—has a larger story. This recognition will assist them now and in the future to comprehend and meet global challenges.

Going Global Matters Because We Are Interdependent. Carbon dioxide emissions from cars on U.S. freeways contribute to a heated atmosphere around the entire planet. Pollution fumes from coal burning energy plants in China ignore national boundaries as they drift across the Pacific Ocean to California. Competing for access to clean water that leads to war

---

[*] United Nations annual report on global food security, 2009

between countries in Africa has ramifications everywhere. Globalization, the Internet, climate change, and our interconnected oceans and waterways place all of us in each other's backyards. Students need this understanding,

Act Local to Go Global

How is going global accomplished? It is imperative to include local action in all service learning experiences. This simply makes sense given what we know about child development. Local service allows students a more up-close and concrete experience. Given that local service is always the starting point, we can then look at three extensions for the global element.

Act Locally ➡ Learn About a Related Global Issue

Add knowledge and awareness of how the local issue being addressed impacts people in a different locale. While working with local hunger, read a newspaper article on hunger caused by drought in India. Books are a critical portal. When students read *In Our Village* (page 192) written by students of Awet Secondary School in Kambi ya Simba, Tanzania, they learn how life expectancy in that community is affected by AIDS, how those students must pay for public education after elementary school, there is limited electricity available in this village, and only one doctor is available for every 50,000 people in Tanzania. Being informed is a prerequisite for thoughtful action.

> Never doubt that a small group of thoughtful, committed citizens can change the world; indeed, it's the only thing that ever has.
> —*Margaret Mead, anthropologist*

Act Locally ➡ Act on a Related Global Issue

While assisting with a local food collection, students may also contribute rice to communities in need through the Free Rice Web site (www.freerice.com). After reading *In Our Village*, students in a Los Angeles middle school decided to collect clothes for a local

family shelter and also send several boxes to Guatemala where a student had relatives and knew there was need. Reading about the kids in Kambi ya Simba inspired the students to extend their response from local to global.

Act Locally ➡ Act with Global Partners

To increase community awareness of international hunger issues, high school students partner with Oxfam International to sponsor a hunger banquet that simulates world hunger statistics at a meal. Additionally, students in over ten countries have read *In Our Village* and joined the *In Our Global Village* community by producing their own book based on the original (www.inourvillage.org). By participating in this international community of young authors, students are constructing knowledge about distant places through peer-to-peer communication. Photographs and student narratives replace misconceptions and stereotypes with accurate information.

Going global in any of these three forms makes sense for our students, for our communities, and for our world.

Curve Balls and Stumbling Blocks in Service Learning

It happens. After all the planning and collaboration and a phone confirmation just two days ago, your well-prepared fourth-grade students arrive at the senior center to begin their oral history interviews. A stop at the information desk reveals that your contact person has suddenly resigned and no replacement has been hired. The oral history interviews? "Sorry, we have nothing in place for you." This situation may seem extreme, but service efforts occasionally go awry. What do you do?

In the case of the "failed" visit to the senior center, the group convened in the parking lot for an emergency discussion. Students asked questions and looked for holes in their thinking and planning. After reviewing their contingency plans, this situation was determined to fall into the category of "truly out of our control." Deterred? No, only delayed. A team of students headed back to the senior center to ask for a brief meeting with the person responsible for scheduling special activities. After describing their plans and exercising their communication skills by using just a little persuasion, they established a new contact and made an agreement to reschedule.

Challenges found in service learning are, not surprisingly, very much like real-life challenges. When students work through these situations, they learn to create options, as well as to develop resiliency, problem-solving skills, persistence, and the concept of having a "plan B"—an important and practical concept. Students of all ages can contribute ideas and strategies that help repair the moment and often improve the original plan. What better time than while in school to learn about meeting a stumbling block with thoughtfulness and resolve?

> We all want to live in the moment but there isn't enough time.
>
> —*David Zasloff, musician*

A completely different kind of challenge you may face is aligning other school or organization programs and practices with service learning. For example, in an elementary school with a strong parent-run community service program, several parents resisted a classroom-based service learning program. The remedy was to educate everyone involved about the benefits of service learning and explain how to collaborate in the best interest of the students. In another school, children received stickers and prizes when they were "caught being good." Although the intention was to promote an ethic of service, children were actually refraining from engaging in kind acts unless they were certain an adult was watching and ready to dole out a reward. When administrators came to realize that the appropriate focus of service learning is the intrinsic reward that comes from cooperation and civic responsibility, the program was eliminated and not one child objected.

Some school administrators and teachers claim there is "no time for service learning" because of other priorities, such as improving math scores or creating a safer school climate. Service learning, however, can be an effective strategy to support many, if not most, important school priorities, including improved attendance, higher test scores, reducing dropout rates, academic improvement, parent involvement, character education, and safety at school (reducing bullying, teasing, and name-calling). More information about these proven service learning results can be found throughout this book and in many of the resources on pages 257–259.

Preserving Our History

Upon nearing completion of this book's revision, I visited a service learning colleague and heard about a splendid service learning experience being developed in Albion, New York. Students studied the lives of people buried in the local cemetery and were bringing these stories to "life" through dramatizations open to the public through "Ghost Walks." This experience combined research skills from history classes with theater and art skills, and students were excited to be connecting the people from the past with their present community. For example, a student might dress as Grace Biddle—the girl who wrote a letter to Abe Lincoln telling him he would look more distinguished with a beard (advice he followed)—and explain how she lived in a house where the hardware store now stands. Another student might "become" the first Santa Claus in New York City's Macy's Thanksgiving Day Parade. The past and present merge as students preserve community knowledge and pride through the telling of unique stories to eager audiences.

Preserving our history builds strong communities; whether in Eureka, California, where students create calendars that show "then" and "now" photographs; in Humble, Texas, where students honor veterans; in Warsaw, Poland, where students document the historic efforts of soldiers hiding in Kaboty Forrest during World War II; in Briggs, Oklahoma, where students are documenting the one hundred years of their school's history; or in Nashville, Tennessee, where first graders chronicle the lives of elders for their public libraries. Students learn as they grow deep roots in a communal history.

In this book, you will find examples of preserving history in the chapter Safe and Strong Communities (pages 197–210). *Safety* is one important part of what must be accomplished in our communities. *Strength* and vitality based on these deep historical roots is the other.

Other challenges you may encounter are more systemic. Is the school schedule flexible enough for service learning experiences? Are any funds available for supplies and transportation? Will the district apply for grants to support staff development and other professional opportunities? If the district or school policy requires that students stay on campus, will there be exceptions for classroom-related service learning outings? Many schools and districts with strong commitments to service learning establish advisory groups to unravel these and other issues. Models and prototypes can be found through state and national education agencies, other service learning organizations, and the Internet. Experienced service learning practitioners are usually more than willing to share ideas and resources.

For more ideas, see the chapter Creating a Culture of Service on pages 238–254.

If you can't make a mistake, you can't make anything.

—*Marva N. Collins, educator*

Establishing Curricular Connections: Points of Entry

1. Identify an existing program or activity to transform into authentic service learning.
   * Select an activity or project already existing on campus.
   * Examine it for cross-curricular learning opportunities that meet or enhance academic standards.
   * Exchange resources and ideas with teachers, students, and community partners.

   Example: Canned Food Drive

   Before students brought in cans of food, classroom activities included studying nutrition, visiting the receiving agency to identify needed foods, and reading related literature. Students led peer discussions on social issues, replacing misconceptions with an understanding of hunger in their community. Graphs showing the food collected along with student-authored articles about the impact and continued need of this service were printed in school and community newspapers.

   Bookshelf suggestions: *The Can-Do Thanksgiving, Soul Moon Soup,* and *Homeless Teens*

2. Begin with standard curriculum, content, and skills, and find an age-appropriate extension into service that meets a community need verified by the students.
   * Identify the specific content and skill areas to be addressed.
   * Select an area of emphasis that supports or adds to classroom learning and addresses learning objectives or state standards.
   * Guide students as they investigate the related community need and create a plan for applying classroom content that improves a situation or benefits others.
   * Look for additional learning opportunities as the plan is transformed into action.

   Example: Learning History through Discussion with Elder Partners

   To be better informed about current events and to improve listening and communication skills, students met weekly with elders at a senior center. Shared experiences included studying news events, learning about aging, interviewing, collaborating on oral histories and photo essays, displaying results in the school and public library, and building a Web page to reach a broader audience.

   Bookshelf suggestions: *Stranger in the Mirror, Growing Older,* and *We Were There, Too! Young People in U.S. History*

3. From a theme or unit of study, identify content and skill connections.
   * Begin with a broad theme or topic, often with obvious service implications.
   * Identify specific standards-based content and skill areas to be developed.
   * Select a service application verified by students as an authentic need, including a baseline of the situation so they can monitor progress.

Example: The Individual's Role in Society

During a lesson about the individual's role in society, teachers encouraged students to consider options for civic participation. Curriculum included reading nonfiction stories of adults and young people contributing to their communities, researching local agency needs, providing regular assistance to an agency, and publishing an informative pamphlet for young people about the agency.

Bookshelf suggestions: *Sisters in Strength: American Women Who Make a Difference* and *Free the Children: A Young Man's Personal Crusade Against Child Labor*

4. Start with a student-identified need.
   * Identify student skills, talents, and interests.
   * Students define a problem, verify a need, and establish solutions, usually with community input.
   * Students lead implementation as teacher facilitates, adding interdisciplinary learning opportunities.

   Example: Transform an Empty Lot into a Community Garden

   A student initiated a conversation about starting a community garden in an empty lot near the school. With teacher guidance, academic standards were met as students communicated with a government agency regarding property use, conducted Internet research to find funding sources, partnered with special needs students to maintain the garden, and donated the harvest to a local shelter.

   Bookshelf suggestions: *Seedfolks, Just Kids: Visiting a Class for Children with Special Needs,* and *A Kid's Guide to Social Action*

5. Start with a community-identified need.
   * Community requests assistance, perhaps through an agency that has worked with the school before.
   * Teacher, students, and community partners identify learning opportunities.

   Example: Tutoring/Literacy

   A school received a request to participate in a citywide book collection to benefit local children. Teachers in several grades collaborated on cross-age projects, in which older students helped younger children write and illustrate bilingual books on mutually agreed-on themes. The books were donated to youth clubs, hospitals, and childcare facilities. Student representatives served on a city committee to plan future literacy activities.

   Bookshelf suggestions: *La Mariposa, Just Juice,* and *Thank You, Mr. Falker*

K–12 Service-Learning Standards for Quality Practice

Meaningful Service. Service-learning actively engages participants in meaningful and personally relevant service activities.

> Students identify, authenticate, and learn about a recognized community need. Student actions are reciprocal, valued by the community, and have real consequences while offering opportunities to apply newly acquired academic skills and knowledge.

Link to Curriculum. Service-learning is intentionally used as an instructional strategy to meet learning goals and/or content standards.

> The process includes deliberate cross-curricular connections whereby students learn skills and content through varied modalities that meet academic standards, and enables the transference of skills and content to new applications. The content informs the service and the service informs the content.

Reflection. Service-learning incorporates multiple challenging reflection activities that are ongoing and that prompt deep thinking and analysis about oneself and one's relationship to society.

> Students participate in systemic varied processes that integrate empathetic response with cognitive thinking related to social issues and their lives. This affective and cognitive blend deepens the service learning as students apply and transfer new understandings of themselves, others, and the world around them.

Diversity. Service-learning promotes understanding of diversity and mutual respect among all participants.

> Student experience affords opportunities to form multidimensional understanding and varied points of view. This process allows students to gain perspective and develop mutual respect and appreciation for others, while replacing stereotypes with accurate information.

Youth Voice. Service-learning provides youth with a strong voice in planning, implementing, and evaluating service-learning experiences with guidance from adults.

> Students experience significant age-appropriate challenges involving tasks that require thinking, initiative, and problem solving as they demonstrate responsibility and decision-making in an environment safe enough to allow them to make mistakes and to succeed.

Partnerships. Service-learning partnerships are collaborative, mutually beneficial, and address community needs.

> Students participate in the development of reciprocal partnerships and share responsibility with community members, parents, organizations, and other students. These relationships afford opportunities to interact with people of diverse backgrounds and experience, resulting in mutual respect, understanding, and appreciation.

Progress Monitoring. Service-learning engages participants in an ongoing process to assess the quality of implementation and progress toward meeting specified goals, and uses results for improvement and sustainability.

> Once students identify and authenticate the need, they use varied methods to observe and track change and improvement as they carry out the service learning process. Advancement toward intended or developing outcomes is examined, along with effectiveness of applied procedures and recognized mutual benefits. Findings are shared with stakeholders.

Duration and Intensity. Service-learning has sufficient duration and intensity to address community needs and meet specified outcomes.

> The length of the experience allows for a complete and thorough process as articulated in the Five Stages of Service Learning, with age-appropriate content, skill development, and depth of material covered.

The Five Stages of Service Learning

Inventory and Investigation

Using interviewing and other means of social analysis, students:
* catalog the interests, skills, and talents of their peers and partners.
* identify a need.
* analyze the underlying problem.
* establish a baseline of the need.
* begin to accumulate partners.

Preparation and Planning

With guidance from their teacher, students:
* draw upon previously acquired skills and knowledge.
* acquire new information through varied, engaging means and methods.
* collaborate with community partners.
* develop a plan that encourages responsibility.
* recognize the integration of service and learning.
* become ready to provide meaningful service.
* articulate roles and responsibilities of all involved.
* define realistic parameters for implementation.

Action

Through direct service, indirect service, research, advocacy, or a combination of these approaches, students take action that:
* has value, purpose, and meaning.
* uses previously learned and newly acquired academic skills and knowledge.
* offers unique learning experiences.
* has real consequences.
* offers a safe environment to learn, to make mistakes, and to succeed.

Reflection

During systematic reflection, the teacher or students guide the process using various modalities, such as role play, discussion, and journal writing. Participating students:
* describe what happened.
* examine the difference made.
* discuss thoughts and feelings.
* place experience in a larger context.
* consider project improvements.
* generate ideas.
* identify questions.
* encourage comments from partners and recipients.
* receive feedback.

Demonstration

Students showcase what and how they have learned, along with demonstrating skills, insights, and outcomes of service provided to an outside group. Students may:
* report to peers, faculty, parents, and/or community members.
* write articles or letters to local newspapers regarding issues of public concern.
* create a publication or Web site that helps others learn from students' experiences.
* make presentations and performances.
* create displays of public art with murals or photography.

See digital content for full-size reproducible pages.

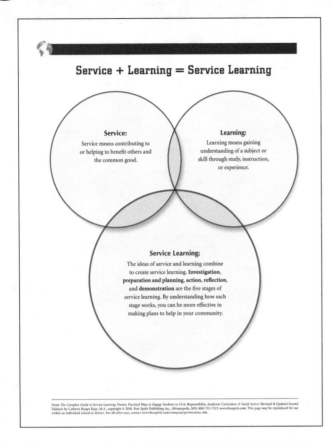

Service + Learning = Service Learning

Service:
Service means contributing to or helping to benefit others and the common good.

Learning:
Learning means gaining understanding of a subject or skill through study, instruction, or experience.

Service Learning:
The ideas of service and learning combine to create service learning. **Investigation, preparation and planning, action, reflection,** and **demonstration** are the five stages of service learning. By understanding how each stage works, you can be more effective in making plans to help in your community.

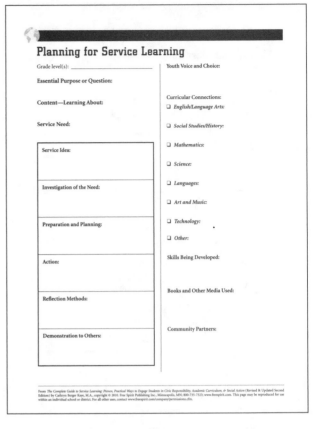

Planning for Service Learning

Grade level(s): _____

Essential Purpose or Question:

Content—Learning About:

Service Need:

Service Idea:
Investigation of the Need:
Preparation and Planning:
Action:
Reflection Methods:
Demonstration to Others:

Youth Voice and Choice:

Curricular Connections:
❑ *English/Language Arts:*

❑ *Social Studies/History:*

❑ *Mathematics:*

❑ *Science:*

❑ *Languages:*

❑ *Art and Music:*

❑ *Technology:*

❑ *Other:*

Skills Being Developed:

Books and Other Media Used:

Community Partners:

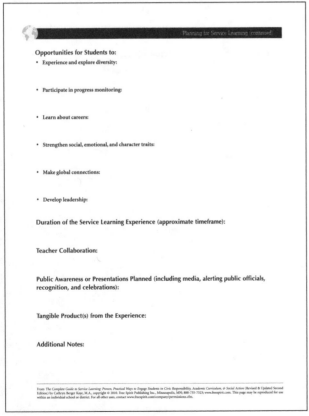

Planning for Service Learning (continued)

Opportunities for Students to:
- Experience and explore diversity:

- Participate in progress monitoring:

- Learn about careers:

- Strengthen social, emotional, and character traits:

- Make global connections:

- Develop leadership:

Duration of the Service Learning Experience (approximate timeframe):

Teacher Collaboration:

Public Awareness or Presentations Planned (including media, alerting public officials, recognition, and celebrations):

Tangible Product(s) from the Experience:

Additional Notes:

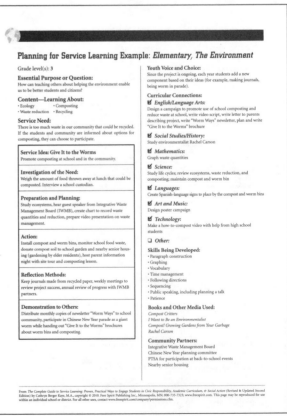

Planning for Service Learning Example: *Elementary, The Environment*

Grade level(s): 3

Essential Purpose or Question:
How can teaching others about helping the environment enable us to be better students and citizens?

Content—Learning About:
- Ecology • Composting
- Waste reduction • Recycling

Service Need:
There is too much waste in our community that could be recycled. If the students and community are informed about options for composting, they can choose to participate.

Service Idea: Give It to the Worms
Promote composting at school and in the community.

Investigation of the Need:
Weigh the amount of food thrown away at lunch that could be composted. Interview a school custodian.

Preparation and Planning:
Study ecosystems, hear guest speaker from Integrative Waste Management Board (IWMB), create chart to record waste quantities and reduction, prepare video presentation on waste management.

Action:
Install compost and worm bins, monitor school food waste, donate compost soil to school garden and nearby senior housing (gardening by elder residents), host parent information night with site tour and composting lesson.

Reflection Methods:
Keep journals made from recycled paper, weekly meetings to review project success, annual review of progress with IWMB partners.

Demonstration to Others:
Distribute monthly copies of newsletter "Worm Ways" to school community, participate in Chinese New Year parade as a giant worm while handing out "Give It to the Worms" brochures about worm bins and composting.

Youth Voice and Choice:
Since the project is ongoing, each year students add a new component based on their ideas (for example, making journals, being worm in parade).

Curricular Connections:
☑ *English/Language Arts:*
Design a campaign to promote use of school composting and reduce waste at school, write video script, write letter to parents describing project, write "Worm Ways" newsletter, plan and write "Give It to the Worms" brochure

☑ *Social Studies/History:*
Study environmentalist Rachel Carson

☑ *Mathematics:*
Graph waste quantities

☑ *Science:*
Study life cycles; review ecosystems, waste reduction, and composting; maintain compost and worm bin

☑ *Languages:*
Create Spanish-language signs to place by the compost and worm bins

☑ *Art and Music:*
Design poster campaign

☑ *Technology:*
Make a how-to-compost video with help from high school students

❑ *Other:*

Skills Being Developed:
- Paragraph construction
- Graphing
- Vocabulary
- Time management
- Following directions
- Sequencing
- Public speaking, including planning a talk
- Patience

Books and Other Media Used:
Compost Critters
I Want to Be an Environmentalist
Compost! Growing Gardens from Your Garbage
Rachel Carson

Community Partners:
Integrative Waste Management Board
Chinese New Year planning committee
PTSA for participation at back-to-school events
Nearby senior housing

See digital content for full-size reproducible pages.

Planning for Service Learning Example: *Elementary, The Environment* (continued)

Opportunities for Students to:

- **Experience and explore diversity:**
  Students used the composting as a way to discuss all the different foods people eat and their cultural connections. After learning more about Chinese New Year, they added another level of understanding diversity. In creating their brochure, students considered who their audience would be and wrote to a range of populations in their community.
- **Participate in progress monitoring:**
  Students measured the reduction in garbage waste at school. They also visited each classroom at the beginning of the year to inform students about the compost, and revisited at the beginning of February to see how many students used the compost and how many planned to use it.
- **Learn about careers:**
  Students learned about careers in waste management and city commissions.
- **Strengthen social, emotional, and character traits:**
  Students strengthened their perseverance and patience. Patience was especially challenging at first since the students wanted results; they wanted everyone to use the compost bins and they wanted to see the compost "magic" happen! By charting progress, they became more patient and saw how the activities and success evolved over time.
- **Make global connections:**
  The connection with Chinese New Year added to our sense of celebration occurring in many parts of the world. This was an exciting notion for the students to understand.
- **Develop leadership:**
  Students worked diligently on organizational skills, which are definite traits of leaders. They planned the collection for the compost, formed speaking teams, and tracked details that were essential to progress.

Duration of the Service Learning Experience (approximate timeframe):
The service began with the commitment of a yearlong effort. With the students' excitement and success, it has grown to an annual experience with ongoing learning opportunities. At the beginning, we spent about a day a week on this, spread out among many subject areas. As the process grew more established, we spent about two to three hours a week doing upkeep and monitoring. Students had roles during lunch and other out-of-class times that they gladly fulfilled.

Teacher Collaboration:
All teachers willingly incorporated into their lessons the books about composting recommended by our class. They welcomed our students for lessons and announcements.

Public Awareness or Presentations Planned (including media, alerting public officials, recognition, and celebrations):
A newspaper article reported on the worm at the Chinese New Year parade. Students made annual presentations and gave tours to parents and community members, including residents of a senior living community.

Tangible Product(s) from the Experience:
"Worm Ways" newsletter, "Give It to the Worms" brochure, how-to-compost video created with high school partners

Additional Notes:
This activity started on a small scale with one elementary school teacher in Palo Alto, California, and grew to involve many more. This plan shows what evolved over four years.

Planning for Service Learning Example: *Middle School, Immigrants*

Grade level(s): **6–7**

Essential Purpose or Question:
Can student learning move from simulation to making a real community impact?

Content—Learning About:
- Immigration to the United States
- Process of becoming a citizen
- Resettlement of refugees
- Civic involvement

Service Need:
Becoming a U.S. citizen requires dedication and hard work that deserves to be honored by the community, which can increase tolerance and understanding between cultures.

Service Idea: In Honor of New Citizens
Sponsor a citizenship swearing-in ceremony at school.

Investigation of the Need:
Interview an official from Immigration and Naturalization Services (INS) to find out about the need for swearing-in ceremonies and community involvement.

Preparation and Planning:
Meet with INS, read about the countries of origin of the people being sworn in, plan the event, get food donations, decorate auditorium and library, arrange for coverage by educational television channel.

Action:
Set up rooms, greet guests, interview the new citizens, and take photographs.

Reflection Methods:
Write in journals, lead discussion groups, identify needs for written materials and resources for children of these families, write a letter to INS to share what has been learned and suggest ideas for next time, send forms to partner agencies for feedback, read and share letters received from new citizen families expressing thanks for the special event.

Demonstration to Others:
Compile interviews and photographs for each family, and make "welcome kits" for the children of these families with: a cartoon-style area map, recommended places for sports and entertainment, a list of after-school and weekend activities, a guide of youth idioms, a small journal, and a pen.

Youth Voice and Choice:
Develop the idea, establish partnerships, organize into committees, plan interviews, design and make welcome kits for children of families.

Curricular Connections:

☑ ***English/Language Arts:***
Write letters for donations and thank-you letters, keep journals, read literature about the immigrant experience, write press releases, learn new vocabulary

☑ ***Social Studies/History:***
Participate in an Ellis Island simulation; hear guest speaker from INS; research the countries of origin of the people being sworn in—their history, current events, and culture (foods, music, traditions); interview immigrants about their transition to citizenship

☐ ***Mathematics:***

☐ ***Science:***

☑ ***Languages:***
Identify greetings in the languages of the countries studied, including the correct pronunciations; use the greetings on banners

☑ ***Art and Music:***
Collect music from many cultures; school choral group participates by singing a medley with cultural references

☐ ***Technology:***

☐ ***Other:***

Skills Being Developed:
- Organization and planning
- Letter writing
- Interviewing
- Problem solving
- Teamwork

Books and Other Media Used:
The Skirt
The Circuit and *Breaking Through*
The Middle of Everywhere: The World's Refugees Come to Our Town (excerpts)
Behind the Mountains
The Whispering Cloth: A Refugee's Story
The Kid's Guide to Social Action
Immigration: How Should It Be Controlled?
A Very Important Day

Community Partners:
Immigration and Naturalization Services (INS)
City multicultural program
Educational TV channel
Portland Press

From *The Complete Guide to Service Learning: Proven, Practical Ways to Engage Students in Civic Responsibility, Academic Curriculum, & Social Action* (Revised & Updated Second Edition) by Cathryn Berger Kaye, M.A., copyright © 2010. Free Spirit Publishing Inc., Minneapolis, MN; 800-735-7323; www.freespirit.com. This page may be reproduced for use within an individual school or district. For all other uses, contact www.freespirit.com/company/permissions.cfm.

Planning for Service Learning Example: *Middle School, Immigrants* (continued)

Opportunities for Students to:

- **Experience and explore diversity:**
  Students researched the immigrants' countries of origin as they were making plans for the swearing-in ceremony. They held discussions about the many different reasons people immigrate to the United States, and the specific circumstances related to people seeking refugee status. They saw the differences in needs from one generation to the next.
- **Participate in progress monitoring:**
  N/A
- **Learn about careers:**
  Students learned about careers in government and nonprofit organizations related to refugee assistance, both national and international.
- **Strengthen social-emotional and character traits:**
  Students replaced stereotypes with accurate information about people within their community. They also gained empathy, compassion, and open-mindedness.
- **Make global connections:**
  Students increased their knowledge of why people immigrate and gained awareness of contemporary global issues in many parts of the world.
- **Develop leadership:**
  This experience presented a tremendous opportunity for youth initiative and creativity. Students had fun learning about other cultures and creating a welcoming environment. They showed initiative in their studies and showed exemplary leadership in making complex issues easier for their peers to understand.

Duration of the Service Learning Experience (approximate timeframe):
Roughly two to three months, with more time spent at the beginning and right before the event. This service experience has been adopted by each class for several years.

Teacher Collaboration:
Teachers school-wide saw the value to their classes and to the entire community and collaborated by allowing release time from class as the event neared. Many classes generously participated by making posters and decorations, helping with translations, and reading relevant literature to become well-versed on the topic.

Public Awareness or Presentations Planned (including media, alerting public officials, recognition, and celebrations):
Students sought donations from the community and educated local businesses about their work and about the need being addressed. Students wrote press releases and invited media to attend the swearing-in ceremony. Students also invited local elected officials and school board members. The event closed with a celebration for the new citizens.

Tangible Product(s) from the Experience:
Welcome kit prototype, area maps, lists of community information

Additional Notes:
This service learning experience took place at Lyman Moore Middle School in Portland, Maine. It evolved from student interest and initiative resulting from an Ellis Island simulation, which taught them more about their community as a resettlement area for people from all over the world. Partnerships with INS and city offices were essential components.

From *The Complete Guide to Service Learning: Proven, Practical Ways to Engage Students in Civic Responsibility, Academic Curriculum, & Social Action* (Revised & Updated Second Edition) by Cathryn Berger Kaye, M.A., copyright © 2010. Free Spirit Publishing Inc., Minneapolis, MN; 800-735-7323; www.freespirit.com. This page may be reproduced for use within an individual school or district. For all other uses, contact www.freespirit.com/company/permissions.cfm.

Planning for Service Learning Example: *High School, Literacy*

Grade level(s): **9**

Essential Purpose or Question:
How do mentoring relationships help students become more cognizant about their own learning styles?

Content—Learning About:
- Interpersonal relationships
- Civic participation
- Child psychology
- Bookmaking
- Being role models

Service Need:
Reciprocal learning occurs in mentoring relationships between older and younger students with mutual benefits; young children need encouragement to read and write.

Service Idea: Book Buddies
Instruct young children in bookmaking and collaborate on making books for the community.

Investigation of the Need:
Interview a kindergarten teacher about the needed products, interaction with young children, and involving a child development specialist.

Preparation and Planning:
Write reflections on childhood and favorite books; participate in an interactive workshop with a child psychologist about learning styles and Gardner's theory of multiple intelligences; read children's books; in small groups, discuss methods of working with young children; design lessons reflecting different types of intelligence; reach consensus on theme for the new books ("friendship" is chosen to combat bullying); get resources for bookmaking; learn bookbinding techniques; arrange logistics and transportation.

Action:
Visit a kindergarten class three times: (1) get acquainted with children and read books, (2) discuss book ideas on the theme of friendship and begin story development, and (3) write and illustrate the story. Copies of the books are given to the children, the school, and public libraries.

Reflection Methods:
Write in journals with peer "journal partners" who read entries and respond; teacher also reads and gives feedback weekly. Engage in a class discussion after each visit, using role plays and problem solving. Write reflective essays on how the theory of multiple intelligences applies to daily student life.

Demonstration to Others:
Present the service experience with the kindergartners at the school district service learning committee meeting.

Youth Voice and Choice:
Created plans, found a partner kindergarten classroom, wrote a proposal for a literacy grant, made phone calls, got donations, and designed activities.

Curricular Connections:

☑ ***English/Language Arts:***
Write a grant proposal; read and analyze children's books for content, format, and style; write a book; write letters requesting donations and reduced-cost supplies

☑ ***Social Studies/History:***
Research child psychology

☑ ***Mathematics:***
Manage a budget of funds received from the school and a literacy grant

☑ ***Science:***
Study how the brain works with multiple intelligences

☑ ***Languages:***
Prepare for working with young bilingual children with assistance from a Spanish language teacher

☑ ***Art and Music:***
Art students make presentations on illustration to inform students about various styles; create illustrations with children; bookbinding

☑ ***Technology:***
Use computer skills to create a design and template for the bookmaking process

☐ ***Other:***

Skills Being Developed:
- Organization
- Leadership
- Planning
- Writing in different styles—proposals, thank-you letters, stories
- Communication—phone calls for supplies, interaction with elementary teachers, interaction in small planning groups, partnerships with children

Books and Other Media Used:
The Sissy Duckling
Toestomper and the Caterpillars
Margarita y Margaret (bilingual)
La Mariposa
Hey, Little Ant!

Community Partners:
Will Rogers Elementary School
Kelly Paper Supplies
School District Service Learning Advisory Committee

From *The Complete Guide to Service Learning: Proven, Practical Ways to Engage Students in Civic Responsibility, Academic Curriculum, & Social Action* (Revised & Updated Second Edition) by Cathryn Berger Kaye, M.A., copyright © 2010. Free Spirit Publishing Inc., Minneapolis, MN; 800-735-7323; www.freespirit.com. This page may be reproduced for use within an individual school or district. For all other uses, contact www.freespirit.com/company/permissions.cfm.

See digital content for full-size reproducible pages.

Panel 1

 Planning for Service Learning Example: High School Literacy (continued)

Opportunities for Students to:

- **Experience and explore diversity:**
  Working with children of many ethnicities and connecting with their interests—often without a common language—led to thoughtful conversations. Students also saw how bilingual development is an advantage and marveled at some of the children who were already fluent in two languages at a young age.

- **Participate in progress monitoring:**
  With each visit to the kindergarten class, students paid specific attention to the interaction on two levels: social comfort and academic growth. They used information from the child psychologist to look for responsiveness from the children and continued positive affect. They also looked at retention, what the children remembered from one visit to the next. At the end of the first two visits they asked, "What do you want to remember from this visit?" and then checked in with the children later. They also asked the teacher after each visit what progress she had noted by observing the children's interactions.

- **Learn about careers:**
  Students learned about careers in child psychology and education (teachers and administrators).

- **Strengthen social-emotional and character traits:**
  Students gained skills in self-reflection, especially when comparing their own learning styles and preferences with those of the children; caring; humor; and supportive interactions with peers and with younger children.

- **Make global connections:**
  N/A

- **Develop leadership:**
  Students revised the initial plans made by their teacher to have them go read books to an elementary class. Students reframed the experience to work with children over time to gain a better grasp of the learning process and to create books for the community. They wrote a new service plan; obtained approval from the principal; and found a class liaison for the elementary school, logistics specialists, a budget manager, and donation solicitors. They also had representatives present at the school district's Service Learning Advisory Committee meeting.

Duration of the Service Learning Experience (approximate timeframe):
The experience lasted three weeks.

Teacher Collaboration:
Teachers collaborated at two different school sites.

Public Awareness or Presentations Planned (including media, alerting public officials, recognition, and celebrations):
Students presented at the school district's Service Learning Advisory Committee meeting and were featured in a local newspaper with a photograph.

Tangible Product(s) from the Experience:
Books for the kindergarten students, with additional copies permanently placed in the school libraries and classrooms.

Additional Notes:
This service learning experience began as a service requirement at Santa Monica High School in California. Through student initiative and planning, the plan changed from a one-time read aloud to elementary children into a three-week reading program and bookmaking venture. An ongoing relationship was established between the classrooms and the schools.

Panel 2

 ### Planning for Service Learning Example: *Middle School, Special Needs and Disabilities*

Grade level(s): PreK–8*

Essential Purpose or Question:
How can children with special needs make a contribution to their community while learning transferable skills?

Content—Learning About:
- Our neighborhood
- Elders
- Life cycle of plants
- Acts of generosity

Service Need:
Two populations are in close proximity with no interaction; communication could be mutually beneficial.

Service Idea: Being Good Neighbors
Give flowering potted plants to elders at a senior residential center

Investigation of the Need:
A group of students with special needs and their teachers visited a neighboring senior center, bringing Halloween decorations. They noticed there were no flowers or plants in the center, except for artificial flowers. They also saw seniors sitting outside next to an empty garden bed. The students were learning about plants and thought the residents needed something fresh and beautiful.

Preparation and Planning:
Study about plants, grow plants from seeds to seedlings, paint and decorate pots with glitter and ribbons, work with high school students in an environmental science class to plant pots.

Action:
Deliver plants, interact with elders, create picture stories to give to the senior center.

Reflection Methods:
Students write or dictate to teachers their reflections on the experience. Teachers reflect and discuss each student's level of participation and development.

Demonstration to Others:
Success led to a follow-up weekend with the students and their families planting an outdoor garden in a courtyard at the senior residence. Elders and staff members helped or watched and interacted with the children. Most parents noted this was the first time their children had participated in community service.

Youth Voice and Choice:
Making choices is a significant skill for autistic children. This project affords many opportunities for choice: selecting colors, choosing plants to grow, and choosing to plant pots for their families.

Curricular Connections:

☑ *English/Language Arts:*
Learn about the life cycle of plants through story books and flannel board activities, make sequence books about plant life cycles, practice conversation skills with elders

☑ *Social Studies/History:*
Learn about the community (the high school and the senior residential center); discuss community involvement, service, and generosity

☑ *Mathematics:*
Measure plant growth and chart data

☑ *Science:*
Plant seeds in plastic bags to watch seedlings sprout, transfer seedlings to soil, draw diagrams of plants

☐ *Languages:*

☑ *Art and Music:*
Draw and label pictures, write picture stories

☑ *Technology:*
Use computer skills in typing stories

☐ *Other:*

Skills Being Developed:
- Art—cutting, pasting, tracing
- Handwriting
- Drawing
- Making choices
- Staying on task
- Transitioning from one setting to another
- Social communication and interaction

Books and Other Media Used:
Jack's Garden
Bud
A Harvest of Color: Growing a Vegetable Garden

Community Partners:
High school environmental science teacher
Senior residential center

* Children with autism were assisted in part by high school students in grades 10 and 11.

Panel 3

 Planning for Service Learning Example: Special Needs and Disabilities (continued)

Opportunities for Students to:

- **Experience and explore diversity:**
  Most students had never been in a senior residential center. This was an opportunity to visit and meet elder people. Through their experience, the students learned they had something to give to the elders. They worked with high school students who helped them prepare the plants they presented to the center.

- **Participate in progress monitoring:**
  The students monitored the growth of their seedlings to determine when the plants were ready to be delivered to the senior center.

- **Learn about careers:**
  Students learned firsthand about the careers of doctors, nurses, caretakers, and cafeteria workers. During a celebration of their work, they each chose an occupation and dressed as if they worked in that profession.

- **Strengthen social, emotional, and character traits:**
  Students practiced social greetings and demonstrated generosity, caring, cooperation, and kindness to others.

- **Make global connections:**
  Students' exposure to elders from different countries led to a class conversation about immigration.

- **Develop leadership:**
  Some students helped their peers who required assistance with the artwork, planting, or delivery. When students and their families planted the garden, they worked together to complete the tasks of digging holes and placing plants in the ground so all students—no matter their skill level—could participate.

Duration of the Service Learning Experience (approximate timeframe):
This project took three to four months, from planting the seedlings to gifting the plants.

Teacher Collaboration:
All teachers and staff members helped in collaborative planning.

Public Awareness or Presentations Planned (including media, alerting public officials, recognition, and celebrations):
N/A

Tangible Product(s) from the Experience:
Each resident of the senior center received a potted plant. The residents had a new garden bed full of flowers and vegetation by their sun deck where many go outside to sit. Students also began volunteer jobs at the center.

Additional Notes:
The senior residential center became a long-term service recipient for our students with special needs at the Giant Steps program in St. Louis, Missouri. We shared holiday decorations with residents, put on holiday shows, performed gymnastic demonstrations, and taught the seniors exercises they could do while seated. One student visited weekly to tell stories to a group of residents. Other students volunteered in the cafeteria setting up the dining room for lunch, and delivering mail, calendars, and newspapers to the residents.
The program is individualized to student ability. The school is on a high school campus; all of the students with autism visited the high school environmental science class and the high school students came to their classrooms. Some students requested extra pots to plant and give to their parents, along with a book of stories written about their service learning experience.

Panel 4

Getting Ready for Personal Inventory

Every student brings interests, skills, and talents to the class. Your task is to discover what those are by doing a personal inventory. Using the Personal Inventory form, you will interview another student to discover abilities and interests that will be helpful to the group. Complete this form to prepare.

Coming to Terms

What's the difference between these three terms?
Interest:

Skill:

Talent:

Active Listening

List three signs that someone is being a good listener.
1.

2.

3.

List three behaviors to avoid when listening:
1.

2.

3.

Form groups of three. One person speaks about a subject for two minutes, one person listens, and one person observes the listener and notes the following:

- Examples of good listening:

- Ideas for improvement:

Now, switch roles and repeat.

See digital content for full-size reproducible pages.

Interviewing

Questions for Getting Information
Look at the Personal Inventory form. What questions will you ask to find out the person's interests?

Encouraging Questions
Sometimes, people need a little encouragement to answer a question. If the person you are interviewing says, "I don't know," be ready with a response like:

1. "Everyone has interests. For example, I'm interested in _____. So, what about you?"

2. Add another response:

3. Add another response:

Probing Questions
A probing question goes deeper. For example, if you ask, "What are your interests?" and the person you are interviewing answers "Music," what would you ask next? *Hint:* A person could listen to music and/or play a musical instrument, and there are many kinds of music.

Write two sample probing questions:
1.

2.

Note Taking Tips
- Write legibly so you can read your writing later.
- Be on the lookout for key words.
- Do not use complete sentences. Notes are meant to be short phrases and words that capture key ideas.
- Add a tip of your own:

Personal Inventory

Interests, skills, and talents—we all have them. What are they?

Interests are what you think about and what you would like to know more about—for example, outer space, popular music, or a historical event like a world war. Are you interested in animals, movies, mysteries, or visiting faraway places? Do you collect anything?

Skills and talents have to do with things you like to do or that you do easily or well. Do you have an activity you especially like? Do you have a favorite subject in school? Do you sing, play the saxophone, or study ballet? Do you know more than one language? Can you cook? Do you have a garden? Do you prefer to paint pictures or play soccer? Do you have any special computer abilities?

Work with a partner and take turns interviewing each other to identify your interests, skills, and talents and to find out how you have helped and been helped by others. Then, compile a class chart of your findings. This will come in handy on your service learning journey.

Interests: I like to learn and think about . . .

Skills and talents: I can . . .

Being helpful: Describe a time when you helped someone.

Receiving help: Describe a time when someone helped you.

Gathering Information About a Community Need

What does your community need? Use the questions in the following four categories as guides for finding out. As a class, you might agree to explore one topic, for example, how kids get along at school, hunger and poverty, or an environmental concern. Or you might decide to learn about general needs at school or in the surrounding area. Form small groups, with each group focusing on one category and gathering information in a different way.

Finding out about _____

Media
What media (newspapers—including school newspapers, TV stations, radio) in your community might have helpful information? List ways you can work with different media to learn about needs in your community.

Interviews
Think of a person who is knowledgeable about this topic in your area—perhaps someone at school or in a local organization or government office. Write four questions you would ask this person in an interview.

An interview with _____

Questions:
1.

2.

3.

4.

Survey
A survey can help you find out what people know or think about a topic and get ideas for helping. Who could you survey—students, family members, neighbors? How many surveys would you want completed? Write three survey questions.

Who to survey: _____   How many surveys: _____

Questions for the survey:
1.

2.

3.

Observation and Experience
How can you gather information through your own observation and experience? Where would you go? What would you do there? How would you keep track of what you find out?

Next Step: Share your ideas. Make a plan for gathering information using the four categories. If you are working in small groups, each group may want to involve people in other groups. For example, everyone could help conduct the survey and collect the results. Compile the information you learn into a list of community needs.

See digital content for full-size reproducible pages.

Who Is Helping?
Government & Community Groups

Who is helping with the community need you've identified? Learning about who addresses this need in the world can help you plan your service learning experience, find partners to work with, and make your contribution count.

Government agencies and community organizations are two kinds of groups that help with community needs. They work to meet immediate needs and to find long-term solutions. Government agencies and community organizations are:

- **local**—in your town and city
- **regional**—in your state or province
- **national**—across your country
- **international**—across the globe (While no single government agency is "international," the United Nations organization is one way the governments of many nations work together to meet needs.)

Where to begin? To learn about government and community groups, contact social service departments or the office of an elected official in your area. You might also start with an organization such as a food bank or animal shelter that helps with the problem.

Research Tips

Phone book—the front pages often list local, state, and national government offices.

The Internet—government offices and many community organizations have easy-to-use Web pages with information about issues and how to learn more.

School office—ask if there are lists of community organizations the school works with already.

Elected officials—they often have people on staff to answer questions and provide contact information and resources.

Phone Call Tips

1. Write a list of questions you want to ask.
2. Practice with a friend before making calls.
3. Begin by introducing yourself and briefly describing what you're working on. Then ask if this is a good time to talk.
4. Let the person know how long the call will take.
5. Follow up with a thank-you card or an email.

Complete the chart on the next page to see how government and community groups help with the need you've chosen. You may decide to work on your own, with a partner, or in small groups.

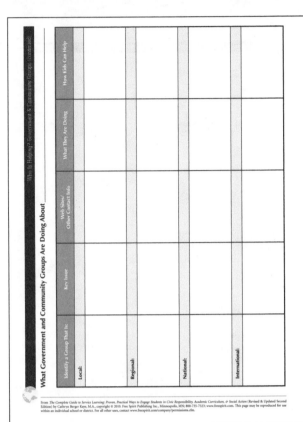

What Government and Community Groups Are Doing About _____

Identify a Group That Is:	Key Issue	Web Sites/ Other Contact Info	What They Are Doing	How Kids Can Help
Local:				
Regional:				
National:				
International:				

Taking Action

Step 1: Think about the needs in our community. Make a list.

Step 2: Identify what you know.

- Select one community need:
- What is the cause?
- Who is helping?
- What are some ways we can help?

Step 3: Find out more.

- What do we need to know about this community need and who is helping?

- How can we find out?

Step 4: Plan for action.

- To help our community, we will:

- To make this happen, we will take on these responsibilities:

Who	will do what	by when	Resources needed

Service Learning Proposal

Students or class:_____

Teacher:_____

School:_____

Address:_____

Phone:_____ Fax:_____ Email:_____

Project name:_____

Need—Why this plan is needed:

Purpose—How this plan will help:

Participation—Who will help and what they will do:

Students:_____

Teachers:_____

Other adults:_____

Organizations or groups:_____

Outcomes—What we expect to happen as a result of our work:

How we will check outcomes—What evidence we will collect and how we will use it:

Resources—What we need to get the job done, such as supplies (itemize on back):

Signatures:

See digital content for full-size reproducible pages.

Our Service Plan

Students or Class: _____

Teacher: _____

School: _____

Address: _____

Phone: _____ Fax: _____ Email: _____

Project name: _____

Our idea: _____

This helps others by: _____

Student names and jobs:

My name _____ My job _____

My name _____ My job _____

My name _____ My job _____

Others who will help:

Students: _____

Teachers: _____

Other adults: _____

Organizations: _____

Supplies needed: _____

Our expectations: _____

Signatures:

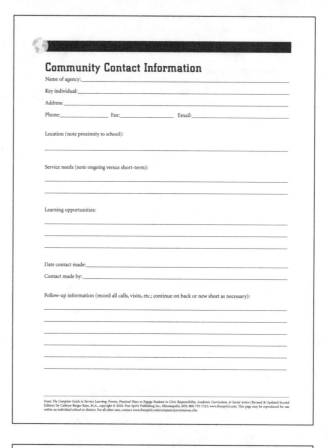

Community Contact Information

Name of agency: _____

Key individual: _____

Address: _____

Phone: _____ Fax: _____ Email: _____

Location (note proximity to school): _____

Service needs (note ongoing versus short-term): _____

Learning opportunities: _____

Date contact made: _____

Contact made by: _____

Follow-up information (record all calls, visits, etc.; continue on back or new sheet as necessary):

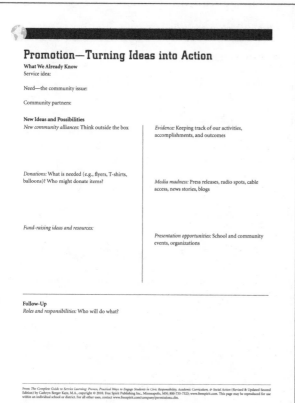

Promotion—Turning Ideas into Action

What We Already Know
Service idea:

Need—the community issue:

Community partners:

New Ideas and Possibilities

New community alliances: Think outside the box

Evidence: Keeping track of our activities, accomplishments, and outcomes

Donations: What is needed (e.g., flyers, T-shirts, balloons)? Who might donate items?

Media madness: Press releases, radio spots, cable access, news stories, blogs

Fund-raising ideas and resources:

Presentation opportunities: School and community events, organizations

Follow-Up
Roles and responsibilities: Who will do what?

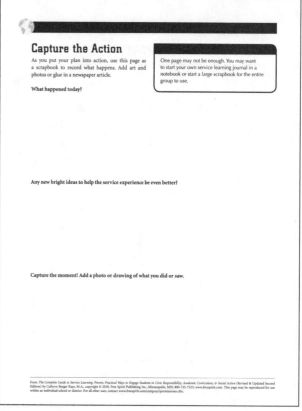

Capture the Action

As you put your plan into action, use this page as a scrapbook to record what happens. Add art and photos or glue in a newspaper article.

One page may not be enough. You may want to start your own service learning journal in a notebook or start a large scrapbook for the entire group to use.

What happened today?

Any new bright ideas to help the service experience be even better?

Capture the moment! Add a photo or drawing of what you did or saw.

See digital content for full-size reproducible pages.

Progress Monitoring

What progress monitoring methods will you use?

❑ Observation
❑ Data Collection
❑ Interviews
❑ Surveys

Other Methods:
❑ _____
❑ _____

Date _____
Step One: Establish your baseline—what is the need?

Date _____
Step Two: What noticeable changes have been made?

Date _____
Step Three: What other changes have taken place?

Date _____
Step Four: Describe evidence of your progress.

Date _____
Step Five: Provide a summary of your findings.

Sequence for Reflection

Use this document as a checklist and to record your own reflections. Remember to align reflection with your essential purpose or question.

In Preparation

As the service learning process begins, find out what students know: What beliefs and assumptions are already in place? Where and how were they learned? What do students expect to happen? What do they expect to learn, and how do they expect to feel? Depending on the situation, you may give students a thought or question to take with them into the service experience. This may encourage them to be more observant or heighten their awareness of a particular need or action being taken.
What happened:

During Action

Be observant. What are the students paying attention to? What comments do you overhear? What behaviors do you see? You may make notes and refer to them later, during the reflection that follows the service. During on-the-spot reflection, students sometimes have insights or make recommendations that improve their experience and the impact of their contributions.
What happened:

Following Service

Vary the reflection methods. Before discussing the service, ask students to first write their responses to discussion prompts. This can protect the integrity of each student's experience and assure that everyone has something to contribute. As students become more adept, ask them to design a reflection process for themselves and their classmates. Have students draw upon their reflections during demonstration of their service learning.
What happened:

Feedback

Provide *nonjudgmental* feedback. If you may read journals, ask if you can write a response in the journal or on an attached piece of paper. Listen well. Ask questions. Appreciate what is being revealed and discovered.
What happened:

Four Square Reflection Tool

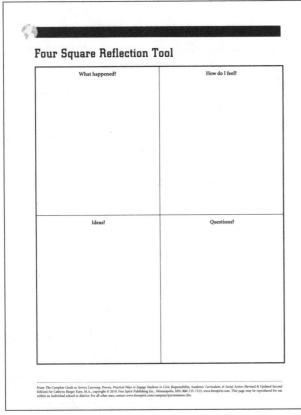

What happened?	How do I feel?
Ideas?	**Questions?**

Community Response

Name of agency: _____
Address: _____
Phone: _____ Fax: _____ Email: _____
Contact person: _____
Teacher/class: _____
Date of visit: _____
Purpose of visit: _____

Please respond to the following questions to help us learn from today's service experience and better meet your agency's needs in the future.

What were the benefits of today's experience for your agency?

What suggestions do you have for future visits or interactions?

What service needs do you have that our school could assist with in the future?

What did you and others at your agency learn about children and our school that you did not know before?

Additional comments are appreciated.

Thank you! Please return this form to the teacher listed above at the following address:

See digital content for full-size reproducible pages.

Once You Know It, Show It!

You've put your plan into action and seen the results. Now it's time for demonstration—the stage where you show others what you've learned about the topic, how you learned it, and what you've contributed to the community. This demonstration of your service learning can take any form you like: letter, article, video, pamphlet, artistic display, performance, or PowerPoint presentation.

To help you make the most of your demonstration, answer these questions:

Who is your audience?

What do you most want to tell about what you've learned?

What do you most want to tell about how you provided service?

Are there any community partners who you might like to participate in the demonstration?

What form of demonstration would you like to use?

On a separate sheet of paper, write your plan for demonstration.

If you are part of a class or youth group, share your ideas for demonstration with the others you're working with. How can you best use each person's talents and skills as part of your demonstration?

Assessment for Service Learning: *Part One*

Service Learning Experience: _____

Respond to the questions relevant to your service learning activities.

Student Learning

• Were the defined content and skill objectives met?

• Were there any unforeseen outcomes?

• Did students show initiative or develop leadership skills?

• Were students able to reflect and place their experience within the larger context of community or society in general?

• Could students identify both their cognitive and affective growth?

Impact of the Service

• Were students able to explicitly state the need and purpose for their service efforts?

• What contribution was made?

• How did the service help or hinder community improvement efforts?

• Is the partner agency satisfied with the interaction?

• Have new relationships been formed?

• Were planned service programs, activities, or products completed?

Process

• How did this experience affect or change how teachers teach and how children learn?

• How effective was the planning process?

• What are your ideas for overall improvement?

• In future activities, how can students take greater ownership?

• How can community partnerships be improved or strengthened?

Assessment for Service Learning: *Part Two*

Service Learning Experience: _____

Identify what methods were used for each stage and whether each standard was present.

Five Stages of Service Learning

Investigation
• Conduct Personal Inventory
• Verify Community Need
• Other:

Preparation and Planning
• Research
• Literature
• Field trips
• Interviews
• Other:

Action
• Direct service
• Indirect service
• Research
• Advocacy

Reflection
• Discussion
• Journals
• Role play
• Other:

Demonstration
• Presentation
• Performance
• Article
• Other:

K–12 Service-Learning Standards for Quality Practice

Meaningful Service.
Service-learning actively engages participants in meaningful and personally relevant service activities.

Link to Curriculum.
Service-learning is intentionally used as an instructional strategy to meet learning goals and/or content standards.

Reflection.
Service-learning incorporates multiple challenging reflection activities that are ongoing and that prompt deep thinking and analysis about oneself and one's relationship to society.

Diversity.
Service-learning promotes understanding of diversity and mutual respect among all participants.

Youth Voice.
Service-learning provides youth with a strong voice in planning, implementing, and evaluating service-learning experiences with guidance from adults.

Partnerships.
Service-learning partnerships are collaborative, mutually beneficial, and address community needs.

Progress Monitoring.
Service-learning engages participants in an ongoing process to assess the quality of implementation and progress toward meeting specified goals, and uses results for improvement and sustainability.

Duration and Intensity.
Service-learning has sufficient duration and intensity to address community needs and meet specified outcomes.

Student Self-Evaluation

Name: _____ Date: _____

Service Learning Experience: _____

Learning

• What information did you learn in preparing to do service?

• What skills did you develop through the activities?

• How did this experience help you better understand ideas or subjects we have been studying?

• Through this service learning experience, what did you learn about:
  – yourself?
  – working with others, including people in your class?
  – your community?

• How will you use what you learned in this experience in different situations?

Service

• What was the need for your service effort?

• What contribution did you make?

• What overall contribution was made by your class?

• How did your service affect the community?

Process

• How did you and other students help with planning?

• In what ways did you make decisions and solve problems?

• Were there any differences between the initial plans and what you actually did?

• What ideas do you have for improving any part of the experience?

See digital content for full-size reproducible pages.

Chapter 3

The Theme Chapters and the Service Learning Bookshelf

Now that you've learned what service learning is and how you can use it, let's get started. You're ready to explore common themes for service and literary resources you can use with your students. Part Two of this guide consists of chapters on thirteen different themes commonly selected for service learning activities, identified through interactions with teachers and students from across the United States. In these theme chapters, you'll find an overview, activities, ideas, curricular connections, and resources that will help you create and tailor service learning experiences around a given theme. A primary part of each theme chapter is the service learning bookshelf, an extensive cross-section of books for different ages you can use with your students. This chapter will explain the structure and resources of the theme chapters and how you can use their content and ideas to enhance your service learning activities.

Getting Oriented: About the Thematic Chapters

As you consider designing a service learning plan, you may be wondering:

- What social concerns are most often addressed through service learning?

- What activities can help prepare my students for service?

- What are some tried-and-true service learning ideas?

- What books can be used to teach young people, motivate them to read, and inspire them to action?

The thematic chapters answer these questions with a wealth of ideas and resources for service learning in action. The theme chapters address: AIDS awareness and education; animal protection and care; elders; emergency readiness; the environment; gardening; healthy lives, healthy choices; hunger, homelessness,

and poverty; immigrants; literacy; safe and strong communities; social change: issues and action; and special needs and disabilities. For convenience, the topics are arranged alphabetically.

Each thematic chapter includes:

- **Introductory comments** regarding this theme and service learning. This will provide you with basic information about the theme and give you an idea of why it's important.

- **Quotes for inspiration.** These quotes have applications throughout the service learning experience as they inspire investigation, preparation, introspection, and may find their way directly into the action. Quotable Quotes (page 72) offers a sequence to use these with your students.

- **Activities** to help you prepare your students for service learning on the theme. Some provoke preliminary thought and discussion, while other activities promote learning and skills development related to the theme. The activities adapt to all age ranges and different grade levels and settings.

- **Organizations and online resources** specific to the content of the theme rather than being general to service learning. They will direct you to reputable organizations or information-rich Web sites that can help you and your students get started on research and planning.

- **A curriculum web** that provides you with a wide sampling of cross-curricular connections you can tailor to the theme.

- **Examples of service learning** that have been successfully carried out by elementary, middle, and high school students. You may find one idea or resource that is just what you've been looking for, or an example might spark another idea that better suits the needs of your students and community. Note that while grade levels are provided as a reference, most examples and ideas transcend age groups and can be adapted to suit younger or older students.

- **A service learning bookshelf** for each theme. Here, you will find a comprehensive listing of literature that helps connect classroom learning and literacy with service to the community. These bookshelves contain more than three hundred book titles that are annotated and categorized for easy identification, reference, and use. Additional titles are found in the digital content—including

ones that are recently published or out-of-print but still worth finding.

As you use the activities in the theme chapters of Part Two, continue to reference Part One especially if the practice of service learning is relatively new, if you are leading staff development workshops to provide others with service learning knowledge, or simply as a reminder of the five stages and the K–12 quality standards of service learning. The reproducible pages at the end of chapter 2 can give you a jump start in planning and organizing as you continue to apply the key concepts.

Quotable Quotes

How can you use the quotes found throughout this book? How can they be used to advance literacy skills and service learning? In our current adult and youth cultures, words are all too often used in a careless manner, flung at one another in ways that can wound, sometimes intentionally. Through education we can reclaim how words are used by modeling and by providing opportunities for kids to use words in uplifting ways. Employing words to elevate a person's sense of self, feelings, and ideas—and then transforming those ideas into action—is fundamentally what service learning is all about.

The ten-step sequence provided on the Quotable Quotes form (page 72) has been used by teachers across the globe with great success. Students of all ages can "draw the quote," for example, revealing interpretative skills and understanding of metaphor, often present in the quotes. Then consider how these drawings can be used as service learning:

- Students toured their school looking for places that could be improved by quotes. By the gym they placed: *"Confidence is contagious. So is lack of confidence."* —Vince Lombardi, coach. And of course the library was the place for this one: *"I must say that I find television very educational. The minute somebody turns it on, I go to the library and read a book."* —Groucho Marx, comedian. Classes took turns changing the quotes on a monthly basis, initiating an exciting scavenger hunt that got everyone on the lookout for quotable quotes.

- As part of computer lab, students created quotable quote screen savers and sent copies to the faculty and school board.

- While visiting elders in a retirement community, students inquired, "What is your favorite quote?" Many elders have quotes or adages they live by, often reflective of their culture or heritage. This question initiated conversations about places of origin and background, and how these words have been influential for a lifetime. On their last visit at the end of the school year, the students presented art of the words shared on the first visit—a thoughtful gift for time well spent.

- What places in your community could be brightened with quote art? From hospital rooms to banks where people stand in line—let students generate a list of places where kids can display their images. Also, this is a great chance for the school to have visibility with a simple tagline, "Quote art brought to you by students from [insert school name]."

As you read through the ten steps, look for ways to expand literacy skills and integrate practical uses of what is created. Ideas are there to be discovered.

The ninth step is, "What quote will I be remembered by?" Teachers have sent samples of these closing quotes by students, and this one, originated by a third grader in Texas, has always been a favorite: "Life is like a stick, don't break it."

About the Service Learning Bookshelf

Clear off a shelf and start collecting! The service learning bookshelf in each thematic chapter is filled with nonfiction books, picture books, and novels selected to enhance your service learning activities. Included on each bookshelf are titles that:

- describe the service experiences of others

- introduce important social themes

- tell stories from history

- provide primary source reference materials

- showcase various genres

- model diverse ways of telling a story

- increase student interest in reading

- promote critical thinking and discussion

- prepare students to interact with diverse populations

- enhance the experiences students have in the community

- inspire students to serve

Whether read aloud or silently, the books included in each bookshelf are guaranteed to make you and your students smile, laugh, cry, think, wonder, dream, plan, hope, and act.

Well-written books can provide many benefits. They tap into students' curiosity and desire to know. They give students the information they need to move to the next level of competency or inspire them to consider important topics. Authors model how to write, how to think creatively, and how to tell one's own story. When the story conveys a concern shared by the students, a range of possibilities for their own actions can emerge.

Reading is to the mind what exercise is to the body.

—*Joseph Addison, poet*

Reading is the foundation of learning, however books can only go so far. In our classrooms, we want books that inspire students to action—that provide knowledge and engagement that stimulates *intrinsic motivation* for service. Each book on the service learning bookshelf has been selected with this in mind. Many of the titles also serve as great resources for teachers, program staff, or family members who want to introduce a topic, expand knowledge, or develop an inquiring mind.

What's on the Shelf? Features of the Service Learning Bookshelf

Each bookshelf includes the following:

- An annotated bibliography of works related to the chapter theme. The list is arranged under the general categories of nonfiction books, picture books, and fiction. Nonfiction and fiction selections include the book's length and recommended grade levels.

- A quick reference chart that classifies the books according to topics within the theme so you can find the books you want more easily.

- Recommendations made by service learning practitioners, with ideas for service learning activities.

- Author interviews to provide the "story behind the story" and more service connections are included in the digital content.

This section describes these features in more detail and suggests ways you can use them. Two other important aspects of titles in the bookshelves are also discussed: artwork and illustrations featured in many books and special selections written by young authors.

A note about bookshelf titles: Books do go out of print—even our favorites. Almost all the bookshelf titles listed were in print at the time of publication. A few out-of-print exceptions are included because of their outstanding content and presentation; these books are identified as out of print in the bookshelves. Libraries and used books stores—including those accessible via the Internet—are good sources for these out-of-print gems. Additional titles are listed in the digital content.

Nonfiction Books

Nonfiction books cover a wide range of topics, coming in a variety of forms from straightforward narrative prose to songs—with everything in between. They can be collections of plays, songs, and poems such as *Cootie Shots: Theatrical Inoculations Against Bigotry for Kids, Parents and Teachers* (Safe and Strong Communities Bookshelf—digital content), a collection that promotes tolerance. They can be photo essays such as *Cycle of Rice, Cycle of Life: A Story of Sustainable Farming* (Gardening Bookshelf), which shows the natural rhythms and life cycles that keep this important staple crop growing. They can even take the form of a coloring book such as *Conversation Starters as Easy as ABC 123: How to Start Conversations with People Who Have Memory Loss* (Elders Bookshelf).

History is frequently a topic for nonfiction books, and a number of nonfiction books link the study of history with events in the present day. *Alone in the World: Orphans and Orphanages in America* (Hunger, Homelessness, and Poverty Bookshelf) includes photographs to illustrate the historical rise and decline of orphanages in the United States. *How Lincoln Learned to Read* (Literacy Bookshelf) shows how education mattered in the lives of twelve influential people including Abraham Lincoln, Helen Keller, and Elvis. *Our Stories, Our Songs: African Children Talk About AIDS* (AIDS Education and Awareness Bookshelf) combines photos, information, and ways to get involved and lend support.

Other books describe acts of service, as in *Nights of the Pufflings* (Animal Protection and Care Bookshelf), which tells how young children rescued small birds from the perils of the city and released them over the ocean waves. Youth activists are profiled in the humorous novel *Scat* (Environment Bookshelf). And students will be amazed to read in *Claudette Colvin: Twice Toward Justice* how a young activist in Montgomery, Alabama, took on civil rights issues even before Rosa Parks refused to give up her seat on the bus (Social Change Bookshelf).

Read books. They are good for us.

—*Natalie Goldberg, author*

Picture Books

Picture books can be read and enjoyed by people of all ages. The language and artwork convey messages that transcend age. As a result, picture books can be effective tools for teaching sophisticated concepts and issues at all grade levels. Older students may be surprised to learn that complex social issues and ideas—such as memory loss or the struggles of refugee children forced into manual labor—can be presented to and understood by young children through the medium of picture books.

Most people like to be read to, yet we usually stop reading aloud to students once they reach middle school. Hearing a story read aloud is different from reading to one's self. Both are necessary processes in whole brain learning. In a class environment, reading a picture book aloud creates a common experience for discussion and stimulates interest or curiosity regarding an important subject. High school students have been known to sit on the edge of their seats listening to the stories of a woman who ran for president against Ulysses S. Grant in *A Woman for President: The Story of Victoria Woodhull* (Social Change Bookshelf—digital content) and a child who suddenly ages in *Stranger in the Mirror* (Elders Bookshelf), and they will laugh out loud when hearing *The Wartville Wizard* (Environment Bookshelf), a hilarious tale of litter flying back to stick to the litterer.

Needless to say, younger children devour picture books, enjoying *All the Way to the Ocean* (Environment Bookshelf) and the thoughtful revelations in *My Diary from Here to There/Mi diario de aquí hasta allá* (Immigrants Bookshelf). These titles also become models for students of all ages about how to write and construct their own stories of service to the community.

Books can also have a direct connection to the service activity. Meeting a child who is blind and plays ball in *Keep Your Ear on the Ball* (Special Needs and Disabilities Bookshelf) is ideal for preparing students of any age to interact with youth with special needs.

Many picture books provide excellent resources for finding subject matter that engages and motivates children. The importance of preserving our natural habitat, for example, is conveyed in *All the Way to the Ocean* (Environment Bookshelf), which examines what happens when a piece of trash goes down the storm drain. There is wonderful storytelling, weaving imagination and reality to help a Spanish-speaking child adjust to an English-only classroom in *La Mariposa* (Literacy Bookshelf). These and other titles are useful for tutoring and language development as well as encouraging young people to learn more about their themes.

An increasing number of picture books convey the powerful and courageous acts of individuals who meet these challenging times through leadership and service. Look for these to inspire and encourage students to follow up with comprehensive research to learn more. Among the many outstanding titles are *Delivering Justice: W.W. Law and the Fight for Civil Rights* (Social Change Bookshelf) and *Passage to Freedom: The Sugihara Story* (Social Change Bookshelf).

Fiction Books

Fiction runs the gamut from easy-to-read beginning chapter books to young adult novels to best sellers for older adolescents. These selections are well-written stories that challenge and compel the reader. In *Hurricane Song: A Novel of New Orleans* (Emergency Readiness Bookshelf), for example, a teen moves into the Superdome with his dad and has harrowing experiences as a community struggles through Hurricane Katrina. *Bone by Bone by Bone* (Social Change Bookshelf) shows a vivid picture of a boy growing up during segregation and confronting the ideas of his racist father. In *Seedfolks* (Gardening Bookshelf), each chapter represents the voice of a different community member bringing his or her seeds and story to

Literature Circle Activity

A service learning Literature Circle (page 72) provides a process to develop students' capacity to explore text that can lead to service learning. Often thought of as something just for language arts and English classes, this Literature Circle process can be adapted for use across the curriculum with the following benefits:

- promotes relevancy of text to self, other books, classroom learning, and service
- models effective communication of ideas
- increases awareness of different and similar interpretations or meanings of text
- requires active listening and conversation skills
- involves leading a discussion and participating as a group member

In groups of four, students take turns leading a discussion for four to six minutes in a designated role:

Personal Connector—This conversation centers on, "What does this text have to do with me and the community or world I know?" Students seek relevance and a safe environment to discuss how content has personal meaning. Relating text to personal situations develops mutual respect and understanding among peers. Students can continue to articulate verbally and in writing about personal meaning derived from literature and academia in general. The Personal

Connector asks questions that connect the story to group members' experiences, such as:

1. Do characters remind you of people you know? How?

2. Have you been in situations similar to what is described in the book? What happened?

3. How have you or people you know resolved similar situations?

Literary Connector—Just as a musician establishes a repertoire of songs, a reader connects one book or story to another. This process assists with retention and is intended to help students value reading. The Literary Connector asks questions that connect this story to other stories group members have read, such as:

1. Which characters remind you of characters from other stories?

2. What situations are similar to what happens in other stories?

3. What would a character in this story say about these other characters or situations? Why?

Service Connector—Every text has a real-world connection to a need and possible response to that need, even fictional texts that may be representing a situation or circumstance. Identifying this actual need promotes relevance, increases student engagement, and may translate into a student response. Ideas may a neighborhood garden, acknowledging real struggles and personal dreams. In *Rules* (Special Needs and Disabilities Bookshelf), a girl whose brother is autistic is compelled by a teen with multiple disabilities to speak out even if it puts her friendships at risk. *I Am a Taxi* and the sequel *Sacred Leaf* (Social Change Bookshelf) describe a boy living in a Bolivian prison with his parents who are falsely accused of a crime. After falling unwittingly into the drug trade, his journey back to his family exposes him to the economic problems facing his country and he becomes a young activist for change. Some novels are ideal to read aloud. Many of the suggested books integrate English and language arts with other academic subjects and develop awareness, sensitivity, and understanding about the human condition and our society.

While high school reading assignments often neglect the riches to be found in young adult literature, hopefully this list will encourage you to look for—or remind you of—the jewels that can be found in this category of books. "Young adult" literature is so named for a good reason. The stories reflect the challenges, dilemmas, and relationships particularly faced by this age group. They offer the complexity and conflicts that often mirror the situations students observe and experience. Whether you choose *The Curious Incident of the Dog in the Night-Time* (Special Needs and Disabilities Bookshelf), *Last Night I Sang to the Monster* (Healthy Lives, Healthy Choices Bookshelf), *The Book Thief* (Literacy Bookshelf), or one of the many other selections, treat yourself and read a young adult novel. You may be surprised at how compelling you find the

develop into student-initiated service learning proposals. The Service Connector asks questions that connect the story to ideas for service by asking:

1. What needs to be fixed in this situation?

2. Did any characters in this story participate in service activities?

3. What service ideas did you think of when you read this story?

Learning Connector—Making classroom connections explicit helps students know how learning in different subject areas is related. Discussing what they are learning and adding the cross-curricular relationships removes false boundaries in academics. One class theme or subject relates to another. Once students recognize this, they are more likely to extend this observation to other learning situations. The Learning Connector asks questions that connect this story to learning, such as:

1. What would you like to learn more about as a result of reading this story?

2. What ideas in this story have you learned about or experienced in school?

3. What do you think people your age would learn from reading this story?

Student roles are explained on Literature Circle Roles (page 72). While having the conversations, students

record their ideas and those of others on the companion Literature Circle form, reinforcing note-taking skills.

As students discuss stories in this Literature Circle format, they explore deeper understandings of text, share the experience of discovery, and engage in peer modeling of how to think about and consider personal and societal connections to text. With experience, students may determine their own discussion roles and questions. This manner of reading and analyzing text can be applied across the curriculum. Teachers have successfully adapted this Literature Circle design to reading historical text, newspapers, scientific information, and math. Nearly any fiction or nonfiction text or even a piece of art can be discussed and analyzed by students with this format.

This Literature Circle activity generally takes twenty to thirty minutes once students know the process; the variable is the time allocated for each Connector role. The initial introductory session usually requires one hour as you model the process. The literature segment may be read aloud or independently as homework. A book chapter, short story, or picture book can be used in its entirety. Adapt the activity for younger children by having students converse in pairs. Students have even led this activity with parents and community study groups as part of a citywide reading program. The possibilities are vast and all lead in the direction of promoting literacy skills and inspiring generations of avid readers.

story and that the power of the words convinces you to include the book and others like it in your service learning curriculum.

Please note: Several bookshelf selections are labeled as having mature themes. Many of these books are read in high schools; however, be sure to review them for content if you have concerns.

Looking It Up: The Bookshelf Charts

The chart in the bookshelf is arranged by topics commonly associated with the service theme and can help you quickly find books that are appropriate for your particular service learning activities. For example, the chart in the Safe and Strong Communities chapter groups books under the topics of personal confidence and safety, bullying, conflict resolution, local violence, hate crimes, our world today, preserving history, and community building. The books under the topics generally include a cross-section of nonfiction, picture books, and fiction and encompass a broad range of reading levels. Books that feature young people in service-providing roles are flagged in the chart. Books that can be used for more than one theme are cross-referenced to where they appear in other themes. Out-of-print—but still worthy—titles are also indicated.

The Importance of Illustrations and Artwork

Visual images communicate the message of a story as much as text. The bookshelf titles employ innumerable illustration techniques and styles that educate as well as inspire. Illustrations and other artwork show us what happened and where it happened. They also sometimes give information not provided in any other way. For example, in Patricia Polacco's *Chicken Sunday* (Safe and Strong Communities Bookshelf—digital content), one image shows an aged shopkeeper with a number tattooed on his forearm, indicating that he was in a concentration camp during World War II; this fact is never mentioned in the story text. The last picture in *Click Clack Moo, Cows That Type* (Social Change

DIGITAL CONTENT

Recommendations from the Field: The Classics and Beyond in Digital Content

"I would like to involve my students in service learning, but we are reading *Romeo and Juliet* this semester. What could I do?"

Substitute any title you like—*The House on Mango Street, Emma, Fahrenheit 451*—and you have identified a quandary for many teachers: how to connect the required classroom literature with service learning. To address this issue, I asked many service learning colleagues—both adults and youth—from around the country to choose and read a curriculum classic and make recommendations for how it could be used in service learning. Reviewers came from across the service learning spectrum and include a fourth-grade student, a college freshman, parent/child teams, K–12 teachers, university professors, program directors, and policy makers. One contributor is autistic.

Most of the books they reviewed are familiar titles, like the kindergarten favorite *Make Way for Ducklings* (Animal Protection and Care Bookshelf) and the high school classic *Siddhartha* (Safe and Strong Communities Bookshelf). Other books stretch the idea of "classics" to include more modern literature that tells a significant story in writing of high quality. Book selection occurred in a variety of ways. Based on research, I provided a list of recommended titles. Many reviewers suggested their own favorite books. Several people said this project gave them a chance to pick up a book they had always meant to read. One contributor was relieved to finally finish reading a lengthy novel that had escaped her during high school; she followed up with a letter to her high school teacher saying, "I finally read the book!"

Each of the recommendations included in the companion digital content provides a summary of the story and offers ideas for service learning connections. Many include questions to initiate discussion regarding service-related themes. Look for these books in most of the thematic chapters, labeled as a "Recommendation from the Field." All of these titles are gathered together for your easy reference in the chart in the digital content.

Is one of your favorite books missing? If so, you have a perfect opportunity to create your own service learning classic connection.

Bookshelf—digital content), illustrated by Betsy Lewin, reveals the resolution of the ducks' quest for a diving board; no words at all appear on the page.

The bookshelf offers an array of options to students exploring ideas and methods for illustrating original stories or helping younger children create a book. Here is a sampling:

- Artist Paul Yalowitz begins the story *Somebody Loves You, Mr. Hatch* (Elders Bookshelf) with dreary colors to match Mr. Hatch's mood. The colors brighten as Mr. Hatch thinks, "Somebody loves me."

- Gerardo Suzán's colorful images in *Butterfly Boy* (Elders Bookshelf—digital content) are a mix of representational and modern art.

- In *My Librarian Is a Camel: How Books Are Brought to Children Around the World* (Literacy Bookshelf), author Margriet Ruurs used the Internet to collect photographs from many distant countries.

- Artist and coauthor Susan Roth makes collages to accompany the story *Listen to the Wind*, the children's version of *Three Cups of Tea* (Social Change Bookshelf).

- Elizabeth Gómez's brilliant use of color and fantastical imagery in *A Movie in My Pillow/Una película en mi almohada* (Immigrants Bookshelf) could inspire murals.

- Lisa Tucker McElroy's *Love Lizzie: Letter to a Military Mom* (Safe and Strong Communities Bookshelf—digital content) integrates text into drawings and uses various angles to show a book in a more free-form letter-writing style.

- Shaun Tan's moving book *The Arrival* (Immigrants Bookshelf) is a wordless graphic novel, perfect for inspiring students to think and construct the stories. Other graphic novels have captured many readers so be sure to seek out *Slow Storm* by Danica Novgorodoff (Emergency Readiness Bookshelf).

> Some painters transform the sun into a yellow spot, others transform a yellow spot into the sun.
>
> —*Pablo Picasso, artist*

Young Authors and Illustrators at Work

Several of the bookshelf titles were written by authors under the age of twenty at the time of being published. These young authors are models that the young people you work with can draw on for inspiration both for

DIGITAL CONTENT

Author Interviews in Digital Content

Have you ever been curious about the story behind the story? Would you sometimes like to pick up the phone, call an author, like Don Madden (Environment Bookshelf), and ask, "So why did you have the Wartville Wizard get the power over trash?" Perhaps you would ask the author to discuss the evolution of the character Alex in *Notes from the Midnight Driver* (Healthy Lives, Healthy Choices Bookshelf) from being self-absorbed to caring for a cantankerous elder fellow he is required to spend time with. Or perhaps you would ask what caused Richard Michelson to tell the story of sustaining language and tradition in *Too Young for Yiddish* (Elders Bookshelf).

The author interviews included in the companion digital content provide the story behind the story of why a person chooses to write. These inspiring essays help readers appreciate the varying reasons people write and the different ways they approach the blank page. Interviews included these questions:

1. What inspired this book?

2. How do you approach the writing process?

3. How do you imagine this book leading students toward service?

Each interview gives a window into the process that goes into creating a story. Each demonstrates the writer's intelligence and desire to reach others and their passion for the written word. All of the writers offer thought-provoking insights into the writing process and the subject matter, and some even describe service learning ideas they've heard about from readers.

Also included are instructions for how to contact an author or illustrator, as well as suggestions for using the author interviews in the classroom.

their own creative endeavors and what they can achieve. If you'd like to highlight the achievements and writings of young authors for your students, here are the titles on the bookshelves that are written, coauthored, or illustrated by young people:

- *Hey, Little Ant* (Safe and Strong Communities Bookshelf), a song-turned-book that ends with the question, "What would you do?"

- *Conversation Starters as Easy as ABC 123* (Elders Bookshelf) and *Increase the Peace: The ABCs of Tolerance* (Safe and Strong Communities Bookshelf—digital content), both in ABC formats.

- *Potato: A Tale from the Great Depression* (Hunger, Homelessness, and Poverty Bookshelf—digital content), by an eight-year-old, telling a story passed down through her family.

- *We Need to Go to School: Voices of the Rugmark Children* and *Free the Children* (Social Change Bookshelf—digital content) about international child labor.

- *In Our Village: Kambi ya Simba through the Eyes of Its Youth* (Literacy Bookshelf) was written by students at Awet Secondary School in Tanzania and has launched an international service learning project, In Our Global Village.

- *Forty-Cent Tip: Stories of New York Immigrant Workers* (Immigrants Bookshelf) by students of three New York international high schools who document the lives of immigrant workers in their city.

- *My Life as a Book* (Literacy Bookshelf) was illustrated by Jake Tashjian with delightfully humorous stick figures.

Using the Service Learning Bookshelf

You can use the service learning bookshelf contents in a remarkable variety of ways throughout your service learning projects. This section will show you how you can use books in every stage of the service learning process, with different partners on a project, and as a source of inspiration for your students. Several charts help you make quick and easy curricular connections and serve as useful cross-references when you're brainstorming ideas and planning. The chart "Connecting the Bookshelf to the Five Stages of Service Learning" (page 65) suggests ideas for linking reading to each service learning stage. The "Bilingual Books" chart (page 68) identifies titles you can use in English and Spanish, while the "History Through the Bookshelf" chart (pages 70–71) lists a selection of bookshelf titles by historical period.

Publish, Publish, Publish

The titles in the service learning bookshelf can inspire students to write about their own service experience and serve as templates for good storytelling about significant social issues. Students' stories and books can be donated to hospitals, libraries, family shelters, and other classrooms. With contributions of time and materials from community partners, students may even be able to publish their book and use it as a fundraiser. Consider having students record audiotapes especially for children or elders who are more able to listen than read. Consider, too, translating the stories for multilingual publications.

Examples of student-generated publications can be found in many of the theme chapters. Read how kindergartners in Hudson, Massachusetts, wrote a book with photographs showing the step-by-step process of holding a drive for a food bank. And how fourth graders in Myrtle Beach, South Carolina, combined art, haiku, and environmental studies to create an exquisite book, *I, Caretta,* to protect sea turtles found along their coast. The ABC format of *Conversations Starters as Easy as ABC 123* (Elders Bookshelf) and *Increase the Peace* (Safe and Strong Communities Bookshelf) has been replicated; this I know because my daughter is the author! We continually receive copies of books from students across the globe using her format to write *The ABCs of Family, Volumes One* and *Two; The ABCs of Homelessness; From Apples to Zucchini: The ABCs of Gardening,* and *The ABCs of Global Warming.* And on the In Our Village Web site (see page 185), you can download student-authored service learning books written in more than twelve countries as part of the In Our Global Village project. Service learning can truly create a world of authors.

Act It Out: The Play's the Thing

Students can also transform favorite stories into plays—or even musicals—that will help the audience learn about social issues. The performance may become an essential part of a service learning activity. The following books are easily adapted into plays and skits:

- *Toestomper and the Caterpillars* (Safe and Strong Communities Bookshelf—digital content) shows how a "rowdy ruffian" is transformed into a kinder fellow by caring for squiggly blue caterpillars.

- *Hey, Little Ant* (Safe and Strong Communities Bookshelf), which began as a song, comes with the sheet music, and has been staged as an opera and a musical.

Connecting the Bookshelf to the Five Stages of Service Learning

During *Investigation*, use books:

- to introduce topics.
- for an overview of the need.
- for examples of how to conduct research.
- for conducting research.

During *Preparation and Planning*, use books:

- to delve into topics for greater awareness.
- for point of view and perspective, particularly involving situations most students will hopefully never experience, for example, as a refugee in a war-torn area or living in a homeless shelter.
- to enhance understanding of a historical time period through parallel reading of a novel or picture book. (See "History Through the Bookshelf" on pages 70–71.)
- to show different approaches to or writing styles on a similar theme.
- to provide documentation of what kids have accomplished.

During *Action*, use books:

- to begin the service activity with a common experience for all involved.
- to help children learn to read.
- to teach concepts or ideas.
- to dramatize for an educational program.

During *Reflection*, use books:

- to introduce inspiring thoughts related to the service experience.
- to share the reflective comments of others.
- to show the results of similar service experiences by others.
- in response to a student's expression of thought or feelings.

During *Demonstration*, use books:

- in a display to show what books were used as resources for student learning.
- to read aloud and share the impact of a story, similar to what the students experienced in class or in other situations.
- in a choral reading format or selected excerpts to read in presentations to tell the scope of the learning and service experience, and emphasize specific information.
- in a list of recommended reading to help others learn more about the subject.

- *Wanda's Roses* (Gardening Bookshelf) follows a girl determined to have her rose bush bloom.

- Even a novel, like *The Misfits* (Safe and Strong Communities Bookshelf) about middle school kids trying to stop name-calling at school, has been transformed into a play.

- *Somebody Loves You, Mr. Hatch* (Elders Bookshelf) is a heartfelt story perfect for a Valentine's Day theme of valuing all community members, particularly those who are isolated and lonely.

- *The Wartville Wizard* (Environment Bookshelf) is a comical depiction of trash sticking to the people who litter in a small town.

- *The Can-Do Thanksgiving* (Hunger, Homelessness, and Poverty Bookshelf) demonstrates how knowing where the can of food is going can make all the difference.

- *How Humans Make Friends* (Safe and Strong Communities Bookshelf—digital content) has built-in scenarios students can perform to model friendship and conflict resolution skills.

- Any of the biographical collections can be adapted for "Living History" productions, where students become the people and tell their stories.

Library Partnerships

Books, too, can be a source of community partnerships. Consider all the possible ways you could collaborate with school and public libraries to promote books with service-learning-related themes. Students can set up displays, provide book reviews, or design bookmarks with recommendations. A first-grade class created an attractive calendar for four local libraries featuring books they enjoyed about gardening. Every month, they promoted a new favorite book. Ask your students what they'd like to do—they will have plenty of ideas.

The future belongs to those who can give the next generation reasons to hope.

—*Pierre Teilhard DeChardin, philosopher*

Tutoring Programs

Many bookshelf titles, particularly ones in the Literacy, Safe and Strong Communities, and Immigrants bookshelves, are helpful in various ways during preparation for or implementation of tutoring programs in which elementary, middle, or high school students tutor younger children or peers.

- Nonfiction books such as *Illiteracy* and *Learning Disabilities* (Literacy Bookshelf—digital content) provide background information.

- Several books describe the frustrations and embarrassment experienced by challenged readers, like *Thank You, Mr. Falker* (Literacy Bookshelf) and *Flight* (Literacy Bookshelf). Such books help students understand how kids may differ by skill, how they are affected by life experience, and how peer teasing and ridicule can present a hurdle.

- Learning English as a second language is hard work and is described in *The Circuit* and *Breaking Through* (Immigrants Bookshelf).

- In *Josias, Hold the Book* (Literacy Bookshelf), a young Haitian boy works the family garden instead of going to school. When Josias realizes that books hold information he needs to get the crops to grow, his father sends him to school.

- *My Name Is María Isabel* (Social Change Bookshelf—digital content) and *Any Small Goodness* (Immigrants Bookshelf) remind students and adults of the importance of treating all children with respect, including in classroom settings.

- Skills such as counting can be reinforced by *How Many Baby Pandas?* (Animal Protection and Care Bookshelf), which contains inspiring photos and information about an endangered species.

- Students may find that the love of words can be contagious when they read the humorous *The Bookstore Mouse* (Literacy Bookshelf—digital content), about a witty fantasy of a mouse with a colorful vocabulary who helps a young medieval scribe rescue storytellers from a dragon.

- In *Dear Whiskers* (Literacy Bookshelf—digital content), a young girl expresses frustration with a partner in a cross-age tutoring project, and comes to recognize appreciation for diversity and learning.

- A classroom with a place for every child, including one who is deaf, can be found in *The Year of Miss Agnes* (Literacy Bookshelf).

- *Sahara Special* (Literacy Bookshelf—digital content) tells of a girl who resists participating in school yet has a secret talent as a writer. This can inspire tutors to look for and encourage the secret (or not so secret) talents of their tutees (and recognize their own "secret" talents as well).

- High school students with low reading skills can develop their own ability while preparing to read quality picture books to younger children.

- Tutors can read books aloud to younger readers to communicate the joy of reading.

- Use the bookshelf to find books of interest to particular tutees. The titles reflect diverse cultures and experiences and should provide something for everyone.

For more information on tutoring and service learning, see the Preparation activity: Cross-Age Tutoring in Reading Skills on page 183. Also, I have written a workbook on the topic entitled *A Kids' Guide to Helping Others Read & Succeed: How to Take Action!*

School, City, and State Reading Programs

Programs that promote literacy and community building through reading are growing in popularity. The bookshelf lists are good sources of material for large-scale reading programs. All middle school students in a district, for example, might read *Any Small Goodness* (Immigrants Bookshelf), a chronicle of an adolescent's experience relocating to East Los Angeles. An entire city might be invited to read *Fahrenheit 451* (Literacy Bookshelf—digital content) or *To Kill a Mockingbird* (Social Change Bookshelf—digital content) and participate in related discussions. A statewide reading program might include *The Grapes of Wrath* (Hunger, Homelessness, and Poverty Bookshelf—digital content) among the selections. Community events associated with such programs might include art exhibits on related themes, staged productions of the book, readings, and speakers.

If a citywide or statewide reading program takes place in your community, get involved. If the selection is geared toward adults, recommend an additional book selection appropriate for young people, with follow-up activities at school or the library. Kids can select the book and design worthwhile and exciting learning opportunities. What may begin as a class or school activity could ultimately have citywide reach. Look at the example from Charleston, Illinois, in the Literacy chapter (page 188) for a description of elementary students leading successful citywide reading programs.

Community Agencies and Organizations

Although the discussion of the service learning bookshelf focuses on school settings, community agencies and organizations can also make use of the lists. Organizations promoting racial diversity and tolerance can refer to the Social Change Bookshelf when looking for recommended readings for a middle or high school class. A staff member at a retirement home may read a book such as *Sunshine Home* (Elders Bookshelf) aloud to elementary children coming for a service activity as part of an orientation to the facility. Many food banks have referenced the Hunger, Homelessness, and Poverty Bookshelf to compile recommended readings in support of annual food drives. Students can compile a list of books to read about special needs (or another theme) for an agency, complete with their original annotations or reviews, and develop analytical and writing skills in the process. Share the booklists with your community partners to find additional ways the resources can be helpful.

High Interest, Easy Reading

Finding books that interest students who avoid reading or who read below grade level can be challenging. That's why I have included some within each of the lists provided in this book. These all have compelling "page turner" stories. Each has the possibility of personal connection, even for a reader who appears dissimilar to the protagonist or other characters. For example, after reading the story of a fifteen-year-old British boy with autism in *The Curious Incident of the Dog in the Night-Time* (Special Needs and Disabilities Bookshelf) a typical student of the same age in Hawaii with nothing overtly in common with this character attested to having "so much" in common with him. Similarly, a parent whose son "never finished a book before" read the book cover to cover. Perhaps in these books we join the characters and the narrative in an exploration, a struggle, and a resolve. Each story has an underlying social issue that enables a heart-mind connection. We want to know whether Arturo in *Any Small Goodness* (Immigrant Bookshelf) will respond with revenge to the act of gang violence aimed at his family. We ask ourselves: can a teen in *Messed Up* (Hunger, Homelessness, and Poverty Bookshelf) who everyone expects to fail prove others wrong? While reading *Cracker!* (Safe and Strong Communities Bookshelf), a young man's experience in the Vietnam War, we witness how his relationship with a dog keeps him focused and helps him survive. And the prose-poetry format of *Soul Moon Soup* (Hunger, Homelessness, and Poverty Bookshelf) makes the story accessible to all of us—whatever our abilities—while

exposing us to the inside of a homeless shelter and examining the act of giving and receiving. And be sure to read *My Life as a Book* (Literacy Bookshelf) that is completely on target for a student who needs a way into reading.

Try this sampling of titles to get started; many others are found among the bookshelf entries within each theme chapter.

Any Small Goodness (page 180)
Bull Rider (page 209)
Cracker! (page 209)
The Curious Incident of the Dog in the Night-Time (page 235)
If I Grow Up (page 168)
Hitch (page 226)
Messed Up (page 168)
My Life as a Book (page 196)
Soul Moon Soup (page 168)
Worth (page 168)

Bilingual Books

Elders Bookshelf
Remember Me? Alzheimer's Through the Eyes of a Child/¿Te acuerdas de mí? Pensamientos de la enfermedad, Alzheimers a travez de los ojos de un niño

Gardening Bookshelf
Carlos and the Cornfield/Carloso y la milpa de maíz
Gathering the Sun: An Alphabet in Spanish and English

Immigrants Bookshelf
A Movie in My Pillow/Una película en mi almohada
My Diary from Here to There/Mi diario de aquí hasta allá

Literacy Bookshelf
Sequoyah: The Cherokee Man Who Gave His People Writing (English and Cherokee)

Safe and Strong Communities Bookshelf
It Doesn't Have to Be This Way: A Barrio Story/No tiene que ser así: Una historia del barrio
A Key to the Heart: A Collection of Afghan Folk Tales (English and Afghani Dari)

Social Change Bookshelf
¡Sí, Se Puede!/Yes, We Can! Janitor Strike in L.A.
That's Not Fair! Emma Tenayuca's Struggle for Justice/¡No Es Justo! La lucha de Emma Tenayuca por la justicia

Special Needs and Disabilities Bookshelf
The Treasure on Gold Street/El tesoro en la calle oro

Need a strategy to capture the reluctant reader? Hand a book to a student and ask, "Could you read the first three chapters and let me know if this is a good book for the class?" A thoughtfully selected book may then be read cover-to-cover.

Graphic Novels

Several entries on the bookshelf are graphic novels and are denoted "GN." These graphic novels may be fiction, nonfiction, or picture books, and they offer rich alternatives for reluctant readers and visual learners.

The Top Ten "Must-Have" Collection

While readers will be attracted to different titles based on their ages and the book's genre and subject matter, the quandary is often the same: So many amazing books! Where to start?

I confess I have hundreds of favorites that I consider "good friends" and are constant companions while spreading the service learning message. However, to simplify your selection process, especially if you are a service learning coordinator, here are my current top ten to accompany you to meet with teachers or as you deliver your own workshops.

1. *The Curse of Akkad* (page 127)

2. *In Our Village* (page 192)

3. *Jakeman* (page 226)

4. *A Life Like Mine: How Children Live Around the World* (Social Change Bookshelf—digital content)

5. *The Long March: The Choctaw's Gift to Irish Potato Famine Relief* (page 167)

6. *The Misfits* (page 209)

7. *Seedfolks* (page 142)

8. *Somebody Loves You, Mr. Hatch* (page 104)

9. *The Summer My Father Was Ten* (page 142)

10. *The Wartville Wizard* (page 131)

History Through the Bookshelf

Refer to this listing when seeking books depicting a particular period or issue. Dates are approximate.

General World History
- *After Gandhi: One Hundred Years of Nonviolent Resistance* (Social Change Bookshelf)
- *Akira to Zoltán: Twenty-Six Men Who Changed the World* (Social Change Bookshelf)
- *Amelia to Zora: Twenty-Six Women Who Changed the World* (Social Change Bookshelf)
- *The House* (Safe and Strong Communities Bookshelf)
- *Vherses: A Celebration of Outstanding Women* (Social Change Bookshelf—digital content)

General U.S. History
- *Denied, Detained, Deported: The Dark Side of American Immigration* (Immigrants Bookshelf)
- *How Lincoln Learned to Read: Twelve Great Americans and the Education that Made Them* (Literacy Bookshelf)
- *Rabble Rousers: 20 Women Who Made a Difference* (Social Change Bookshelf—digital content)
- *We Were There, Too! Young People in U.S. History* (Social Change Bookshelf)

The Middle Ages
- *A Company of Fools* (Healthy Lives, Healthy Choices Bookshelf)
- *The Bookstore Mouse* (Literacy Bookshelf—digital content)
- *Run Far, Run Fast* (Healthy Lives, Healthy Choices Bookshelf)
- *When Plague Strikes: The Black Death, Smallpox, AIDS* (AIDS Education and Awareness Bookshelf)
- *The White Witch* (Healthy Lives, Healthy Choices Bookshelf)

World History
1800–1865
- *The Adventurous Chef: Alexis Soyer* (Hunger, Homelessness, and Poverty Bookshelf)
- *Black Potatoes: The Story of the Great Irish Famine, 1845–1850* (Hunger, Homelessness, and Poverty Bookshelf)
- *Feed the Children First: Irish Memories of the Great Hunger* (Hunger, Homelessness, and Poverty Bookshelf)
- *The Forbidden Schoolhouse: The True and Dramatic Story of Prudence Crandall and Her Students* (Literacy Bookshelf)

- *The Long March: The Choctaw's Gift to Irish Famine Relief* (Hunger, Homelessness, and Poverty Bookshelf)
- *The Narrative of the Life of Frederick Douglass* (Literacy Bookshelf—digital content)
- *Sequoyah: The Cherokee Man Who Gave His People Writing* (Literacy Bookshelf)

1865–1910
- *I Could Do That! Esther Morris Gets Women the Vote* (Social Change Bookshelf)
- *Indian School: Teaching the White Man's Way* (Literacy Bookshelf)
- *They Came from the Bronx: How the Buffalo Were Saved from Extinction* (Animal Protection and Care Bookshelf)
- *A Train to Somewhere* (Hunger, Homelessness, and Poverty Bookshelf)
- *A Woman for President: The Story of Victoria Woodhull* (Social Change Bookshelf—digital content)

1910–1939
- *The Donkey of Gallipoli: A True Story of Courage in World War I* (Safe and Strong Communities Bookshelf)
- *Orphan Train Rider: One Boy's True Story* (Hunger, Homelessness, and Poverty Bookshelf)
- *Winnie's War* (Healthy Lives, Healthy Choices Bookshelf)
- *The Gardener* (Gardening Bookshelf)
- *Esperanza Rising* (Immigrants Bookshelf)
- *The Grapes of Wrath* (Hunger, Homelessness, and Poverty Bookshelf—digital content)
- *Hitch* (Social Change Bookshelf)
- *That Book Woman* (Literacy Bookshelf)

1939–1955
- *Alan's War: The Memories of G.I. Alan Cope* (Safe and Strong Communities Bookshelf)
- *The Book Thief* (Literacy Bookshelf)
- *Boxes for Katje* (Safe and Strong Communities Bookshelf—digital content)
- *Brundibar* (Social Change Bookshelf)
- *The Cat with the Yellow Star: Coming of Age in Terezin* (Safe and Strong Communities Bookshelf)

History Through the Bookshelf (continued)

1939–1955 (continued)

- *Eyes of the Emperor* (Safe and Strong Communities Bookshelf—digital content)
- *The Grand Mosque of Paris: A Story of How Muslims Rescued Jews During the Holocaust* (Safe and Strong Communities Bookshelf)
- *Left for Dead: A Young Man's Search for Justice for the USS Indianapolis* (Safe and Strong Communities Bookshelf—digital content)
- *One Thousand Tracings: Healing the Wounds of World War II* (Safe and Strong Communities Bookshelf)
- *Passage to Freedom: The Sugihara Story* (Social Change Bookshelf)
- *Six Million Paper Clips: The Making of a Children's Holocaust Memorial* (Safe and Strong Communities Bookshelf—digital content)
- *Slap Your Sides* (Social Change Bookshelf—digital content)
- *The Victory Garden* (Gardening Bookshelf)

1955–1968 (Civil Rights Era)

- *Across the Alley* (Social Change Bookshelf)
- *Birmingham, 1963* (Social Change Bookshelf—digital content)
- *Bone by Bone by Bone* (Social Change Bookshelf)
- *Claudette Colvin: Twice Toward Justice* (Social Change Bookshelf)
- *Delivering Justice: W.W. Law and the Fight for Civil Rights* (Social Change Bookshelf)
- *Goin' Someplace Special* (Literacy Bookshelf)
- *To Kill a Mockingbird* (Social Change Bookshelf—digital content)
- *Through My Eyes* (Social Change Bookshelf—digital content)
- *Remember: The Journey to School Integration* (Social Change Bookshelf—digital content)
- *We Are One: The Story of Bayard Rustin* (Social Change Bookshelf)

Recent and Current Events

Latin America

- *In the Time of the Butterflies* (Social Change Bookshelf—digital content)

Eastern Europe

- *Girl of Kosovo* (Safe and Strong Communities Bookshelf—digital content)
- *Notes for a War Story* (Safe and Strong Communities Bookshelf—digital content)

Southeast Asia

- *The Clay Marble* (Immigrants Bookshelf)
- *Cracker! The Best Dog in Vietnam* (Safe and Strong Communities Bookshelf)
- *Shooting the Moon* (Safe and Strong Communities Bookshelf)
- *Tangled Threads: A Hmong Girl's Story* (Immigrants Bookshelf)
- *The Things They Carried* (Safe and Strong Communities Bookshelf—digital content)
- *The Whispering Cloth: A Refugee's Story* (Immigrants Bookshelf)

Iraq and Afghanistan

- *Afghan Dreams: Young Voices of Afghanistan* (Safe and Strong Communities Bookshelf)
- *Bull Rider* (Safe and Strong Communities Bookshelf)
- *Children of War: Voices of Iraqi Refugees* (Safe and Strong Communities Bookshelf)
- *The Librarian of Basra: A True Story from Iraq* (Literacy Bookshelf)
- *The Photographer: Into War-Torn Afghanistan with Doctors Without Borders* (Social Change Bookshelf)
- *Silent Music: A Story of Baghdad* (Safe and Strong Communities Bookshelf)
- *Sunrise Over Fallujah* (Safe and Strong Communities Bookshelf)

September 11, 2001

- *14 Cows for America* (Safe and Strong Communities Bookshelf)
- *Bifocal* (Social Change Bookshelf)
- *Shine, Coconut Moon* (Social Change Bookshelf)

Hurricane Katrina

- *Hurricane Song: A Novel of New Orleans* (Emergency Readiness Bookshelf)
- *Two Bobbies: A True Story of Hurricane Katrina, Friendship, and Survival* (Emergency Readiness Bookshelf)

Literature Circle Roles

Form groups of four to discuss a story.

Assign each person in the group one of the "connector" roles below. Each connector's job is to lead a group discussion about the story from a specific point of view. He or she asks the questions listed (along with others that come to mind) and encourages group members to respond. Write notes and ideas on the Literature Circle.

To begin, review these tips:

Tips For Effective Group Discussions
• Use active listening skills
• Ask questions
• Take turns speaking
• Welcome all comments

Personal Connector

Ask questions that connect the story to group members' experiences, such as:
1. Do characters remind you of people you know? How?
2. Have you been in situations similar to those described in the book? What happened?
3. How have you or people you know resolved similar situations?

Literary Connector

Ask questions that connect this story to other stories group members have read, such as:
1. Which characters remind you of characters from other stories? Why?
2. What situations are similar to what happens in other stories? Why?
3. What might a character in this story say about these other characters or situations? Why?

Service Connector

Ask questions that connect this story to ideas for service projects, such as:
1. What needs to be fixed in this situation?
2. Did any characters in this story participate in service activities?
3. What service ideas did you think of when you read this story?

Learning Connector

Ask questions that connect this story to learning opportunities, such as:
1. What would you like to learn more about as a result of this story?
2. What topics in this story have you learned about or experienced in school?
3. What do you think people your age would learn from reading this story?

Literature Circle for _____

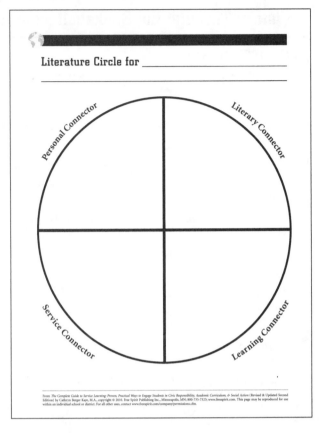

Quotable Quotes

Choose a quote and follow these ten steps.

Step 1: Draw the quote

Make a picture that visually represents the quote. Integrate the words of the quote into the picture or the frame. Consider unique ways to display the finished art piece.

Step 2: Find the meaning

Write a paragraph explaining what the quote means to you.

Step 3: Opinions & feelings

What do you *think* about the quote? Do you agree or disagree with it? Write your thoughts in a paragraph. How does this quote make you *feel*? Describe your feelings in a separate paragraph.

Step 4: Be creative!

Write a poem, short story, song, or other creative work that includes the quote.

Step 5: Who in history?

Find out who made the quoted statement and when. How was the statement influenced by world events at the time, and what relevance does it have today?

Step 6: The moral of the story is . . .

Write a brief story with a conflict between two characters; characters can be people, animals, or objects. End your story with a life lesson that can be explained through the quote. Conclude with the line, "The moral of the story is [insert the quote]."

Step 7: Comparative study

Select a second quote to compare with the first one. How are their messages alike and different? Consider, for example: "Education is not preparation for life; education is life itself." —John Dewey, and "Life is either a daring adventure or nothing." —Helen Keller.

Step 8: Putting the quote into practice

How can the quote be used to teach or influence others? How could it be used in a service learning activity?

Step 9: What quote will I be remembered by?

Write a quote of your own for which you'd like to be remembered.

Step 10: Reflect by answering one of these questions.

• What about this quote is most memorable to you?

• Write a letter to the author of this quote, sharing both your thoughts and feelings.

• Who would you like to give this quote to, and why? Describe how you could present the quote to this person so that it has the effect you intend.

See digital content for full-size reproducible pages.

Part Two

Service Learning Themes

Chapter 4

AIDS Education and Awareness

No war on the face of the Earth is more destructive than the AIDS pandemic.

—*Colin Powell, former U.S. Secretary of State*

Education is the primary prescription for preventing the spread of HIV and AIDS. With education, we can equip youth for the challenges that confront them, their society, and our global population. In this continually shrinking world, our neighbors are the folks down the block *and* in Africa, Asia, and South America, where the numbers of people who are HIV positive or living with AIDS are increasing at a staggering rate. Even with medical advances in more affluent countries, the problem is far from being under control. Consider these facts from 2007*:

- Globally, 33 million people were living with HIV/AIDS.

- 2 million people died from AIDS, the majority of them in sub-Saharan Africa.

- 270,000 of these people were children (down from the peak of 320,000 in 2003, a result of increased antiretroviral therapy and a decline of new infections among children).

The impact of HIV and AIDS extends well beyond issues of health. Consider what occurs when a child becomes infected. He or she can face discrimination, isolation, loss of education, and in many countries, homelessness. Limited resources can cut short a young life. To create well-being and opportunities for every child, learning about HIV and AIDS becomes a necessity.

In uncertain times, we can help young people deal with facts like these by providing information, resources, and prevention strategies. We can equip them to make healthy personal choices, be advocates for a healthy society, and promote well-being in all parts of the world. We must be involved, continue to create educational opportunities based on current

* All statistics from The Living Proof Project, 2009, and the Joint United National Programme on HIV/AIDS

information and resources, help young people separate fact from fiction, and act for prevention.

Preparation: Getting Ready for Service Learning Involving AIDS Education and Awareness

 The following activities can be used in the preparation stage to promote learning and skill development related to HIV and AIDS education and awareness. These activities can be used with different age ranges during investigation, preparation, and planning to help your students examine key issues through research, analyze community needs, and gain the knowledge they need to effectively contribute to the design of their service plan. Since literature is often an important part of preparation, you can find recommended titles on this theme in the AIDS Education and Awareness Bookshelf later in this chapter.

Activity: Understanding Leads to Action. Providing age-appropriate information helps students gain knowledge that can lead to action. For young children up to third grade, AIDS education is often included with information concerning other health problems. The emphasis is on staying healthy—eating well and getting adequate exercise and sleep. Children are also often taught to differentiate between communicable and noncommunicable diseases. While most children know they can "catch" a cold, young children can be assured that being friends and playing with a child who is HIV positive or living with AIDS is safe.

Young people can also have great empathy for people who are receiving care in hospitals, or who are taken to emergency rooms or clinics. By revisiting

74

their own experiences with being sick or going to the doctor's office, students can come up with ideas to reach out to others who are affected by HIV or AIDS. Guide your students' empathy with readings from the bookshelf, research, and class discussions. Start looking for organizations in your community that assist people living with HIV or AIDS or who are working to stop the spread of AIDS. Early collaborations with these kinds of agencies can help students develop project ideas that meet real local, or even global, needs. Project ideas that could result include:

- younger students writing "Have a Good Day" greeting cards to be inserted in lunches to be delivered to people living with HIV or AIDS

- making blankets for babies living with HIV or AIDS

- collecting materials for, assembling, and decorating holiday gift baskets for people living with AIDS

- developing programs to replace myths about HIV and AIDS with accurate information

- older students helping to assemble and deliver meals, providing pet care, or participating in other forms of outreach to people living with HIV or AIDS

Activity: Discussion and Research. Through reading, students can continue to learn about the ever-changing world of education, research, and prevention of AIDS. What is the most current information regarding the spread of HIV and AIDS, strategies for prevention, and the search for a cure? Students can begin by reading one of the nonfiction books listed in this chapter, such as *When Plague Strikes: The Black Death, Smallpox, AIDS*, holding small-group discussions, and generating questions. If needed, you can add any of the following to their list:

- How much funding is allocated to research?

- Do socioeconomic factors affect who is getting treatment for AIDS and what treatments are available?

- How do developing countries cope with the spread of HIV and AIDS?

- What populations are most susceptible to contracting HIV and AIDS?

- What are the resources for children, particularly in developing countries where many have the disease or have been orphaned by AIDS?

In groups, students can use the Internet, newspapers and journals, and local organizations to find answers to these questions and then share their findings. They might consider interviewing a person of knowledge in the community—someone well versed on current medical and societal programs. This research helps students determine worthwhile and meaningful activities that can help educate others to stop the spread of AIDS or that can assist people in the community or in other parts of the world who are affected by HIV. Learning about the impact of AIDS in the local and global context helps students understand the challenges facing people particularly in Third World countries.

Find Out More About AIDS Education and Awareness

To learn more about these issues and to get ideas for service and action, visit these Web sites and organizations online:

UNICEF (www.unicef.org/programme/hiv/overview.htm) works closely with national governments, nongovernmental organizations, and other United Nations agencies to improve the lives of children, youth, and women.

The Kaiser Family Foundation (www.kff.org/hivaids/index.cfm) serves as a resource for information about HIV/AIDS policy, public opinion and knowledge about the disease, and media-based partnerships.

The Centers for Disease Control (www.cdc.gov/hiv/dhap.htm) is a good source for current information and statistics on HIV and AIDS. They have a Frequently Asked Questions section that answers general questions about what causes AIDS, how it's transmitted, and how it can be prevented. It also has a page devoted to debunking common hoaxes and rumors about HIV and AIDS.

Making Connections Across the Curriculum

Some service learning activities naturally lend themselves to interdisciplinary work and making connections across the curriculum. These connections strengthen and broaden student learning, helping them meet academic standards. More than likely, you'll be looking for these connections and ways to encourage them well before the students ever start working on service learning activities. As with the entire service learning process, it helps to remain flexible, because some connections can be spontaneously generated by the questions raised throughout and by the community needs identified by the students. To help you think about cross-curricular connections and where you can look for them, the curricular web for this chapter (page 77) gives examples of many different ways this theme can be used in different academic areas. (The service learning scenarios in the next section of the chapter also demonstrate various ways that this theme can be used across the curriculum.)

Service Learning Scenarios: Ideas for Action

Ready to take action? The service learning descriptions that follow have been successfully carried out by elementary, middle, or high school students in schools and with community organizations. Most of these scenarios and examples explicitly include some aspects of investigation, preparation and planning, action, reflection, and demonstration, and all have strong curricular connections. These scenarios can be a rich source of ideas for you to draw upon. Keep in mind that grade levels are provided as a reference; most scenarios can be adapted to suit younger or older students, and many are suitable for cross-age partnerships.

The Universal Language of Theater in Ethiopia: Grades 1–12

Sharing information to prevent AIDS is serious business all over the world. In Ethiopia, children perform as part of the Awassa Children's Project and One Love Theater. Through fund raising, many of the child performers, themselves orphaned by AIDS, reside at the Awassa Children's Center. They receive education, food, and clothing as they take their lifesaving message across their country. Service has provided new opportunities for the youth while giving them an important role to play. See their work at www.awassa.org.

Blankets for Babies: Grade 4

Fourth-grade students took turns bringing in news articles for class discussion. One student brought an article about babies born with AIDS. The class agreed they wanted to help in some way and decided to make baby blankets. They looked at pictures of quilts made by pioneer women and decided to use similar patterns for decoration. Using soft fabric and fabric markers, they worked with geometric patterns in soothing colors. A parent volunteer sewed the edges, and the completed blankets went on "tour" in the school to teach others about this important subject. Students created mini-lessons to make their classroom presentations interactive. They received a letter of thanks from the organization that received the blankets.

Teaching Respect: Grade 5

After learning about people being mistreated because of illnesses such as AIDS, fifth-grade students considered various ways to get across a message of respect for all people. They decided to create a comic book character who would teach younger children to be thoughtful toward people living with HIV or AIDS. After consulting with a local health organization, students developed several story lines, combined them into one magazine, and made copies for younger children. These were distributed in school and at a community health fair.

Using the AIDS Memorial Quilt: Grade 7

While studying ways to prevent HIV infection and AIDS, two middle school classes in Pennsylvania decided to bring information to the community. After learning about the AIDS Memorial Quilt—an ongoing community art project that includes more than 47,000 three-by-six-foot memorial panels, each commemorating a person who has died from AIDS—they wanted to participate. After receiving names and biographies of eleven individuals who died from AIDS and were not yet represented in the quilt, the students made and contributed eleven panels. They mastered sewing, silk screening, and the art of gathering and recycling

AIDS Education and Awareness Across the Curriculum

English/Language Arts

- Discuss the importance of friendship with children who are living with HIV or AIDS
- Read written material from a clinic offering HIV/AIDS prevention information and adapt it to a teen or younger child's version
- Study the impact of media coverage, entertainment, and/or mass marketing campaigns to eliminate misconceptions about people living with HIV or AIDS

Social Studies/History

- Create an AIDS historical timeline
- Study medieval history and the pattern of scapegoating (irrational intolerance toward certain people or groups) during plagues
- Compare approaches to AIDS prevention by different governments

Languages

- Find out how HIV/AIDS impacts countries internationally
- Read HIV/AIDS information in the language being studied as prepared by different countries
- Translate HIV/AIDS prevention information for community organizations and outreach

Theater, Music, & Visual Arts

- Research how theater and storytelling have been used to teach about social issues, including AIDS awareness in the United States and abroad
- Find out how music has influenced HIV/AIDS prevention both through fund raisers and messages in songs
- Examine how the AIDS Memorial Quilt has grown as an international art project

AIDS Education and Awareness

Math

- Research the cost of hospital stays for various ailments
- Graph the funds allocated by governments to research and prevent HIV/AIDS
- Review the statistics of HIV and AIDS by age and sex

Physical Education

- Research the role of exercise in healthy living
- Have a physical therapist demonstrate adaptive exercise programs
- Create a simplified exercise protocol for children or teens who have health limitations

Computer

- Design pocket-size information cards with community health resource information
- Create a multimedia presentation on an HIV/AIDS–related subject
- Use the Internet to learn how African nations are responding to the AIDS crisis

Science

- Learn about the body's regulatory and immune systems and healthy life habits
- Interview doctors at a local health clinic about epidemics
- Research the transmission factors that put young people at risk

assorted fabrics and materials. Students proudly displayed their artwork to the community.

Connecting Science to Action: Grades 7–8

The seventh and eighth grades at the Brandeis Hillel Day School in San Francisco connected science units on HIV and AIDS with community action. In addition to their academic studies, students heard from speakers about the complexity and human impact of HIV and AIDS. The seventh-grade class partnered with Project Open Hand, a grassroots organization that provides nutrition services. Eighth graders visited the National AIDS Memorial Grove in Golden Gate Park, donating gardening services while learning from Grove representatives about the role of the memorial in the lives of people affected by HIV and AIDS.

Informational Brochures: Grade 8

An English teacher read *Too Far Away to Touch* to his middle school students to stimulate a conversation about HIV and AIDS in our society. This sparked a lengthy discussion of personal experiences involving both losses and new research. Students were allowed to choose a project that would involve developing and using persuasive writing skills, and they decided to help break down some of the myths surrounding AIDS. They found an HIV/AIDS quiz on the Internet and got permission to use it as a teaching tool. Working in small groups, they created brochures, which included the quiz, and informational packets that were used in several schools in their area.

Live Safe–A Filmmaking Experience: Grades 8–12

A Native American youth filmmaking project on the dangers of HIV and AIDS involved teens ages thirteen to eighteen in all aspects of production work. They learned about Native American history and culture and the AIDS impact on this population. Students rotated through many jobs to gain a cross-section of experience. Conducted after school and led by the Media Arts Center San Diego, their ten-minute documentary titled, "It's Your Life, Live It Safe," takes viewers through the experience of a Native teen who decides to take an HIV test. Native elders from the community would visit and offer their wisdom to the diverse group of students. The film screened for the elders and in Native American film festivals.

> Once every generation, history brings us to an important crossroad. Sometimes in life there is that moment when it's possible to make a change for the better. This is one of those moments.
>
> —Elizabeth Glaser, founder of the Pediatric AIDS Foundation

Building Awareness: Grade 9

Using *AIDS: Can This Epidemic Be Stopped?* plus Internet research, high school students in Oakland, California, worked in small groups to plan a series of activities concerning issues affecting people with HIV/AIDS. They conducted an Awareness Day with speakers, in-class workshops, and presentations; prepared a short unit to teach in a ninth-grade health class; and wrote an editorial to the local paper advocating greater respect for persons living with HIV/AIDS.

Tolerance Campaign: Grade 10

Reading *When Plague Strikes: The Black Death, Smallpox, AIDS* as a class text, students in Minnesota learned how people have been blamed for the spread of diseases throughout history. A parallel study emerged of ways in which some teens were scapegoats in their school. Students formed strategy groups to plan campaigns to help eliminate the ridicule and harassment that undermines confidence and isolates their peers. Strategies included public service announcements, meetings with administrators to discuss policy issues, a proposal for "safe school guidelines," and a "teach-in" devoted to music and poetry about building tolerance among teens. The students conducted a survey to find out how the school population was responding to their efforts. The survey indicated that a substantial number of students had become more thoughtful about their actions and were also more likely to interrupt disrespectful actions by their friends.

Get Cookin': Grade 10

Two classes collaborated to prepare meals to be delivered to people living with AIDS in their upstate New York community. Both were biology classes, one was a regular biology class, the other was for students with special needs. To prepare for the project, each class learned about AIDS, nutrition, special diets, what to expect, and how to work together as a team. Everyone assumed the kids in the regular class would take the lead, however, one young man in the special needs class who, even though he couldn't speak, could cook. He ran the kitchen, assigning jobs, showing how to slice and dice, and impressing everyone. Both classes were eager to collaborate again.

Taking a Stand for Youth Voice: High School

Students have a vested interest in participating in developing ideas and strategies to help teens avoid HIV and AIDS. This was the position of high school students in upstate New York as they requested positions on a school district AIDS advisory committee. After making a strong case to the local school board, with a concerted expression of ideas and ways they truly "represent the voice of youth," several students (identified by the youth) were appointed to the advisory group.

Teams for Understanding: High School

High school students who were HIV positive or living with AIDS collaborated with uninfected peers to form speaking teams to teach middle and high school students about the disease. With guidance from professionals, students developed basic scripts and practiced public speaking skills. They rehearsed with their classes how to respond to questions and developed a handout with facts, figures, myths, truths, and Web sites to provide more information.

Dream to End AIDS Benefit Ball: High School

More than one hundred teens from twelve public high schools joined Fight AIDS in Africa, a program developed by the Youth Empowerment Project (YEP), a nonprofit organization created by teens in Michigan. This ongoing program involves YEP teens using the Internet to provide West African youth with information about education and leadership to enable them to help prevent the spread of the disease in thirty villages in their country. The "Dream to End AIDS Benefit Ball" proceeds purchased laptop computers, video equipment, electricity generators, and related technology to make ongoing communication more effective. The benefit included jazz and poetry readings in "The Ouagadougou Cafe," named after the capital of Burkina Faso. Decorations had an African theme and video displays offered valuable information about AIDS in Burkina Faso.

Theater Works: High School

After research and study, and with guidance from local AIDS activists, high school students in northern Missouri prepared and presented skits depicting young people in situations requiring that choices be made. Because the skits called for audience participation, debate and discussion followed. Through performance, students hoped to reinforce healthy behavior, give strategies for dealing with peer pressure, and promote community awareness. Ongoing role playing and reflection helped the actors refine their skills and deal with challenging teaching situations and audience reactions.

World AIDS Day: High School

In California, Murrieta Valley High School clubs recognized World AIDS Day using song, poetry, dance, and statistics to illustrate that the deadly virus continues to wreak havoc. As the choir sang, images showing young people infected with AIDS flashed across a screen. Members of the school's Si Si Puede and Ballet Folklorico clubs offered poems in English and Spanish, along with statistics on how AIDS affects Latinos. The Health Occupation Students of America, National Honor Society, Poetry and Black Student Union clubs also meshed statistics on AIDS with poems and music to spread awareness. Together they led a challenge to spread the information and grow awareness to minimize the impact of AIDS.

Learning About Policy and Speaking Out: High School

Youth activists attended an international AIDS conference to make their voices heard, since 50 percent of new HIV infections worldwide occur in young people ages fifteen to twenty-four.* Through workshops, students learned about policy and current strategies. They returned to their communities to write articles for the school paper, form study groups, and help design an informational brochure about confidential testing for a local AIDS prevention organization.

A Mural to Remember: High School

Fifteen participants in a New York City youth program whose lives had been touched by AIDS designed a mural to face a busy city street. The entire teen group helped paint and create this 150-foot long, 10-foot tall

---

* *Listen, Learn, Live! World AIDS Campaign with Children and Young People: Facts and Figures*, UNAIDS Joint United Nations Programme on HIV/AIDS

masterpiece, unveiled to the community on World AIDS Day. Elected officials, community members, parents, and friends gathered to see the art and hear the poetry written by these young people.

The AIDS Education and Awareness Bookshelf

The AIDS Education and Awareness Bookshelf contains a modest number of selections compared with other themes. Still, these selections represent a range of opportunities to learn and develop meaningful service connections. To help you find books relevant to your particular projects, the book chart classifies the titles into several topic areas: historical overview, our stories, and relationships.

In general, the bookshelf features:

- An annotated bibliography arranged and alphabetized by title according to the general categories of nonfiction (N), picture books (P), and fiction (F). For nonfiction and fiction, length and recommended grade levels are included. The entries in the picture book category do not include suggested grade levels, since they can be successfully used with all ages.

- A chart organized by topic and category to help you find books relevant to particular projects.

- Recommendations from service learning colleagues and experts that include a book summary and ideas for service learning connections. (The number of recommended books varies in each bookshelf.)

AIDS Education and Awareness Bookshelf Topics

Topics	Books	Category
Historical Overview What do we already know about this disease that continues to spread at an alarming rate?	Fighting the AIDS and HIV Epidemic: A Global Battle Frequently Asked Questions About AIDS and HIV HIV and AIDS: Coping in a Changing World A Life Like Mine: How Children Live Around the World * (See Social Change Bookshelf—digital content) When Plague Strikes: The Black Death, Smallpox, AIDS	N N N N N
Our Stories The voices of the people living with HIV or AIDS or those close to people who are infected add personal experience to the facts and statistics.	Chanda's Secret The Heaven Shop Our Stories, Our Songs: African Children Talk About AIDS * Quicksand: HIV/AIDS in Our Lives You Can Call Me Willy: A Story for Children About AIDS	F F N N P
Relationships Meaningful relationships demonstrate the caring response of family and community to the AIDS crisis. Learning of these interactions reminds us to reach out and create similar relationships.	The Beat Goes On * Far and Beyon' Positively Too Far Away to Touch ‡	F F F P

Page references are given for books that appear in the bookshelf lists of other chapters.
* These books include examples of young people in service-providing roles.
‡ These books are out of print but still worth finding.

- *Please note:* additional titles for this category are listed in the digital content; some of these were out of print at time of publication but still worth finding.

From what we get, we can make a living; what we give, however, makes a life.
—*Arthur Ashe, athlete*

Nonfiction: AIDS Education and Awareness

Fighting the AIDS and HIV Epidemic: A Global Battle
by Maureen J. Hinds (Enslow Publishing, June 2007). In this comprehensive text, the author explains how HIV and AIDS first emerged and describes the devastation that has followed. Included is information about prevention, treatment, possible future courses of the illness, and its impact on our world. 128pp., grades 3–6

Frequently Asked Questions About AIDS and HIV
by Richard Robinson (Rosen Publishing Group, 2009). Being informed is the first step toward making sound choices and being respectful of others. By framing the information about HIV/AIDS through a series of questions, students find out what they need to know as they develop curiosity to find out more. 64pp., young adult

HIV and AIDS: Coping in a Changing World
by Paula Johnson (Rosen Publishing, 2007). With more than 40 million people in the world living with AIDS, it is now recognized as the most devastating disease in human history. This coping manual defines the disease, explains how it operates in the body, discusses treatments, and advises on prevention. Also included is a comprehensive guide for teens who either live with the disease or know someone who does. 112pp., young adult

Our Stories, Our Songs: African Children Talk About AIDS
by Deborah Ellis (Fitzhenry & Whiteside 2005). A combination of photos, information, and ways to get involved, this outstanding compilation is easily accessible to students. The author spent many months in several African countries working with local relief organizations and meeting families and children. Even in light of this devastating epidemic, Deborah Ellis's insightful work offers opportunity for awareness and action. 104pp., grades 4–12

Quicksand: HIV/AIDS in Our Lives
by Anonymous (Candlewick Press, 2009). The author chose anonymity out of respect for her brother-in-law who contracted HIV. With the continued stigma regarding people contracting this virus, they deemed keeping their privacy necessary. The format is helpful: information followed by the typical questions most people want to know about that particular topic. From "False Fears" to "Slowly Stealing Life" to "Lifelines." Even though "Jay" succumbs to his ailment and dies, the final chapter, "A Vision of Hope," expresses the author's desire that soon "no one with HIV/AIDS has to remain anonymous anymore in America or anywhere." 103pp., young adult

When Plague Strikes: The Black Death, Smallpox, AIDS
by James Cross Giblin (HarperCollins, 1995). This compelling study of three deadly epidemics, separated by centuries, shows the similarity of social, political, and cultural reactions. Each disease brought medical advances. At the same time, in each case, blame was placed on people where none was deserved. The insights into the human condition are as provocative as the studies of history and medical advances. 212pp., grades 6–12

Picture Books: AIDS Education and Awareness

Too Far Away to Touch
by Lesléa Newman (Clarion, 1995). Little Zoe and her Uncle Leonard enjoy adventures together. While at the Planetarium, Zoe asks, "How far away are the stars?" "Too far away to touch, close enough to see," her uncle answers. When Leonard becomes weaker due to AIDS, the message from the Planetarium has special meaning.

You Can Call Me Willy: A Story for Children About AIDS
by Joan C. Verniero (Magination Press, 1995). Willy tells about her life with AIDS. She describes the care she receives from her grandmother, her best friend, and other adults. Most of all, she wants to have friends and play baseball.

Fiction: AIDS Education and Awareness

The Beat Goes On
by Adele Minchin (Simon & Schuster, 2001). When Leyla learns the older cousin she admires most has HIV, she breaks down. But soon she begins supporting her cousin through the shock of diagnosis and process of treatment. When a relationship begins with a guy she likes, Leyla realizes this diagnosis changed her life forever and that silence and shame contributes to the problem. So she takes action, being part of a youth center where teens can be teens without labels. 224pp., grades 10–12

Chanda's Secrets

by Allan Stratton (Annick Press, 2004). This informed, moving narrative unflinchingly describes the shame and abuse surrounding the AIDS epidemic in Africa, through the courage of a girl whose love and pride causes her to defy the cruelty of the status quo. When her family members are stricken and many die, Chanda breaks the social taboo of acknowledging this virus so she and those remaining can live with dignity. The author traveled in South Africa, Botswana, and Zimbabwe in preparation for writing the book. 196pp., young adult

Far and Beyon'

by Unity Dow (Aunt Lute Books, 2002). Set in Botswana, this novel draws from the author's experience in the women's rights struggle while sharing a contemporary family's loss due to AIDS. This is a family in conflict, both between and within individuals. At the center is Mora, age seventeen, who watched her two brothers die, and is torn between her ancestral traditions and the influence of western medicine and culture. After a pregnancy and an abortion, Mora returns to school, only to face the abuse of female students in the corrupt school system. But Mora takes a risk, and joined by other female students, makes a dramatic stand to stop the violence and obtain dignity. 199pp., grades 9–12

The Heaven Shop

by Deborah Ellis (Fitzhenry & Whiteside Limited, 2007). Thirteen-year-old Binti has a remarkable life in Malawi: she is a radio celebrity! When the community learns that her father, just like her mother, died of AIDS, Binti and her siblings are sent to live with relatives far from home. Life as she has always known it ends abruptly. Through this realistic portrayal of the plight of African families living with and dying with AIDS, young people can develop empathy and choose to become involved. 186pp., grades 5–9

Positively

by Courtney Sheinmel (Simon and Schuster, 2009). After her mother dies, Emerson feels lonely and lives with her dad and his wife. She is sure they can't understand what being HIV-positive is like. Surprisingly, going to Camp Positive where other kids might understand really does make the change she needs. 224pp., grades 5–9

DIGITAL CONTENT

**Interviews with Authors:
The Story Behind the Story**

In the companion digital content, you'll find interviews with James Cross Giblin *(When Plague Strikes: The Black Death, Smallpox, AIDS)* and Allan Stratton *(Chanda's Secrets)* that tell the "story behind the story" of their books.

Chapter 5

Animal Protection and Care

Every individual matters. Every individual has a role to play. Every individual makes a difference. And we have a choice: What sort of difference do we want to make?

—*Jane Goodall, primatologist and anthropologist*

Nature is all about balance, and maintaining a desirable balance in nature depends on the survival of a web of species. For animals, the world is shrinking. Threatened by human development, our expansive lifestyles continue to encroach on natural habitats and disrupt migratory patterns. Honoring the symbiotic relationship among the species requires awareness, education, and action. If we are to prevent extinction and preserve biological diversity, it is important to understand our options while they still exist.

If we don't change our direction, we're likely to end up where we are going.
–*Chinese proverb*

Children seem to be naturally drawn to animals, eager to learn about the Asian elephant, blue whale, and giant armadillo. Students often express surprise that animals in their own region may be rare, threatened, vulnerable, or endangered. When they find out about such situations in distant places or learn about overcrowded animal shelters, they are usually eager to get involved. As they observe, compare and contrast, categorize, analyze, and report findings about animals in their own backyard or regions, young people develop scientific inquiry practices and apply their knowledge. The controversies that students may come across in their research enliven social studies, civics, and government classes and familiarize them with local and national advocacy groups.

As more animals face extinction on every continent due to global warming, the changing climate, and increased animal abandonment during challenging economic times, we must act. Protecting and caring for animals—the need exists and we must respond.

Preparation: Getting Ready for Service Learning Involving Animal Protection and Care

 The following activities can be used to promote learning and skill development related to animal protection and care. These activities are easily adapted to different grade levels during investigation, preparation, and planning to help your students examine key issues through research, analyze community needs, and gain the knowledge they need to effectively contribute to the design of their service plan. They can often be integrated into reflection and demonstration as students can lead the activities with others to build awareness. Since literature is often an important part of preparation, you can find recommended titles on this theme in the Animal Protection and Care Bookshelf later in this chapter.

Activity: Assisting Wildlife Rehabilitation. Wildlife rehabilitators rescue and care for animals and then release them back to the wild. Young people have been of great assistance to the local nonprofit organizations doing this important work. Students can conduct research in their region to find any such agencies and establish an ongoing relationship with them.

How can youth be involved with wildlife rehabilitation? Author Shannon K. Jacobs (*Healers of the Wild*) offers these suggestions for ways to help rehabilitation centers and protect animals in the wild.

- Ask for a "wish list" from local rehabilitators. A variety of activities can result when students find out needs and start looking for ways to meet them. They could collect supplies by gathering donated produce daily from grocery stores, picking up fallen fruit under fruit trees and unwanted produce from community gardens, or organizing donations from the community of other supplies the rehabilitation center may need.

- Ask what kinds of help the rehabilitation center needs. They may need help cleaning cages. Or perhaps they might welcome assistance with fundraising and publicity efforts, which could lead to students writing articles, letters to the editor, and press releases, or painting native animals for display or sale. Or maybe they would welcome students setting up and maintaining computer programs that assist with tracking volunteer hours, data about admission/discharge of animals, donations, and the budget.

- Do research and consult with rehabilitation experts, so that students can learn how to design and build birdhouses, bat houses, or cages for mammals.

- Research and consultation could also result in: school presentations and community programs about fascinating native wildlife and how to protect them; the creation of materials to help younger students develop compassion for wildlife; inviting wildlife rehabilitators to speak at school; or the design and organization of a cleanup campaign to pick up litter from school yards, parks, and shorelines.

Activity: From Headlines to Research to Action. Because the well-being of animals is a favorite topic of kids, use their natural desire to know more to engage them in research. Newspaper and magazines articles provide many headlines that inspire ideas and are supported with research using a variety of sources. Ask students to scan newspapers and magazines to develop a topic and an action plan. Perhaps they'll write a series of newspaper articles. Or create a presentation for a local group of animal lovers, a podcast, radio spots for their favorite station, or a billboard design. The following headlines are adapted from the news:

- Kids Hope to Find Homes for Abandoned Dogs

- Animals Trained for Law Enforcement

- Arrests Made in Dog Fighting Operation

- Along Local River Bird Population Falls

- Bears Out West Searching for Food

- More Animals Added to Threatened List

- Animals Trained for Movies—Are They Treated Well?

Find Out More About Animal Protection and Care

To learn more about these issues and to get ideas for service and action, visit these Web sites and organizations online:

ASPCA Professional (www.ASPCApro.org), a Web site of the American Society for the Prevention of Cruelty to Animals (ASPCA), provides quality materials and resources for educators, students, and parents that aid in the realization of ASPCA's mission.

Kids' Planet (www.kidsplanet.org) is the youth Web site of Defenders of Wildlife, an organization dedicated to the protection of all native wild animals and plants in their natural communities. This Web site offers extensive information about endangered species worldwide.

The Nature Conservancy (www.nature.org) is the world's leading conservation organization. Check out their Web site for numerous examples of animals being saved in their natural habitat on every continent.

Roots & Shoots (www.rootsandshoots.org) is the Jane Goodall Institute's international environmental and humanitarian program for young people. The program encourages all participants to do service learning aimed at improving situations for animals, people, and the environment. Many resources can be found at their Web site and in their frequent newsletters.

Students can work in pairs or teams on a topic they choose. Review the "Five Ws" of good journalism: Who? What? Where? When? Why? Students should look for different sources. If a newspaper or magazine article is used, can students contact the writer with more questions or to find out his or her sources? Can they look up any agencies referenced in the article?

Review the different research methods of media, interview, survey, observation, and experiences. Which methods will students use?

Making Connections Across the Curriculum

Some service learning activities naturally lend themselves to interdisciplinary work and making connections across the curriculum. These connections strengthen and broaden student learning, helping them meet academic standards. More than likely, you'll be looking for these connections and ways to encourage them well before the students ever start working on service learning activities. As with the entire service learning process, it helps to remain flexible, because some connections can be spontaneously generated by the questions raised throughout and by the community needs identified by the students. To help you think about cross-curricular connections and where you can look for them, the curricular web for this chapter (page 86) gives examples of many different ways this theme can be used in different academic areas. (The service learning scenarios in the next section of the chapter also demonstrate various ways this theme can be used across the curriculum.)

Service Learning Scenarios: Ideas for Action

Ready to take action? The service learning descriptions that follow have been successfully carried out by elementary, middle, or high school students in schools and with community organizations. Most of these scenarios and examples explicitly include some aspects of investigation, preparation and planning, action, reflection, and demonstration, and all have strong curricular connections. These scenarios can be a rich source of ideas for you to draw upon. Keep in mind that grade levels are provided as a reference; most scenarios can be adapted to suit younger or older students, and many are suitable for cross-age partnerships.

Animal Care: Kindergarten

Most children love animals and enjoy learning about how to provide them with the best possible care. Kindergarten children listened to many books on animals, including *Nights of the Pufflings* and *Before You Were Mine*. An animal specialist and the owner of a hospital companion dog visited their classroom, and the children also took a field trip to an animal rescue organization. The children helped plan and promote a school-wide collection of old bedding for donation to the rescue group and made dog bandanas to be sold by the local Society for the Prevention of Cruelty to Animals (SPCA).

A Helping Hand—A Receiving Paw: Grades K–5

Social studies, math, science, language arts—all combined in service learning experiences related to lending a helping paw. At Bailey Lake Elementary in Michigan, the C.A.T.S. project (Connecting Academics Through Service) involved the whole school: Older students made toys and blankets and collected supplies; younger students assembled bags for new pet owners. Everyone wrote thank-you cards for people who adopted animals. And the learning continued when an endangered species expert visited the school.

Ducks and Organic Rice: Grade 1 with High School Partners

Wildlife-friendly agriculture in the Central Valley of California led to community partnerships on a river preserve where nearly one thousand acres of organic rice are farmed each year. After the rice is harvested in the fall, fields are flooded providing a superb habitat for migrating ducks, swans, geese, and cranes. In spring, ducks nest in the fields before they are plowed and planted. Five first-grade classes integrated a duck egg rescue experience into their study of animal life cycles. Students visited the preserve wetlands in the fall, observing shorebirds and waterfowl. Over the next few months, students learned about the life cycles of many types of animals. In April, just before plowing, the students returned to the preserve. Led by the farmer, with help from preserve staff, volunteers, and a high school biology class, first-grade students walked

Animal Protection and Care Across the Curriculum

English/Language Arts

- Find books to read to younger children that teach respect for animals
- Create an ABC book of endangered animals and ways to help
- Write essays from the perspective of endangered animals seeking human assistance

Social Studies/History

- Visit an animal shelter or zoo to learn about its role in the community
- Research the government agencies that oversee endangered animals
- Learn about the Progressive Era (1890–1913) and the inception of organizations to protect animals

Languages

- Find out about animal rescue projects run by kids in different countries and correspond by email
- Create multilingual informational brochures about a local endangered animal
- Make presentations to other classes in the language being learned on a topic related to protecting animals

Theater, Music, & Visual Arts

- Write and perform plays with animals as characters teaching about their care or how to protect them
- Learn and perform songs that show respect for animals and nature
- Using drawing, painting, photography, or any visual art medium, create an art show of animals in both dangerous and protected environments

Animal Protection and Care

Math

- Develop a budget for the weekly cost of pet care
- Study the math concepts used to build small animal shelters or create a bird habitat
- Compare statistics on changes in the status of an endangered animal

Physical Education

- Do exercises that you've developed or drawn from yoga or other movement systems, that mimic the ways animals naturally move
- Learn how domesticated animals are affected when they don't get exercise
- Conduct research locally to find community needs for animal walkers or runners

Computer

- Find out how computers are used to track migratory patterns
- Create a Web site to help advertise and promote pet adoption
- Research and inform classes about Web sites with information about endangered animals

Science

- Research pet care, including nutrition, physiology, and psychology; also learn about and compare to their relations in the wild
- Learn about endangered animals in your region and groups that work to rescue and restore
- Visit a natural wildlife habitat to make observations, learn about the ecosystems, and ways to protect the animals living there

through the fields rescuing several nests from the tractor. Eggs were taken back to school and hatched in incubators. Students kept incubation logs, plotted duckling growth and development, and read many duck- and bird-related stories and poems, including *The Nights of the Pufflings*, a true story of very young children rescuing baby birds in Iceland. The first graders also read books to their ducks! Office and administrative staff volunteered to help with weekend feeding duties. Volunteers working with the state waterfowl association raised the ducks during the summer. The ducks were then banded and released into the wild on the preserve. These students set a precedent for an annual quality environmental action collaborative experience.

If you think you're too small to have an impact, try going to bed with a mosquito.

—*Anita Roddick, businesswoman*

Taking Giant Steps for Animals: Grades 1–8

Students in Giant Steps, a school for kids with autism, learned about an animal rescue and retirement farm outside St. Louis, Missouri, called The Shannon Foundation. With one hundred animals calling this farm home—including cats, dogs, horses, deer, pigs, donkeys, and llamas—help was certainly needed. The Giant Steps children learned about the different animals and how they receive care. They made lists of needed items and began collecting, sorting, and folding used towels, blankets, and comforters. To raise funds for items needing to be purchased, students baked and sold dog biscuits. Initially, they thought the biscuits would be a short-term effort, however, popular demand made this ongoing.

For the first visit to the Shannon Foundation, a reporter came along to see how the kids and animals would interact. Upon returning, students brought more towels needed for bedding and a cash donation from their continued dog biscuit sales. The students helped groom the horses and clean their hooves; and they brushed the dogs and socialized with two litters of rescued puppies. Learning life skills became easier when doing for others. A giant success for everyone!

Zoo Story: Grade 2

A second-grade teacher in Santa Monica, California, connected community studies with her science theme of "living things" through a zoo project: students made "brain challenges" for primates. Research shows that animals are healthier when mentally active rather than bored. With student help, animals would be challenged to get food out of containers. The children eagerly agreed to assemble papier-mâché tubes and pine cones stuffed with food for primates. On their first zoo visit, the students learned about primates and zoo life. Back at school, they determined ways to collect supplies: paper tubes, sugar-free cereal, dried fruits, and pine cones. They distributed flyers about their project to school families and neighbors and decorated bins to collect donations at two local supermarkets. The students researched and wrote reports on primates, made graphs to chart items received and needed, solved mathematical equations about what they could assemble, mimicked body movements of gorillas and lemurs, and determined methods for storing vast quantities of paper tubes. They discussed why they had more donations of recycled goods (tubes and pine cones) than of more costly items (sugar-free cereal and dried fruits). Then, on the second trip to the zoo, they worked with zoo educators to stuff food into paper tubes and cover them with papier-mâché and to put peanut butter and dried fruit into pinecones. Both sets of primates—those at the zoo and the children—mastered brain challenges through this project.

Turtle Artists, Authors, and Protectors: Grade 4

The Myrtle Beach Intermediate fourth-grade class partnered with a local gallery that specializes in art using recycled materials. These students had studied turtles and how they were in danger along the South Carolina coast. They combined their study of the threatened species of loggerheads with the study of haiku and art and published the book *I, Caretta*. *Caretta* is the Latin name for this turtle. Each page spread blends art, poetry, and a practical tip for caring for these sea turtles.

Wildlife Habitat at School: Grade 5

As part of their fifth-grade science program, students in Mount Vernon, Washington, learned about the migratory patterns of birds in their region. They constructed bird nesting boxes and feeders to attract and support the birds. Parents joined students on weekends to construct the feeders just outside the classroom. As birds arrived, the students moved quietly to the windows to watch and logged their observations in notebooks. Art projects showed a greater awareness of colors and detail of these feathered guests, as well as a greater appreciation and knowledge of nature.

Don't Mess with the Lizards: Grade 5

When fifth-grade students in San Angelo, Texas, were selecting an endangered animal to study they wanted to study something close to home. They chose the Texas horned lizard. After extensive research, students became experts on the subject and were invited to speak at a community college class and appear on local access cable television. To demonstrate their knowledge, they prepared "Don't Mess with the Texas Horned Lizard" kits, complete with a lizard constitution (linked to studying government) and ways to protect their spiky, brown friends. These were distributed to every fifth-grade class in their school district.

Compassion for Animals: Grade 6

In Brookline, Massachusetts, sixth-grade teachers read students excerpts from the book *straydog* about a teen volunteering in an animal shelter, and *Saving Lily* about students working to save an abused circus elephant. They visited a shelter for a firsthand look at the hardships shelter animals face and learned from the staff about mistreatment and proper care of pets. After considering ways to help, students took ownership of planning. They decided to collect donated linens to increase the comfort of shelter animals. To publicize their drive, they made written and oral announcements, wrote letters to the school community, and designed posters. They named their ever-growing linen pile "Donation Mountain." Students organized two bake sales and raised more than $700. They learned about publicity, event management, and appropriate pricing. After studying the shelter's budget allocations, they decided to dedicate their money from the bake sale to the shelter's emergency medical fund. Students worked with the technology teacher to develop several videos to help educate younger children about pet care. After every video and slideshow presentation, the sixth graders handed out bookmarks with a reminder about how to care for animals. Students also posted their videos online and shared them with friends and family. And they exchanged letters with one of the book authors. Preparing materials for different audiences and through different media helped develop students' communication skills. Administrators and teachers were inspired by how passionate and engaged students were throughout the project and by the great compassion they expressed for the shelter animals.

Land and Water Appreciation: Grades 6–8

Taking advantage of its rural setting in Middleburg, Florida, a middle school developed environmental service learning projects to teach students personal responsibility and how to take care of natural resources. For example, students worked with the local water management district to maintain and develop a 900-acre nature preserve for public use. Students built an eagle observation site at the preserve so visitors could view an active nest from a safe distance and learn about eagle needs and habits. The experience helped students recognize the necessity for preserving precious land and water resources.

No Horsing Around! Grades 6–8

Middle school students in New York City learned of the death of a hansom cab horse on their streets. They researched the issues of working horses in the city and created an action plan. They wanted to influence the city council by creating a petition to educate others about the situation. They proposed better oversight of the carriage horse industry and limits on where and when the horses could work. A good lesson in civic involvement.

Canine Commandos: Grades 6–8

Fifty middle school students in Merritt Island, Florida, eagerly board buses to local animal shelters every month. Many dogs in these shelters are overlooked for adoption because of their excitement or "untamed behavior" that occurs when they see people. Half of the students work on teaching the dogs five basic commands: "Watch me," "Sit," "Down," "Stay," and "Come." The rest of the students use clickers to train dogs to stop barking and jumping. With training from these dedicated students, these animals are more adoptable.

Simply Natural—A Preservation Project: Grades 6–12

In partnership with Texas Parks and Wildlife, students in Omaha, Texas, learned how to preserve an open field behind their school as an animal habitat. They focused their efforts on the deer that lived there. Since no hunting is permitted on school property, students aimed to create a safe area for deer during hunting season. Using hidden motion-detecting cameras, students observed deer behavior and determined what food they prefer—deer corn is the favorite! Students provided food for the deer during the winter, while the rest of the year, the animals are able to fend for themselves. Students continued to improve the area with a nature walk and nature-friendly sculptures (by art classes), while agriculture students built an outdoor pavilion. All students helped with tree planting. The overall result? A harmonious place for *all* life to coexist peacefully.

International Exchange: Grade 7

Students visiting the Cosumnes River Preserve in central California in the fall and winter observed magnificent sandhill cranes that travel thousands of miles to winter in these wetlands. As students learned about cranes and their amazing life story, wetland restoration efforts become even more significant. In class, students read about cranes from around the world, studied crane anatomy and physiology, and wrote stories and poems about the bird, which is a symbol of peace and beauty in many cultures. In collaboration with the International Crane Foundation, students created over 200 pieces of artwork and poems to be displayed at the Sandhill Crane Festival in Ciego de Avila, Cuba. At the same time, they had the opportunity to contribute much-needed school supplies to Cuban children. Four local biologists and educators visited Cuba to collaborate with Cuban teachers on crane curriculum and to teach lessons on cranes and wetland conservation. Cuban elementary students got involved in service learning, joining biologists in the search for the rare and endangered Cuban sandhill cranes as part of the annual crane census. Students recorded sightings, crane behavior, and calls.

Animal Enrichment Activities: Grades 7–9

Students in Trinidad and Tobago got together with experts from the local zoo to develop enrichment projects for the animals at the zoo. Students worked in teams and selected a variety of animals, from otters to ocelots. The group who chose otters created a feeding ring for a river otter and also purchased a ball for the otter to play with in the water. Students documented the animals' behavior before and after the enrichment activity was introduced.

Save Our Species: Grade 8

A middle school group focused its efforts on a local species with a declining population—the Channel Island fox, a small canine found on six of the eight California islands. They developed an Island fox sponsorship form, presented educational assemblies, and established an annual Fox Festival at the Santa Barbara Zoo. This dedicated group made a presentation to the school board, received numerous awards, and gained recognition from the city and the National Park Service.

Lost Animals: Grade 9

A ninth-grade English class for remedial readers wrote a book called *What Happens When an Animal Gets Lost?* Working with the county animal shelter and the Society for the Prevention of Cruelty to Animals, the students developed educational materials stressing the importance of licensing and identification tags. They also taught kindergarten and second-grade classes and spoke on local television.

> I ask people why they have deer heads on their walls. They always say because it's such a beautiful animal. Well, I think my mother is attractive, but I just keep photographs of her.
>
> —*Ellen DeGeneres, actor and comedian*

Writing Children's Books: Grades 9–11

For an end-of-term high school biology class project, students have a choice of activities. The most popular was writing a story for children about an endangered or extinct species. The assignment was twofold: research what makes an engaging children's book, and learn enough about the chosen animals to make the book informative. The teacher used *Pipaluk and the Whales* and *Intimate Nature: The Bond Between Women and Animals* to show a variety of storytelling approaches. Students agreed to produce three copies—one to keep and two to donate to local schools or organizations of their choice. In their journals, students described this as a favorite activity.

Pet Population Control: Grades 9–12

High school students described as "at risk" were working on strategies to improve reading and writing. Their teacher introduced them to the world of nonfiction through articles on local community problems related to pet overpopulation. They analyzed the articles to develop questions to help them write a report on the subject without plagiarizing. Questions generated included: Why is there a problem? What can be done? What are the consequences of too many cats and dogs? After practicing social skills, especially how to talk with adults, the students invited two speakers, an animal control officer and a veterinarian, to address the class. The students decided to develop lessons for kindergarten children, with each group focusing on a different problem: dog care, cat care, avoiding dog bites, and being respectful to wildlife. Students wrote and taught five lessons for each theme. To demonstrate what they had learned, students made a presentation with recommendations on pet overpopulation to the city council. Students also assisted at rabies clinics in the area, used Spanish language skills to teach people why they need to spay or neuter pets, and made public service announcements in Spanish.

Science and Government Connections: Grades 10–12

What recreation activities threaten our endangered species or disturb sensitive habitats? High school students began to investigate this question in science classes, which led them to approach their government teacher for assistance. Through phone calls and email, students found state officials willing to provide information about state policy. They also partnered with local parks and recreation staff to prepare brochures on safe use of local recreation areas. Students made coloring books about the endangered animals in the area to be given to any young visitors coming to the park.

African Bushmeat Identification: Grades 10–12

The students of the Conservation Forensics class at High Tech High in San Diego went far from their local community to apply their scientific skills to help stop illegal wildlife poaching in Africa. First, the students studied the use of DNA as a means of species identification in the bushmeat crisis. In collaboration with local scientists at the Zoological Society of San Diego, Life Technologies, and other partners including Jane Goodall, the students simplified the techniques needed for species identification. Their DNA barcoding method will enable scientists and environmental groups to trace illegal bushmeat back to its localized animal

populations. Next, the students were able to travel to Africa to conduct field studies in the regions affected. They lived among three tribes (Maasai, Iraqw, and Hadza) where they learned about wildlife management practices. They interviewed anti-poaching officials and developed ongoing partnerships with agencies and universities. The students and the African Bushmeat Expedition returned to Tanzania and conducted a Bushmeat Identification Workshop. They continue their awareness campaign through their inspirational award-winning film "Students of Consequence" and their Web site (www.africanbushmeat.org), which provides a wealth of information and shows how young people are truly changing the world.

A Field Guide to Birds: Grades 10 and up

Teens and young adults in Mbeya, Tanzania, noticed changes in their community. As more people settled in the area, the more birds left. Construction, farming, livestock keeping, cutting trees for firewood, charcoal production, and noise pollution from people, cars, and music were all greatly impacting the area. As part of the local Roots & Shoots club—the Jane Goodall Institute's global, environmental, and humanitarian program for young people—the Mbeya teens told the story of their birds through words and colorful drawings in a bilingual book (written in Kiswahili and English) called *A Field Guide to Birds of Mbeya*. Researching for and publishing this book helped the teens think more deeply about the natural world surrounding them and how daily actions can impact the fragile ecological systems. Part of the In Our Global Village project, see page 190.

Young Scientists: Grades 11 and 12

Science students in Crystal River, Florida, conducted surveys and collected data from government agencies regarding animal populations in a wetland area near the school to track the patterns of migratory wildlife. The students analyzed the information and distributed it in a brochure during an open house at school and at community environmental events. Extended activities also included helping with adoption and release of redfish, water protection programs, and demonstration lessons at primary schools. Ongoing partners included state parks, an animal hospital, a mariculture center, and government fish and wildlife agencies.

The Animal Protection and Care Bookshelf

The Animal Protection and Care bookshelf (page 92) adds much to the process of finding out about threatened species and caring for the other creatures on our planet. Reading about animals teaches us about all aspects of life, including the environment and the partnership between the species. All participants in our ecosystems have a place and a role. Sometimes *Cats Up a Tree* need help to get down. Sometimes what is learned in school about mistreatment of circus animals creates unsuspecting rescuers as in *Saving Lilly*. Herds of buffalo have been raised in the east and sent on trains out west by a consortium of people who wanted to preserve a nearly extinct animal, in *They Came from the Bronx: How the Buffalo Were Saved from Extinction*. Perhaps caring for animals reminds us to simply care for all life. To help you find books relevant to your particular projects, the book chart classifies the titles into several topic areas: for the future, rescue and restore, and caring relationships.

In general, the bookshelf features:

- An annotated bibliography arranged and alphabetized by title according to the general categories of nonfiction (N), picture books (P), and fiction (F). For nonfiction and fiction, length and recommended grade levels are included. The entries in the picture book category do not include suggested grade levels, since they can be successfully used with all ages.

- A chart organized by topic and category to help you find books relevant to particular projects.

- Recommendations from service learning colleagues and experts that include a book summary and ideas for service learning connections. (The number of recommended books varies in each bookshelf.)

- *Please note:* additional titles for this category are listed in the digital content; some of these were out of print at time of publication but still worth finding.

Nonfiction: Animal Protection and Care

Animal Survivors of the Wetlands

by Barbara Somervill (Watts Library, 2004). Step into the wetlands to meet animal populations threatened by a disappearing habitat and discover how human intervention can help. Learn facts about animals and their environments, and the actions of government organizations, scientists, and individuals to save these communities. 63pp., grades 4–7

Breakfast in the Rainforest: A Visit with Mountain Gorillas

by Richard Sobol (Candlewick Press, 2008). Fewer than 700 mountain gorillas remain in the world; all reside in national parks in central Africa. Through photographs of their environment and close-ups of the gorillas, we learn about their family habits and behaviors and about the people working to protect them. An afterword by Leonardo DiCaprio details the threats that keep these animals at high risk. 44pp., grades 1–6

How Many Baby Pandas?

by Sandra Markle (Walker & Company, 2009). In this charming counting book, the photos and information about panda bears living in the Wolong Giant Panda Breeding Center in China will inspire every reader to want to protect our endangered species. Read about why "Giant Pandas Are Cool," and what happened to these pandas in the May 5, 2008, earthquake that struck close to where they live. 32pp., grades preK–3

Just for Elephants

by Carol Buckley (Tilbury House, 2006). This book chronicles Shirley's retirement as a circus elephant and her move to a new home at the Elephant Sanctuary where she can live freely and roam with other elephants. The photography and narrative tell of the physical transference and the change in personality as the large animals thrive. 32pp., grades 3–6

Kids Making a Difference for Animals

by Nancy Furstinger and Sheryl Pipe (Wiley Publishing, 2009). A blend of information and examples show kids helping to keep animals in good health and care. These inspiring stories set wonderful examples for kids. 96pp., grades 4–6

Nights of the Pufflings

by Bruce McMillan (Houghton Mifflin, 1995). Travel to Heimaey Island, Iceland, where children stay up all night when the pufflings are ready to take flight for the first time. Many birds, confused by the village lights, head toward town instead of the open sea. The children rescue the birds from the dangers of cats and cars and set them on their proper course. 32pp., grades K–4

The Race to Save the Lord God Bird

by Philip Hoose (Farrar, Straus, Giroux, 2004). A suspense-filled story about a modern endangered animal, the ivory-billed woodpecker. How have politics, environmental laws, and habitat reduction driven this bird to near-extinction? Find out who

Animal Protection and Care Bookshelf Topics

Topics	Books	Category
For the Future Books in this category discuss issues that we must think about as we consider how to protect animals from extinction.	Gone Wild: An Endangered Animal Alphabet When the Wolves Returned: Restoring Nature's Balance in Yellowstone	P N
Rescue and Restore Many organizations and individuals actively work to protect, rescue, and save animals from extinction, giving us models for our own work. Notice that young people are included among the activists.	Animal Survivors of the Wetlands Breakfast in the Rainforest: A Visit with Mountain Gorillas Buffalo Music Eating Animals Evangeline Mudd's Great Mink Rescue Flash Point How Many Baby Pandas? Just for Elephants Mr. Wellington Night of the Spadefoot Toads Nights of the Pufflings The Nine Lives of Travis Keating The Race to Save the Lord God Bird They Came from the Bronx: How the Buffalo Were Saved from Extinction	N N P (see page 153) F F N N F F N F N P
Caring Relationships This category includes stories, fiction and nonfiction, about people whose lives are touched by their animal neighbors.	Before You Were Mine Don't Shoot! Chase R.'s Top Ten Reasons NOT to Move to the Country Highway Cats How to Heal a Broken Wing Kids Making a Difference for Animals Make Way for Ducklings (see digital content) Mama Pennies for Elephants Pony Island Saved: Rescued Animals and the Lives They Transform straydog Up-Close: Jane Goodall Winter's Tail: How One Little Dolphin Learned to Swim Again	P F F P N P P P P N F N N

Page references are given for books that appear in the bookshelf lists of other chapters is helping and how budding activists can take lessons learned and apply them in future situations. 208pp., young adult

Saved: Rescued Animals and the Lives They Transform

by Karin Winegar (Da Capo Press, 2009). A collection of twenty-eight true stories from coast to coast about people healing the damage done to animals, and animals healing the suffering of humans. 256pp., grades 4–12

Up-Close: Jane Goodall

by Sudipta Bardhan-Quallen (Viking, 2008). From her love of the classic children's book *Dr. Dolittle*, to her childhood determination to work with animals in Africa, to her revolutionary fieldwork in the jungle of Gombe, this book tells the story of Jane Goodall. A pioneer in her studies, this inspiring biography depicts how she creatively crafted a personal life around her supreme passion: protecting animals and our environment. 218pp., grades 5–8

When the Wolves Returned:
Restoring Nature's Balance in Yellowstone

by Dorothy Hinshaw Patent (Walker Books, 2008). Our ecosytems require a natural system of balance. This was dramatically seen at Yellowstone National Park when the wolves were eliminated. See how the ecosystem changed during the time the wolves were gone and the changes that occurred ten years after they were reintroduced back to the park. An excellent guide to considering an ecosystem's interworkings wherever you live. 40pp., grades 3–5

Winter's Tail: How One Little Dolphin
Learned to Swim Again

by Juliana Hatkoff, Isabella Hatkoff, and Craig Hatkoff (Scholastic, 2009). Imagine a three-month-old bottlenose dolphin with a severely damaged tail rescued from a crab trap. Could she survive? This is Winter's story, a feisty dolphin who, with the care and support of her rescuers, visitors to her aquarium residence, and fan mail from all over the world, and a custom-made prosthesis, is swimming again. The technology used in her prosthesis is being used to develop prosthetics for war veterans with sensitive injuries. 30pp., grades 2–6

Picture Books:
Animal Protection and Care

Before You Were Mine

by Maribeth Boelts (Putnam, 2007). A boy wonders what his new puppy's life was like before his family rescued him from the shelter. How hard and sad to imagine his dog had been homeless or perhaps treated poorly! However, when it comes to creating a home for his new puppy, he knows just what to do.

Buffalo Music

by Tracey E. Fern (Clarion Books, 2008). Based on a true story from the 19th century, a woman and her husband realize the familiar noise of hunters' guns is causing their neighboring buffalo population to disappear. Strong-headed Molly begins raising two orphan calves that friends bring to her to help restore the population.

Gone Wild: An Endangered Animal Alphabet

by David McLimans (Walker & Company, 2006). This marriage of pictograms and letters comprises an alphabet of endangered or near-endangered species. The stark and elegant illustrations express a simple hope for the survival of each.

How to Heal a Broken Wing

by Bob Graham (Candlewick Press, 2008). In this urban fable a boy sees an injured bird amid the city traffic and, with his parents, cares for the bird until he is released once more: ". . . and with a beat of its wings, the bird was gone." Few words and a big heart make this story very touching.

DIGITAL CONTENT

Recommendation from the Field

Make Way for Ducklings by Robert McCloskey (Viking, 1941).

Mama: A True Story in Which a Baby Hippo Loses His Mama During a Tsunami but Finds a New Home and a New Mama

by Jeanette Winter (Harcourt Books, 2006). A young hippo swimming with "mama" and the rest of their pod is in harm's way when a tsunami strikes. With sparse narration and vivid imagery, we watch the baby clinging to survival through the night while in search of its mother. In the morning, the baby is found by wildlife officials and brought to the local zoo where the little hippo adopts a surprising surrogate mama.

Pennies for Elephants

by Lita Judge (Hyperion, 2009). The year is 1914, the place Boston, Massachusetts. And children need to raise $6,000 to purchase three trained elephants for their zoo. All over New England, children volunteered their savings and worked to add every cent to their cause. Based on the newspaper headlines of the day, the author shows determination, ingenuity, and a true collaborative spirit.

Pony Island

by Candice F. Ransom (Walker & Company, 2009). Chincoteague ponies living on an island off Maryland and Virginia inspired this poetic story. While it's uncertain how they arrived, the small horses and their "pony penning" is now part of the local tradition and so is the care they receive from local volunteers.

They Came from the Bronx:
How the Buffalo Were Saved from Extinction

by Neil Waldman (Boyds Mills Press, 2001). On an October morning in 1907, a Comanche grandmother and her grandson await a train that carries a herd of buffalo for reintroduction to Oklahoma. Two stories interweave: one that shows the near destruction of this mighty animal, and one that shows the rescue efforts led by concerned conservationists. In the historical note, other efforts to restore the buffalo to their native lands in Canada and the United States are described.

Fiction: Animal Protection and Care

Don't Shoot! Chase R.'s Top Ten Reasons NOT
to Move to the Country

by Michael J. Rosen (Candlewick Press, 2007). Chase's family has moved from an urban to a rural community, a monumental shift for a teenager. Fortunately, he has his computer and uses email to stay connected with his city friends. Unfortunately, he is caught in a complex dilemma regarding local hunters and their prey. Will Chase come to terms with hunters and hunting? 160pp., young adult

Evangeline Mudd's Great Mink Rescue

by David Elliot (Candlewick Press, 2006). Evangeline Mudd and Alexy Alexy, the world's highest jumping dancer, begin an adventure to set free the animals held by Evangeline's cousin at Mudd's Marvelous Minks. Can they trick Evangeline's mean guardian Ratsputin? Can Evangeline and Alexy ride their unicycles to the secret location where the minks are caged? Evangeline is the most unusual animal rights activist. 192pp., grades 3–5

Flash Point

by Sneed B. Collard III (Peachtree, 2006). In Heartwood, Montana, Luther just wants to finish school each day in time to ride his bike to help at the wildlife reserve. Though his parents and friends would prefer he compete on the football field like he used to, Luther has found his calling in nature in the company of his favorite birds. However, while trying to impress Alex, the new girl he really likes, life backfires in every way possible. When a fire threatens the entire reserve, Luther takes tremendous risk to do what is right. 214pp., young adult

Highway Cats

by Janet Taylor Lisle (Philomel, 2008). A group of cats living on their own in a wooded area are shocked to observe three kittens who, abandoned on the highway median, magically survive the treacherous highway crossing to the trees. These kittens continue to cast a loving magical spell as the older, but not always wiser, felines conspire to save their woods from a sprawling strip mall and greedy developers. 118pp., grades 3–5

Mr. Wellington

by David Rabe (Roaring Brook Press, 2009). A sweet story with an important message told in two voices—one being "Mr. Wellington," a young squirrel who fell from a tree and the other, Jonathan, the teen who rescues the squirrel. Well-meaning intentions by Jonathan and his older brother to care for the fragile squirrel don't work, so they contact a wildlife rehabber who recommends they bring in the squirrel as soon as possible. She explains, "He belongs outside in the trees and with other squirrels, . . . Your smells, the smells in the house, the sounds, all of it is unnatural for him and I'm sorry to say—threatening." 87pp., grades 3–6

Night of the Spadefoot Toads

by Bill Harley (Peachtree, 2008). Ben has moved from his beloved deserts of Arizona to cold, wet Massachusetts. His new science teacher fosters his love of the outdoors by introducing him to the spadefoot toad, which mates only once a year when conditions are exactly right. But developers want to eradicate the toads' breeding ground, a vernal pool, and build houses where many wild creatures live. Ben discovers courage and contacts a local environmental agency for help. Ben's story reminds us that one young individual can make a difference in this fragile environment, dramatically affecting an ecosystem in danger. 224pp., grades 3–7

The Nine Lives of Travis Keating

by Jill MacLean (Fitxhenry & Whiteside, 2008). Travis has reluctantly agreed to live in Newfoundland with his dad for 365 days. His grief about his mother's death and the attention from the school bully make matters unbearable. However, after finding a colony of abandoned cats, Travis starts to care for the animals, his surroundings, and the people he meets. With plenty to overcome, will Travis use all of his "nine lives"? 192pp., grades 3–7

straydog

by Kathe Koja (Speak, 2004). Teenage Rachel volunteers at an animal shelter. When a feral dog arrives, Rachel feels a bond that motivates her to risk a rescue that fails miserably. This book gives a voice to Rachel and "Grrl," the name she gives this animal who is unable to be tamed. 128pp., young adult

---

DIGITAL CONTENT

Interviews with Authors:
The Story Behind the Story

In the companion digital content, you'll find an interview with Kathe Koja that tells the "story behind the story" of her novel *straydog.*

Chapter 6

Elders

Imagine what a harmonious world it could be if every single person, both young and old, shared a little of what he is good at doing.

—*Quincy Jones, musician and producer*

The intergenerational connection has a long and vibrant history in service learning—young people and older people naturally fit together. Their interactions are often based on shared interests and result in personal growth for everyone involved. Service and learning flow easily in both directions as an older person tutors a child or an adolescent teaches computer skills to a retiree. These partnerships evoke caring and provide an exchange that matters. The two groups often discover similarities more profound than their differences: a love of baseball or gardening, appreciation of music, caring for families, or pleasure in traditions.

Young people benefit from getting to know active elders in their communities as well as those who are infirm or suffering from memory loss. Each population offers unique ways to interact and create meaningful relationships. It is often said that our mobile society separates the generations within families. While the relationships created through service learning are not substitutes, they are rich with their own rewards and exchanges and offer opportunities for contact between generations that might otherwise be missing.

Through intergenerational experiences, young people can explore:

- the learning of life's lessons.

- how different cultures treat older populations.

- how to stay healthy in body and mind.

- the joy of living.

- history related through personal experience and knowledge, which is hard to find in textbooks.

- the mutually beneficial relationships that can be achieved between people of different ages.

When preparing for intergenerational situations and activities, make sure that both your students and the elders are willing participants or recipients. A key purpose of service learning is creating mutually respectful relationships. When combining generations, be particularly attentive to the potential for imbalance or even condescension. It's important to explore and state the value of both the young people and the elders involved in the experience and to be sure that the service is directed toward an actual need rather than an assumed one.

Preparation: Getting Ready for Service Learning Involving Elders

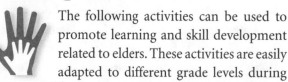 The following activities can be used to promote learning and skill development related to elders. These activities are easily adapted to different grade levels during investigation, preparation, and planning to help your students examine key issues through research, analyze community needs, and gain the knowledge they need to effectively contribute to the design of their service plan. They can often be integrated into reflection and demonstration as students can lead the activities with others to build awareness. Since literature is often an important part of preparation, you can find recommended titles on this theme in the Elders Bookshelf later in this chapter.

Activity: Coming to Know the Elder Population. Who makes up the elder population in your community? How do they spend their time? Answering these questions and others can help generate possibilities for service learning. Sometimes the best way to acquire the information you need is to go straight to the source. Invite several elder community activists to class—business people, volunteers, educators, historians—and aim for a ratio of one for every five to seven students. To find potential visitors, ask students or other teachers for referrals, or check with the local volunteer or senior center. Before the visit, ask each of the older community members to submit a brief personal biography or résumé. In small groups, have students read the biographies to prepare questions for an interview session. You and your students might discuss conversation topics that have a direct connection to classroom learning; inform the guest about this topic ahead of time. You might plan for multiple visits to provide time for both interviews and topic discussions. As a result of these meetings, students and their elder guests may decide to collaborate on social action projects. For younger children, one or two classroom visitors is ample to create a discussion. Have students develop their questions prior to the visit, and be certain every child has a turn to participate.

Activity: Preparing for Oral History Projects. Bringing people together from different generations can be most gratifying, especially when everyone is prepared. For oral history projects, if possible try to colead the activities with an agency partner who has experience with elders. Many books in this chapter's bookshelf can also be helpful, for example, *Mr. Williams* is the oral history of a family friend heard at the author's kitchen table when she was a child. Years later, these memorable descriptions became a splendid book. Many oral history collections are now posted at school or community Web sites. To get your oral history project off to a good start, try the following process.

Begin by meeting separately with the students and the elders. With the students, ask, "What do you think of older people?" Most students think that elders have a disability. Present information—or have students conduct research—to demonstrate that this is not true. Many seniors are healthy, and even those with infirmities may lead active lives.

Similarly, members of the older group can be asked, "What do you expect from the students?" Often, they expect students to be rude or impolite; they may also express concern about safety issues when visiting a high school. Take this opportunity to present accurate information.

To prepare for the first interaction, students can work in small groups to develop questions that "break the ice." Students can role-play the initial meetings, from welcoming the guest to practicing introductions. Inform the older group that the students will be asking questions to help everyone become acquainted.

Consider this list of questions developed and used by high school students:

- What should I call you?
- What inspired you to come today?
- Do you have a favorite quote or proverb that means a lot to you?
- How many decades have you experienced? (a variation on, "How old are you?")
- Do you have children or other close family members?
- As a child, what did you want to be when you grew up?
- What was the time of your life that you most enjoyed?
- What are some of your hobbies?
- How did you meet your significant other or others?
- What would you like to change about your life?
- What has changed in the world since you were a teenager?
- What are major historical events that you lived through/participated in? How did these influence your life choices?

Allow time for interaction and, at the conclusion, for feedback about the process. Reflection for this initial meeting can be held separately so each group can express any concerns as well as happiness about their new relationships.

Even very young children have successfully created oral histories in collaboration with elder partners. Younger children who cannot yet write may need to dictate their stories for older students or others to transcribe. Sometimes the books take the form of shared histories—for example, "We both like . . . " or "Our favorite animals are . . . " Preparation also includes getting acquainted with their older student helpers.

Find Out More About Elders

To learn more about these issues and to get ideas for service and action, visit these Web sites and organizations online:

Generations United (www.gu.org) is a national organization promoting intergenerational strategies, programs, and policies.

Senior Corps (www.seniorcorps.org) is a network of programs that tap the experience, skills, and talents of older citizens to meet community challenges, including young and old people serving their communities together.

Making Connections Across the Curriculum

Some service learning activities naturally lend themselves to interdisciplinary work and making connections across the curriculum. These connections strengthen and broaden student learning, helping them meet academic standards. More than likely, you'll be looking for these connections and ways to encourage them well before the students ever start working on service learning activities. As with the entire service learning process, it helps to remain flexible, because some connections can be spontaneously generated by the questions raised throughout and by the needs of the experience. To help you think about cross-curricular connections and where you can look for them, the curricular web for this chapter (page 98) gives examples of many different ways this theme can be used in different academic areas. (The service learning scenarios in the next section of the chapter also demonstrate various ways that this theme can be used across the curriculum.)

> The human contribution is the essential ingredient. It is only in the giving of oneself to others that we truly live.
>
> —*Ethel Percy Andrus, founder of AARP (formerly the American Association of Retired Persons)*

Service Learning Scenarios: Ideas for Action

Ready to take action? The service learning descriptions that follow have been successfully carried out by elementary, middle, or high school students in schools and with community organizations. Most of these scenarios and examples explicitly include some aspects of investigation, preparation and planning, action, reflection, and demonstration, and all have strong curricular connections. These scenarios can be a rich source of ideas for you to draw upon. Keep in mind that grade levels are provided as a reference; most scenarios can be adapted to suit younger or older students, and many are suitable for cross-age partnerships.

First-Grade Historians: Grade 1

An elementary teacher in Tennessee described how, for more than twenty years, her first-grade students have documented the lives of local senior citizens and placed the collected stories in the public library. The teacher and students identified candidates to interview through newspaper stories about contributions made by older community members (read aloud to the class by the teacher) and by publicizing the project on a flyer at the local senior center. The class developed a list of questions and conducted about ten interviews, adding drawings of the older persons and illustrations of their activities. Parents took photographs of the interviews, and a display was mounted in the library when the book is donated. The stories and art are enjoyed and appreciated every year.

Shared Moments: Grades 1–3

Elder volunteers in Iowa attended a three-part workshop on reading with young children hosted by a local agency (a school district can also sponsor the workshop). The volunteers were then placed in classrooms as Reading Buddies to help students at all

Elders Across the Curriculum

English/Language Arts

- Discuss: Why should younger people care about elders?
- Take dictation and compose letters and other correspondence for elders
- Read and discuss a classic text with an elder partner

Social Studies/History

- Learn about Medicare, social security, and Medicaid
- Establish a current events discussion group with elders at a senior center
- Conduct interviews with older people about community history or significant historical events

Languages

- Contact senior centers to find elders who are fluent in the language being studied to visit and speak with the class
- Compare how elders are regarded by different cultures and countries
- Learn about colloquial expressions or proverbs used by elders in the language

Theater, Music, & Visual Arts

- Create a dramatic reading of passages written by people of all ages
- Learn and perform music enjoyed by a previous generation
- Study and learn to do folk or traditional arts from your community or region

Elders

Math

- Find out and graph statistics on the population of your region by age
- Learn about tax forms and help prepare tax returns for elders
- Create a "true or false" survey about elders and find out peer group opinions; create a statistical report and use this to teach others

Physical Education

- Learn and teach armchair exercises
- Research athletic programs and competitions for elders; observe and cheer participants
- Arrange for an intergenerational athletic or exercise experience

Computer

- Document elders' memories, pictures, and stories on a Web page
- Conduct Internet research on careers in gerontology and geriatrics
- Survey seniors about their attitudes toward and their uses of technology

Science

- Educate elder people about nutrition
- Study health care and dietary needs of elders; compare with those of youth
- Plan ahead and grow corsage flowers for a "senior senior" prom

levels to advance in their skills and literature appreciation. The students wanted to show appreciation to their buddies, so they wrote special stories, which they read aloud and then gave to their partners. Each story was accompanied by a piece of art showing the buddy and the student together. The elder participants described this experience as a "true exchange between the generations."

Oral History Projects—Variations on a Worthwhile Theme: Grades 1–12

This tried-and-true service learning activity enables young people and other community members to learn from the collective experience of elders. Careful preparation will produce meaningful long-term partnerships. Literature connections can be made through many of the bookshelf titles. The epilogue of *Pink and Say*, for example, attests to the importance of keeping stories alive from generation to generation. *Too Young for Yiddish* illustrates what can be easily lost—or preserved. *Growing Older* presents anecdotal remembrances of older adults with very different backgrounds. Many books explore memory and the beauty of tapping into the stories of our elders.

A Poetic Journey: Grade 4

Fourth-grade students in Maryland had a long-term, year-round collaboration with older people in the community. At the beginning of the school year, the students gave a "welcoming tea" party. Poetry sessions followed; seniors and students wrote poetry, produced a poetry book, and made poetry posters that were displayed in storefronts. The students and their senior partners had a holiday party, made collages, participated in science experiments with the support of college students, made scrapbooks, and had a storytelling event. The year concluded with a potluck dinner in honor of the senior partners.

A Gift of Tradition: Grades 4–8

More than a hundred students in northeast Oklahoma participated in a cultural event sponsored by the Cherokee Nation. Community volunteers worked with the students as they learned how to craft objects once used in daily life and now viewed as art forms, including stickball sticks and baskets. Students also made cornhusk dolls, traditional Cherokee dolls mothers and grandmothers make as playthings for children. Students met with representatives from the Cherokee Nation to determine appropriate places to donate the cornhusk dolls. Student representatives from every grade level went on field visits to personally give the gifts; one group went to local preschools, and the other went to a local nursing home. At each site, the students demonstrated how the dolls were made. Among the elder recipients were many Cherokee men and women who shared their own recollections of making these and other items.

Knitting Past and Present Together: Grade 5

As part of a unit of study, "Schools of the Past," students in Vermont learned how children helped during World War II by sewing blankets and knitting socks to be sent to soldiers overseas. They decided to learn to knit, which was described as extremely difficult by many children. They also found out that residents of a nearby nursing home had themselves made sweaters and blankets during the war. The class agreed this would be the ideal place to donate their creation, a handmade knitted blanket. The students sent a letter describing their project and asking if the facility would like to receive the blanket and if residents would be willing to meet and discuss their World War II experiences with the class. During a visit to the nursing home, the students listened as the older people described their experiences in the 1940s. Another benefit: The small-motor skills used in knitting improved the students' cursive handwriting.

Bingo Buttons: Grade 5

Fifth graders in New York City who visited a convalescent home each week noticed that while their older friends enjoyed playing bingo, they had difficulty picking up the bingo markers. They brainstormed ways to make the game easier to play. After conferring with the center's staff, they began to collect buttons to replace the traditional bingo chips. When the class initiated a school-wide button collection, the entire school learned about the visits and how much the students enjoyed the time spent in intergenerational activities. The button gathering culminated in an original rap song, a ceremony in which the song was presented to the seniors, and the best bingo game ever.

A Dance for All Ages: Grade 5

Two populations joined together to create a multimedia performance that combined the written word and movement. Elders and fifth graders in Maryland who were interested in movement, writing, and collaboration were recruited for the project. A series of workshops led by a high school dance teacher brought the two groups together. The older people wrote about "what it is like to be old," and the elementary students wrote about "what it might be like to be old." Dances were then created to accompany the written words and the multimedia performance was presented at a school PTA event, the senior center, and a state intergenerational conference.

Time Online: Grade 6

Sixth-grade students read and discussed *Doing Time Online* and reflected on many aspects of the novel: a student required to correspond online with a nursing home resident as the result of a joke that cased harm, the student's original skepticism, and the surprising benefits and relationship that developed. Students talked about finding their own "senior email pals" and began to research possible community sources of such partnerships. They found eight older people who had computers at home and four who regularly went online at the senior center and began to correspond with these elders via email. Sometimes the students or the seniors were slow in responding, and a few of the seniors had to leave the program. Still, there were benefits: companionship, an exchange of experiences, and face-to-face conversations in three gatherings during the school year.

Holidays of Old: Grade 7

A math teacher in Alvin, Texas, brought an idea to a faculty meeting with teachers from the various disciplines that made up the school's seventh-grade teaching team. Having recently visited her elder aunt in a nursing home, she thought that a visit to a similar local facility would make a good addition to the students' learning about "Holidays of Old." Through collaboration, all disciplines participated. Students eagerly contributed ideas and showed leadership. Even a young student with a history of discipline problems "shaped up" so he could go along. English teachers used literature to examine how older people are perceived—the book *Notes from a Midnight Driver* was

a particular favorite. In history class, students planned and practiced interviewing so they could interview residents about what Texas was like during World War II and how the residents celebrated special events and holidays. Health classes found out about residents' dietary restrictions and distributed appropriate recipes to volunteer bakers. Math students constructed geometric holiday ornaments for tree decorations and science classes studied the aging process. Art students made papier-mâché picture frames to leave as gifts. Before the visit, residence staff members provided orientations for the students and the elders who chose to participate. The visit far exceeded the expectations of all involved, and the teachers became staunch advocates of service learning.

A Senior Register: Grade 7

Students collected oral histories from older African Americans who attended a church that was being closed. In preparation, students studied the era when the church was built. Interviews were transcribed into stories, and photos were taken of all contributors. Students wrote letters to help get the church placed on the historic register and preserved. At a final celebration, each elder was given a copy of the book. Copies were given to numerous organizations, historical societies, and libraries as well.

Project Cook 'n' Serve: Grade 7

Middle school teachers in Massachusetts were concerned that many of their students lacked the social skills and manners to have appropriate conversations with peers and adults. They decided to build on an existing partnership with a senior center, and Project Cook 'n' Serve was born. Through collaboration between senior center staff and teachers, seventh graders and senior citizens studied nutrition together (this met an academic standard) and took a cooking class together. The students then interviewed their older partners about rules of etiquette, reported their findings in class, and practiced what they had learned. For a finale, the students prepared lunch at the senior center, served the food with proper manners, and had lovely conversations. But the program did not end—the students and seniors decided to collaborate on a community cookbook. After the cookbook was completed, students maintained communication with their senior friends through frequent emails and occasional visits.

Teachers observed an increase in polite and appropriate verbal exchanges student-to-student and student-to-teacher. In their reflection journals, students noted that reading *Handbook for Boys: A Novel* added to their understanding and appreciation for older people and what can be learned through friendships.

Poetry Partners: Grade 7

As the culmination of a poetry unit, middle school students in Wisconsin invited their grandparents and other elders from a local senior center to participate in a poetry event. The students performed poetry, shared music as poetry, and engaged in poetry activities, such as creating the longest alliterative sentence. Then intergenerational "poetry partners" composed collaborative poems: teens wrote on the theme "when I'm old, I'll . . . " and grandparents wrote "looking back on my life." After lunch, some read their poems aloud, and each student presented a previously written poem "Ode to My Grandparent/Grandfriend" to his or her guest.

Stimulating Conversations: Grade 8

Time spent with elders in convalescent centers or day-care facilities for people with memory loss can be designed to provide stimulation and interaction opportunities. After reading *Stranger in the Mirror* and *Conversation Starters: How to Start Conversations with People Who Have Memory Loss*, middle school students raised questions and concerns about working with this population. They learned more about Alzheimer's disease by viewing a video and attending three informational sessions led by staff from the partner day-care facility for people with memory loss. Students had time to develop and try out ideas for helpful activities, including crafts, musical programming for sing-a-longs, and current events discussions. From their journals, the students made a display and booklet for the agency with original poetry and art. They also presented their program to other classes in their school to familiarize students with service learning and to teach about Alzheimer's disease.

Where Were You When? Grade 8

The strategy for a "Where Were You When?" oral history project begins with finding out what subjects interest the senior citizens who will be interviewed. A simple survey of participants at the senior center in Maryland revealed a range of intriguing subjects: a woman who knew Rosa Parks wanted to discuss civil rights, a woman whose brother repaired Charles Lindbergh's airplane had photographs to share, a man wanted to discuss how the Kennedy assassination had affected his life, and a woman was ripe with stories of her experience as a riveter during World War II. Eighth-grade students reviewed the list, and each selected a topic of interest. The students researched their topics to prepare for the first visit, a combination interview and lunch. The preparation created a level of comfort and facilitated exchange for all. During the next visit, the seniors heard the reports written by the students. A compilation of these conversations was given to each participant and the library.

Intergenerational Technology: Grades 9 and 10

What to do with your unwanted computers? A non-profit organization in Maryland came up with an idea: bring high school students and senior citizens together and provide them with training in repairing and rebuilding computers. A technology center was created at a high school. With skilled volunteer trainers, equipment to repair, and needy recipient agencies and individuals, the center went into operation. Students completing the training program also earned credits toward graduation.

Intergenerational Learning: Grades 9 and 10

Thirty high school students and thirty senior citizens in Maryland formed a mini-university to learn about each other and about topics of mutual interest. Before the groups came together, each had workshops to express concerns about soon-to-be partners, as described in the "Coming to Know the Elder Population" activity on pages 95–96. A committee with representatives from each group selected the topics and planned the workshops, which were usually led by group members. At each monthly class, two topics were presented. For example, in the "Let's Cook" program, participants (1) prepared and brought their favorite recipes to share and (2) watched a cooking demonstration by a local chef. For ESL students and seniors with limited English-speaking skills, the program provided a safe environment for improving conversational abilities. In addition, high school students learned about careers in fields that involve elders. They also learned grant-writing skills as they sought the funding needed to support the program. The seniors favorably commented on their relationships with their new teen friends. As a result of this project, students developed other service activities, such as a "senior prom," that were greatly appreciated.

Tennis, Anyone? Grades 9–12

Senior citizen tennis players were looking for a good game in preparation for a local tournament, and they found one—at the high school. They became regulars at the school, working out once a week with the tennis team during practice. The high school players became the cheering section at the tournament, and the seniors surprised the young athletes with a donation that helped them get team sweatshirts.

There Is a Bridge: Grades 9–12

Students from Roberto Clemente High School in Chicago Public Schools participated in the Memory Bridge program. Students were paired with a "buddy" at a residential facility for people living with Alzheimer's disease and memory loss. During a twelve-week series of interactive sessions, students explored concepts around memory loss, empathetic communication, and identity. They watched videos, role-played, and asked questions in preparation for their first of four visits with their buddy. During the first visit, students shared photographs brought from home to help stimulate memory; asked about family, travel, pets, and important historical occurrences; and most importantly, followed the thread of their buddies' communications wherever it led. Even if students didn't receive verbal responses from their buddies, they were taught to remain attentive and emotionally engaged with their buddy by being attuned to observing nonverbal communication. After the twelve weeks, the Roberto Clemente school staff noticed that all the Memory Bridge participants had improved behaviors—they demonstrated the ability to hold respectful conversations, exhibited more patience with themselves and others, and integrated aspects of reflection into their daily actions. These students became great role models for the next group of Memory Bridge participants and continued to be active in service learning. (See www.memorybridge.org.)

Tell Me Your Story: Grade 10

A tenth-grade "American Experience" class began an oral history project in partnership with a local neighborhood association to record histories of people who had lived in the school's community in Spokane, Washington. To help students prepare, a local news reporter taught them interviewing skills. Through a community meeting, the students identified people who had lived in the neighborhood in the 1930s and 1940s. The students then collected oral histories that reflected community life in those decades. Students recorded the histories, transcribed them, and gave copies of the written histories and recordings to participants. Copies were also kept in the archives of the partnering community organization. Letters from several of the participating older people described their appreciation for the opportunity to share their stories and for having copies of the interview audiotapes to give to their children.

At the Internet Café: Grades 10–12

At the senior citizen center "Internet café," high school students acted as Internet coaches. As the students refined their skills, they helped the elders feel more comfortable going online. The assistance helped many older people stay connected with family members who lived in different regions. The seniors said they especially enjoyed writing to and hearing from their grandchildren.

A Matter of Health: Grades 10–12

High school students who were learning about health sciences took their knowledge and skills directly to the senior citizens in their community of Sarasota, Florida. During six visits, relationships formed between students and their elders as tenth through twelfth graders practiced skills by measuring blood pressure and demonstrating CPR and choking relief measures. Students were well prepared through aging sensitivity training, and through extensive research and discussion of aging, the illnesses affecting older people, and death and dying. Time was always made for socializing, which included the young people learning line dancing from their older friends. Students kept journals throughout the year and demonstrated academic competencies beyond the course requirements.

Advocates for Elders: Grades 11–12

High school students completely absorbed in reading the state regulations for convalescent homes? While this may not sound "normal," it did occur. After making several visits to a residential care and convalescent facility to conduct interviews, students in Minnesota became upset by what they perceived as poor care. Upon reviewing state regulations and debating interpretations, students composed a letter outlining their concerns and suggesting ways in which they could provide assistance to the facility. They added that they were prepared to send a copy of the letter to the state licensing agency. The response was favorable. The residential care director took the recommendations seriously, outlined a course of action, and even thanked the students, inviting them to return. Two students were hired for summer jobs.

Remember the Women and Children! Grade 12

For an oral history project focusing on World War II, students in a government class divided into groups to interview veterans. Then a student asked, "What about the women?" Responding to this inquiry expanded the activity to include collecting stories from women who were at home during the war as well as adults who were children in the early 1940s. Questions included: "What different roles did you assume?" "What were some unexpected effects of the war?" One result of the project was a unique publication illustrating multiple perspectives on and memories of living through times of war.

We have to reinvent the wheel every once in a while, not because we need a lot of wheels; but because we need a lot of inventors.

—Bruce Joyce, educator

The Elders Bookshelf

Our elder generations offer wisdom and insights gained from years of experience. The titles found in the Elders Bookshelf (page 105) can provide knowledge and support to inspire and sustain intergenerational interactions. To help you find books relevant to your particular projects, the book chart classifies the books into several topic areas: an overview of elders, active elders, intergenerational relationships, and memory loss and/or nursing homes.

In general, the bookshelf features:

- An annotated bibliography arranged and alphabetized by title according to the general categories of nonfiction (N), picture books (P), and fiction (F). For nonfiction and fiction, length and recommended grade levels are included. The entries in the picture book category do not include suggested grade levels, since they can be successfully used with all ages.

- A chart organized by topic and category to help you find books relevant to particular projects.

- Recommendations from service learning colleagues and experts that include a book summary and ideas for service learning connections. (The number of recommended books varies in each bookshelf.)

- *Please note:* additional titles for this category are listed in the digital content; some of these were out of print at the time of publication but still worth finding.

Nonfiction: Elders

Conversation Starters as Easy as ABC 123: How to Start Conversations with People Who Have Memory Loss
by Devora Kaye (ABCD Books, 2000). Written by an eighth-grade student, this ABC coloring book is a friendly guide for young people who are interacting with people who have memory loss. 29pp., all ages

Growing Older: What Young People Should Know About Aging
by John Langone (Little, Brown and Company, 1991). By 2025, American teenagers will be outnumbered two to one by people 65 and older. This book clears up myths and misconceptions about aging and provides information about cultural differences and physical ailments. It also asks, "What kind of old person will you be?" Out of print but worth finding. 162pp., grades 6–12

Picture Books: Elders

Grandma's Records
by Eric Velasquez (Walker, 2001). Eric loves summer with Grandma in Spanish Harlem. During the hot days, Grandma fills the apartment with the salsa and merengue music that she grew up with in Puerto Rico. When her nephew Sammy Ayala, a percussionist for Rafael Cortijo's band, "the best band in Puerto Rico," comes to town, Grandma and Eric are special guests at

their first New York concert. The performance strengthens the bond between the generations.

The Memory Box

by Mary Bahr (Albert Whitman, 1992). When Gramps realizes he has the beginnings of Alzheimer's disease, he starts a "memory box" with his young grandson, Zach, to keep memories of all the times they have shared.

Mr. Williams

by Karen Barbour (Henry Holt and Company, 2005). Simply narrated and elegantly drawn, the author relates stories she heard from Mr. Williams about growing up on a Louisiana farm during the Great Depression. Describing a typical day, week, and year, we witness simple joys, seasonal anxieties, and sometimes harsh injustices that one black family in the South experienced in 1930s America. An inspiring and replicable example of capturing an oral history.

Mrs. Katz and Tush

by Patricia Polacco (Bantam, 1992). A young African-American boy gives a lonely Jewish widow a kitten named Tush. The cultural and age differences between the boy and the older woman only add to their special friendship, which grows and lasts throughout their lives.

Remember Me? Alzheimer's Through the Eyes of a Child/¿Te acuerdas de mí? Pensamientos de la enfermedad, Alzheimers a travez de los ojos de un niño

by Sue Glass (Raven Tree Press, 2003). A young girl is perplexed. She cannot understand why Grandfather no longer remembers her. Did she do something wrong or make him angry or hurt his feelings? When she tells her mother about this problem, her mother explains about Alzheimer's disease. They both learn that sharing the knowledge about what is happening to a family member is better for everyone involved. In English and Spanish.

Singing with Momma Lou

by Linda Jacobs Altman (Lee & Low, 2002). Nine-year-old Tamika is frustrated with visiting her grandmother at the nursing home each week, especially now that Alzheimer's disease has robbed Momma Lou of so much memory. When Tamika begins to bring and show her grandmother old photos and yearbooks, and newspaper clippings related to her grandmother's arrest during a civil rights demonstration, the sparks of memory and relationship are rekindled.

Somebody Loves You, Mr. Hatch

by Eileen Spinelli (Aladdin, 1996). An anonymous valentine turns unsociable Mr. Hatch into a friend of everyone in the neighborhood. When he learns the valentine was meant for someone else, Mr. Hatch reverts to his old ways until his true friends come to the rescue. A wonderful book to dramatize with children.

Stranger in the Mirror

by Allen Say (Houghton Mifflin, 1995). Sam, an Asian-American boy, does not want to get old like his grandpa, but one morning he awakens with the face of an old man. His family, teacher, and friends treat him as if he is not the same person on the inside. "Who cares what I look like. I am Sam. Nobody can change that." A subtle and perceptive look at societal views on aging.

Sunshine Home

by Eve Bunting (Clarion, 1994). Timothy visits his grandmother, who has broken her hip. Timothy and his parents have a hard time leaving Gram at the nursing home. They know that an aging person with physical difficulties still needs love.

Too Young for Yiddish

by Richard Michelson (Charlesbridge, 2002). Aaron loves his *zayde* (grandfather), though he is embarrassed by his funny accent and arm-waving gestures. Aaron longs to read Zayde's treasured books, which are written in Yiddish, but Zayde says, "You are too young . . . speak English like everyone else." As the years pass, Aaron and his grandfather realize the importance of preserving family history and culture, agreeing that you are never too young—or old—for Yiddish. Includes a glossary and author's notes.

Fiction: Elders

Doing Time Online

by Jan Siebold (Albert Whitman, 2002). A "practical joke" that led to an elder woman's injury leaves twelve-year-old Mitchell remorseful. As a consequence of his actions, he is required to participate in a police program involving twice-a-week online chats with a nursing home resident, Wootie Hayes. Despite initial misgivings, Mitchell grows to depend on Wootie for advice, and a valued relationship grows. 90pp., grades 4–7

The Graduation of Jake Moon

by Barbara Park (Aladdin, 2000). Fourteen-year-old Jake Moon treasures his relationship with his grandfather, Skelly. The past four years have been difficult, though, because Alzheimer's disease has changed everything. Now roles are reversed, and Jake is a caregiver. Although Jake rebels, his love for his grandfather remains. And when the elder man wanders off, Jake is determined to find him. 115pp., grades 4–7

Handbook for Boys

by Walter Dean Myers (HarperCollins, 2002). The wisdom of age becomes apparent to reluctant Jimmy as he meets three elder men. After school, sixteen-year-old Jimmy must spend his afternoons at a barbershop, Duke's Place, in a "community mentorship" program as an alternative to a juvenile facility. As these "old guys" talk about their lives, Jimmy begins to think for himself about staying out of trouble, about making better choices, and about true success. 179pp., grades 6–12

Elders Bookshelf Topics

Topics	Books	Category
An Overview of Elders Aging happens, actually, day by day. The "big picture" shows the complexity of aging and includes health concerns, family life, and cultural and societal changes.	*Growing Older: What Young People Should Know About Aging ‡*	N
Active Elders Recognizing the many roles played by elders enriches our lives and corrects misconceptions.	*A Day's Work* (See Immigrants Bookshelf— digital content) *Edwina Victorious* * *Mr. Williams* *Rainbow Joe and Me* (See Special Needs and Disabilities Bookshelf—digital content) *Tuck Everlasting* (see digital content)	P (see page 225) P P F
Intergenerational Relationships These books continue the theme of active elders but also emphasize the relationships between generations, capturing something special that occurs between young and old.	*Chicken Sunday* (See Safe and Strong Communities Bookshelf—digital content) *City Green* * *Doing Time Online* * *Grandma's Records* *Handbook for Boys* *The Hundred Penny Box* (see digital content) *Makeovers by Marcia* *Mrs. Katz and Tush* *Petey* * *Somebody Loves You, Mr. Hatch* *The Summer My Father Was Ten* *Too Young for Yiddish*	P (see page 142) F P F F F P F P (see page 142) P
Memory Loss and/or Nursing Homes With aging can come loss of memory or other conditions leading to a need for assistance. These stories share a range of experience and memories with respect and dignity.	*The Bonesetter's Daughter* (see digital content) *Conversation Starters as Easy as ABC 123* *The Graduation of Jake Moon* *The Memory Box* *Remember Me? Alzheimer's Through the Eyes of a Child/¿Te acuerdas de mí? Pensamientos de la enfermedad, Alzheimers a travez de los ojos de un niño* *Singing with Momma Lou* *Stranger in the Mirror* *Sunshine Home*	F N F P P P P P

Page references are given for books that appear in the bookshelf lists of other chapters.

* These books include examples of young people in service-providing roles.

‡ These books are out of print but still worth finding.

Recommendations from the Field

The Bonesetter's Daughter by Amy Tan (Ballantine Books, 2001). 403pp., young adult

The Hundred Penny Box by Shannon Bell Mathis (Viking, 1986). 47pp., grades 1–4

Tuck Everlasting by Natalie Babbitt (Farrar, Straus and Giroux, 1985). 139pp., grades 5–8

Interviews with Authors: The Story Behind the Story

In the companion digital content, you'll find author interviews with Eve Bunting *(Sunshine Home, A Train to Somewhere, One Green Apple,* and *Our Library)*, Richard Michelson *(Too Young for Yiddish),* and Eileen Spinelli *(Somebody Loves You, Mr. Hatch* and *Hero Cat)* that tell the "story behind the story" of their books.

Petey

by Ben Mikaelson (Hyperion, 2000). In 1922, at the age of two, Petey is placed by his parents in the state's insane asylum when he was actually suffering with severe cerebral palsy. His life in institutions continues to age seventy, with brief moments when his caretakers recognize his ability to communicate and his passion for learning and living. In his advancing years, while living at a nursing home, Petey meets Trevor, an eighth grader who is frustrated by a lack of friends and minimal parental attention. The depth of their relationship offers both companionship and much joy. Based on a true story, this book delves into the tragedy of misdiagnosis and inappropriate care. 256pp., grades 5–9

Chapter 7

Emergency Readiness

Want of foresight, unwillingness to act when action would be simple and effective, lack of clear thinking, confusion of counsel until the emergency comes, until self-preservation strikes its jarring gong—these are the features which constitute the endless repetition of history.

—*Winston Churchill, former Prime Minister of the United Kingdom*

Hurricanes, tornadoes, ice storms, floods—nature causes emergency situations often when we least expect it. Even when scientists and others inform us of the likelihood that such an event will occur, are we ready? During both the tsunami that hit Southeast Asia and Hurricane Katrina, which pummeled the southern United States, the general populace swarmed into action with rescue teams, food, and water. Children and teens across the globe asked, "What can we do?" and joined in varied long- and short-term responses that made a world of difference.

While Mother Nature will always be a force that creates large and small impacts on the environment, human impact is of great concern. Perhaps at one time Mother Nature was the sole culprit, however, farming changed human land use, which contributed to soil erosion. Human-made dams shifted waterways, causing unexpected flooding. And the industrial revolution spawned oil tankers, which occasionally have hazardous spills that take years to clean up, polluting oceans and beaches, harming wildlife, and leaving behind toxic waste for future generations. Environmentalists, scientists, and policy makers continually evaluate how our day-to-day choices that maintain our quality of life may place our environment at risk while heightening "natural" disasters to unnatural proportions.

These events and experiences reach every corner of the globe, and so in every community the question remains: What does being ready really look like? How can people—including young people—be informed

ahead of time and able to respond? What unique ways can the ideas and talents of even the youngest children become contributions? Fortunately, the field of service learning refuses to stand by passively; *we act.* And we have established a precedent for enabling our children to mitigate disaster, solve problems, and be "response-able" members of our global society.

Preparation: Getting Ready for Service Learning Involving Emergency Readiness

The following activities can be used to promote learning and skill development related to emergency readiness. These activities are easily adapted to different grade levels during the investigation stage and the preparation and planning stage, to help your students examine key issues through research, analyze community needs, and gain the knowledge they need to effectively contribute to the design of their service plan. They can also be integrated into reflection and demonstration as students lead the activities with others to build awareness. Since literature is often an important part of preparation, you can find recommended titles on this theme in the Emergency Readiness Bookshelf later in this chapter.

Activity: A World of Caring. "Why should we care? We don't know what a tsunami is or where Indonesia is on a map!" A middle school teacher reported this student comment during a faculty service learning professional development session I led recently. The resulting discussion became: What makes kids care when others suffer from a disaster? This school-wide conversation is worth having within any faculty. Consider these responses as you develop a well-prepared student population that is willing and eager to become involved when needed:

- **Begin local, extend to global.** Every community has some history of disaster and can face difficulties in the future. Examining local history and what everyday citizens did to respond builds understanding and can lead to students studying other locales and determining what puts them at risk and what people can do.

- **Map the world.** By using newspapers, the Internet, books, and other resources, students can discover what puts people at risk on every continent. The book *Environmental Disasters* provides a world map showing six locations where disasters have taken place, including the infamous Chernobyl disaster in the Ukraine and a deadly gas leak in Bhopal, India.

- **Place real people in real situations.** The book *A Life Like Mine: How Children Live Around the World* (Social Change Bookshelf—digital content) introduces students of any age to young people living in familiar and very unfamiliar situations, with a range of circumstances that may make them easy targets for disasters. In another exceptional book, *Tsunami: Helping Each Other*, readers encounter two young survivors who, with the assistance of volunteers from around the world, rebuilt their lives that were torn apart by a tsunami. Both books use photographs to bring the world into close-up view.

- **Catalog careers.** Who are the professionals who help in emergencies? The end of every chapter in the book *Natural Disasters: Hurricanes, Tsunamis, and Other Destructive Forces* includes a list of careers and a brief explanation of job responsibilities for each. Further investigation could prompt students to make podcasts about these careers and inspire them to consider these occupations.

- **Step inside their shoes.** Select a novel from the list beginning on page 114 to read aloud or assign for independent reading. Each story places characters in challenging situations that will surely create opportunities for conversation and further research. For example, students may choose to learn more about the history of the 1935 hurricane on the Florida Keys after reading *Blown Away*, or to discuss the more contemporary event portrayed in *The Killing Sea*. You might also read a selection of one of the novels as part of a Literature Circle (pages 60–61), which can often inspire students to read the entire book.

- **Add celebrity role models.** A teacher recently offered this helpful idea at a service learning forum: "I recorded a news segment of a popular VJ (video jockey) who flew to the affected region of Indonesia and spent time alongside other volunteers helping out. My class could relate to him and this made them want to help." There are recognizable people taking on issues and responding when emergencies occur, and by helping students see these people as role models, you may inspire them to action.

Activity: At the Ready. The U.S. Federal Emergency Management Agency (FEMA) suggests keeping in mind four areas when developing plans for emergency readiness: Mitigation and Prevention, Preparedness, Response, and Recovery. Familiarize students with these approaches and have them consider which ones seem most appropriate or necessary for their intended project. Provide students an example of each approach to assist them in understanding the concepts and then have them create definitions for the key terms. Evelyn Robinson, service learning coordinator of Lake County Schools in central Florida, outlined this process for a Florida Learn and Serve publication as part of their statewide initiative to address "Hometown Safety."* Here are examples of each approach from the Lake County students' service learning effort "Operation Blown Away":

- **Mitigation and Prevention:** Students created an emergency supply room and educated students and the community about being prepared for

---

* *A Guide to Engaging Students in Service-Learning Projects Addressing Hometown Safety: Lessons from Florida SPaRC*, Second Edition 2007

emergencies. These efforts will help to prevent anxiety, confusion, and potential chaos and physical distress during a future disaster.

- **Preparedness:** Students stocked their emergency supply room with appropriate supplies, and instructed students and community members about what to do before another disaster occurs.

- **Response:** Students prepare to help run the emergency shelter during a disaster, including distributing supplies and comforting younger students. They also create special books to read to young children to help keep them calm.

- **Recovery:** Students will evaluate how the shelter operates during a disaster, make recommendations for improvement, and implement those changes.

Making Connections Across the Curriculum

Some service learning activities naturally lend themselves to interdisciplinary work and making connections across the curriculum. These connections strengthen and broaden learning, helping students meet academic standards. More than likely, you'll be looking for these connections well before students ever start working on service learning activities. As with the entire service learning process, it helps to remain flexible, because some connections can be spontaneously generated by the questions raised throughout and by the community needs identified by the students. To help you think about cross-curricular connections and where you can look for them, the curricular web for this chapter (page 110) gives examples of many ways this theme can be used in different academic areas. (The service learning scenarios in the next section also demonstrate various ways this theme can be used across the curriculum.)

> Everyone plays a role in preparing for, responding to, recovering from, and mitigating the effects of disasters—and everyone is needed!
>
> *—Alex Amparo, Director of Legislative Affairs, Emergency Management and Inclusion, Volunteer Florida*

Find Out More About Emergency Readiness

To learn more about these issues and to get ideas for service and action, visit these Web sites and organizations online:

American Red Cross (www.redcross.org/disaster/masters) has a Disaster Education section at their Web site that includes valuable preparedness education tools for both teachers and families, including a full "Masters of Disaster" curriculum available for download.

Save the Children (www.savethechildren.org) Emergency Response, under the What We Do category, includes information detailing emergency hotspots around the globe and what can be done to help protect and assist kids living in those areas.

FEMA and the U.S. Department of Homeland Security (www.ready.gov/kids) team up to provide the "Ready Kids" Web site that guides young people through a four-step process to create a readiness kit, make a plan, know the facts, and take a quiz to "graduate from Readiness U."

Discovery Education

(readyclassroom.discoveryeducation.com) offers free K–8 learning resources for emergency readiness, including interactive maps, for many kinds of situations. High school students will also find this helpful when preparing materials for families and younger children.

Emergency Readiness Across the Curriculum

English/Language Arts

- Read stories of how animals have come to the rescue of people in difficult situations
- Adapt emergency readiness information for younger children
- Prepare oral presentations that could be adapted for different populations, such as young children, elders, or parent groups on what to do in case of an emergency

Social Studies/History

- Create a map of where community emergencies have occurred in the past and may likely occur in the future
- Compare the role of local, state, and national agencies when responding to emergency situations such as Hurricane Katrina
- Read about how people have responded to emergencies throughout history, and how communities rallied to help

Languages

- Study the response terms in different languages
- Create a bilingual community presentation to educate people on what to do in an emergency
- Chart the emergency threats of the country where the language being studied is spoken

Theater, Music, & Visual Arts

- Help stage a simulation of an emergency and act out a response; make a video from this experience that can be a teaching tool
- Create music with a message to use in public service announcements
- Create a media campaign honoring people who respond to emergencies and keep our communities safe

Emergency Readiness

Math

- Study the use of perimeter and area measurements to create defensible space around the school
- Look at how math is used in predicting earthquakes, charting hurricane movement, controlling fires, and preparing for potential disasters within the community
- Look at how prediction and probability are used to determine the likelihood of disasters

Physical Education

- Get physical at school or in the community by removing dead brush that is a fire hazard
- Participate in a CPR training
- Re-create an old-fashioned "fire line," where people quickly pass buckets of water down a line to put out fires. How much water remains in the bucket by the end of the line? How much physical strength is required?

Computer

- Find out how GPS systems are used in mapping a community for the local fire department or other emergency responders
- Use Google Maps to find locations of Red Cross shelters and hospitals, and make this information available to the community
- Learn new technology for tracking hurricanes or other disasters

Science

- Compare and contrast natural and human-caused factors that contribute to disasters
- Find out about the importance of fire to the health of a forest
- Discuss with emergency responders how to care for pets in a challenging evacuation situation

Service Learning Scenarios: Ideas for Action

Ready to take action? The service learning descriptions that follow have been successfully carried out by elementary, middle, or high school students in schools and with community organizations. Most of these scenarios and examples explicitly include some aspects of investigation, preparation and planning, action, reflection, and demonstration, and all have strong curricular connections. These scenarios can be a rich source of ideas for you to draw upon. Keep in mind that grade levels are provided as a reference; most scenarios can be adapted to suit younger or older students, and many are suitable for cross-age partnerships.

Together We Can Grow: Grades 1–5

After Hurricane Rita devastated their community, Dolby Elementary students in suburban Lake Charles, Louisiana, developed a school beautification plan and then took the plan to local nursing homes. They created gardens with benches, birdhouses, flowers, weather instruments, and much more. As a representation of their service learning experience, students also painted a set of ceiling tiles to illustrate their unique community. Why focus on beautification? Upon surveying students, community pride following the hurricane remained low. Through this service learning experience, students increased their understanding of environmental needs (which enhanced their science studies) and also helped rejuvenate community morale.

Smart Envelopes: Grade 3

After learning firsthand about hurricanes, weather patterns, and the potential impact of climate change, children in a Florida school were ready to help others in their community be prepared. They designed large envelopes to hold the important papers people need to take with them during an emergency evacuation. They clearly listed on each envelope the documents to keep inside. They also added advice for keeping pets safe during an emergency situation. Once finished, the students distributed these practical resources throughout their community.

A Bilingual Weather Book: Grade 5 with Grade 1 and High School helpers

Here's an idea for meeting state academic standards. Small groups of fifth graders at a school in Florida learned about natural disasters—from earthquakes to hurricanes—and wrote a short narrative about their causes. After doing research on the Internet, the students added visuals to their narrative. As part of their studies of myths and legends, students wrote original mythologies of these natural disasters. They read their stories to first graders, who added their own illustrations. Finally, high school students translated this exceptional student-authored book into the languages they were studying.

Get Safe! Grade 5

At the Center for Inquiry, a K–5 magnet school in Columbia, South Carolina, students travel to school from across the district, most via car. Fifth-grade students took action to make these commutes safer by participating in Youth Organized for Disaster Action (YODA), a service learning program that helps young people prepare their families, schools, and communities for unexpected emergencies. The students created carpool patterns, researched and revised student safety patrol guidelines, developed multimedia training materials for safety patrol members, developed safety guidelines for parents, and established a safety system for kindergarten students to travel to the middle school cafeteria. Learning activities were connected to math, technology, and language arts.

Gulf Coast WalkAbout: Grades 5–8

In a multistate effort, Mississippi, Louisiana, and Texas students participated in the National Youth Leadership Council's Gulf Coast WalkAbout program following the hurricane devastation. Young people involved had experienced the upheaval and were now responding by becoming community leaders and rebuilding many things they had lost. Using community mapping, students came up with ideas. Teachers connected the projects to environmental science, oral history, and emergency preparedness. Students improved academic skills through journaling, research, and communications with neighbors. Here are a few examples of the many accomplishments:

• In New Orleans, Louisiana, Capdau Charter School students rebuilt bus benches that had been destroyed and also became reading mentors to elementary students.

- In Picayune, Mississippi, students placed birdhouses throughout their community to help restore wildlife to their natural habitats.

- In Port Arthur and Groves, Texas, students were given supplies and funds from local businesses so they could clean up and restore a street.

For more information, visit www.nylc.org, click on "Programs," and "WalkAbout Service-Learning Program."

I Can Help: Grades 6–12

Middle and high school students from Miami-Dade County Public Schools, first responders, and elder group leaders in Miami, Florida, formed a partnership to create a safer environment. They designed fire and life safety education and public awareness projects that target young people and elders. Local fire officials and other first responders taught students about fire safety risks, accident prevention tips and techniques, and public education needs of the local fire departments. Students helped install smoke detectors in homes of low-income independent seniors. Other student teams developed puppet shows for preschool through second grades to introduce children to basic fire safety, including the use of stop, drop, and roll; crawling in smoke; burn dangers in the kitchen; and consequences of playing with fire. Students designed a kit with games to help parents and grandparents familiarize their grandchildren with smoke detectors, teach them how to follow a family escape plan, and demonstrate the importance of not hiding during a fire. Students also designed a coloring book using puppet show characters to reinforce fire safety tips.

Emergency Preparation: Grade 8

When earthquakes, tornadoes, or hurricanes occur in their community, students usually learn firsthand the meaning of "being prepared." They may also learn that people of lower socioeconomic groups lack the resources for preparation. In partnership with a social service agency, students in California took part in a countywide survey to find out what natural emergency resources were available for low-income families and elders, and what was missing. Their campaign included collecting donated merchandise, preparing emergency kits, and notifying the public of the kits' availability. In language classes, students assisted with the translation of promotional flyers and instructions for use of the kits. Students made presentations in adult education programs and set up displays at high school sports events. The community response was overwhelmingly favorable.

GPS Mapping: Grades 9–12

Students at Central Alternative School in Libby, Montana, worked closely with county officials, FEMA, and others to improve the county GPS database and disaster response. With training in GPS technology, students were able to assist officials in local mapping that was needed to ensure community preparedness for a possible flood. This work involves the highly technical creation of new data layers and error assessment. Such work has major ties to math, science, technology, social studies, and geography, and teaches skills often reserved for college level. Along the way students were exposed to careers in emergency response and developed social skills and confidence as they interacted with the adult community.

A Community Story—Flood and Ice: Grades 9–12

Within a year, communities in northeastern Oklahoma faced unprecedented weather—two ice storms and a flood. Students wanted to tell their story. A journalism class created a newspaper devoted to students whose lives were affected by the disasters, history classes conducted surveys, English classes wrote poetry, art classes produced posters, and civics classes wrote essays. With community support and assistance from Cherokee Nation Learn and Serve, the collective result was *Disasters: Flood and Ice*, a book of images, photos, and writings that give voice to the community.

> We had over five feet of water damage. We got "red tagged," which means you can't rebuild or move back in. We lost our most prized possession, our home.
>
> —*from* Disasters: Flood and Ice

Operation Blown Away: Grades 9–12

With their school becoming an emergency shelter in their central Florida location, students designed a survey to find out how to make South Lake High School a better crisis shelter. Using the results from community respondents, they set out to complete the necessary improvements and give presentations to participating classes and appropriate community organizations. Math students took measurements for storage shelves for emergency kits, drafting students created blueprints, and construction students built the shelves. Economics and youth council students gathered emergency supplies. English classes wrote stories and created crossword puzzles and coloring books about hurricanes. Art classes illustrated the books, and language classes translated them. Service learning students read with reading buddies about hurricanes, other natural disasters, and helping others in need. They placed the books in the shelter. Frequent discussions and reflection opportunities allowed students to make improvements along the way. To demonstrate their work, students created a documentary for school TV announcements and contacted newspapers and TV networks for coverage.

Mentors for New Orleans:
Grades 9–12 with college students

In St. Paul, Minnesota, students at Hamline University and Avalon High School teamed up to mentor New Orleans middle school students identified as lagging several grades behind after experiencing the devastation of Hurricane Katrina. The St. Paul students made a ten-day visit to Martin Luther King Science and Technology Magnet School located in the Ninth Ward of New Orleans, Louisiana. They taught the younger students technology skills—navigating the Web, "blackboard," word processing. They also used art for self-expression and created spoken-word presentations. After returning home to Minnesota, the students continued to mentor the New Orleans students via the Internet for the rest of the school year.

Organizing and Informing: Grades 9–12

At Gorton High School in Yonkers, New York, students studied health and safety. Members of the school's Youth Organized for Disaster Action (YODA) program developed and assembled 150 disaster readiness kits for distribution at Gorton's Family Day. They partnered with the Yonkers Office of Emergency Management to certify sixty students in First Aid and CERT (Community Emergency Response Teams) and trained over 140 community members in CPR and the use of an AED (Automatic External Defibrillator). Students also developed informational literature and presentations for Career Technology Education Day and for a health fair that reached over 2,000 members of the Yonkers community.

The Emergency Readiness Bookshelf

In preparation for emergencies, books provide information and examples of people (and even animals) who join in the process of recovery. Whether the disaster was a fire, tsunami, or oil spill, reading about what has occurred in the past gives awareness and encourages us to take action in thoughtful ways. Part of this awareness comes from learning about others' experiences such as in *Hurricane Song: A Novel of New Orleans*, where the characters entered the chaotic Superdome after Hurricane Katrina devastated New Orleans. The Emergency Readiness Bookshelf (page 114) covers a host of topics in two basic categories: what a disaster and to the rescue. Please note that most of these books are relevant to both of these categories, but they have been placed within the category that is most significant.

In general, the bookshelf features:

- An annotated bibliography arranged and alphabetized by title according to the general categories of nonfiction (N), picture books (P), and fiction (F). For nonfiction and fiction, length and recommended grade levels are included. The entries in the picture book category do not include suggested grade levels, since they can be successfully used with all ages.

- A chart organized by topic and category to help you find books relevant to particular projects.

- Recommendations from service learning colleagues and experts that include a book summary and ideas for service learning connections. (The number of recommended books varies in each bookshelf.)

Emergency Readiness Bookshelf Topics

Topics	Books	Category
What a Disaster! Disasters happen, whether caused by nature or human actions.	Blown Away	F
	Environmental Disasters	N
	Eyewitness: Hurricane & Tornado	N
	Eyewitness: Volcanoes & Earthquakes	N
	Fire! The Renewal of a Forest	P
	Fire and Drought	N
	Hurricane!	P
	I'll Know What to Do: A Kid's Guide to Natural Disasters	N
	The Killing Sea	F
	Natural Disasters: Hurricanes, Tsunamis, and Other Destructive Forces	N
	Tornadoes!	P
	Wildfire	N
To the Rescue Disasters require varied responses to match the specific occurrence and to help the community repair and heal.	Animal Heroes: True Rescue Stories	N
	Firefighters! Speeding! Spraying! Saving!	P
	Hero Cat	P
	How to Build a House	F
	Hurricane Song: A Novel of New Orleans	F
	Mama	P
	Slow Storm	F (GN)
	Tsunami	P
	Tsunami: Helping Each Other	N
	Two Bobbies: A True Story of Hurricane Katrina, Friendship, and Survival	P

(GN) These books are graphic novels.

Nonfiction: Emergency Readiness

Animal Heroes: True Rescue Stories

by Sandra Markle (Millbrook Press, 2009). Mike Hingson was led by his seeing-eye dog Roselle down seventy-seven flights of stairs in Tower 1 of the World Trade Center on September 11. On an overnight hike in the winter, a dog's body warmth helped the hikers survive. A pod of dolphins saved swimmers from sharks. Each astounding story in this collection shows how animals assist us in ways we hardly can expect. They encourage, protect, and provide strength in the most unlikely circumstances. Meet these extraordinary animals through photographs and narrative. 64pp., grades 2–8

Environmental Disasters

by Michael Woods and Mary B. Woods (Lerner Publications, 2008). This book explores the human errors that have taken tremendous tolls on our planet. For example, a decision to change crops in Uzbekistan and the building of canals to divert water created a disaster affecting five million people in the region. A ship off the coast of Spain sank in 2002 and spilled two million gallons of oil into the water. 64pp., grades 4–12

Eyewitness: Hurricane & Tornado

by Jack Challoner (DK Publishing, 2004). This up-close look at these catastrophic events includes a glimpse at the eye of a cyclone, giant hailstones, how unexpected floods can occur in minutes, and how a lightning rod really works. The book provides a history of weather forecasting that sheds light on techniques used today. Readers will also learn what humans do that causes weather patterns to change. 72pp., grades 4–7

Eyewitness: Volcanoes & Earthquakes

by Susanna van Rose (DK Publishing, 2008). Powerful visuals set the stage for learning more about how volcanoes and earthquakes occur. An effective blend of many subjects, such as science, geography, history, and math. 72pp., grades 4–7

Fire and Drought

by Blake Education (A & C Black Publishers, 2007). This book contains what kids want to know and understand about these disasters, framed with charts, graphs, photographs, maps, timelines, and even ideas for experiments. 32 pp., grades 3–5

I'll Know What to Do: A Kid's Guide to Natural Disasters

by Bonnie S. Mark, Ph.D., and Aviva Layton (Imagination Press, 1997). This guide offers suggestions for how to best ready oneself in the face of unforeseeable disasters, while explaining how natural disasters come about. The book also gives advice for dealing with the psychological aftermath of these crises. 64 pp., grades 3–6

Natural Disasters: Hurricanes, Tsunamis, and Other Destructive Forces

by Andrew Langley (Kingfisher, 2006). This comprehensive digest packs information into every inch of the page with fascinating facts and illustrations depicting every kind of disaster. Each chapter has a summary, Web site resources, descriptions of relevant careers, and museum listings. An exceptional resource. 64pp., grades 4–12

Tsunami: Helping Each Other

by Ann Morris and Heidi Larson (Lerner Publications, 2005). One typical winter day in Thailand, two young brothers played on the beach near their home. A huge sound startled them. They quickly climbed two tall trees and watched giant waves crash, recede, and reemerge. After desperate hours clinging to the trees for survival, they returned to where their home once stood and found their mother. Though their father didn't survive, they rebuilt their lives with generous contributions and support from countless volunteers. This photo essay portrays the process of response to enormous catastrophe. Portions of the book proceeds go to the Tsunami Relief Network. 32pp., grades 3–6

Wildfire

by Taylor Morrison (Houghton Mifflin, 2006). Learn all about wildfires—the historical cases, prevention, and ways people work concertedly when they occur to predict, spot, manage, and control them before they cause unexpected havoc on a community. Find out how plants and animals naturally protect themselves. Integrates science and math. 48pp., grades 4–7

Picture Books: Emergency Readiness

Fire! The Renewal of a Forest

by Celia Godkin (Fitzhenry & Whiteside, 2006). This book shows what occurs in a forest when lightning strikes causing a blaze. In the fire's aftermath, life gently returns—the natural order of renewal. Following the poem-like story is a two-page illustrated spread showing "A View of a Wilderness Forest" and all its parts, such as old and new growth forest. The next spread similarly shows "How Life Returns to a Forest After a Fire." The Author's Note provides more information and resources.

Firefighters! Speeding! Spraying! Saving!

by Patricia Hubbell (Marshall Cavendish, 2008). Simple art and simple words help even the youngest children understand the people in the community who help every day and also when emergency needs arise. Also see: *Police: Hurrying! Helping! Saving!*

Hero Cat

by Eileen Spinelli (Marshall Cavendish, 2006). According to the author, *Hero Cat* is based on "the true story of a homeless cat who rescued her kittens from a burning building." Making repeated trips while the firefighters fought the flames, "Hero Cat" became recognized for her valiant deed and ended up in a loving home.

Hurricane!

by Celia Godkin (Fitzhenry & Whiteside, 2006). A Florida coastal town is portrayed in this story of animals and humans seeking refuge as a hurricane nears. Special attention is paid to a mangrove swamp and the animal life supported there. Excellent information follows the story accompanied by detailed art and a map showing worldwide distribution of mangroves and locations of major tropical storms.

Mama: A True Story in Which a Baby Hippo Loses His Mama During a Tsunami but Finds a New Home and a New Mama

by Jeanette Winter (Harcourt Children's Books, 2006). Simple words: "Mama" and "Baby" are all that are needed in this gentle story based on a hippo family separated by a tsunami in Kenya.

Tornadoes!

by Gail Gibbons (Holiday House, 2009). This jam-packed book tells all about tornadoes, from the meaning of the word (from the Spanish *tronada*, meaning thunderstorm), to how the air and winds combine to create the funnel. Gibbons describes the

Tornado Scale and illustrates what each level represents. Learn about tornado alley and how ninety-six tornadoes ravaged an area in 1999, and find out what to do in an emergency.

Tsunami

by Kimiko Kajikawa (Philomel, 2009). In a remote Japanese village, a wise elder one day stated, "Something does not feel right," and stayed home. He predicted an earthquake and it came. Then he saw a bizarre sight in the distance: "The sea was running away from the land!" This was a tsunami wave and the elder chose to sacrifice his wealth to save 400 people's lives. The book's collage art of paper, straw, and fabric builds the tension and contributes to the drama.

Two Bobbies: A True Story of Hurricane Katrina, Friendship, and Survival

by Kirby Larson and Mary Nether (Walker Books, 2008). A cat is a dog's best friend? During the terrible hurricane that struck New Orleans, these two animals' unlikely friendship kept both alive. People forced to flee reluctantly left this pet dog and cat behind. After four months on their own, the animals found the care they needed and were taken to a temporary animal shelter. When placed in separate rooms, they made it clear to the volunteers that they needed to be together. Then someone realized the cat, nicknamed "Bob Cat," was blind, and her companion Bobbi was actually her seeing-eye dog.

Fiction: Emergency Readiness

Blown Away

by Joan Hiatt Harlow (Aladdin, 2007). In 1935 on the Florida Keys, Jake lives with his family enjoying the summer as any thirteen-year-old would, until a hurricane—the "Storm of the Century"—arrives with devastating results. In the afterword, the author describes the actual event that is the basis for the novel. 272pp., grades 3–7

How to Build a House

by Dana Reinhardt (Wendy Lamb Books, 2008). Seventeen-year-old Harper Evans decided to spend the summer away from her family woes, which included her father's divorce, her confusing relationship with a guy, and a seemingly irreparable rift with her stepsister. She lands in Bailey, Tennessee, a rural community trying to recover from tornado damage. She joins other teens from across the United States with a mission: to build a house. She sees firsthand what disasters can do—those caused by nature and by humans—and she may even find "home." Family, friendships, romance, and hard labor yield exceptional results in this novel. 240pp., grades 8–12

Hurricane Song: A Novel of New Orleans

by Paul Volponi (Viking, 2008). Miles recently came to live with his musician father in New Orleans, and he loves football as much as his dad loves jazz. But life takes a frightening turn when his uncle's car breaks down as they're trying to escape Hurricane Katrina, and they end up in the Superdome. As people file in, supplies dwindle, gangs threaten and harm people, and police and military fail to create order, Miles learns that caring for family and community means more to his father than he ever imagined. 160pp., grades 8–12

The Killing Sea

by Richard Lewis (Simon & Schuster, 2006). Two stories weave together in this fictionalization of events when a great tsunami hits Southeast Asia. Set in the Aech region on a devastated island, it follows two teens—an American visitor terrified of losing her entire family and a local teen searching for his father. On their reluctant adventure they battle threats of wild beasts, rebel forces, journalists, and their own prejudices. 256pp., grades 6–10

Slow Storm

by Danica Novgorodoff (First Second, 2008). It's tornado season in rural Kentucky. Lightning strikes. A barn burns. This graphic novel weaves together the stories of an illegal immigrant from Mexico who may be caught in the fire, and the brother and sister firefighters whose rivalry places them both at tremendous risk. As firefighter Ursa aids the immigrant, their fleeting relationship reflects the complexity of society and shows how our assumptions often cause us to miss out on personal connections and true understandings of others. Stunning and haunting, this is a book that teens will read many times. 176pp., grades 10–12, mature language and themes

DIGITAL CONTENT

**Interviews with Authors:
The Story Behind the Story**

In the companion digital content you'll find interviews with authors Danica Novgorodoff (Slow Storm; Refresh, Refresh) and Dana Reinhardt (How to Build a House) that tell the "story behind the story" of their books.

Chapter 8

The Environment

When one tugs at a single thing in nature, one finds it attached to the rest of the world.

—John Muir, naturalist and author

Majestic redwood trees, waves cresting near tidal pools, deserts with cacti and coyotes—these images from diverse landscapes make up our environment. To define this all-encompassing term, we need only look at the word. At the center of "environment" is the Latin root *viron*, meaning "circle." This simple yet profound image reveals the interconnectedness of air, water, plants, animals, and all of our ecosystems.

Recent years have revealed human encroachment on these natural spaces and the consequences of global warming. This "hot topic" appears as headline news, whether it's a drought in sub-Saharan Africa, an ice shelf collapsing into the ocean, coral reef destruction, warmer temperatures causing the spread of malaria, or the Siberian tundra spewing gases. Some populations are less affected and think, "This doesn't have much to do with me." But for others, these changes dominate their daily lives and the option to ignore the issue does not exist. Voices across the globe are joining the call for innovative solutions and are taking action to reverse the trend of environmental decline. The call for environmental service learning is loud. We teach our children: "If you make a mess, clean it up."

At all ages, young people can develop understanding of and respect for our environment. They can acquire a vocabulary that will allow them to participate in conversation and develop informed ideas about such topics as acid rain, ozone depletion, alternative energy sources, watersheds, erosion, ocean acidification, and carbon consumption. Knowing the earth is dynamic, they can consider which of our human actions protect and preserve and which cause irreparable harm. Knowledge and the ability to respond can join to create a citizenry prepared to ensure a healthy environment for generations to come.

The frog does not drink up the pond in which he lives.

—Sioux proverb

Preparation: Getting Ready for Service Learning Involving the Environment

 The following activities can be used to promote learning and skill development related to the environment. These activities are easily adapted to different grade levels during investigation, preparation, and planning to help your students examine key issues through research, analyze community needs, and gain the knowledge they need to effectively contribute to the design of their service plan. They can often be integrated into reflection and demonstration as students can lead the activities with others to build awareness. Since literature is often an important part of preparation, you can find recommended titles on this theme in the Environment Bookshelf later in this chapter.

Activity: Moving from Litter Reduction to Simply Using Less. Young people have been the best advocates for eliminating litter and promoting recycling. How can your school or class join in or expand your participation? Investigating and addressing the issue of litter at school can lead to more complex projects that raise awareness about how trash is processed in the community or region, and then can encourage people to recycle, reuse, and simply use less. The following suggestions have successfully helped elementary, middle, and high school classes get started in the environment right around them—school.

- Create a school survey to identify litter "hot spots" (usually near the lunch area). Students can walk around the school campus at different times of the day—at breaks or lunch or just after passing periods in middle or high schools—to find out where the trash accumulates. Students can make posters to designate these places as "hot spots" to be cleaned up.

- Establish a litter-free zone in one specific area of the school. Add to the beauty of this area—for example, plant flowers. Students can make signs and promote this campaign through public-address announcements at school. If different classes each adopt litter-free zones, all zones will add up to a litter-free school.

- Use books such as *The Great Trash Bash*, *The Wartville Wizard*, and *I Want to Be an Environmentalist* as resources to develop campaign ideas for cleaning up litter. From these and other books, develop plays or choral readings to educate other students and school community members.

- Consider that in the United States, about 4.6 pounds of garbage is produced per person each day—in total, that is the weight of nearly two Empire State Buildings.* What's your school's per person average? In a math class, maintain records about the quantities of trash produced by the school—a good way to teach about graphs, statistics, and percentages. Guide students into thinking about how much trash is produced by their community, their city, even their country and what can be done to reduce it.

- Have students come up with ideas for reusing rather than buying more. Can both sides of paper be used before it's recycled? Could juice cartons from the school cafeteria be used to make tote bags in art class?

Once the school is on its way to being litter-free, establishing recycling, and cutting down on consumption, students can take their expertise into the community through public service announcements and mass messaging. Promote your students as social entrepreneurs who can offer their services to other schools, offices, and organizations in the community.

Activity: Take the Climate Change and Global Warming Challenge. Where does your community stand on the issue of global warming? Are campaigns in place for decreasing energy consumption, such as light bulb exchanges or plans to reduce car usage? Are alternative energy sources like solar panels, wind power, or biofuels being considered? Find out the "hot topics" in your community and how local officials, government agencies, nonprofits, and businesses are collaborating. Use newspapers and the Internet, and interview people in the know to find out what's going on. Conduct a survey to find out what information or resources would assist others in the community. Pick a topic that is currently affecting your locale. Learn about all sides of the issue.

Consider these categories and facts. What questions might each of these provoke? Have students move from facts, to questions, to seeking more information regarding local impact and then develop a Taking Action plan (see page 52).

PEOPLE FACT: During the 1900s, the world population multiplied nearly four times, however, our carbon emissions multiplied by twelve.

PLANTS FACT: Plant species are being forced to migrate to higher elevations due to the increase in global temperatures.

ANIMALS FACT: Caribou in western Greenland depend on seasonal vegetation for food and are struggling to find enough to eat.

WEATHER FACT: Anticipated droughts could leave up to 250 million Africans short of water.

LAND & WATER FACT: Covering over seventy percent of the planet, oceans hold increasing amounts of heat from the atmosphere, leading to the death of many coral reefs.

HEALTH FACT: Increased rainfall and warmer climates at higher elevations benefit mosquitoes, which carry malaria and other diseases.

FOOD FACT: After food is grown, it is packaged and transported usually over 1,500 miles before being consumed.

* *USA Today*, June 8, 2009. Environmental Protection Agency, Census Bureau, www.esbnyc.com.

First I thought I was fighting for the rubber tappers, then I thought I was fighting for the Amazon, then I realized I was fighting for humanity.

—*Chico Mendez, rain forest activist*

Find Out More About the Environment

To learn more about these issues and to get ideas for service and action, visit these Web sites and organizations online:

The Earth Day Network (www.earthday.org) includes environmental education curriculum and resources for K–12 teachers and promotes the April 22 annual Earth Day event that began in 1970.

EarthEcho International (www.earthecho.org) is a nonprofit organization whose mission is to empower youth to take action that protects and restores our water planet.

Earth Force (www.earthforce.org) is a youth-driven organization, engaging young people in problem solving to discover and implement lasting solutions to environmental issues in their communities.

At the **National Arbor Day "Nature Explore"** Web site (www.arborday.org/explore), you can find many activities, plenty of resources, and programs and projects all across the country that encourage tree planting.

The National Resources Defense Council (www.nrdc.org) has easy-to-read information and photographs on a variety of environmental topics, including wildlife and fish, global warming, energy use, and clean air, water, and oceans.

Rare Organization (www.rareconservation.org) launches social marketing campaigns on environmental issues, such as biodiversity conservation, with a successful track record in more than fifty countries to date.

Making Connections Across the Curriculum

Some service learning activities naturally lend themselves to interdisciplinary work and making connections across the curriculum. These connections strengthen and broaden student learning, helping them meet academic standards. More than likely, you'll be looking for these connections and ways to encourage them well before the students ever start working on service learning activities. As with the entire service learning process, it helps to remain flexible, because some connections can be spontaneously generated by the questions raised throughout and by the community needs identified by the students. To help you think about cross-curricular connections and where you can look for them, the curricular web for this chapter (page 121) gives examples of many different ways this theme can be used in different academic areas. (The service learning scenarios in the next section of the chapter also demonstrate various ways that this theme can be used across the curriculum.)

Think of what we ourselves are doing. When we see that part of the problem, we can become part of the solution.

—*Wangari Maathai, 2004 Nobel Peace Prize winner*

Service Learning Scenarios: Ideas for Action

Ready to take action? The service learning descriptions that follow have been successfully carried out by elementary, middle, or high school students in schools and with community organizations. Most of these scenarios and examples explicitly include some aspects of investigation, preparation and planning, action, reflection, and demonstration, and all have strong curricular connections. These scenarios can be a rich source of ideas for you to draw upon. Keep in mind that grade levels are provided as a reference; most scenarios can be adapted to suit younger or older students, and many are suitable for cross-age partnerships.

From Frogs to Petroglyphs: Grades K and 2

Four classes of kindergartners and second graders in El Cerrito, California, set out to learn more about their neighborhood creek and park. Naturalists took the students on nature walks to teach observation skills. They listened to Pacific Chorus frogs singing at dusk, found tiny hummingbird nests, and raised buckeyes, oaks, and willows for creek restoration projects. After discovering a "plucking tree" where Cooper hawks deposit tiny feathers of the birds they hunt and catch, students gathered samples of the feathers and sent them to the Golden Gate Raptor Observatory, where scientists conduct research about what the hawks eat. They studied the petroglyphs etched into the boulder next to the pond and learned some of the history of the area and the people who once lived along the creek. Finally, they published an illustrated guidebook—"From the Tops of the Trees to the Bottom of the Pond"—and delivered copies to all the homes in the neighborhood to encourage others to make wonderful discoveries at the creek.

Preserving Chemung River: Grades 1–6

The Chemung River divides Elmira, New York, into north and south sides. Students bridged this divide using the river as an opportunity to learn about local history, environmental issues, animal and plant life, and recreation in the area. Three schools shared their Chemung River knowledge with others.

- *Hendy Avenue Elementary.* Each fourth-grade class had a unique response. One group wrote a puppet show to tell the river's history and demonstrate the need for animal habitat preservation. Another class designed brochures for community distribution. One group presented information at a Town Hall gathering. And another class constructed a giant water bottle filled with empty water bottles and an information label telling how water bottles affect the environment.

- *Beecher Elementary.* Students became junior curators at the Chemung Valley History Museum. They designed displays, including a water exhibit. The students served as docents to the public and talked about their learning. A newspaper reporter interviewed students and published an article encouraging others to visit.

- *Coburn Elementary.* A first-grade class made an ABC book of the Chemung River to share with local agencies. Students researched the area, learned about habitats from experts who visited their class, participated in a river cleanup day, and took a field trip to the Elmira Water Board. The first graders also staffed an information booth at a community River Fest.

Cancel a Car: Grades 1–6

At Bacich Elementary School in Kentfield, California, an interactive kiosk in the library allows students to monitor solar energy generated and used at the school. Their "cancel a car" initiative allows students to accumulate at-home energy savings. When they reach 12,000 pounds of carbon dioxide, it's like taking a car off the road for a year. In six months, they cancelled sixty-six cars. Homes produce twice as much greenhouse gases as our cars. Congratulations to Kentfield School District, the first all-solar school district in the nation.

Oak Forest Sprouts: Grades 2–12

Students and other members of one central California community are working together to protect and restore forests of valley oaks, the largest of all oak trees in North America. A local river preserve has the best remaining examples of these oak forests, which once flourished in California's Central Valley. Most of the preserve is left to natural regeneration; however, active restoration efforts are needed in some areas. During one school year, more than a thousand students from four elementary schools and a high school participated in oak forest restoration field trips. Second and third graders gathered over 14,000 acorns. Fifth and sixth graders washed, sorted, counted, and bagged the acorns. Students from all four elementary schools and the high school helped plant nearly five acres of land that one day will return to oak forest. This project was successful because of the cooperative efforts of the Nature Conservancy, Bureau of Land Management, California Department of Fish and Game, and many parent and community volunteers. In-class lessons that related to the project crossed all curriculum areas, including math, language arts, science, social studies, and fine arts. Several schools also hosted their own tree-planting activities.

The Environment Across the Curriculum

English/Language Arts

- Interview local elders about how the environment used to be; write stories comparing these perspectives with your perspectives on how it is now
- Read biographies of environmentalists then create a "living museum" where students take on the identities of these people and tell their life stories
- Study how advertising is being used to promote awareness of environmental themes

Social Studies/History

- Study different Native American tribes' relationships with the land they lived on, how they interacted with the environment, and their concepts of "owning" land
- Examine how climate change impacted events in world history and how global warming continues to have irreversible impacts
- Research government policy on an environmentally sensitive area or issue in your region; discuss and debate the policy

Languages

- Find out the words for "reduce, reuse, and recycle" in many languages and create a poster
- Compare the political positions of different countries with U.S. policies on environmental issues
- Compile a book of original poetry in different languages about the environment

Theater, Music, & Visual Arts

- Prepare a skit or play about the environment to be performed in a natural setting
- Create and perform jingles or raps to promote clean schools and playgrounds
- Decorate trash bins at school to make them attractive receptacles

The Environment

Math

- Present environmental statistics on the public-address system at school each morning
- Analyze the pattern of waste disposal at school
- Review the water or electrical bills at school and develop a conservation program to reduce costs

Physical Education

- Study the effect of pollution on the lungs and overall health
- Create a public service announcement on outdoor activities
- Plan a field trip to a nature reserve or park and hike

Computer

- Design and make flyers of recycling tips for the community
- Find out what happens to discarded computers in your community and research options for re-use
- Research and discuss: Does computer use result in less paper being used?

Science

- Learn about and then make recycled paper
- Study the progress made on deep water exploration that has led to discoveries about chemosynthesis and furthered the need for ocean conservation
- Find out how environmental issues and economics intersect to impact who makes decisions and how decisions are made about waste disposal, dump and incinerator placement, and toxic site clean ups

Plant trees. They give us two of the most crucial elements for our survival: oxygen and books.

—A. Whitney Brown, writer

Give It to the Worms: Grade 3

A composting effort that began in one Palo Alto classroom grew over four years to involve many teachers and students and resulted in promoting the benefits of composting to the entire school and surrounding community. As part of the science curriculum students learned about ecosystems, and after hearing a guest speaker from the Integrative Waste Management Board, students wanted to get involved. They created a chart to record waste at school and brainstormed ideas for waste reduction. They prepared a video presentation and spoke to other classes about ecology, especially how to reduce food waste through composting. The kids became composting and worm bin experts. They collected school food waste and watched as it was transformed into deep, rich soil that they used in their school garden and donated to gardeners who lived in a nearby senior residential facility. The students' next step was community outreach. They hosted a parent information night with a site tour and composting lessons. They distributed monthly copies of their newsletter, "Worm Ways," in the neighborhood and participated in the local Chinese New Year parade, where—costumed as a giant worm—they handed out informational pamphlets on worm bins and composting called "Give It to the Worms!"

Environmental Curriculum + Cost Savings = E-Squad: Grade 4

Ten-year-olds at Parker Whitney Elementary School in California formed the E-Squad, and made weekly checks to find out the efficiency and use of classroom lights, computers, and air conditioners. The purpose of the E-Squad was to make kids more aware of energy waste at their school and homes and to minimize their carbon footprints. Some teachers now turn on only half the lights in their classroom. E-Squad members also created posters about saving energy and wrote an article for the school newsletter to increase parent involvement.

Lessons from Trash: Grade 4

Fourth graders in New Jersey analyzed school trash during a recycling effort that included practice computing with fractions and percentages. They determined that 85 percent of the trash could have been recycled. As part of a campaign for awareness and school change, the students put up posters and created PowerPoint presentations to teach others in their school. Learning continued in math as the students tracked and charted their household garbage for a week. In science class, they learned about renewable versus nonrenewable resources. The next step was to compost lunch leftovers adding earthworms to help. This resulted in newly enriched soil for the vegetable gardens planted by the kindergarten classes.

What's Your Footprint? Grade 5

Coppell, Texas, fifth graders attending Denton Creek Elementary formed groups to find out their carbon footprints. Through Internet research, they measured the approximate amount of carbon dioxide their daily activities released into the atmosphere and learned how that impacted the earth. They were astonished to discover that in order to have enough natural resources for the whole world to live as they did, there would need to be about six Earths! So the students improved their recycling program, discussed food waste on a school news program, and initiated "Walking Wednesdays," asking students and their families to walk or ride bikes to school or work. These ideas combined into an assembly to teach the entire school and visiting parents about reducing their carbon footprint.

Too Much Water, Water Everywhere: Grade 5

"How much water do you use?" This question led a class of fifth-grade students to a formidable task: evaluating school and home water usage. In school the students learned to read water bills, and they took a walking tour of the school to identify, with assistance from maintenance staff, ways to conserve water. At home, the students developed a survey to record how much water each family member used per week; they compared the results with the average use (in the United States) of between 80 and 100 gallons of water each day. After hearing a guest speaker describe "water use reduction in the home" and conducting research through literature and the Internet, students created and distributed a family-friendly guide, "Save

Water—We Need Every Drop." Their next challenge? Cutting back on electricity.

Yonkee Ranch Creek Reclamation: Grades 5–9

Students in an after-school and summer prevention program participated in "Yonkee Ranch Creek Reclamation" sponsored by Youth Emergency Services in northeast Wyoming. The intent was to teach the value of conservation and reclamation of a natural habitat. During the spring and summer, students went to Yonkee Ranch twice a week for two to three hours per visit. They learned why the creek is drying out (over grazing, old existing trees, drought conditions, new tree growth getting trampled); learned how to reclaim creeks (fencing off land from grazing animals, replanting of new trees, promoting new vegetation growth); and planted and watered trees and observed how trees did when they were watered from a methane well versus from the creek. The students also were taught weed, insect, and tree identification, and heard several lectures presented by partners from National Resources Conservation Services and the owner of the ranch. As a result, students learned to be more proactive in protecting natural habitats and getting involved in its reclamation.

Our Forest: A Community Web Site: Grade 6

Students from all around the world attend the American School of Warsaw. One aim of the school is to develop students into responsible world citizens. After a sixth-grade class field trip to Powsin Park and Las Kabaty Forest, students decided to create a Web site in English to provide information to the global community about the park. During the field trip, students were assigned different roles such as historian, biologist, poet, journalist, recreation enthusiast, and geologist to learn about the park from a perspective that would benefit others. Students came up with questions and decided more research in the community would help them find answers. Students spoke with people at Town Hall, the Agriculture College, the Warsaw Uprising Museum, and the Botanical Garden, and used the photo archives. They also interviewed a park ranger and WW II veteran. In math class, students created a survey to poll 300 people at the local mall to find out what they already knew about Las Kabaty Forest and Powsin Park and whether they thought a

Web site would be useful. From the survey, students discovered the main uses of the park, that only 2 percent of those surveyed knew which animals and plants were indigenous to the area, that 76 percent wanted to know the park's history, and that the majority of the people wanted to preserve the park for future generations. The students' Web site included:

- A catalog of all trees in the park written in Polish, English, and Latin

- Information on the park's indigenous plants and animals

- The history of the park, including how the forest was a place where resistance fighters hid during WW II

- The recreational opportunities at the park

- Maps of park trails with highlights (GPS units were used for accuracy)

- Photographs and poetry inspired by the park

An International Mobile Science Classroom: Grades 6–8

The PAWS mobile—Purification of Air and Water Systems mobile class—was designed by students in Valdosta, Georgia, with assistance from peers in Great Britain. Elementary teachers provided a list of academic state standards that are most difficult for elementary kids to grasp. Middle school students, with their British partners, used the Internet to communicate and create lesson plans for hands-on learning activities. The younger students used equipment to collect and analyze data and solve problems. They learned about pollution—noise, air, water—and formulated solutions. When students from England visited from across the ocean, they joined in as teachers, too.

Promoting Community Awareness: Grades 6–8

Science students at Silvio Conte Middle School in North Adams, Massachusetts, wondered if they could do anything to promote community awareness of global warming and climate change. For several weeks, eight students worked through lunches and after school trying to answer the question, "What is global warming?" They contacted local legislators and received a document outlining their state's plans.

Students researched the greening of state schools and wind energy, and visited a small wind farm in Vermont. They learned about location of wind mills, wind speed, tornadoes, harm to the environment, and noise. With a college student as a partner, the high school students helped publicize a global warming town event held at Williams College. Sixty guests, including a state senator, attended. Others tuned in on local cable access. Key topics included an overview of global warming, green buildings (including schools), and wind power. The events were videotaped and shown on local cable television and copies were forwarded to several state government officials to communicate concerns about these issues.

Be Girl Scout Green: Grades 6–12

Through Project FLOW (Future Leaders of Watersheds), the Girl Scouts of Shawnee Council in West Virginia have been involved with the "Be Girl Scout Green" service learning project. Several troop members began participating in a youth focus group that provided the leadership necessary to structure the overall initiative. As a result, a wetland management program for the White Rock Girl Scout Camp in Capon Bridge, West Virginia, was developed. The girls learned how wetlands are created, the habitat they provide for animals, and the purpose wetlands serve for humans. The girls charted the growth of the wetlands by measuring the land and water. They collected macro invertebrates and amphibians to gauge animal growth in the wetlands. The girls removed invasive species at the wetlands and held several removal events. The focus group participants shared their new knowledge with the younger girls during stream monitoring, wetland activities, and general watershed education at Girl Scout–sponsored events.

There are no passengers on spaceship earth, only crew.

—Marshall McLuhan, author, educator, and philosopher

Bringing Back the American Chestnut Tree: Grades 6–12

In 2001, Carroll County Public Schools, Maryland, entered into a partnership with the Thorpewood Environmental Center and the Maryland Chapter of the American Chestnut Foundation to aid in reforestation efforts of the American chestnut tree. This partnership provided science students and teachers in Carroll County with an issue to study, helped develop scientific research skills, and taught students and community members how to be environmental citizens. The experiences connected to a variety of courses as part of the STEM program—an initiative to increase students' interest in the careers of science, technology, engineering, and mathematics. Students collected important data, identified advance microbiology topics from the chestnut research, and established native chestnut orchards throughout their school campuses.

Environmental Heroes: Grades 7–8

The LaBranche Hurst Middle School Wetland Watchers in Destrehan, Louisiana, took a comprehensive approach to service learning. A group of 300 seventh- and eighth-grade students participated in a variety of service activities to improve their local habitat and community. Students worked with experts to test water and soil quality, identify plants, grow and plant trees, pick up trash, and create the first public nature trails in the region. Academics from every curricular area were incorporated in the service experiences, from writing descriptive essays in English, to reading journals of French explorers comparing past and present use of land, to using historical area maps with grid overlays to calculate percentage of land loss on the shoreline over the past fifty years, to writing rap songs on conservation for choral presentations. Students used the knowledge they gained from these hands-on experiences to host service trips for over a thousand younger students during the school year. Students also coordinated three weekend conservation events that involved community volunteers and spoke to thousands of people through outreach events. Through education, service, and awareness, students led a community effort for wetland conservation. One seventh grader reflected on her experience this way: "If the plants and animals could talk, I think they would say we are their heroes. That is what I feel like when we are working in the wetlands."

A Skyline Project: Grades 7–12

The Appalachian region houses one of the most environmentally devastating practices—mountain top removal, which clear-cuts trees, blasts away land, and negatively impacts the local watershed and natural ecology. In Appalachia, over sixty percent of electricity is generated from coal-fired power plants. Within a thirty-mile radius of these power plants, over 5.5 million people, including 1.2 million children, are exposed to harmful pollutants. The use of coal also produces many other harmful emissions, including greenhouse gases which contribute to global warming. As part of Global Youth Service Day, the Girl Scouts of Virginia Skyline Council set high ambitions and met them. Among their accomplishments:

- increased resource efficiency in the community through the distribution of energy-efficient light bulbs to Habitat for Humanity homes and other community housing

- reduced the pollution within Southwest Virginia through a "turn off the lights" campaign

- planted local native plants and trees within the community to help offset some of the negative effects of coal-fired power plants. The trees preserve the skyline and serve as an investment in the future to reduce pollution in the area and help fight global warming through carbon dioxide conversion.

Ocean Activists: Grades 9–12

Through science-oriented and cross-curricular studies, students at Coral Shores High School have made significant progress with ocean preservation in the upper Florida Keys. Students have:

- created an underwater video guide to John Pennecamp Coral Reef State Park

- done water quality testing in the Everglades (testing is ongoing)

- studied and reported on the flora and fauna in the Dry Tortugas

- bred conch to replace the tourist-ravaged population

- repaired coral reefs with artificial reef balls

- in shallow lagoons where reefs are scarred by boat propellers, installed PVC pipes and attached a block of planted seagrass seedlings; the local birds—cormorant, anhinga (snake bird), sea gulls, and pelicans—perch on the pipes and defecate as they feed, which fertilizes the seagrass and increases the rate of its growth

It's not that you *can* make a difference; it's that everything you *do* makes a difference.

—*Philippe Cousteau, EarthEcho International*

Alaska Youth—Taking Action! Grades 9–12

What can six kids do? Start a national campaign! Alaska Youth for Environmental Action (AYEA) began with a commitment to educate others about environmental issues; now over 1,200 young people are involved across the state. In addition to raising awareness, they have gathered signatures urging federal action on global warming and gone directly to Washington, D.C., to spread their message. They train leaders, promote green jobs, and are currently a program of the National Wildlife Federation. Visit www.ayea.org.

This Earth is not ours; it is a treasure we hold in trust for future generations.

—*African proverb*

A Power-ful Solar Alliance: Grades 9–12

In California, Santa Monica High School students started a bike-to-school movement. Within a year, they increased the number of students cycling to school from 20 to 120, participated in city biking improvement planning, and increased awareness of the impact of school-related trips on congestion, air pollution, health, and global warming. Students now lead parent and community volunteers in the Safe Routes to School program to promote bike safety skills, helmet use, and funding.

Leave No Trace: Grades 9–12

In rural Eastern California, Eastern Sierra Academy High School students worked with staff from the United States Forest Service to create an edgy, humorous video that conveyed outdoor ethics and presented the concept of "Leave No Trace." The students met with and questioned wilderness rangers and wildlife biologists to learn more about "Leave No Trace." The students created storyboards and wrote scripts and incorporated the project into a scheduled overnight backcountry trip where they also studied the biology of macroinvertebrates and the geology of the Eastern Sierra with the Forest Service and other local experts. On a two-night trip to the nearby Hoover Wilderness, the students collected rocks and minerals for geological classification, took water samples to determine the health of the local watershed, and filmed their movies. They edited their scripts and storyboards in the field and filmed scenes of themselves showing the importance of respecting the wilderness. Back at school they assembled their shots into thirty-second public service announcements that are used by the Forest Service in their presentations and are available on the Internet.

An Energetic World Café: Grades 10–12

Alternative energy sounds good, but do we want windmills in our backyard? With alternative energy sources coming to the upstate New York community of Albion, students led conversations that matter. About eighty stakeholders arrived in April 2008 for a World Café. This innovative approach used a café model: four participants sat at a small table and were given a question by the high school student facilitators to discuss. After spending twenty minutes with introductions and sharing their ideas in response to targeted questions, and writing down ideas on a large piece of butcher paper, it was time to move. One person remained at the table, the others scattered to different tables. With this new group of four, each person shared the highlights of the previous conversation, added to the butcher paper, and discussed a second question. The process of discussion and movement was repeated three times. This process led everyone to have a voice and input into local decision making. To learn about leading a World Café in your community, visit www.theworldcafe.org.

Hydraulic Research Station: High School with 2nd- and 3rd-Grade Partners

In Auburn, Alabama, a high school science class was interested in hydraulics and wanted to do an experiment with fish. The high school students divided into three- to four-member teams. First they drew plans and built small fish tanks by using PC pipe, a pump, a five-gallon bucket, a one-gallon bucket, and a translucent plastic box. They wanted to include second- and third-grade students from four local elementary schools, so they went to the elementary schools and invited them to be science research stations. Each of the twelve participating classes received a tank and was given an ID such as Field DR5. Serving as field managers, elementary students used water test strips to test water quality of their tank. Each class received a male and female cichlid, a South American fish that reproduces quickly. A Web site was created for classes to report data. Twice a week, second and third graders fed the fish and posted data on the Web. The high school students compiled the data and determined if the water quality was healthy or poor. The elementary students asked questions via the Web and the high school students made suggestions on how to improve water quality. Approximately 250 elementary students participated in the scientific experiment. High school and elementary students learned various forms of math through graphs and charts, engineering, and science through inquiry and questioning.

> The elders were wise. They knew that man's heart, away from nature, becomes hard; they knew that lack of respect for growing, living things, soon led to lack of respect for humans, too.
>
> —*Chief Luther Standing Bear of the Lakota Sioux*

The Environment Bookshelf

It's a big world out there. Clearly, "the environment" covers many aspects of the planet, and this breadth is reflected in the Environment Bookshelf (pages 129–130). To help you find books relevant to what your students are learning and doing, the book chart classifies the titles according to several topic areas: learning from history, overview of the environment, natural resources, recycling, appreciation, and activism.

In general, the bookshelf features:

- An annotated bibliography arranged and alphabetized by title according to the general categories of nonfiction (N), picture books (P), and fiction (F). For nonfiction and fiction, length and recommended grade levels are included. The entries in the picture book category do not include suggested grade levels, since they can be successfully used with all ages.

- A chart organized by topic and category to help you find books relevant to particular projects.

- Recommendations from service learning colleagues and experts which include a book summary and ideas for service learning connections. (The number of recommended books varies in each bookshelf.)

- *Please note:* additional titles for this category are listed in the digital content; some of these were out of print at the time of publication but still worth finding.

Nonfiction: The Environment

Acme Climate Action

by Provacateur (Fourth Estate, 2008). This unique climate change book and kit is filled with information, postcards, stickers, carbon counter spinning wheels, and more. Pour over the pages; each generates ideas to cool off the planet. 64pp., all ages

The Boy Who Harnessed the Wind:
Creating Currents of Electricity and Hope

by William Kamkwamba and Bryon Mealer (William Morrow, 2009). At age fourteen, William Kamkwamba took discarded items and produced a windmill. This is the true story of a community with famine and poverty and plenty of wind, and one teenager determined to turn wind into freedom. 288pp., grades 8–12

Climate Change

by Shelley Tanaka (Groundwood Books, 2007). This guide to climate change examines the causes, risks, and recommended sacrifices needed to alter the course of global warming. Well-documented with examples of strategies worth considering. 144pp., young adult

The Curse of Akkad: Climate Upheavals
that Rocked Human History

by Peter Christie (Annick Press, 2008). An original and informative examination of previous human encounters with drastic climate change, this book explains the relationship between historical events like migration and war to climate. From the days of Macedonia through witch hunts in Eastern Europe to Hitler's quest for power, changing climate impacted our history in dramatic ways and includes information about how we can act now to curb the looming climate change disaster. 160pp., young adult

The Down-to-Earth Guide to Global Warming

by Laurie David and Cambria Gordon (Orchard Books, 2007). This covers the global warming topic by giving scientific information in easy-to-grasp language, reminds us what's at risk, and gives suggestions for how to become involved. Familiar faces, from Sponge Bob to Leonardo DiCaprio, make appearances. 128pp., grades 4–7

Earth-Friendly Design

by Anne Welsbacher (Lerner Publications, 2008). This book explores some of the exciting designs that are changing the way people consume energy. It introduces readers to cars, homes, and gardens that have changed not only how we live in relation to the planet but also how we live in relation to one another. 72pp., grades 4–8

Earth-Friendly Energy

by Ron Fridell (Lerner Publications, 2008). This explains the various energy resources that could be tapped to supply the world with its energy needs. Each section discusses the pros and cons of the particular resource and gives examples of its use so far. It's an exploration of how industry and individuals can make changes using alternative energy such as biofuels or wave-farming. 72pp., grades 4–8

Generation Green: The Ultimate Teen Guide
to Living an Eco-Friendly Life

by Linda Sivertsen and Tosh Sivertsen (Simon Pulse, 2008). Written by a mother-son team, this book is for any teenager who wants to know more or who is becoming a green activist. Topics include: Eating Green, Green Begins at Home, Guilt-Free Shopping, Hanging Out Green, Greener Schools and Careers, and Step Up and Speak Out. With teen culture imbedded in every page and resources throughout, it's easy to join the Green Generation. 272pp., grades 8–12

Going Blue: A Teen Guide to Saving
Our Oceans, Lakes, Rivers, & Wetlands

by Cathryn Berger Kaye with Philippe Cousteau (Free Spirit Publishing, 2010). This book seeks to inform young people about the issues surrounding our waters and provide the strategies and examples they need to see themselves as change agents. With the aid of lively photos and illustrations, along with practical suggestions and activities, kids follow the five stages of service learning in an effort to benefit our planet's water system. 128pp., grades 6–12

Gone Fishing: Ocean Life by the Numbers

by David McLimans (Walker and Co., 2008). With its bright blue color reminiscent of the oceans, we are drawn into this counting book that uses the shape of animals to count one to ten and back again. Each represents sea life threatened by human encroachment. Filled with information, statistics, and resources—definitely something for everyone. 40pp., all grades

Heroes of the Environment: True Stories of People Who Are Helping to Protect Our Planet

by Harriet Rohmer (Chronicle, 2009). From the community activist saving West Virginia's oldest mountains to bringing solar power to the Hoi Indian Reservation, read about twelve individuals who are taking a stand for change. Included is service learning teacher Barry Guillot (see page 124) who transforms his students into heroes for the wetlands and a Rhode Island teenager who helped write environmental laws. 110pp., grades 4–8

An Inconvenient Truth: The Crisis of Global Warming

by Al Gore (Viking, 2007). This book, "adapted for a new generation" is the young readers' version of the documentary and book of the same name. Brilliant charts, maps, and photographs accompany the text, which ultimately leads to the conclusion that we all have to "change the way we live our lives." 192pp., grades 4–8

John Muir: America's First Environmentalist

by Kathryn Lasky (Candlewick Press, 2008). This book outlines the course of John Muir's life and fascination with the natural world, and his work founding national parks and promoting environmentalism. Follow Muir's life from a young boy in a meadow in Scotland to an old man advocating for the preservation of American wilderness. Illustrations lend beauty to broad landscapes as well as small details such as a snowstorm. 48pp., grades 2–5

Mission: Planet Earth: Our World and Its Climate—and How Humans Are Changing Them

by Sally Ride and Tam O'Shaughnessy (Roaring Brook Press, 2009). Dramatic photographs highlight this overview of climate change that begins with an astronaut's-eye view of the globe as the environment changes and the earth warms. It describes how life and climate intertwine, what human negligence has done to cause disastrous changes, how these changes affect other species and our own, and what we can do to save our planet. Companion guide also available. 80pp., grades 4–6

Mission: Save the Planet: Things You Can Do to Help Fight Global Warming

by Sally Ride and Tam O'Shaughnessy (Roaring Brook Press, 2009). An interactive guide with practical ways kids (and others) can change habits and lifestyle patterns to use less and be "more green." The exercises guide students to integrate these suggestions into their everyday thinking. 64pp., grades 4–6

Not a Drop to Drink: Water for a Thirsty World

by Michael Burgan (National Geographic, 2008). Using timelines, photographs, charts, and a glossary, this book presents one of the greatest issues of our time: the need for clean, accessible water. The reader learns science (robot ocean floor exploration), history (retrieving ocean fossils), current events (the war in Darfur), global awareness (water consumption throughout the world), and innovative ways this dilemma is being addressed (Salt Solutions). Excellent for considering careers that address our water concerns. 64pp., grades 4–8

Oil

by James Laxer (Groundwood Books, 2008). In this world so dependent on oil, this book helps the reader understand the politics, the corporate realm, and the influence of oil on humanity as we face a dwindling supply. It also discusses climate change and how burning coal and petroleum affects our lungs and planet. 144pp., young adult

One Well: The Story of Water on Earth

by Rochelle Strauss (Kids Can Press, 2007). The simple language and art are depictions of what happens to water during its various cycles. Many subject areas converge in this informative resource including habitats, issues of access, demands, pollution, conservation, and "Becoming Well Aware" with ideas for social action and engagement. 32pp., grades 4–8

Protecting Earth's Water Supply

by Ron Fridell (Lerner Publications, 2008). Water, water everywhere? Unless we are more cautious about our water supply, our planet is at risk. Human induced pollution and global warming is threatening our water supply. This book tells about innovative solutions for collecting water from fog and water from air, and how a ten-year-old from Aluva, India, developed her own rainwater harvesting system to help local farmers. 72pp., grades 4–7

Ryan and Jimmy and the Well in Africa that Brought Them Together

by Herb Shoveller (Kids Can Press, 2008). When six-year-old Ryan Hreljac heard about the lack of portable water in Africa, he thought, "I will get money from my parents to buy a well." His hard work and optimism led to the creation of Ryan's Well Foundation, which has raised thousands of dollars for wells in Africa and South America. Ryan also traveled to Uganda, the location of the first well. There he met Akana Jimmy, his pen

The Environment Bookshelf Topics

Topics	Books	Category
Learning from History What we learn from the past can assist us in moving forward as we reclaim, protect, and restore our fragile environment.	The Curse of Akkad Into the Deep: The Life of Naturalist and Explorer William Beebe John Muir: America's First Environmentalist * What Darwin Saw: The Journey that Changed the World	N P N P

Overview of the Environment
These "big picture" books cover a range of environmental topics. Ecosystems, climate change, and global warming are highlighted in many of the titles.
	Climate Change
	The Down-to-Earth Guide to Global Warming
	Earth-Friendly Design
	Generation Green: The Ultimate Teen Guide to Living an
	    Eco-Friendly Life *
	An Inconvenient Truth: The Crises of Global Warming
	A Life Like Mine: How Children Live Around the World *
	    (see Social Change Bookshelf—digital content)
	Mission Planet Earth: Our World and Its Climate and How
	    Humans Are Changing Them
	Trout are Made of Trees
	We Are the Weather Makers: The History of Climate Change
		N
		N
		N
		
		N
		N
		
		N
		
		N
		P
		N

Natural Resources These books focus on life-sustaining resources that are at risk and need to be used more wisely.	All the Way to the Ocean Arctic Tale The Boy Who Harnessed the Wind: Creating Currents of Electricity and Hope * The Carbon Diaries 2015 Earth-Friendly Energy Gone Fishing Leaf Not a Drop to Drink: Water for a Thirsty World Oil One Well: The Story of Water on Earth Protecting Earth's Water Supply	P F N F N P P N N N N
Recycling Reduce, reuse, recycle: This is the mantra of the recycling movement. These books tell of the subject from various perspectives.	Stuff! Reduce, Reuse, Recycle The Wartville Wizard	P P

Page references are given for books that can be found in the bookshelf lists of other chapters.
* These books include examples of young people in service-providing roles.
(GN) These books are graphic novels.

The Environment Bookshelf Topics (continued)

Topics	Books	Category
Appreciation Taking time to appreciate our planet and our resources is part of the environmental story.	*The Bee Tree* *The Blind Faith Hotel* *The Tree*	P F P
Activism These books tell the story of transforming the ideas into action and inspire others.	*Acme Climate Action* * *Earthgirl* * *Going Blue: A Kids' Guide to Saving Our Oceans and Waterways* * *Heroes of the Environment: True Stories of People Who Are Helping to Protect Our Planet* * *The Last Wild Place* *Mission: Save the Planet: Things You Can Do to Help Fight Global Warming* * *Planting the Trees of Kenya: The Story of Wangari Maathai* * *Ryan and Jimmy and the Well in Africa that Brought Them Together* * *True Green Kids: 100 Things You Can Do to Save the Planet* *Scat* * *Your Planet Needs You!* *	N F N N N N P N N F F (GN)

Page references are given for books that can be found in the bookshelf lists of other chapters.
* These books include examples of young people in service-providing roles.
(GN) These books are graphic novels.

pal. Jimmy, an orphan, lived under the threat of being abducted by the Lord's Resistance Army as a child soldier. His fortunate escape and the good will of caring adults led him across the ocean to join Ryan's family permanently. Learn more at www .ryanswell.ca. 56pp., grades 3–6

True Green Kids: 100 Things You Can Do to Save the Planet
by Kim McKay and Jenny Bonnin (National Geographic, 2008). This book has 100 short segments on what any green activist would want to know and countless ideas for doing them. This book will cause you to think about your actions at home, school, with friends, and may even influence what "stuff" you buy. Photographs show kids involved in service. Includes an index of useful resources. 144pp., grades 2–7

We Are the Weather Makers: The History of Climate Change
by Tim Flannery, adapted by Sally M. Walker (Candlewick Press, 2009). Written to "the generation who will act on global warming," this thorough overview explains the carbon cycle and greenhouse story, and reviews many endangered habitats.

Each chapter has a "Call to Action," plus 14 chapters on "What's to Come?" The final chapter has stories of youth who took action. 320pp., young adult

Picture Books: The Environment

All the Way to the Ocean
by Joel Harper (Freedom Three, 2006). A dropped gum wrapper down a storm drain leads to an explanation of where that small piece of trash goes—all the way to the ocean. These unnecessary pollutants harm our wildlife, close our beaches, and taint our drinking water. Two boys organize a school yard cleanup and ask the reader, "What are some of the things you and your friends can do in your community to help prevent storm drain pollution?"

The Bee Tree
by Diana Cohn and Stephen Buckmann (Cinto Puntos Press, 2007). Based on a Malaysian proverb, this book tells the tale of Nizam, the grandson of the leader of their honey hunting clan.

Nizam takes the first daunting steps to succeed his grandfather in the honored position of honey hunter. He will climb the Tualang trees—so tall that the top cannot be seen—to retrieve honey in the dead of a moonless night. He learns the stories, traditions, and values of the clan. The final pages include a general overview about Malaysia, its people, and its environment and natural resources, including the honey bee.

Into the Deep: The Life of Naturalist and Explorer William Beebe

by David Sheldon (Charlesbridge, 2009). A young boy's passion for animals develops into a profession as "a pioneer in the field of ecology, deep-sea exploration, and conservation." Follow Beebe's exciting journeys into the wilds of the jungle and ocean depths. Through writings and lectures, his life's work became promoting conservation of our vanishing wilderness and endangered animal species.

Leaf

by Stephen Michael King (Roaring Brook Press, 2009). A boy discovers a plant growing on his head and does all he can to keep the spore alive. This funny and touching cartoon about nurturing random encounters through the imagination shows the lasting creations those acts produce.

Planting the Trees of Kenya: The Story of Wangari Maathai

by Claire A. Nivola (Farrar, Straus and Giroux, 2008). This book recounts the experiences of Wangari Maathai, the first African woman to receive the Nobel Peace Prize. Before she left to pursue her education in the United States, Wangari's native Kenya was covered in a rich and green landscape. When she returned, she found that the land had been depleted nearly into a desert, and even the sacred fig trees had been cut down. Instead of looking to the government for answers, she offered her people a very simple solution: they would plant the earth back into productivity.

Stuff! Reduce, Reuse, Recycle

by Stephen Kroll (Marshall Cavendish, 2009). Pinch, a pack rat who is an actual rat, wants to keep everything he has. His friends convince him to donate his stuff to a community tag sale. His selling inspires others, and they donate their profits to help plant a dozen trees!

The Tree

by Karen Gray Ruelle (Holiday House, 2008). Looking at history through the lens of an elm tree and the land where it grows, we see 250 years pass by in Madison Square Park in New York City. The tree stood through the inauguration celebration of George Washington. It stood by the riots and demonstrations of the early 1900s. The tree survived Dutch elm disease and the growth of the urban sprawl. Though its dying limbs were removed, the trunk still stands as a monument in the heart of the city.

Trout Are Made of Trees

by April Pulley Sayre (Charlesbridge, 2008). Two children follow the ecological food web centered in streams and rivers and discover the interconnectedness of nature. The book also includes suggestions children can do to help conservation and for being a "Stream Hero!"

The Wartville Wizard

by Don Madden (Aladdin, 1993). A man turns "wizard" to fight a town of litterbugs by making litter stick to the person who dropped it! A memorable and colorful tale of how people learn about the consequences of their actions. Easily adapted to an amusing play with an important message.

What Darwin Saw: The Journey that Changed the World

by Rosalyn Schanzer (National Geographic, 2009). Join twenty-two-year-old naturalist Charles Darwin on his scientific journey around the world that lasted four years, two months, and two days. The illustrations and text work perfectly to show the details that influenced Darwin's theory of evolution. Science, history, culture, geography—it's all included in this book.

Fiction: The Environment

Arctic Tale

by Barry Varela (National Geographic, 2007). A companion to the movie of the same name, readers discover the perspective of a polar bear family, following their daily activities and the suppositions of what they might be thinking and feeling. Through this point of view, we gain a glimpse of how global warming affects our wildlife. 132pp., grades 3–8

The Blind Faith Hotel

by Pamela Todd (Margaret K. McElderry Books, 2008). Fourteen-year-old Zoe is not interested in this Midwest town, this rundown old house her mother inherited, or school. She simply wants to return to the Northwest coast and be with her father. Instead she gets caught shoplifting and has to complete community service at a nature preserve. Surprisingly, her world there makes sense, and she develops a deep appreciation for nature as she begins to make sense of the relationships around her. 320pp., young adult

The Carbon Diaries, 2015

by Saci Lloyd (Holiday House, 2009). The year is 2015, the place London, England, and fifteen-year-old Laura is keeping a diary. She is not pleased that after a great storm hits London, "the gov volunteered Britain to be the stupid guinea pig freak and ration carbon." The whole world is watching this experiment. As you read excerpts from Laura's year, consider how limiting the amount of carbon that you, your family, and your friends could use would change your life. Gripping, relevant, edgy. Also read the sequel, The Carbon Diaries, 2017. 330pp., grades 8–12

Earthgirl

by Jennifer Cowan (Groundwood Books, 2009). A car driver carelessly tosses McDonald's leftovers out her window. The plum sauce lands on sixteen-year-old Sabine as she's riding her bike to meet friends. In a drastic turn of events, Sabine becomes a blogging, eco-emphatic teenager who changes her job, friends, opinions, and almost gets caught way over her head in political activism. 192pp., grades 7–10

The Last Wild Place

by Rosa Jordan (Peachtree, 2008). Chip Martin's life in Florida is pretty good until his family seems to be changing. In fact, he's noticing many changes, folks displaced by the hurricane are now taking shelter in the community center and a construction crew wants to build in a nearby woodsy marsh of the Everglades. Can he mobilize his best friend Luther and other kids in his middle school class to become activists? Can they protect a family of Florida panthers that have settled in the marsh? Follow Chip and Luther as they lead their friends to protect the environment and the animals. 256pp., grades 4–8

Scat

by Carl Hiaasen (Knopf, 2009). A great eco-thriller by a master storyteller. Maybe Nick and Marta should be relieved that Ms. Starch, the feared biology teacher, has gone missing after a field trip to Black Vine Swamp, but something definitely feels amiss. Could the "class delinquent," Smoke, be behind this? What about the Florida panther that may be on the prowl? And could a self-centered wannabe oilman be causing all of these problems? A real page-turner. 384pp., grades 5–8

Your Planet Needs You!

by Dave Reay (Macmillan, 2009). As superhero Maximus heads off on a mission to stop the planet from heating up, he comes across two knowledgeable kids—Henry and Flora—who become his expert guides. Using his superpowers, this dynamic three-o fly over the globe to see the rain forests getting ravaged, Bangladesh flooding, and tundra melting. Experiments and graphic comic pages spice up this humor-filled book about taking action. 176pp., grades 2–5

DIGITAL CONTENT

Interviews with Authors:
The Story Behind the Story

In the companion digital content you'll find interviews with authors Laurie David (coauthor of *The Down-to-Earth Guide to Global Warming*) and Don Madden *(The Wartville Wizard)* that tell the "story behind the story" of their books.

Chapter 9

Gardening

I'm a big believer in community gardens, both because of their beauty and for their access to providing fresh fruits and vegetables to so many communities across this nation and the world.

—*Michelle Obama, First Lady of the United States*

Sweet peas and cucumbers, tomatoes and daffodils, strawberries and corn. A garden is a place to watch—and help—things grow, where nature's cycles become apparent, and the impact of care and neglect are dramatic lessons in cause and effect. *Planting, growing,* and *transformation* are just a few of the words in a common language used to describe gardening as well as human development and relationships. Gardens bring people together with meaning and often delectable purpose.

Have you noticed? Gardens are sprouting up everywhere. On rooftops, in pocket parks, on front lawns and back lawns, and on the White House grounds in Washington, D.C. School and community gardens provide active classrooms a place where many hands can tend plants. All ages can work cooperatively to make a garden grow. Even reluctant students or urban youth who have never planted a seed can usually find a connection in the garden with the other gardeners, as well as with the soil, plants, flowers, and produce.

Learning possibilities abound in gardening. Science literally comes alive as students identify the parts of plants in real life and diligently observe the stages of their garden's life cycle unfold. Students use computers and math skills to design a garden, measure their plot, and estimate the cost of materials. They have serenaded plants with music, painted murals to keep their garden in bloom year-round, and planted poetry alongside the radishes and lettuce. Issues of health, hunger, and poverty in the community and the region

are covered when harvested food is shared with shelters and food banks. Young people can partner with elders and refugees to learn from others how to care for all living things. Environmental issues can be raised when students start figuring out whether to grow an organic garden or how pesticides can affect our planet's health. Through service learning, students come to appreciate and understand how agriculture, farm workers, and environmental issues interconnect through the process of planting and maintaining a garden. Planting, growing, transformation: How will your garden grow?

Preparation: Getting Ready for Service Learning Involving Gardening

 The following activities can be used to promote learning and skill development related to gardening. These activities are easily adapted to different grade levels during investigation, preparation, and planning to help your students examine key issues through research, analyze community needs, and gain the knowledge they need to effectively contribute to the design of their service plan. They often can be integrated into reflection and demonstration as students can lead the activities with others to build awareness. Since literature is often an important part of preparation, you can find recommended titles on this theme in the Gardening Bookshelf later in this chapter.

Activity: An Old Fashioned Almanac. Beginning in 1792, farmers turned to printed almanacs for a variety of information concerning agriculture, including sunrise and sunset tables, planting charts, weather patterns and predictions, and recipes. Students can learn a great deal by reviewing the almanacs available in most libraries. The students can identify topics to research in preparation for creating their own gardens and their own version of an almanac, which can be distributed to community members. The students' almanac could include a planting schedule, tips from gardeners, strategies for dealing with pests, recipes tested by students, and a problem-solving section. Students could even create short scenes based on their almanac to perform for younger students or community members in (where else?) the garden.

Activity: Community Gardens and Other Social Movements. Community gardens are much more than a pretty neighborhood scene. They bring people together, encourage physical exercise, create opportunities for collaboration, and provide a valuable healthy resource: fresh produce.

Delve into history or find present day examples of how gardens can become social movements. For example, the Victory Gardens of World War II, when the United States government asked the general populace to plant gardens to free up commercial growers to provide for the military. Today, students are planting sunflowers to use for biofuel, and in Africa, women are learning how to create gardening co-ops to increase their incomes and create more time with their families. And composting has become commonplace in many communities as a way to reduce waste and enrich the soil. When economic times are hard, many people look to planting as an affordable way to have vegetables and fruits for their families, and their surplus often is donated to local food shelves or shelters.

Before initiating a community garden, many questions may come up: Does our community already have any community gardens? If so, what are the land use policies in the gardens? How do people reserve or share garden plots? What help is needed to maintain the gardens or to expand the opportunities for participation? Who in the community could benefit from the garden's produce? How could one be started? Many national and local organizations support the development of community gardens with funds and expertise. They also can be good sources of information for students conducting research. In addition to planning their own garden, students can become advocates for garden programs, collaborating with local government agencies and schools. Gardens are not only about seeds, compost, plants, and harvesting, they are also about people and building community.

Find Out More About Gardening

To learn more about these issues and to get ideas for service and action, visit these Web sites and organizations online:

Junior Master Gardeners (www.jmgkids.us) is an international youth gardening program whose mission is to grow good kids by igniting a passion for learning, success, and service through a unique gardening education.

KidsGardening! (www.kidsgardening.org), a program of the National Gardening Association, offers a host of gardening resources including books, curriculum, more Web connections, and grant opportunities.

The National Wildlife Federation's Garden for Wildlife (www.nwf.org/gardenforwildlife/create.cfm) program teaches students about the wildlife right in their own backyard or school yard and includes resources to create gardens that are habitat-based learning sites in school yards.

Making Connections Across the Curriculum

Some service learning activities naturally lend themselves to interdisciplinary work and making connections across the curriculum. These connections strengthen and broaden student learning, helping them meet academic standards. More than likely, you'll be looking for these connections and ways to encourage them well before the students ever start working on service learning activities. As with the entire service learning process, it helps to remain flexible, because some connections can be spontaneously generated by the questions raised throughout and by the community needs identified by the students. To help you think about cross-curricular connections and where you can look for them, the curricular web for this chapter (page 137) gives examples of many different ways this theme can be used in different academic areas. (The service learning scenarios in the next section of the chapter also demonstrate various ways that this theme can be used across the curriculum.)

Service Learning Scenarios: Ideas for Action

Ready to take action? The service learning descriptions that follow have been successfully carried out by elementary, middle, or high school students in schools and with community organizations. Most of these scenarios and examples explicitly include some aspects of investigation, preparation and planning, action, reflection, and demonstration, and all have strong curricular connections. These scenarios can be a rich source of ideas for you to draw upon. Keep in mind that grade levels are provided as a reference; most scenarios can be adapted to suit younger or older students, and many are suitable for cross-age partnerships.

Schoolwide Community of Gardeners: Grades K–5
The gifted and talented students and two fourth-grade classes, along with community partners, developed the Glen View Elementary School Community of Gardeners project in Ruston, Louisiana. They set out to build beds to grow strawberries and herbs. The strawberries were delivered to a local nursing home and the herbs were potted and sold at a local business to benefit a domestic abuse center. As part of cross-curricular study, they integrated academic concepts related to science, math, language arts, social studies, health, nutrition, and economics. For example, students researched the history of farm equipment and made sure their garden only had indigenous plants. The older students created lessons about what they learned for the kindergartners and first graders. The fourth-grade students honed their writing skills through documentation and writing summaries. The entire school became engaged in studying nature, learning work habits, and developing environmental awareness. Students who otherwise would not be exposed to gardening had a chance to "feel the earth move under their feet"—and to grow in new ways.

International Collaboration: Grades K–6
Students from Iowa State University and Makerere University in Uganda collaborated on plans to increase nutrition at the 700-student Namasagali Primary School in the rural Kamuli district of Uganda. Eating the same corn meal porridge for lunch every day, these young students were not receiving enough nutrients in their diets, and they were not learning anything at school about farming, likely their future profession. Via the Internet, the university students and faculty collaborated with teachers, parents, and leaders at the elementary school and they developed plans for a huge garden to be created at the primary school. The garden had a June launch date, and when the primary school students returned to school, vegetable nurseries, two acres of cassava, two acres of maize, and a field of soybeans were waiting for them. The young students were responsible for weeding and watering the garden, and their parents formed a garden management committee and provided labor and materials for a fence to keep out animals. The joint effort yielded a new school garden, a well for drinking and cooking water, and a chicken house. In addition to being a great outdoor laboratory for studies and teaching about farming, the garden also served as a supplement for the school lunches. The children gained a positive perspective on agriculture as a profession, and shared their gardening experiences and planting materials with their own families.

Gardening Takes Root in an Entire District: Grades K–12
In one school district, gardens became an important part of student life at several schools. Students found many different ways to contribute to their gardens and to use the produce that was the result of their efforts. Students at one elementary school began to eat plenty of leafy greens after harvesting certified organic produce from their on-site garden, adding the tastes of bok choy and arugula to the cafeteria food. At another elementary school in the district, students took surplus produce to a homeless shelter each week. At yet another elementary school with extensive gardens, students progressed through various gardening tasks by

grade level, moving from raising berries and vegetables to building ponds and garden structures. Greenhouses at the district middle schools allowed students to start seedlings for the elementary students, and high school students planned nutrition classes and a health fair to teach students across the district about gardening, cooking, and nutrition. The younger students contributed ideas about what to plant, while high school students planned and organized all aspects of the health fair from fund-raising to publicity. Benefits extended in all directions. One school, for example, included a large population of Hmong and Hispanic students, who sometimes had a difficult time sharing expertise at school. The garden provided a way for Hmong and Hispanic families who worked in the agricultural industry to participate. Local businesses (such as nurseries and excavation companies, which provided topsoil) and local nonprofit organizations became collaborators and assisted with the building of garden beds.

A Giving Garden: Grades 1–3
with Middle and High School Helpers

Three first- through third-grade classrooms in West Salem, Wisconsin, designed, constructed, planted, maintained, and harvested a garden on school grounds, with help from middle and high school students and community members. After hearing a speaker from the food pantry talk about the pantry and the needs it addressed, the students came up with the idea of planting a garden to help serve their community. The garden was intended to produce vegetables for fifty families per month who used the local food pantry. Students would experience community participation by providing opportunities to work with teachers, parents, and other community members. In addition to learning gardening skills, the students learned about the relationships between people, plants, and wildlife and practiced leadership skills in work crews. Students from the junior high constructed benches for the garden, and high school students helped with planting. Classroom reflection included discussion of the concept of community and the reasons a community might need a food pantry, such as job loss and poverty. Students wrote journals throughout the process. And to keep the garden healthy year-round, the students created a weekly schedule for families to work in the garden during the summer.

It is not enough to be busy; so are the ants. The question is: What are we busy about?

—*Henry David Thoreau, philosopher*

A Poetic Garden Adds a Mural: Grades 2–4

An elementary school garden added beauty to a Los Angeles neighborhood. Students who were planting, tending seedlings, or harvesting would strike up conversations with neighbors passing by. The neighbors commented on the poetry "planted" among the vegetables. Students explained how they had read books about gardening and had been inspired to write poems by the curly pea vines and the large zucchini leaves. Their poems, mounted on boards and laminated, were interspersed with the greenery. During the off-season, however, the area looked pretty dull. The students gathered in their garden to think about what could be done. They designed and received approval to make a garden mural so the beauty of things growing would be present all year long.

Planting a Butterfly Garden: Grades 2 and 7

After elementary students read *Butterfly Boy*, they wanted to create a butterfly garden alongside a local senior center, which was located in a park. The teacher thought the job seemed too large for her class alone, so when she contacted the city parks and recreation department for permission to plant the garden, she also asked for assistance. She was referred to the middle school, and a seventh-grade class at the school offered to help. Their teacher wove the experience into literature by selecting *Butterflies and Lizards, Beryl and Me* for her students to read. Many groups assisted, including the senior citizens, a community college life-sciences class, and a local conservation group. Students conducted research to identify the appropriate plants. The teacher also asked the students for ideas to begin a relationship with members of the senior center. As a result, the students hosted a "butterfly" party at the center and, with assistance from the center's art director and the elders who used the center, made three-dimensional butterflies to display in the local library.

Gardening Across the Curriculum

English/Language Arts

- Research and write about gardens and herbs
- Write letters soliciting donations for community gardens
- Write poetry about the flowers, fruits, or vegetables (or aspects of the garden) to "plant" or display in the school garden

Social Studies/History

- Research the indigenous plants in your area and Native American gardening methods
- Learn about local gardening organizations
- Study World War II Victory Gardens

Languages

- Learn the vocabulary of gardening in the language of study
- Research fruits and vegetables grown in the country where the language is spoken
- Make multilingual signs for the garden identifying the plants; or translate community gardening materials and distribute them

Theater, Music, & Visual Arts

- Create and perform a dramatization to teach about gardening
- Perform songs about plants and growing
- Design and paint a mural to create a year-round garden

Gardening

Math

- Create a budget and price list for plants and materials to purchase
- Measure space for planting
- Chart observations of plant growth and change; calculate expected yields and compare to actual harvest

Physical Education

- Prepare a warm-up exercise routine to do before working in the garden
- Research the impact on the body of bending and lifting and other gardening movements, then find the healthiest ways to do these activities
- Plan a garden tour for very young children that includes pretending that they are seeds that grow and grow into a plant

Computer

- Read and research software and literature on garden design
- Create a computer slide show on garden development
- Use the Internet to learn about careers in landscape architecture, horticulture, topiary design, and agriculture

Science

- Identify and compare seeds and plants, then observe and record life cycle of plants
- Examine and test soil
- Study invasive exotic plants

A Safe Habitat: Grade 3

While studying about habitats, two third-grade classes at Mary O. Pottenger School in Springfield, Massachusetts, watched a film about a group of students that created a habitat for an injured bird. Afterward, the third graders wanted to create a community garden safe for creatures and critters, and for people, too. This idea launched a cross-curricular gardening experience with many partners. Students worked with a local landscape designer to develop the plans. Students then wrote letters to twenty local businesses, including nurseries, asking for donations. In the spring, working side-by-side with local college students, they planted the garden. But an unfortunate incident happened a month later: the garden was vandalized, and many costly plants were lost. More donations came pouring in from parents, businesses, and the community. Today, the garden thrives year-round. Children in the summer after-school program tend to the garden during summer break, and in the fall, a new batch of third graders takes over. Visit the school and you can sit on a park bench and enjoy the butterfly bush, petunias, hydrangeas, lilies, cypress bushes, and pink pushpin flowers.

The Wrong Way and the Worm Way: Grade 3

In Humble, Texas, at Humble Elementary, you might think the third graders are successful business people who have been reduced in size: They started their own business making and selling worm poop. Having become composting experts, the students took science to a new level and designed advertising and marketing, manufactured a product, and taught the broader community about worms and composting. Their business helped engage them in learning and raised their science test scores at school.

To Learn, to Share, to Experience Peace: Grades 3–5

Sometimes a garden has many purposes. In Dulles, Oregon, an elementary garden serves three needs. First, the garden offers numerous hands-on learning experiences for children. The students manage the greenhouse, weather station, worm garden, and composting, and grow flowers and vegetables. Second, the produce and flowers are given to people in need within the community. And third, the garden is a place for reflection and peace where students can sit quietly and write in journals or simply enjoy the beauty and peace around them.

Singing for Plants: Grade 4

Students at one Illinois elementary school were interested in planting some native species around their school. To raise money to help them buy the necessary supplies, they decided to do what youngsters do well—sing loudly! They planned a concert and chose songs that pertained to plants and their importance to people, animals, and the earth. The students sold tickets to the concert and used the money they raised to help them buy several varieties of native flowers, vegetables, and herbs. Students planted a beautiful garden around their school and also learned how to care for the plants by weeding and watering the garden.

History That's for the Birds: Grade 5

Fifth-grade students in Galt, California, put hammer to nail as they worked on rebuilding a chicken house. While helping the local historical society develop a living history ranch, they learned construction methods of the past and present. They also planted several acres of pumpkins that were enjoyed by kindergarten classes during fall harvest activities.

From Worm Bins to Radishes: Grade 5

Fifth graders in West Hollywood, California, who began the school year with little, if any, knowledge of gardening had green thumbs by year's end. During science lessons, they planted and cared for seedlings, charting growth and changes. That was just the beginning, then they: read books about gardens, such as *Carlos and the Cornfield/Carlos y la milpa de maíz* and *Wanda's Roses*, to younger students; built compost bins at school and collected appropriate food waste during lunch time; tasted their first radishes; displayed worm bins at the local farmers' market; lead tours for visitors and had them write comments in the guest journal; and published a brochure, "How to Start a Container Garden," for distribution throughout the community. What was left? The next year, the gardeners created a coloring book called "From Apples to Zucchinis: The ABCs of Gardening" to share their expertise and inspire other young gardeners.

Recipes and Remedies: Grades 5–8

Good food grown in gardens may taste even better when used in recipes that teach about culture and tradition. After students in Oklahoma researched traditional plants used by Native Americans for cooking and for herbal remedies, they cooked up a cookbook with art and detailed information to share their new knowledge and recipes with the community.

Planting to Grow and Learn: Grade 6

What are the correlations between the life cycle of plants and the life cycle of humans? Sixth graders in Sheffield City Schools in Alabama integrated their knowledge of plants with character education. They studied the cyclic growth of plants, how green gasses operate, and gerontology. Then they planted various types of flowers and plants and learned how to take care of them through a partnership with a local greenhouse. Students went on a field trip to a local nursing home and shared the plants with the elders. Students wrote a paper about the correlations they discovered between the growth of plants and people. They shared their stories and what they learned with partners. In the process, students were exposed to careers in medicine, including being a nurse, researcher, or doctor, and also in horticulture.

Language Skills and Gardens Grow: Grades 6–8

Student and adult volunteers in Houston, Texas, created an urban garden with dual objectives: to grow fresh produce for a local food pantry and to learn Spanish related to gardening. In this "speak Spanish" garden, students learned Spanish words for various tools and vegetables and even the vitamins in the produce. The students also learned how to talk to community members in Spanish about why a garden is important and how to get a garden started.

A Fruitful Process: Grades 6–8

Pollard McCall Jr. High students in Alabama wondered if fruit trees could grow in their community. They researched whether fruit had been grown there before and the time required for trees to bear fruit. They studied life cycles of trees and responses to potential problems. Seventh and eighth graders helped sixth graders understand the process and plant new trees. Once their first crop was harvested, students needed to decide what to do with the fruit. While churches purchase fruit to give to shut-in elders in the community during holidays, the students thought homegrown fruits would be more special. Students delivered baskets with oranges, tangerines, and kumquats. Throughout

the project, students completed narratives, expository writing, and persuasive papers, paying particular attention to descriptive elements. They also identified questions for scientific investigation. After each stage (planting, tending to the trees, harvesting), students reflected on the process, describing what occurred and why. Many skills were in play: observation, note taking, social, and reading, and students learned about different careers such as farmers, business owners, entrepreneuers, scientists, and conservationsists.

A Victory Garden: Grade 7

As middle school students were preparing to plant a garden, their teacher read aloud chapters of *The Victory Garden* to learn about how communities across the United States grew produce during World War II. This led students to conduct research using history books and having conversations with community members who have memories of dirt under their fingernails from those days. The students then considered what their garden could represent or commemorate from their lives. They decided to plant a garden to honor the people who died in the terrorist attacks on September 11, 2001. To recognize the fact that people of many different ethnic groups lost their lives, the students included plants from different parts of the world in their peace garden.

A Neighborly Garden: Grade 8

As part of a community cleanup around the school, eighth-grade students in Texas spruced up an elder neighbor's front yard. The invitation to "come back again" began a relationship that grew. Students received permission to create a garden in this new friend's backyard and walked over several times each week to do the necessary work. The students found that their older friend greatly enjoyed their companionship—as well as the produce from the garden, which was also shared with the local food bank. Students helped deliver and return library books for their neighbor as well.

All plants are our brothers and sisters. They talk to us and if we listen, we can hear them.

—*Arapaho saying*

Two Cultures Growing: Grade 8

In partnership with a historical society, an eighth-grade class in Wisconsin created Native American and European gardens to show the difference between the two cultures. Activities expanded with student input to include making Native American tools, writing brochures about the gardens, and creating a display case. During the summer, the gardens were maintained by young students from Somalia who had come to the community as refugees. One outcome of this project was that the Somalis planted their own community garden. For this group, the garden helped in the transition from an agricultural society.

Gardening Partnerships: Grades 9 and 10

Environmental biology students stopped building virtual gardens and created a greenhouse on their Santa Monica, California, school campus to try out their ideas and to grow produce for a local shelter. Once the greenhouse was operational, the students addressed the larger challenge of taking what they had practiced into the community. A nearby residential facility for active seniors contacted the high school asking for help in creating an on-site garden. When students visited the facility with their plans, they found a huge flaw: the residents would be unable to bend down to work in a garden. With assistance from shop classes, the students found a solution: raised-bed gardens. This solution led to another dilemma. The elder gardeners wanted to invite elementary classes to visit and receive gardening tips, but the raised-bed gardens where too high for the children! The shop class constructed easy-to-move platforms that would bring the children up to dirt level.

A Touch Garden: Grades 9–12

As part of a dropout prevention program, high school students in Fort Myers, Florida, were given responsibilities and the necessary skills and knowledge to create a "children's touching garden." This required a comprehensive education about planting and plant care, the construction of pathways, and building benches. Students were mentored by master gardeners and other community volunteers. They also created a children's brochure. Once open, thousands of young children had visual and tactile experiences in this colorful and well-planned garden.

Profits Keep Growing: Grades 9–12

Inner-city high school students in Los Angeles transformed themselves into entrepreneurs as they transformed their garden into a business by growing most of the ingredients for a salad dressing. Local business people contributed time and expertise to guide the students in many necessary tasks, from recipe development to promotion. Profits were divided: half goes back into the business and the rest goes to a college scholarship fund. The students have visited many schools to share their knowledge and inspire others.

A book is like a garden carried in the pocket.

—*Chinese proverb*

The Gardening Bookshelf

Books from the Gardening Bookshelf (page 141) can teach us the fundamentals of gardening and frequently show how gardens illuminate many aspects of life and community. Seedlings, like infants, need careful nurturing. By harvest time mature plants can seem like old friends. Bonds can form with the garden and among the people providing care. The garden can be a source of beauty that grows the soul as well as the produce that feeds the body. To help you find books relevant to your particular activities, the book chart classifies the books into two topic areas: planting and growing, and transformation.

In general, the bookshelf features:

- An annotated bibliography arranged and alphabetized by title according to the general categories of nonfiction (N), picture books (P), and fiction (F). For nonfiction and fiction, length and recommended grade levels are included. The entries in the picture book category do not include suggested grade levels, since they can be successfully used with all ages.

- A chart organized by topic and category to help you find books relevant to particular projects.

- Recommendations from service learning colleagues and experts that include a book summary and ideas for service learning connections. (The number of recommended books varies in each bookshelf.)

- *Please note:* additional titles for this category are listed in the digital content; some of these were out of print at the time of publication but still worth finding.

Books are the bees which carry the quickening pollen from one to another mind.

—*James Russell Lowell, author*

Nonfiction: Gardening

Cycle of Rice, Cycle of Life: A Story of Sustainable Farming
by Jan Reynolds (Lee & Low, 2009). Take this literary trip to Bali, Indonesia, to see the natural way rice is planted and grown. For generations, the Balinese have used an intricate system of water and crop rotation to become the world's leading producer of rice. This method of sustainable agriculture respects the balance of wildlife and nature. Through photographs and text, readers gain an awareness of how we farm today and the effects that can have on our world tomorrow. 48pp., all ages

Edible Schoolyard: A Universal Idea
by Alice Waters (Chronicle Books, 2008). Chef Alice Waters makes a convincing case for the creation of gardens on school campuses through the idea of Edible Education, integrating academics with growing, cooking, and sharing wholesome, delicious food. Beautiful color photographs show children in the process of learning, creating, eating, and commenting on the experience. Recipes and lessons learned are part of this story. 80pp., all ages

Grow Your Own Pizza: Gardening Plans and Recipes for Kids
by Constance Hardesty (Fulcrum Publishing, 2000). Want a pizza? Grow one! A practical guide with information about easy, medium, and more challenging gardening ventures. 128pp., grades 1–4

Wildlife Gardening
by Martyn Fox (DK Publishing, 2009). Visually appealing guide to open kids' eyes to the world around them, how things grow, and the possibilities of interacting with the "wild." 80pp., grades 2–5

Gardening Bookshelf Topics

Topics	Books	Category
Planting and Growing Methods for planting and providing care are featured in these selections, along with the strong, hardworking people who work the fields.	Cycle of Rice, Cycle of Life: A Story of Sustainable Farming	N
	Edible Schoolyard: A Universal Idea	N
	Gathering the Sun: An Alphabet in Spanish and English	P
	Grow Your Own Pizza: Gardening Plans and Recipes for Kids	N
	Wildlife Gardening	N
Transformation In a garden, change happens; a small seed becomes a huge green watermelon or a juicy red tomato. People can change along with the plants. These are their stories.	Carlos and the Cornfield/Carlos y la milpa de maíz	P
	City Green *	P
	The Curious Garden	P
	The Gardener	P
	How Groundhog's Garden Grew	P
	A Place to Grow (see Immigrants Bookshelf—digital content)	P
	Seedfolks *	F
	The Summer My Father Was Ten	P
	Vegetable Dreams/Huerto Soñado	P
	The Victory Garden *	F
	Wanda's Roses	P
	Xóchitl and the Flowers/Xóchitl, la niña de las flores	P

Page references are given for books that can be found in the bookshelf lists of other chapters.
* These books include examples of young people in service-providing roles.

Picture Books: Gardening

Carlos and the Cornfield/Carlos y la milpa de maíz

by Jan Romero Stevens (Rising Moon, 1995). Young Carlos tries to rush the planting process when he cares more about the money he will earn than the corn he will grow. His conscience causes him to set things right. *Cosechas lo que siembras*—you reap what you sow. English and Spanish text.

City Green

by DyAnne DiSalvo-Ryan (Morrow, 1994). Marcy's plan to turn a vacant lot into a city garden inspires everyone to pitch in, except grouchy, elder Mr. Hammer. Then a few surprises bloom!

The Curious Garden

by Peter Brown (Little, Brown and Company, 2009). Young Liam sees a struggling garden. He's inspired to keep the growing going and to expand it all over the community.

The Gardener

by Sarah Stewart (Farrar, Straus Giroux, 1997). The hard times of the Depression force Lydia to move to an unfamiliar city to stay with her Uncle Jim, a baker with a frown. With determination, she brightens her corner of the world and her uncle's life with flowers.

Gathering the Sun: An Alphabet in Spanish and English

by Alma Flor Ada (HarperCollins, 2001). Twenty-seven poems pay tribute to farm workers and to nature's delicious gifts. Using the Spanish alphabet as a guide, the book takes us into the fields and orchards to learn about people and the pride they carry for their culture. Includes a historical reference to César Chavez. Illustrator Simón Silva grew up in a farm worker's family.

How Groundhog's Garden Grew

by Lynn Cherry (Blue Sky Press, 2003). A wealth of information about planting and plants is packed in the illustrations of this sweet story about a groundhog whose healthy appetite leads him into Squirrel's garden. Fortunately, Squirrel is a fine teacher and guides Groundhog in the process of planting and growing and sharing with others. A fine Thanksgiving feast for all the animals illustrates the collaboration and spirit of giving.

The Summer My Father Was Ten

by Pat Brisson (Boyds Mills Press, 1998). Every year, as the narrator and her father plant their garden, she hears the story "about Mr. Bellavista and the summer my father was ten." What starts as a joke—using a tomato as a baseball—becomes a careless act of vandalism in a neighbor's garden. The elder immigrant neighbor simply asks, "Why?" The next year, to make amends, her father asks to help replant the garden. An act of forgiveness begins a lifelong friendship and a family tradition.

Vegetable Dreams/Huerto Soñado

by Dawn Jeffers (Raven Tree Press, 2006). When Erin's parents think she is too young to plant a garden, an elder neighbor is delighted to lend the tools and time for growing vegetables and friendship. The soft pastel colors match the summer growing season perfectly. In Spanish and English.

Wanda's Roses

by Pat Brisson (Boyd Mills Press, 1994). When Wanda discovers a thorn bush in an empty lot, she is sure it is a rosebush ready to bloom. She clears away trash and waters her "bush." When no roses appear, her neighbors and friends have a surprising solution.

Xóchitl and the Flowers/Xóchitl, la niña de las flores

by Jorge Argueta (Children's Book Press, 2003). Young Xóchitl and her parents, immigrants from El Salvador, work hard to transform a garbage filled backyard into a blooming nursery to provide income for their family. When their landlord tries to stop them, Xóchitl discovers the value of community in her new home in the United States. Based on a true story, this book is written in English and Spanish.

Fiction: Gardening

Seedfolks

by Paul Fleischman (HarperCollins, 1997). These short stories introduce the people in a diverse urban Cleveland neighborhood. People of varying ages and backgrounds transform a city lot filled with garbage into a productive, beautiful garden. In the process, they are also transformed. 69pp., grades 5–10

The Victory Garden

by Lee Kochenderfer (Delacorte, 2002). Teresa Marks and her entire Kansas town await news that World War II will end soon. Many serve, like her older brother Jess, a fighter pilot. To keep busy, Teresa and her dad, like people all over the United States, plant a victory garden to provide fresh produce so other foods can be sent to troops overseas. In spring, when her neighbor is hospitalized, Teresa rallies her friends to tend his garden. As she tries to raise prize-winning tomatoes, Teresa questions the purpose of gardens and of war. She also finds that her garden grows new friendships. 166pp., grades 6–8

DIGITAL CONTENT

**Interviews with Authors:
The Story Behind the Story**

In the companion digital content, you'll find an interview with author Pat Brisson that tells the "story behind the story" of her books, *The Summer My Father Was Ten* and *Wanda's Roses.*

Chapter 10

Healthy Lives, Healthy Choices

Keeping your body healthy is an expression of gratitude to the whole cosmos—the trees, the clouds, everything.

—*Thich Nhat Hanh, peace activist*

Creating a healthy life involves an ongoing series of personal choices. Kids are faced with a wide range of decisions, such as: *What will I eat for lunch? Should I play outside or watch television? I don't like wearing a bike helmet . . . should I leave it at home? Other kids are doing drugs . . . do I want to? Some people say to wait to have sex until I am older or married, but with so many mixed messages, how do I decide what to do?* Many situations require kids of all ages to consider options, seek helpful information, and make choices that promote personal and collective well-being, even when these choices could be difficult or unpopular.

To make matters even more complicated, circumstances can sometimes create enormous challenges and require an immediate call to action. When a loved one has a life threatening illness, families and friends may have to find new strengths and support. If a classmate is injured in a drunken driving accident, a new cause can arise to prevent this from happening again.

The idea of healthy lives, while having many personal aspects, also reaches into the community. Are there parks where kids can play outdoors in every neighborhood? Do local markets sell affordable fresh fruits and vegetables? Is the water toxic in the stream where children play after school? Every community can create a map that shows what is already good and what is ready for change, and kids can instigate or be contributors to this exploration, which can lead to action.

These days, discussing health brings up a host of other topics—many of which are chapter themes in this book. For example, you might end up talking about the environment and how global warming causes drought, which in turn causes illness. Or you might discuss how over-fishing is damaging our waters

and causing a lack of food supplies for future generations. Health also relates to issues of class and poverty, for instance, when the cost of fresh, healthful food is prohibitive, or the basic need for physical education in schools is not being met in some communities.

What we *can* do is become knowledgeable about how to optimize our own health. We can become sensitized to what others are experiencing and respond in thoughtful, caring ways. We can recognize that service learning provides a process to extend what we learn to a broader community where young people—and everyone they reach and teach—can benefit.

He who has health has hope, and he who has hope has everything.

—*Arabian proverb*

Preparation: Getting Ready for Service Learning Involving Healthy Lives, Healthy Choices

The following activities can be used to promote learning and skill development related to healthy lives and choices.

These activities are easily adapted to different grade levels during investigation, preparation, and planning to help your students research key issues, analyze community needs, and gain the knowledge they need to effectively contribute to the design of their service plan. They can often be integrated into the reflection and demonstration stages also, as students lead the activities with others to build awareness. Since literature is often an important part of preparation, you can find recommended titles on this theme in the Healthy Lives, Healthy Choices Bookshelf later in this chapter.

Activity: The Picture of Health. You likely have heard that phrase, "Oh, isn't she *the picture of health!*" What exactly does that look like? This preparation activity easily adapts to a range of grades and abilities. Begin a discussion by asking questions like, "What does health look like?" or "What images come to mind when you hear the word *health* or *healthy*?" Even these two words might evoke different visuals or thoughts. Then have students brainstorm what mediums they might use to construct a representation of this "picture." Depending on materials and resources, students could create magazine collages, draw, take photographs, or use abstract images. Once the visuals are created—and they may all be completely different—discuss how they could be used. With technology, they could be digitally photographed or scanned into documents, which could be turned into posters for a media campaign related to health. Consider having a display of all the "pictures of health." Have students look at their visuals and recommend slogans that could be provocative and eye catching if placed at bus stops, on billboards, or in community centers, or given to influential organizations looking to help the community live healthily. Perhaps there is a sequence to these pictures, so they could be displayed in a particular order or rotated to tell a story.

Students may develop their ideas and their visuals individually, in pairs, or in small groups with same-age or cross-age partners depending on the purpose of the experience. While they are immersed in the creative process, urge them to think personally and practically. Have students consider: What does this have to do with me? In what ways am I already making healthy choices? Have students use their visuals to create lists: What I already do to be healthy; What would be easy to start doing; and What requires more long-term commitment. As the students launch their campaign, they will be able to say, "We are moving toward becoming our own 'picture of health'!"

> Health and good humor are to the human body like sunshine to vegetation.
>
> —*Jean Baptiste Massillon, bishop*

Activity: A Range of Possibilities. With so many issues related to health, what's a young person to do? In schools, with all the academic standards and benchmarks to meet, how can all of these health issues be addressed? For example, students learn about health issues in science class studying anatomy and nutrition. In social studies, they read about plagues or influenzas that affected large populations. In mathematics, they may study insurance costs related to teens and driving. In physical education, the intent is often to develop personal health. Each of these examples can be connected to service learning: Students might create multilingual brochures educating people about free community talks on healthy eating. Students may raise community awareness and contribute to the organization Nothing But Nets, to help mitigate the spread of malaria. Students could campaign to reduce car accidents caused by texting. Or students might create exercise videos for children living in shelters or group homes to promote physical activity.

Consider the ways young people around the globe are responding to health issues:

- **A School-Wide Event**. Many schools participate in events like Pennies for Patience or Jump for Heart in which students earn or collect money for a cause. These experiences can go further to follow the five stages of service learning. Otherwise, adults may end up doing more than their fair share, while young people miss the opportunity to learn about the topic and find answers to questions such as: How does the heart pump differently when I am sitting at a computer compared to when I jump rope? Always keep these events noncompetitive so everyone is working toward a common cause.

- **An Unexpected Circumstance**. When an illness strikes a member of a family or the school community, people want to help. Even when the response must happen immediately—such as a fundraiser for a family with burdensome medical expenses—everyone will move immediately to the "planning" and "action" stages, and rightfully so. However, keep in mind that all of these situations generate questions and concerns. Young people crave information and resources to make sense of the world around them. As you read the interview with author Jordan Sonnenblick in the digital content, note how he was approached by a parent of a student in his class whose sibling had cancer— this parent was looking for a book to help her daughter understand. Students benefit significantly when they are able to ask questions, meet with knowledgeable people, access helpful literature, and reflect to place all the pieces into a context.

• **An Issue of Common Concern.** Young people have rallied around issues they care about and have even astounded adults in the process. In diverse settings, both urban and rural, kids and teens have worked to create recreation centers or coffee houses where they can congregate for healthy social times together. Students have taken initiative to clean up toxic dumps near their schools. And youth clubs have led major citywide biking campaigns to support healthy lifestyles.

Find out what matters most to your students. Provide the support and guidance they need to develop skills and to experience the process of activism. Then let them begin! While younger children may need more structure and assistance, this is an opportunity for youth leadership to evolve for upper elementary students and adolescents. Remember, the process of service learning incorporates ongoing student reflection, so check in and stay attune to their needs and progress.

Making Connections Across the Curriculum

Some service learning activities naturally lend themselves to interdisciplinary work and making connections across the curriculum. These connections strengthen and broaden students' learning, helping them meet academic standards. More than likely, you'll be looking for these connections and ways to encourage them well before the students ever start working on service learning activities. As with the entire service learning process, it helps to remain flexible, because some connections can be spontaneously generated by the questions raised throughout and by the community needs identified by the students. To help you think about cross-curricular connections and where you can look for them, the curricular web for this chapter (page 146) gives examples of many ways this theme can be used in different academic areas. (The service learning scenarios in the next section of the chapter also demonstrate various ways this theme can be used across the curriculum.)

Find Out More About Healthy Lives, Healthy Choices

To learn more about these issues and to get ideas for service and action, visit these Web sites and organizations online:

Farm to School (www.farmtoschool.org) connects schools (K–12) and local farms with the objectives of serving healthy meals in school cafeterias; improving student nutrition; providing agriculture, health, and nutrition education opportunities; and supporting local and regional farmers.

It's My Life (www.pbskids.org/itsmylife) is a place kids and teens can find informative articles about issues they face, share their stories, play games, take quizzes, watch videos, get advice from peers and experts, and contribute their own comments and questions.

KidsHealth (www.kidshealth.org/kid) is the largest and most-visited site on the Web providing trusted health information for kids of all ages.

MyPlate.gov (www.choosemyplate.gov) is a project of The Center for Nutrition Policy and Promotion whose mission is to advance and promote dietary guidance for adults and children.

Healthy Lives, Healthy Choices Across the Curriculum

English/Language Arts

- Read a picture book or novel, and look at the choices made by the characters that contributed to their well-being
- Create a persuasive speech to convince a target audience (elders, young children, parents) about healthy habits
- Examine how marketing has been used to promote smoking cigarettes and to stop people from smoking cigarettes

Social Studies/History

- Compare global diets and lifespans
- Study the health traditions and folk remedies of different cultures
- Learn about the economics of local farms versus factory or industrial farming
- Find out about the "slow food" movement
- Interview elders to find out how popular diets have changed since their childhoods

Languages

- Read recipes in different languages and learn about the food ingredients from various cultures
- Examine how language barriers interfere with health care in developing countries and among immigrant populations
- Look at media campaigns in different countries to address a variety of healthy life choices of interest to students

Theater, Music, & Visual Arts

- Create dramatizations of challenging situations with "what would you do?" moments, and include examples of healthy responses
- Find lyrics of current songs that illustrate some of the difficult choices young people face and create a musical response
- Using photography, capture images of community health

Math

- Compare health care costs in rural, suburban, and urban communities
- Compare food labels for a variety of products
- Chart the percentage of fat, protein, sodium, and carbohydrates eaten in daily diets
- Find statistics regarding the reaction time of braking in a vehicle while under the influence of drugs and alcohol

Healthy Lives, Healthy Choices

Physical Education

- Develop workout routines for different age groups and for people with various physical restrictions
- Use pedometers and chart physical activity of students in a class
- Interview athletes for information about how food choices and exercise can build strength and endurance

Computer

- Research how increased recreational computer use (video games, social networking, etc.) impacts young people's health
- Design screen savers with positive messages about healthy choices and distribute to students and the community
- Create a template for keeping track of daily health habits

Science

- Find out how weather can affect the health of people living with conditions like asthma
- Learn what blood pressure is and how to check it
- Study the impact of cigarettes and alcohol on the body

Service Learning Scenarios: Ideas for Action

Ready to take action? The service learning descriptions that follow have been successfully carried out by elementary, middle, or high school students in schools and with community organizations. Most of these scenarios and examples explicitly include some aspects of investigation, preparation and planning, action, reflection, and demonstration, and all have strong curricular connections. These scenarios can be a rich source of ideas for you to draw upon. Keep in mind that grade levels are provided as a reference; most scenarios can be adapted to suit younger or older students, and many are suitable for cross-age partnerships.

A Child-Friendly Hospital: Kindergarten

A kindergarten teacher in North Adams, Massachusetts, listened to her students describe their fears of going to the hospital. The class decided this was an important issue and contacted the regional hospital about how they could help sick children be more comfortable. The plan: to create a special place for children in one of the emergency treatment rooms. Using math skills and lots of masking tape, students measured and marked the amount of space they were provided. They brainstormed a list of things children would like to have and then began to actualize their ideas. The children brought games, a chalkboard, safe toys, decorative murals, and self-portraits to the hospital. They even included an original book with photographs telling the story of how the room was created. A hospital administrator visited the class several months later and brought along a restraining device previously used to strap down children in the emergency room to keep them calm. She reported that since the new child-friendly room had been in use, the restraining device had not been used at all. She also described an elder patient who was quite distraught about his health and was left alone for a while in this special room. When the nurse returned, the patient was all smiles—busy enjoying the children's portraits and photo album. What came next? Another year, this teacher's class created a child-friendly waiting room in the emergency registration area.

Knit One, Save One: Grade 3

Children who take part in the Knit-for-Service Club at Westwood Elementary in Friendswood, Texas, participated in a national campaign to knit caps for newborn babies overseas. The need for warm clothing is great in developing countries, especially for babies with low birth weight who don't have access to blankets and incubators. This can have a life-saving impact on newborns. Based on what students learned, they extended their action to advocacy. Serving as a Westwood Ambassador, a student knitter, along with a parent and a school counselor, lobbied on Capitol Hill in Washington, D.C., with international organization Save the Children to recruit sponsors for the Newborn, Child, and Mother Survival Act (HR1410). Students also wrote letters (which met academic standards) to President Obama asking for his help to combat the staggering infant mortality rate. These letters were hand delivered to the President's Senior Staff. With knitting, these students exercise their fine motor skills, and with advocacy they exercise their First Amendment rights!

Getting Physical: Grade 3

Third graders in West Hollywood, California, got into all sorts of positions while studying yoga, but the one they enjoyed most was collaborating with senior citizens. In weekly visits to the local senior center, students shared their yoga skills with the older people, and together, the two groups learned how to modify the yoga positions for people who are less agile. Students used their writing and communication skills to produce "We Love Yoga" brochures for community distribution. To reach more elders, students created a series of public service announcements (PSAs) on exercise for daily broadcast on local cable television.

> No matter what accomplishments you make, somebody helps you.
>
> —Wilma Rudolph, athlete

Taking Pennies for Patience to a New Level: Grade 5 (and school-wide)

The students at Ronald L. Sodoma Elementary School in Albion, New York, did not hold your typical penny drive. With a pro-service-learning attitude, a fifth-grade class transformed a run-of-the-mill Pennies for Patients coin collection drive into action stemming from knowledge. The cause was children with leukemia, and students met academic standards while researching leukemia, understanding statistics and health issues involved, developing questions for interviews with healthcare providers, reading the novel *Sadako and the Thousand Paper Cranes* by Eleanor Coerr, and using technology to prepare interactive presentations for every classroom in the school. Do you think the school raised more or fewer pennies than in prior years? Apparently they broke local records, so a member of Pennies for Patients called with good news: the class had been awarded a pizza party! The students' unanimous response was: Give the money to the cause instead. For Albion students involved in service learning, the intrinsic experience is what counts. After this story was published in a local paper, a parent wrote to the class congratulating them on their efforts and telling them what a good organization they were supporting. She explained that her son had leukemia and was almost through with his treatments. She also developed a Web site that charted her son's journey with the disease, so the Albion students were able to connect to someone just a few miles away and watch his progress as he went through treatment.

Taking a Stand: Grades 6–8

Tacoma Park Middle School students in Silver Spring, Maryland, addressed the cruel treatment of animals in the food industry. As part of the process, they led a campaign that included research, community outreach and awareness, and advocacy through policy development. Students researched groups seeking to prevent animal cruelty. They set out to teach other students how their economic decisions directly affect the treatment of animals. Their message: Promote farms, meat processors, and grocers that produce, process, and stock meats from animals that were treated humanely. Students then posted advertisements and held a fair to promote businesses that support humane practices. They raised funds for organizations and wrote letters to restaurants and grocers asking them to check their sources and buy humane. Students also made a presentation to Silver Spring's City Council asking that cruel practices be prohibited, and to the Maryland Board of Education requesting that only humanely produced meats be served in the state's schools. The students

kept journals, wrote articles for a newsletter and Web site, and reflected frequently on their effectiveness.

Kids' Health Matters: Grade 7

The poor nutritional habits of teens and the consequences of those habits have become headline news. But obesity and diabetes aren't the only health threats facing kids. Asthma, often linked to air pollution, is the third-ranking cause of hospitalization among kids under 15. Domestic violence also remains a silent stalker. And for children living in areas with high housing density, low socioeconomic status, and no safe play environments, getting hit by a car is a real concern. The injury rate among black children is almost twice that of white children.* Seventh graders at the Lang Youth Medical Program in Manhattan created four sixty-second public service announcements about these pressing health concerns. Their PSAs combined photographs with audio that they composed, performed, and edited.

Break from Boredom: Grade 8

"There's nothing to do in this boring town." This is a common refrain heard from teens in a typical small town. Students in Eldorado, Texas, were no exception. Six years ago, a group of at-risk students in an eighth-grade language arts class wrestled with a solution to this problem. Out of that discussion, the Eagle Arcade Youth Center was born. Once the students knew their purpose, they began to work on the plan. They crafted a proposal, appeared before the county commissioners' court, and received the green light to proceed with their proposal. The county commissioners allowed the students to convert a basement room in a building adjacent to the courthouse into a teen's dream room! Each student brought his or her idea of what to include in the room. Then they created a school-wide survey and polled the student body. After determining which items were most popular, the students priced pool tables, foosball games, ping-pong tables, and other items on their list. The county commissioners committed to a modest yearly stipend, and local individuals contributed money as well. After several shopping trips and many hours of set up time, the Eagle Arcade Youth Center opened its doors to a curious and

---

* National SAFE KIDS Campaign (NSKC). Pedestrian Injury Fact Sheet. Washington, DC: NSKC, 2004.

excited group of teens and tweens. Six years later, the center still exists. The dreamers in that eighth-grade class have graduated, but their contribution to their community continues.

> It is our choices, Harry, that show who we truly are, far more than our abilities.
>
> —*Professor Dumbledore, in* Harry Potter and the Chamber of Secrets

Knowing the Triggers: Grades 7 and 8

Confidence, stress reduction, and homework completion are interwoven topics covered by middle school students in Hialeah, Florida. First semester, seventh and eighth graders studied stress reduction methods and anger management to overcome tension and anger that interfere with learning. After learning the triggers for emotional conflict, they wrote lessons for mentoring projects and taught third graders homework strategies. School counselors had identified third grade as the time when learning good homework habits was essential for the transition to the upper elementary grades. Second semester, the tutoring continued every week.

Beauty Is More than Skin Deep: Grades 9–12

If "we are what we eat," does it also matter what we put *on* our bodies in the form of cosmetics? Based in Marin County, California, the Teens for Safe Cosmetics Web site states that many cosmetics expose consumers to toxic chemicals. Do we suffer from complacency about environmental toxins? Influenced by parent organization Search for the Cause, a group that aims to "investigate how exposures in our daily lives increase the risk of cancer," Teens for Safe Cosmetics focused on spreading awareness among young people about potentially carcinogenic ingredients found in personal care and beauty products. According to the Teens for Cosmetics Web site, the average teen is exposed to about 200 chemicals a day through personal cosmetic products like eye shadow, mascara, shampoo, and deodorant. Since our skin is our largest organ, should we be paying more attention to these products? On the site, teens posted their "Dirty Dozen"—twelve toxic chemicals and the everyday products they are found in.

Though young, these activists were seriously engaged in study and sharp political analysis to address the sixty-billion-dollar cosmetics industry head-on. Their work took them to California's state capitol to lobby for a new law that requires the reporting of cosmetic ingredients to the government. This law passed in January 2007. Visit the Teens for Cosmetics Web site at www.teensturninggreen.org to see what's next for these kids determined to have both health and beauty!

Get Up, Power Up: Grades 9–12

Teens in North Anson, Maine, not only got up early, they also got in shape and influenced their peers to do the same. Making adolescent obesity their challenge—an issue that has troubled the nation's top health experts—this group of high school athletes set out to reverse the trend by starting before-school exercise groups. Along the way, they hoped to discover some factors that prevent teens from keeping fit. Students used electronic Body Composition Monitors and learned to measure their percentages of body fat and muscle mass and chart their metabolic rate. To monitor progress and outcomes, the teens charted the progress of members and nonmembers of the exercise groups to determine whether physical fitness relates to such indicators as school attendance, academic achievement, or disciplinary referrals. Their aim was to combine factual education and tough physical conditioning with the influential social networking that characterizes the high school years. What was learned from this combination? One student stated, "We learned a lot about how to make better choices in our lives—like eating right and not drinking on the weekends. And we learned to 'do the right thing,' which means treating people fairly and helping each other out."

Lessons from the Middle Ages: Grades 9–12

High school teachers in Berkeley used *When Plague Strikes: The Black Death, Smallpox, AIDS* to address issues of tolerance on their campus. The book discusses the issues of intolerance, blame, and scapegoating as they relate to the diseases in the title. Students have used their studies to plan a tolerance campaign at their high school, educating their peers about the perils of scapegoating and the possibilities of creating a more tolerant and inclusive campus.

Walk, Bike, Serve in Idaho: Grades 9–12

Biking and walking along the Portneuf River has become more enjoyable for the residents of Pocatello, Idaho, thanks in part to New Horizon High School students. These alternative school students adopted a trailhead and created a path for community access. With help from a local foundation, they created the trail, cleared brush and litter, and installed signs explaining local geology. The students involved are members of the Alameda Bike Club, an elective course that empowers young people through engagement in bike-related service learning projects. Students also fix up bikes during class for "Free Bike Rides" at the local Visitor's Center.

Subsistence Living and Community Renewal: Grades 9–12

Food is expensive in rural Alaska. Yupik Eskimo teens in Russian Mission, Alaska, designed a process to research the village's eating habits to determine what portion of foods people eat are caught in the wild. With a research grant from the nonprofit What Kids Can Do and the Bill and Melinda Gates Foundation, students surveyed all eighty households in the village (some sheltering three or more generations). Their results showed an increase in subsistence eating, and the survey began an impromptu community dialogue on the subjects of food, nutrition, and health. Students realized the added value from subsistence living—eating locally grown food. A community member noted, "We used to think we had to have [food] from the store, things we've seen on TV. Now we enjoy more what we can get here—salmon, moose, berries, and all the food that we have to prepare for the winter. We are teaching this to the grandkids again, so they can live a better life." The grant also sponsored students' travel to nearby native villages to present their learning at schools and tribal councils. Nine junior high school students traveled to Tokyo, Japan, to the Ecoplus International Symposium on the Environment, where they danced, drummed, and made presentations to place their culture into global and historical perspective.

Responding to Drug Use with Care: Grades 9–12

Franklin County Community Education Center operates seven high schools in Russellville, Alabama. Each school supports Youth Organized for Disaster Action (YODA) service learning activities. Students partnered with the Franklin County Sheriff's Department to be trained in Methamphetamine Awareness and Community Education. YODA students were particularly interested in providing services for children removed from homes where methamphetamine was used, because no personal items can be removed due to contamination. Students designed educational pamphlets discussing the dangers of methamphetamine use for distribution in their community. They also researched, designed, and compiled YODA Care Bags containing personal items, such as shampoo, soap, and toothpaste, for distribution by the Alabama Department of Human Resources to these affected children.

Fast, Yes . . . But Healthy? Grade 11

A high school junior in the Los Angeles area wanted to enjoy a meal out with her family. The problem: both her parents had diabetes and in her low-income neighborhood there were only fast-food restaurants. So she began a campaign with support from her high school civics teacher. She contacted her city council member about ways to control what new restaurants open in the area. She created flyers for restaurants with information about diabetes and asked them to note "health-friendly" items on their menus. As support grew and other students became involved, they all realized they could make better choices themselves. They also learned that consumer influence can be more powerful in numbers.

Setting the Stage for Drug-Free Youth: Grades 11 and 12

In rural Guntersville, Alabama, students formed the Drug Free Marshall County Youth Council, a coalition designed to present drug prevention education through peer interaction and one-on-one mentoring. These busy eleventh and twelfth graders were trained in drug prevention education to serve as role models and positively influence children in kindergarten through sixth grade. Drug task force police officers and prevention specialists provided the training, so the youth leaders could present information to students during Red Ribbon Week. Their activities included drug-free bingo, reading books, artwork, poster contests, and sidewalk chalk messages. They also provided tutoring to the younger kids, and contributed to other art and summer programs.

Driving Safe in Pennsylvania: Grades 11–12

Car crashes are a leading cause of death for U.S. teenagers. The New Castle Senior High School Project Ignition Team in Pennsylvania made "Driving Safe" a multiyear message. What was their message? They encouraged safe driving habits through increased seat belt use, increased adherence to traffic controls and laws, and decreased driving distractions, while emphasizing the dangers of drinking and driving. Like many teens, they knew the pain of losing friends from car crashes caused by speeding, distractions, and not wearing a seat belt. So they took their message and spread it to their school, surrounding community, and across Pennsylvania, targeting community events with large crowds like football and basketball games, parades, and Election Day at the polls. To inspire other youth advocates, New Castle hosted a Safety Summit for teens from four counties. To influence young kids, they created a coloring book for local elementary schools to teach school bus safety. Visit the State Farm Web site for more details.

Let's Talk About Sex: High School

High school students enrolled in Blackstone Academy Charter School's Community Involvement course chose to meet with Planned Parenthood Rhode Island to learn about sex-related health problems and needs in their community. The students embarked on a service learning project with Planned Parenthood—educating community teens about safe sex practices. For several weeks, students participated in a comprehensive Peer Educator program, learning about safe sex practices and sexually transmitted diseases. Students then brainstormed potential topics and formed small groups to choose particular issues. Each group researched ideas and planned workshops. Students studied presentation and leadership styles, conducted dress rehearsals, and adjusted their presentations according to group feedback. Through offering workshops at local schools, at KIDS Consortium's annual Student Summit in Maine, and at a local World AIDS Day event, and by hosting a Pregnancy Prevention Day at their school, they educated over 300 area teens about safe sex practices. For more information visit www.kidsconsortium.org.

The Healthy Lives, Healthy Choices Bookshelf

In developing healthful life styles and influencing others to do the same, books become one of the best resources. Either factual or fiction, books are a way to find out what other people know or are doing, even if these people are characters in a story. To help you find books relevant to the health-related community issues students choose to learn about and address, the book chart (pages 152–153) classifies the titles according to several topic areas: what history shows us, journeys to health, teen concerns, what we need to know, and taking action, supporting a cause.

In general, the bookshelf features:

- An annotated bibliography arranged and alphabetized by title according to the general categories of nonfiction (N), picture books (P), and fiction (F). For nonfiction and fiction, length and recommended grade levels are included. The entries in the picture book category do not include suggested grade levels, since they can be successfully used with all ages.

- A chart organized by topic and category to help you find books relevant to particular projects.

- Recommendations from service learning colleagues and experts that include a book summary and ideas for service learning connections. (The number of recommended books varies in each bookshelf.)

- *Please note:* additional titles for this category are listed in the digital content; some of these were out of print at the time of publication but still worth finding.

Nonfiction: Healthy Lives, Healthy Choices

Chew on This: Everything You Don't Want to Know About Fast Food

by Eric Schlosser and Charles Wilson (Houghton Mifflin, 2006). This critical history of the U.S. fast-food industry tells captivating anecdotes including the vast preference among New Yorkers for cow tongue and spinach over hamburgers in 1925. It traces the growth of the fast-food industry, the questionable working conditions that have kept the products so cheap, and the life-threatening health problems that have arisen from addiction and dependence on fast food. 304pp., grades 6–12

Healthy Lives, Healthy Choices Bookshelf Topics

Topics	Books	Category
What History Shows Us Look back in time to find people striving for healthy lives and meeting considerable challenges in these stories of strength and perseverance.	A Company of Fools Run Far, Run Fast Small Steps: The Year I Got Polio When Plague Strikes: The Black Death, Smallpox, AIDS The White Witch Winnie's War	F F (GN) N (see page 81) F F
Journeys to Health Whether fact or fiction, these tales show how people move toward health even when facing obstacles along the way.	Bluish Brushing Mom's Hair Cold Hands, Warm Heart The Dot Hole in My Life I Get So Hungry My Great Big Mamma Notes from the Midnight Driver Wilma Unlimited: How Wilma Rudolph Became the World's Fastest Woman	F F F P N P P F P
Teen Concerns As they are growing and aiming to clarify their identity and place in the world, young people struggle with issues surrounding relationships, drugs, and sex; literature offers a portal for discussion and reduces isolation.	Apart Breathing Underwater Club Meds Cheater: A Novel Food, Girls, and Other Things I Can't Have Hole in My Life How to Build a House Inexcusable Jumping Off Swings Last Night I Sang to the Monster A Room on Lorelei Street Shooting Stars Slam The Way	F F F F F N (see page 116) F F F F F F F

What We Need to Know These selections help students see the "big picture" of health and learn information that can support them in finding ways to help others.	Chew on This: Everything You Don't Want to Know About
	    Fast Food
	Eating Animals (see digital content)
	Eat Right! How You Can Make Good Food Choices
	Food for Thought: The Stories Behind the Things We Eat
	Lunch with Lenin
	Made You Look: How Advertising Works and Why You
	    Should Know
	Nana, What's Cancer?
	The Omnivore's Dilemma: The Secrets Behind What You
	    Eat (see digital content)
		N
		N
		N
		N
		F
		
		N
		N
		
		N

Page references are given for books that can be found in the bookshelf lists of other chapters.
(GN) These books are graphic novels.

Healthy Lives, Healthy Choices Bookshelf Topics (continued)

Topics	Books	Category
Taking Action, Supporting a Cause At the core of these books is social action—the gestures, the work, and the results.	*Drums, Girls, and Dangerous Pie* *Healing Our World: Inside Doctors Without Borders* *Melissa Parkington's Beautiful, Beautiful Hair* *Sadako and the Thousand Paper Cranes* *Taking Action Against Drugs*	F (see page 222) P F N

Page references are given for books that can be found in the bookshelf lists of other chapters.
(GN) These books are graphic novels.

DIGITAL CONTENT

Recommendation from the Field

Eating Animals by Jonathan Safran Foer (Little, Brown, 2009). 341pp., grades 11–12

Eat Right! How You Can Make Good Food Choices

by Matt Doeden (Lerner Publications, 2008). This easy-to-read guide builds our appetite to think about the food we eat and helps us make healthier choices by presenting the facts of nutrition and food science. 64pp., grades 4–7

Food for Thought: The Stories Behind the Things We Eat

by Ken Robbins (Flash Point, 2009). Students will want to read this fascinating book cover to cover. They will find out the history behind some of their favorite produce, such as the likelihood that oranges were first grown by the Chinese, who were also responsible for a sauce called kat siap that we put on French fries today. Readers learn the history of expressions such as, "You're the apple of my eye," and facts like this one: 24 billion pounds of bananas are grown and eaten in India every year. 48pp., grades 1–5

Hole in My Life

by Jack Gantos (Farrar, Straus, and Giroux, 2004). In this frank memoir, author Jack Gantos carries us through his teen and young adult years when his choices grew from mistake to tragedy. Always striving to be a writer, he thought he lacked experience and adventure. Jack spent his high school years living on his own in south Florida, and later he crewed a boat loaded with drugs from the Virgin Islands to New York City where he learned the trip was a setup. He reveals the horrors of federal prison and how writing saved his life, providing the means for him to reconcile with his past and build his future. 208pp., grades 9–12, mature themes

Made You Look: How Advertising Works and Why You Should Know

by Shari Graydon (Annick Press, 2003). Finally, a book for teens to help them become media savvy and know how to avoid the grips of advertising. This book explains "ad power" so readers understand who ads are targeting and how. And for activism? Many ideas are included for speaking out, taking on issues, and getting really good at "kid power." A must-read. 120pp., grades 5–9

Nana, What's Cancer?

by Beverlye Hyman Fead and Tessa Mae Hamermesh (American Cancer Society). When her grandmother was diagnosed with stage IV cancer, ten-year-old Tessa was filled with questions. The book captures the heartfelt conversation between the two generations with honest answers and insights. 55pp., grades 4–8

DIGITAL CONTENT

Recommendation from the Field

The Omnivore's Dilemma: The Secrets Behind What You Eat (Young Readers Edition) by Michael Pollan (Dial, 2009). 352pp., young adult

---

Taking Action Against Drugs

by Jacqui Bailey (Rosen Publishing, 2009). Did you know that until 2005 caffeine was listed as a banned substance by the Olympic Committee? According to this book, drugs are pervasive in society. News coverage includes drugs in sports, drug cartels, tobacco companies targeting youth, and young children experimenting with drugs, sometimes putting their lives at risk. An informative book that will get kids thinking and talking. 48pp., grades 5–8

Picture Books: Healthy Lives, Healthy Choices

The Dot

by Peter H. Reynolds (Candlewick Press, 2003). At the end of art class, Vashti's page is blank. Her teacher proves to her that she can in fact make a mark, and the next day Vashti finds the "dot" she made hanging on the wall. Soon her one dot turns into many, many colorful dots and circles. When a boy marvels at her paintings and laments that he cannot even draw a straight line, she has him try so he can see for himself!

I Get So Hungry

by Bebe Moore Campbell (Putnam Juvenile, 2008). When Nikki tells her mom she wants to try to lose weight, her mom tells her she comes from a long line of big-boned women. When Nikki joins her teacher on morning walks, soon she and her mom are taking weekend walks together. Nikki's story teaches readers of all age groups that the time is always right to make the lifestyle changes necessary for happier and healthier living.

Melissa Parkington's Beautiful, Beautiful Hair

by Pat Brisson (Boyds Mills Press, 2006). Melissa has beautiful hair, which everyone notices. So why is Melissa complaining? "I want to be seen for something beyond my hair!" she says. Melissa's determination leads to her cutting her hair for Locks of Love, a nonprofit organization that makes human hair wigs for cancer patients. Now Melissa is certain her hair will be of great value for someone else, and Melissa is just fine with that.

My Great Big Mamma

by Olivier Ka (Groundwood Books, 2008). The heart-warming story of a mother who decides to go on a diet, and her son who loves her in all her abundance and would have her no other way.

Wilma Unlimited: How Wilma Rudolph Became the World's Fastest Woman

by Kathleen Krull (Voyager Books, 1996). Wilma Rudolph had many hurdles to overcome before proving her athletic skills in the 1960 Olympic Games. She was born very tiny—too tiny, some thought—to survive. She became sick easily and often, which was especially problematic in the southern United States where the standards were poor for medical care for African Americans. This gracefully illustrated book brings to life the moving story of one woman's triumph over countless adversities.

Fiction: Healthy Lives, Healthy Choices

Apart

by R. P. McIntyre and Wendy McIntyre (Groundwood Books, 2007). High school senior Jessica didn't suspect that an ad she placed in a newspaper to find her missing father would lead to a letter from Sween, a teen living on the other side of Canada. This novel in letters traces the yearlong correspondence in which the two teens share their deeply troubling stories. Jessica writes about her dysfunctional family, including an often-absent father with erratic and illegal behaviors, a brother with autism, and a mother who abdicates her role. Sween struggles with being bipolar and is unable to fit within his family, despite their wealth and status. Facing challenging choices as they move toward adulthood, these two friends find support and solace in their letters. Will finally meeting face-to-face put all of this at risk? 176pp., grades 7–12, mature themes

Bluish

by Virginia Hamilton (Scholastic, 1999). Natalie is different from other fifth graders in Dreenie's class. She arrives in a wheelchair wearing a wool cap and holding a dog on her lap, and her pale skin has a bluish tint from chemotherapy. Dreenie's journal describes her fears and fascination as she develops a close friendship with a girl struggling with illness and moving toward health. And then there is Tuli, Dreenie's biracial friend who so wants to be a beautiful Latina. Overall, this is a story of three girls who learn, laugh, and grow together. 128pp., grades 4–7

Breathing Underwater

by Alex Flinn (HarperTeen, 2002). Teenager Nick has hit his girlfriend, has a restraining order filed against him, and tries to make sense of his actions and his life. Seeing the pattern of violence in Nick's home, the reader recognizes the difficulties teens and young males in particular may have these days when turbulent lives result in uncontrolled choices. 272pp., young adult

Brushing Mom's Hair

by Andrea Cheng (Wordsong, 2009). Told in first person, this easy-to-read book of poems leads us through the experience of a girl whose mother has cancer. Worry seems to overcome this fourteen-year-old. Dance, art, and kind adults help dispel the loneliness and remind her that life is still there to enjoy. 59pp., grades 5–8

Cheater: A Novel

by Michael Laser (Dutton Juvenile, 2008). Karl Petrofsky gets 100s on tests and an A+ on every paper and he makes learning look too easy. For this eleventh grader, life in school is seen from the outside. While admiring the life of the popular kids, Karl's eye catches Blaine Shore looking at his cell phone during a test. Was he cheating? With a war on cheating set by the principal and the chance to finally be popular by helping in a high-tech cheating ring, what's a "geek" to do? This novel has plenty of humor and unexpected plot twists, making the ethics of decisions brilliantly come to life. 240pp., grades 7–12

Club Meds

by Katherine Hall Page (Simon Pulse, 2006). Jack needed to start taking prescription medication when he was in third grade. Club Meds is a support group for kids on medication at Busby Memorial High School. The friendships formed in

Club Meds help members as they deal with isolation, teasing, and bullying by other students. Sam faces the school bully with courage and everyone learns about respect and acceptance. 176pp., grades 6–10

Cold Hands, Warm Heart

by Jill Wolfson (Henry Holt, 2009). When an athletic teen, Amanda, suddenly dies, and Dani, born with a heart on the wrong side of her body, receives Amanda's heart as a transplant, a host of lives are touched and changed. This story interweaves the network of family and friends impacted by this life-giving generosity, tells of other young people awaiting the possibility of being a transplant recipient, and provides a real context of friendship, budding romance, and hospital realities. 256pp., grades 8–10

A Company of Fools

by Deborah Ellis (Fitzhenry & Whiteside, 2007). In the Abbey of St. Luc near Paris in 1349, Henri, Micah, and Brother Bart show great courage and compassion as the plague sweeps through Europe. The two boys and others in the Abbey's choir sing, laugh, and care for the sick. In spite of the plague, Henri and Micah have grand adventures and joy. This story tells how people coped with fear and death as they struggled through a year in history in which 25 million people died. A great read that encourages hope. 192pp., grades 5–8

Drums, Girls, and Dangerous Pie

by Jordan Sonnenblick (Scholastic, 2006). Meet Steven Alper, a typical eighth grader, except he is an exceptional drummer. Life appears fairly normal until his younger brother falls and is diagnosed with leukemia. Steven tries to keep others from knowing and stay afloat through his mother's complete absorption and his father's retreat. He finally realizes that being part of a caring community really does make the difference, and he draws needed support from his friends while raising community awareness of leukemia. The author's wit and his characters' resilience make this a book readers want to finish and share with others immediately. 288pp., grades 5–8

Food, Girls, and Other Things I Can't Have

by Allen Zadoff (Egmont, 2009). It's sophomore year and Andy Zansky knows he's doomed to repeat the same mistakes as last year, when he was the overweight geek and butt of jokes ... unless he makes a different choice. One choice will lead Andy to the Model U.N. with his best friend, while another choice will take him to football tryouts. Can he make the varsity team, get the girl, and make all the problems disappear—including his parents' divorce—by making this one choice? 320pp., young adult

Inexcusable

by Chris Lynch (Altheneum Books, 2007). This haunting story is about dating, intimacy, and trust. It is a powerful read about individual perception and perspective. Did Keir do something wrong? Is he a good guy or is he a rapist? A disturbing story that will make young men and women think about intimate relationships. 176pp., grades 9–12, mature themes

Jumping Off Swings

by Jo Knowles (Candlewick Press, 2009). Four high school students tell their stories, all surrounding the ramifications of an unexpected and unwanted pregnancy. Meet Ellie who wants desperately to be loved, her friend Corinne who sticks by her, Caleb the boy who always cared, and Josh who would do anything to take back that one night. 240pp., grades 9–12, mature themes

Last Night I Sang to the Monster

by Benjamin Alire Sáenz (Cinco Puntos Press, 2009). This exceptional novel tells in first person the experience of eighteen-year-old Zach. He should be in high school, but instead he's in rehab for alcoholism and can't recall how he got there. In fact, he doesn't want the memory of what happened, because he's sure it's all bad. He doesn't want to feel. Through his therapy and relationships with other residents, Zach makes amazing self-discoveries and learns that his heart can experience joy and love again. A realistic and compelling page-turner. 304pp., grades 9–12, mature themes

Lunch with Lenin

by Deborah Ellis (Fitzhenry & Whiteside, 2008). These ten short stories are based on the real lives of young people all over the world affected by the drug trade and substance abuse. The connections stun the reader, while the storylines have engaging twists. An Afghan family loses their livelihood when poppy fields are destroyed. A boy seeks marijuana for his ailing grandmother. By drawing together stories from diverse settings, Ellis leads readers to recognize the global issues that urgently require response. 192pp., grades 7–12

Notes from the Midnight Driver

by Jordan Sonnenblick (Scholastic Press, 2006). Alex Gregory is fed up and decides to drink and drive (he's underage) and tell off his father who is living with Alex's third-grade teacher. As he steers the car to the end of the block, Alex decapitates a neighbor's lawn gnome and recognizes trouble is afoot. He later appears in court, and the judge gives him an option for his punishment. Alex chooses to complete community service hours by spending time with an elder man with emphysema in a nursing home. To Alex's surprise, Solomon Lewis becomes the best thing that ever happened to him. Includes recurring characters from *Drums, Girls, and Dangerous Pie*. 288pp., grades 8–12

A Room on Lorelei Street

by Mary E. Pearson (Henry Holt and Co., 2005). Seventeen-year-old Zoe faces an unexpected venture into adulthood when she rents her own apartment to get away from her alcoholic mother. She still wants to be cared for, but must learn how to make smart choices and recover from mistakes along the way. 272pp., grades 9–12

Run Far, Run Fast

by Timothy Decker (Front Street, 2007). Provocatively illustrated in comic-strip style, this black and white graphic novel tells of the pestilence that struck fourteenth-century Europe. When a family is quarantined, the mother sneaks her young daughter through a hole in the wood beams so she can make her way alone through the dismal world. The daughter eventually returns to salvage something of her family. 40pp., grades K–3

DIGITAL CONTENT

Recommendation from the Field

Sadako and the Thousand Paper Cranes by Eleanor Coerr (Puffin, 2004). 80pp., grades 4–7

Shooting Star

by Fredrick McKissack Jr. (Atheneum, 2009). Jomo Rogers is just looking for that little "edge" to improve his talents. How dangerous could enhancement drugs really be? As Jomo's life spins out of control, he finds out. 288pp., young adult

Slam

by Nick Hornby (Putnam Juvenile, 2007). *Slam* explores teenage pregnancy and nontraditional family relationships, narrated by a young father who is a skateboarder and Tony Hawk fan. Through the father's conversations with a poster of Hawk and "flash forwards," the reader gains a deep appreciation of his situation. For teachers comfortable with this subject matter (and explicit language about condom use), *Slam* is an effective discussion starter about teen pregnancy. The author presents both the challenges of becoming a teen parent and the deep feelings of love and responsibility that come with the territory. 304pp., young adult, mature themes

Small Steps: The Year I Got Polio

by Peg Kehret (Albert Whitman, 1996). Peg led a normal life until the day in 1949 when she suddenly fell ill. The doctor gave the dreaded diagnosis: polio. At age 12, Peg was isolated from her family and friends in a hospital with an unknown prognosis. In this memoir, the author chronicles the following eight months, where, aided by doctors and therapists, a supportive family, and courageous roommates, she regains the ability to walk. 184pp., grades 4–6

The Way

by Joseph Bruchac (Darby Creek Publishing, 2007). Cody goes unnoticed most of the time—except now, at Long River High, he has become the target for bullying. Suddenly an uncle he has never met arrives, bringing Native American folklore and teachings along with martial arts. As he and his uncle help each other, Cody arrives at an understanding of "The Way"—a path to peace in the midst of anger. 156pp., grades 7–12

The White Witch

by Janet Graber (Roaring Brook Press, 2009). Since her mom died, Gwendolyn Riston usually ignores the whispers that her mother was a witch. With a terrible plague stretching across England in the mid-1600s, blame falls on her young shoulders. Hidden away by her father before he travels, Gwendolyn observes how the villagers behave—their scapegoating, their deaths—and she finally comes forward to stand her ground. The language and imagery brings the reader into the time, and a glossary of old English words is included. 160pp., grades 5–9

Winnie's War

by Jenny Moss (Walker Books for Young Readers, 2009). The Spanish Influenza epidemic of 1918 has arrived in Houston, Texas, some thought brought from Europe by soldiers returning from war overseas. All Winnie cares about is keeping the disease away from her troubled momma and two frail sisters. Just twelve years old, Winnie has more than enough to deal with—all the funerals her father builds coffins for, her social-climbing grandmother, and the anti-Semitism aimed at her best friend's family. 192pp., grades 5–8

DIGITAL CONTENT

Interviews with Authors: The Story Behind the Story

In the companion digital content, you'll find an interview with author Jordan Sonnenblick that tells the "story behind the story" of his books *Drums, Girls, and Dangerous Pie; Notes from the Midnight Driver;* and *After Ever After.*

Chapter 11

Hunger, Homelessness, and Poverty

If you don't like the way the world is, you change it. You have an obligation to change it. You just do it one step at a time.

—Marian Wright Edelman, founder, Children's Defense Fund

Hunger and homelessness are global concerns. They are sometimes considered urban ills, but the reality is they are found in every country and in every community, rural and urban. Hunger and homelessness have many different causes. People throughout history have been uprooted and left without homes because of war or famine. Indigenous groups such as the Native Americans in the United States have been driven from their ancestral lands. Natural disasters also take a toll: floods, droughts, tornados, hurricanes, earthquakes, and fires can all devastate a community or destroy crops. Sometimes, events that do not affect entire communities create havoc in individual lives: People may face poverty and homelessness after losing their jobs or because of unexpected medical expenses, a downturn in the economy, or an advance in technology that replaces traditional work skills.

Children are frequently those most affected by poverty in modern society. Many children live at or below the poverty level.

- In the United States, almost 14 million children live in poverty.[*]

- More than 1.5 million U.S. children are without a home—that's 1 in 50 kids.[**]

- Worldwide nearly 650 million children live in extreme poverty.[***]

Other children may see people living on the streets, in cars, and in shelters and wonder why. During their first years of school, children learn about people's basic needs: food, clothing, and shelter. Yet some of the same children lack these basic necessities, and most are cognizant that many people live and struggle without them.

Peace, in the sense of absence of war, is of little value to someone who is dying of hunger or cold. Peace can only last where human rights are respected, where people are fed, and where individuals and nations are free.

—Tenzin Gyatso, the Fourteenth Dalai Lama

Through service learning, students examine conditions that cause poverty and lead to hunger and homelessness. They can become familiar with local needs and the services that address them. Studying history through the lenses of hunger, homelessness, and poverty makes issues of politics, power, and class struggles come alive by placing real people in real situations. Literature, both fiction and nonfiction, also vividly depicts events and the people who live in difficult circumstances, and can help clarify the myths and erroneous assumptions that create greater distances between people on different sides of the issue. Today, young people around the globe are contributing to the immediate needs related to this theme and becoming more adept at examining systems, questioning existing policies, and being part of the long-term meaningful response.

[*] *Basic Facts About Low-Income Children: Children Under Age 18*, Vanessa R. Wight and Michelle Chau, National Center for Children in Poverty, 2009
[**] The National Center on Family Homelessness, 2009
[***] The Global Study on Child Poverty and Disparities (Bangladesh: UNICEF, 2007–2009)

Preparation: Getting Ready for Service Learning Involving Hunger, Homelessness, and Poverty

 The following activities can be used to promote learning and skill development related to hunger, homelessness, and poverty. These activities are easily adapted to different grade levels during investigation, preparation, and planning to help your students examine key issues through research, analyze community needs, and gain the knowledge they need to effectively contribute to the design of their service plan. They can often be integrated into reflection and demonstration as students can lead the activities with others to build awareness. Since literature is often an important part of preparation, you can find recommended titles on this theme in the Hunger, Homelessness, and Poverty Bookshelf later in this chapter.

Activity: What Shape Is Your Pyramid? From the four food groups to the food pyramid, is there really one shape for all of us? Ask students to share their families' particular relationship to eating and nutrition. In diverse communities, students will have the opportunity to learn about a range of foods, from bok choy and dal to grits and falafel, and to find out how different cultures and communities address their dietary requirements. This can help students develop appreciation for the diversity in their communities and better analyze and understand the needs of those communities.

Activity: Learning About the Issues. How do we put a face on hunger and homelessness? How do we separate fact from fiction, myth from knowledge? You can try one or all of the following activities to start your students thinking.

- Give each student a piece of drawing paper and a crayon or marker (keep this simple). Ask students to draw a picture of somebody who is hungry. Let them know they can make a simple drawing and that they will have five minutes to finish. Encourage them to work individually and quietly. When everyone is done, ask students to place their drawings where others can see them. Ask the students to describe the person they drew—young, old, single, part of a family, man, woman, child—and how this person portrays hunger.

- Have students work in small groups. Assign each group one population: senior citizens, veterans, immigrants, families with children, unemployed people, people who are homeless. The students will spend five minutes thinking why this particular population might be hungry and

---

Find Out More About Hunger, Homelessness, and Poverty

To learn more about these issues and to get ideas for service and action, visit these Web sites and organizations online:

Free Rice (www.freerice.com) is a nonprofit Web site run by the United Nations World Food Program to help end hunger. By providing correct answers to trivia questions on the home page, rice grains are donated where needed across the globe.

Habitat for Humanity's youth programs (www.habitat .org/youthprograms) offer ways for young people to get involved in the organization's mission to eliminate poverty housing and homelessness and make decent shelter a matter of conscience and action.

Oxfam America (www.oxfamamerica.org) and **Oxfam International** (www.oxfam.org) are dedicated to finding long-term solutions to poverty, hunger, and social injustice around the world. Visit their "Cool Planet" site (www.oxfam.org.uk/coolplanet/kidsweb) for kid-friendly activities and stories.

Share Our Strength (www.strength.org) mobilizes individuals and industries to lend their talents to raise funds and awareness for the fight against hunger and poverty, addressing immediate and long-term solutions. Their Great American Bake Sale program offers educational curriculum and opportunities to work toward eliminating childhood hunger in America.

might need assistance with food. They will then share their thoughts with classmates, who can ask questions. As a follow up, you or a guest speaker can present facts on these populations (provided by local, state, or national agencies), *and/or* each small group can research its assigned population to gather information about hunger and poverty to be presented to the class.

- Invite a representative from a local agency who works with people who are in need of assistance with food to help answer questions and brainstorm ways the class can provide meaningful assistance.

The outrage of hunger amidst plenty will never be solved by "experts" somewhere. It will only be solved when people like you and me decide to act.

—*Frances Moore Lappe, author*

Making Connections Across the Curriculum

Some service learning activities naturally lend themselves to interdisciplinary work and making connections across the curriculum. These connections strengthen and broaden student learning, helping them meet academic standards. More than likely, you'll be looking for these connections and ways to encourage them well before the students ever start working on service learning activities. As with the entire service learning process, it helps to remain flexible, because some connections can be spontaneously generated by the questions raised throughout and by the community needs identified by the students. To help you think about cross-curricular connections and where you can look for them, the curricular web for this chapter (page 160) gives examples of many different ways this theme can be used in different academic areas. (The service learning scenarios in the next section of the chapter also demonstrate various ways this theme can be used across the curriculum.)

Service Learning Scenarios: Ideas for Action

Ready to take action? The service learning descriptions that follow have been successfully carried out by elementary, middle, or high school students in schools and with community organizations. Most of these scenarios and examples explicitly include some aspects of investigation, preparation and planning, action, reflection, and demonstration, and all have strong curricular connections. These scenarios can be a rich source of ideas for you to draw upon. Keep in mind that grade levels are provided as a reference; most scenarios can be adapted to suit younger or older students, and many are suitable for cross-age partnerships.

Activists and Authors: Grade K

In Hudson, Massachusetts, kindergarten students were serious about meeting community needs. They listened astutely to the facts and information presented by adults, including the district superintendent. They visited the food bank and recorded how much food was on the shelves. Back in class, they improved their math skills while calculating what quantities were needed by the food bank. Then, they conducted a food drive that matched what the agency needed. Following their sizeable contribution, they took digital photographs to document each step in the food drive process and created a book to inform others about the importance of service learning and to let the public know what still needs to be done.

A Community Collaboration: Grades K–12

Eight hundred public school students in Rhode Island have worked together in a cross-age service learning project to produce food that will feed people who are hungry in their community. The local food bank has received five tons of produce from the students' gardening efforts over four years. While older students teach younger ones about civic involvement, the environment, and how everyone can have a role in ending hunger, both groups enjoy working in the gardens and greenhouse—the latter built through the support of local businesses and volunteers. The broad scale of this project has encouraged the whole community to explore how food, agriculture, abundance, hunger, and society interconnect.

Hunger, Homelessness, and Poverty Across the Curriculum

English/Language Arts

- Define "home" and its attributes; contrast with "homelessness"
- Research myths and facts about homelessness and use them in a persuasive writing piece to share information
- Find examples of how people who are homeless or living in poverty are depicted in literature

Social Studies/History

- Study historical events that led to hunger or homelessness such as the Irish famine
- Interview a city council member or deputy about the government's role in providing services for people in need
- Conduct a demographic and economic study of people who are hungry or homeless in your community

Languages

- Look at and compare the statistics for poverty and hunger in different countries
- Discuss issues of poverty and government programs in a country where this language is spoken
- Study the different kinds of structures used for homes in different countries and learn the associated vocabulary

Theater, Music, & Visual Arts

- Adapt literature that features a person who is homeless into a performance piece with opportunities for discussion with the audience
- Compose simple songs that teach basic concepts like numbers or colors; record and distribute them to a family shelter
- Research what art supplies are needed at a local shelter and prepare art kits

Hunger, Homelessness, and Poverty

Math

- Read food labels to find out serving quantities and nutritional values
- Create a statistical chart to compare national and local statistics on hunger; discuss how statistics can be used in a food drive campaign
- Chart how many cans or pounds of food are needed and received by the local food bank in order to serve their target population

Physical Education

- Discuss the effects of malnutrition on physical health and well-being
- Create a child-friendly exercise video for a family shelter
- Visit a food bank and "get physical" while sorting cans and stocking shelves

Computer

- Develop a brochure for a local food shelter
- Type résumés for people who are looking for work and have no computer access
- On the Internet, find slogans and quotes to use in a marketing campaign for a food drive

Science

- Learn about the food pyramid and nutritional needs of children and adults
- Study the effect of hunger on student achievement in school and on adults trying to enter the workforce
- Compare the nutritional value of different foods and the associated costs

Quilting: Grade 2

In a second-grade class, a teacher read *The Teddy Bear* to initiate conversation about people who are homeless. Students eagerly discussed people they had observed in their semi-rural Washington state community who seemed to have no residence. The children expressed concern and wanted to know who helped people who were homeless in their community. A speaker from a local shelter was invited to answer prepared questions and listen to students' ideas for helping. The class decided to make two quilts that could be used at the shelter. Students applied math and art skills and learned to sew. With parental assistance, they delivered two quilts for permanent use at the shelter.

Children's Hunger Network: Grades 4 and 5

In Los Angeles, Westwood Elementary students in a fourth/fifth-grade combined classroom created a Children's Hunger Network to study national geography, to explore issues of hunger and poverty around the United States, and finally to work on these issues in their own Los Angeles community. To start their geography unit, they identified a school in each of six regions in the United States. Through letters, faxes, and email, they challenged participating classrooms to learn about hunger and homelessness in their communities, find out what organizations were already helping, find a way to make a difference, and report back what they had learned. A local college student helped document the results, and copies were sent to all participating classrooms. For the initiating classroom, U.S. geography came alive as students connected with peers across the country who also wanted to help others. A variety of methods—speakers, field trips, books, and journals—were part of the learning process. The students' direct service included conducting an art exchange with children who lived in a shelter and donating art supplies for their use.

An Art-Full Environment: Grade 6

After a food bank relocated, its coordinator visited a class and described how "sterile and unwelcoming" the new waiting area appeared with its rows of chairs and bare white walls. The middle school students made posters and art work to decorate the area and created a childcare area stocked with donated art supplies.

A Garden That Serves: Grades 6–8

What began as a garden for a class science project expanded when students wanted to continue planting, weeding, and harvesting. After five years of year-round participation at school, the students continue to tend an organic garden in a community lot to provide fresh produce for families in need and hundreds of residents of local shelters. A partner agency assists with food distribution.

What Is Hunger? Grade 7

Everyone says it: "I'm hungry!" Is "hungry" a growling stomach before the lunch bell or a longing for an after-school snack? Students in social studies classes discussed hunger and came to understand how the word is experienced by people in poverty. They found out that people who don't eat, or who don't eat regular, nutritionally balanced meals, have impaired immune systems and may get sick more often. Their ability to study or work is reduced, too. These effects can lead to a downward economic spiral unless intervention and assistance are provided. Students partnered with local agencies to prepare written materials for distribution at schools, libraries, youth clubs, and other organizations. The materials provided facts about local hunger, ways in which people can help, and tips for running food and clothing drives.

Kids Sew for Kids: Grade 8

In an eighth-grade home economics class, students working in pairs selected an outfit to make for a child at a homeless shelter. The outfits were color coordinated, and each partner sewed one piece. Outfits ranged from sweat suits to shorts sets. Some students also made backpacks for school. To fund the project, community partnerships were established with local fabric stores.

Functional Math: Grade 8

Middle school students combined math lessons with studies of homelessness to provide community assistance. The students learned about the business math concepts of profit, loss, gross, net, discounts, taxes, and so forth and then applied these skills in a fund-raiser aimed at buying food to make bag lunches for a local soup kitchen. Partnerships were created among the students, the school, community food wholesalers, potential donors, and the soup kitchen itself.

Understanding Poverty: Grade 8

At Einstein Middle School in Seattle, Washington, 120 eighth graders did more than read about poverty. In English class, they read *Slake's Limbo*, a novel about a boy living on the streets. Students in math classes looked at the financial side of poverty, for example, costs associated with housing and employment statistics. And in science classes, students learned about the effects of poverty on health, from malnutrition to inadequate medical attention. They then led an Oxfam Hunger Banquet during which their peers were placed in groups and fed different meals based on actual world hunger statistics. Guest speakers talked about poverty in their community. Knowing this background, students volunteered in downtown Seattle agencies preparing and serving food, giving pedicures, and collecting needed hygiene supplies. Students next wrote reports, published zines, created digital video, and conducted an evening exhibition to extend their outreach. Visit www.oxfamamerica.org for more information about the Oxfam Hunger Banquet.

Working with Orphans in Tajikistan: Grades 8–11

In Tajikistan in Central Asia, students in grades eight through eleven joined Youth Leadership Clubs. They gathered ideas from kids in different parts of Tajikistan and put together Ready to Help. Volunteers from different organizations gathered on Global Youth Service Day to prepare and serve meals for children who are disabled and homeless in orphanages. The students also played games and made art with the children. For information about Global Youth Service Day, visit www.gysd.org.

Eagles Soar High! Grades 9–12

In Georgetown, Texas, the Georgetown High athletic director decided he wanted to get the "eagles," as the athletes were known, involved in service learning. The district service learning coordinator met with about 1,000 athletes and homelessness emerged as a critical issue, especially after the athletes learned that 100 students from their school had nowhere to sleep. They collaborated to open an on-campus pantry, "Eagle Locker." The students stocked the shelves with snack foods, clothes, toiletries, school supplies, and more. The track team replaced costly plaques and awards they used to hand out to teammates with a certificate stating, "In honor of your achievement, we have donated funds to assist Eagle Locker." This added up to thousands of dollars! Before competitions, visiting sports teams received brown paper bags with information about supplies needed for the Locker—three fifty-five-gallon bins were filled with supplies in one day. The first home game of any sport was Eagle Locker Night, which built a community tradition of participation. Photojournalism students ran infomercials about Eagle Locker on the big screen at football games. The students' next project, in partnership with Georgetown Project, a local nonprofit, is to open "Eagle's Nest," a local teen shelter. The students' motto: Georgetown Eagles Working Together On and Off the Field.

Monthly Dinners: Grades 8–12

In addition to advocating for service learning in schools, a youth service learning advisory board in Maryland plans, buys ingredients for, and prepares dinners for the women and children at a shelter twice each month.

Shelter Help: Grades 9–11

After helping a shelter for women and children with room decorations, students in Maryland asked what else they could do to be helpful. The agency and student representatives met to discuss needs and ideas. Students acted on several ideas, including making journals to give to the young people when they arrive and constructing dollhouses for use in play therapy.

From Activity Center to Family Album: Grades 9–11

At a "drop in" agency in San Pedro, California, that helps to find temporary housing, food, and other services for families in need, young children often waited for hours with nothing to do. High school students created an activity center with shelves of games and books. On the day they set up the center, the students played games with and read to the children on-site. One student took photographs, careful not to take pictures of the children because of issues concerning confidentiality. However, one parent approached the photographer, asking, "Can you take a picture of my child? I have no pictures of my children." Students then took the initiative to address this situation. They secured donations of an instant camera and film and returned on a regular basis to keep the games and books in good shape and to take photos of the children to give to their parents.

"Gotta Feed Them All": Grades 9–12

The "Gotta Feed Them All" citywide canned food drive was designed by alternative high school students for West Hollywood, California, and coordinated through their partnerships with city government, schools, and the local food bank. After helping to sort and stock food supplies at a local food bank, the students learned that the food bank is always low on supplies during spring and summer months. The students' campaign, held in April, has become an annual event. It is publicized through street banners and with specially marked containers placed by markets, in schools, and at city hall. This event has been a welcome windfall for the food bank.

As a result of their homelessness, children are struggling in school, their health is hindered, and they are not getting enough to eat.

—*Homes for the Homeless, a program of The Institute for Children and Poverty*

Donated Eggs: Grades 9–12

Students raising chickens for an agricultural project found that the local food pantry was an appreciative recipient of their eggs. After learning more about the needs of the community, the students helped organize and promote the collection of other needed resources.

A Video Donation: Grade 10

Following a tour of a food bank, several students expressed interest in doing more than just "donating food." They worked to develop a video for the agency that featured a video tour of the facility and an interview with a woman who had experienced poverty. The students, with help from their teacher and agency staff, wrote a four-page curriculum with suggestions on how to use the video with upper elementary, middle, and high school classes. This video is now used to educate the local community on poverty and hunger.

Making Connections—A "Novel" Experience: Grades 10–11

In September, at Cathedral High School in Indianapolis, a service learning coordinator and teacher determined that significant value could come from connecting an Advanced Composition class text

to community action. By October, students were immersed in understanding Cormac McCarthy's post-apocalytic novel *The Road* and becoming more skillful at time management as they arranged to work at a local food bank. Experience became a journal topic and papers were written making the connection between *The Road* and the service provided at the food bank. Use of math came into play as students determined the number of people who would benefit from the tons of canned food collected and sorted. Students created a DVD for faculty meetings and for submission to a National Service Learning Partnership video contest. See the Recommendation from the Field for *The Road* (in digital content).

Teaching at a Shelter: Grades 11–12

Through research, high school students in Chicago learned that children who live in extreme poverty or are homeless often are ill prepared for kindergarten. The students contacted a shelter for women and children and prepared educational activities such as workbooks and game boxes for preschoolers. With support from teachers and agency personnel, the high school students led educational lessons with the children while learning valuable skills themselves.

A Book Club: Grades 11–12

Students in a class on contemporary issues read fiction and nonfiction literature about poverty and homelessness. After hearing the director of a shelter for men speak about the facility and the programs available for the residents, the students discussed unmet needs. One student commented on the speaker's remarks about how many of the men spend their evenings reading. The class submitted a proposal to the shelter to start a book group in which the male teens and the men in the facility would read the same fiction and would meet two evenings per month for discussion. The reflective writings of the students showed the respect they developed for the men and their knowledge, courage, and resilience.

What do we live for, if it is not to make life less difficult for each other?

—*George Eliot, author*

The Hunger, Homelessness, and Poverty Bookshelf

Whether describing the past or examining the present, the works in the Hunger, Homelessness, and Poverty Bookshelf (pages 165–166) show us that these conditions have touched many lives in many places. To help you find books relevant to your particular projects, the book chart classifies the titles into several topic areas: learning from history, communities today, national perspective, and international needs.

In general, the bookshelf features:

- An annotated bibliography arranged and alphabetized by title according to the general categories of nonfiction (N), picture books (P), and fiction (F). For nonfiction and fiction, length and recommended grade levels are included. The entries in the picture book category do not include suggested grade levels, since they can be successfully used with all ages.

- A chart organized by topic and category to help you find books relevant to particular projects.

- Recommendations from service learning colleagues and experts that include a book summary and ideas for service learning connections. (The number of recommended books varies in each bookshelf.)

- *Please note:* additional titles for this category are listed in the digital content; some of these were out of print at the time of publication but still worth finding.

Nonfiction: Hunger, Homelessness, and Poverty

Alone in the World: Orphans and Orphanages in America
by Catherine Reef (Clarion Books, 2005). With captivating photographs and images of children throughout the nineteenth and twentieth centuries, this is a short and vivid history of the rise and decline of orphanages in the United States. 144pp., young adult

Black Potatoes: The Story of the Great Irish Famine, 1845–1850
by Susan Campbell Bartoletti (Houghton Mifflin, 2001). The Irish potato famine of 1845–50 had international repercussions. The Irish people were starving to death. Approximately one million died and two million fled Ireland, with many of those immigrants coming to the United States. The history of this disaster unfolds in vivid text that draws from news reports and first-person narratives. 160pp., grades 6–10

Feed the Children First: Irish Memories of the Great Hunger
by Mary E. Lyons (Simon & Schuster, 2002). The great Irish potato famine, caused by a fungus that wiped out the staple potato crop, was one of the worst disasters of the nineteenth century. More than a quarter of Ireland's country's eight million people died or emigrated. First-person accounts evoke the time and place, the suffering, and the survival. The introduction includes an overview and examples of the aid received. *The Long March*, also listed in this bookshelf, describes the contribution made by the Choctaw to Irish famine relief. 48pp., grades 4–12

If I Had a Hammer: Building Homes and Hope with Habitat for Humanity
by David Rubel (Candlewick Press, 2009). From his background in Plains, Georgia, as a member of the Future Farmers of America, Jimmy Carter knew how to use a hammer. However, as former President of the United States, Carter used that hammer for a different purpose: to help Habitat for Humanity build homes in more than ninety countries. With photographs and narratives, this book makes the process and the people involved come to life. 148pp., grades 4–12

DIGITAL CONTENT

Recommendation from the Field

Nickel and Dimed: On (Not) Getting By in America by Barbara Ehrenreich (Metropolitan Books, 2001). 221pp., young adult

---

Orphan Train Rider: One Boy's True Story
by Andrea Warren (Houghton Mifflin, 1996). "Children without Homes"—so read the signs announcing the arrival of the Orphan Trains that left New York City heading west. Children on board were orphans or had been abandoned by families who could no longer care for them. Over 200,000 children made such journeys to the Midwest from 1854 to 1929. This book tells the story of one boy, providing an important historical account of societal conditions that predated foster homes and homeless shelters. 80pp., grades 4–8

Taking Action Against Homelessness
by Kaye Stearman (Rosen Publishing, 2009). An informative book with facts, questions, and discussion starters. Includes an international perspective. 48pp., grades 5–8

Hunger, Homelessness, and Poverty Bookshelf Topics

Topics	Books	Category
Learning from History Is hunger new? Or homelessness? Poverty? Through the lens of history, find out what occurred in the past and what lessons we can learn.	*The Adventurous Chef: Alexis Soyer* ‡	P
	Alone in the World: Orphans and Orphanages in America	N
	Black Potatoes: The Story of the Great Irish Famine, 1845–1850	N
	Feed the Children First: Irish Memories of the Great Hunger	N
	Grapes of Wrath (see digital content)	F
	The Long March: The Choctaw's Gift to Irish Famine Relief *	P
	Orphan Train Rider: One Boy's True Story	N
	A Train to Somewhere	P
	Worth	F
Communities Today In our own modern times and our own communities, social problems lead too many people into lives of homelessness or hunger. The stories in this category show a variety of situations and needs.	*Beneath My Mother's Feet*	F
	The Can-Do Thanksgiving * ‡	P
	A Castle on Viola Street *	P
	The House on Mango Street	(see page 226)
	The Hundred Dresses	F
	If I Grow Up	F
	The Magic Beads	P
	Messed Up	F
	Money Hungry	F
	Pitch Black	F (GN)
	The Road (see digital content)	F
	A Shelter in Our Car	P
	Shifty	F
	Sketches	F
	Soul Moon Soup	F
	The Teddy Bear *	P
	Three Little Words: A Memoir	F
	Uncle Willie and the Soup Kitchen * ‡	P
	Where I'd Like to Be	F

Page references are given for books that can be found in the bookshelf lists of other chapters.

* These books include examples of young people and adults in service-providing roles.

‡ These books are out of print and still worth finding.

(GN) These books are graphic novels.

Hunger, Homelessness, and Poverty Bookshelf Topics (continued)

Topics	Books	Category
National Perspective How does a nation respond to the needs of people who are homeless? What are the underlying issues, controversies, and possible solutions? As public debate and planning continue, how do people who live on the streets survive?	*How to Build a House* * *Nickel and Dimed: On (Not) Getting By in America* (see digital content) *Taking Action Against Homelessness* *	(see page 116) N N
International Needs Hunger and homelessness have no boundaries. These stories take place across the globe.	*Dream Freedom* * (see Social Change Bookshelf—digital content) *First Crossing: Stories About Teen Immigrants* *If I Had a Hammer: Building Homes and Hope with Habitat for Humanity* * *A Life Like Mine: How Children Live Around the World* * (see Immigrants Bookshelf—digital content) *Sélavi: A Haitian Story of Hope* *Those Shoes* *What the World Eats*	F (see page 181) N N P P N

Page references are given for books that can be found in the bookshelf lists of other chapters.

* These books include examples of young people and adults in service-providing roles.

‡ These books are out of print and still worth finding.

(GN) These books are graphic novels.

Three Little Words: A Memoir

by Ashley Rhodes-Courter (Atheneum, 2008). At the age of four, Ashley is taken from her mother and forced to live in the foster care system. She is treated with disrespect and unkindness in most of the fourteen homes that take her in. She is transferred from school to school and she has many caseworkers. In spite of manipulation, humiliation, and loneliness, Ashley finds the courage to live a life of contribution. 336pp., grades 9–12

What the World Eats

by Faith D'Aluisio and Peter Menzel (Tricycle Press, 2008). What do people buy? What do people eat? The authors take you to twenty-one countries to see their shopping lists and what's on their table. Clearly, a rural family, one living near urban markets, and a family living in a refugee camp all eat quite differently. We see the connection between nutrition and politics and circumstance. And perhaps this will help us also consider that with the rise of diabetes and obesity in America, we need to look at food in a whole new light. 160pp., all ages

Picture Books: Hunger, Homelessness, and Poverty

The Adventurous Chef: Alexis Soyer

by Ann Arnold (Farrar, Straus and Giroux, 2002). In this unique biography, meet Alexis Soyer, flamboyant chef and inventor of kitchen tools, who defied tradition, improved cooking methods, and helped people in need. His philanthropic work led him to create the soup kitchen model in Dublin during the Irish potato famine and to work alongside Florence Nightingale to reform and improve military cooking methods during the Crimean War. Out of print but worth finding.

The Can-Do Thanksgiving

by Marion Hess Pomeranc (Albert Whitman, 1998). When Dee brings a can of peas to school for the canned food drive, she keeps asking, "Where do my peas go?" Her persistent questioning results in a class project to prepare and serve food for people in need at Thanksgiving. An excellent resource for transforming the traditional canned food drive into a service learning project.

A Castle on Viola Street

by DyAnne DiSalvo-Ryan (HarperCollins, 2001). On Viola Street, a family joins Habitat for Humanity volunteers as they restore a home. In time, they learn that another home will be restored for them. As the father says, "Big dreams are built little by little," and many generous hands have helped in the dream building.

The Long March: The Choctaw's Gift to Irish Famine Relief

by Marie-Louise Fitzpatrick (Tricycle Press, 1998). The year is 1847, and Choona, a young Choctaw, has learned of a famine in Ireland. From what precious little they have, the Choctaw collect $170 to help the starving Irish. As Choona learns the terrible truth about his own tribe's long march, he must decide whether to answer another people's faraway cry for help. Based on actual events.

The Magic Beads

by Susan Nielsen-Fernlund (Simply Read Books, 2007). When Lillian moves to a new school in second grade, she is so nervous about show-and-tell. When she asks her mom to buy her something so she can present to her new class, her mother reminds her that she is saving money so they can get their own place. Lillian and her mom are living in a shelter. Lillian discovers she might have something even more special to share than the fancy toys that other kids brought in: her magic beads and the imagination that imbues them with the power to help her cope with such a scary ordeal.

Sélavi: A Haitian Story of Hope

by Youme Landowne (Cinco Puntos Press, 2004). Based on the actual efforts of young children living on the streets in Haiti, they were determined to make a home for themselves. Believing that if they shared their resources there would be more for each of them, they found work whenever they could, and they created a home wherever they could. After police allowed their first home to be burned, they defiantly rebuilt and expanded it, adding a radio station from which they broadcast stories, songs, and interviews about their experiences. The station operates to this day.

A Shelter in Our Car

by Monica Gunning (Children's Book Press, 2004). Vividly illustrated, this is the story of Zettie and her mother who are living in their car while Mama looks for a steady job. They miss the comforts of Jamaica and the company of her father, but they also know that through it all they have each other.

The Teddy Bear

by David McPhail (Henry Holt, 2002). A special teddy bear, lost by his little boy, is found and loved by an elder man who lives on the street. Months later, the boy is amazed to find his bear sitting on a park bench. Reunited with his bear at last, the boy hears the cries of a bearded man, "My bear! Where is my bear?" The boy's actions show understanding and compassion.

Those Shoes

by Maribeth Boelts (Candlewick Press, 2007). Almost everyone in school has pricey name brand shoes. But when Jeremy's grandma takes him to buy a pair, she sees the price and sits down in shock. On a trip to a thrift store, Jeremy purchases a too-small pair with his own money, keeping them unworn by his bed. When he notices Antonio on the playground with torn soles like his own, Jeremy has to make a decision: whether or not to give the too-small shoes to the only boy who did not laugh at the replacement pair his guidance counselor gave Jeremy during recess.

A Train to Somewhere

by Eve Bunting (Clarion, 1996). In 1878, a young girl rides the Orphan Train out west hoping somehow to find her mother, who has abandoned her. With each stop she watches other children being adopted. At the last stop, in the town of Somewhere, she finds a home.

Uncle Willie and the Soup Kitchen

by DyAnne DiSalvo-Ryan (Morrow, 1991). When Willie's nephew works at the neighborhood soup kitchen preparing and serving food, he gains admiration for people who lend a hand. Out of print but worth finding.

Fiction: Hunger, Homelessness, and Poverty

Beneath My Mother's Feet

by Amjed Qamar (Atheneum Books for Young Readers, 2008). Nazia is a young girl growing up in a working class family in Pakistan. When troubles befall her family, she and her mother must work as "masis"—women who clean houses for a living. Nazia has to give up attending school and exchange her love of learning for the challenges of accepting cultural traditions and her changing role from a masi to a "memsahib"—the lady of the house. Nazia finds herself questioning her allegiance to her mother and family and to her own dreams. 198pp., young adult

The Hundred Dresses

by Eleanor Estes (Harcourt, 1944). Wanda Petronski is teased by classmates for living in a poor part of town and wearing the same dress every day. One girl, Maddie, is confused by the taunting and by Wanda's insistence that she has "one hundred dresses at home." When Wanda's dad moves the family to escape the relentless teasing, Maddie and her friends face up to their behavior and see Wanda's dresses. A true classic. 80pp., grades 3–7

DIGITAL CONTENT

Recommendation from the Field

The Grapes of Wrath by John Steinbeck (Penguin, 1939/1992). 619pp., young adult

If I Grow Up

by Todd Strasser (Simon & Schuster, 2009). Every day DeShawn tries to avoid the gangs that are running the inner-city project where he lives. He does well in school, but all his best intentions dissolve when he realizes that the money he needs to support his family cannot be had by any other means. For DeShawn, gangs stop being about right or wrong—they are about survival. The author, known for his gritty stories of urban life, interviewed gang members and residents of the projects around New York City. 240pp., young adult

Messed Up

by Janet Nichols Lynch (Holiday House, 2009). At age fifteen, R. D. appears to be an innocent bystander in his life. His father disappeared when he was a toddler, his mother is in prison, and his grandmother has gone off with her new boyfriend, leaving R. D. under the care of Earl, his grandmother's ex. When Earl suddenly dies, R. D. decides he's best off fending for himself. He applies himself to school (he's repeating eighth grade), stays out of trouble (he's surprisingly helpful to school administrators), makes unexpected friends (and a few he'd rather not have), and learns how to cook. An inside view of a Mexican American young man's struggle with his past to build a future. 250pp., grades 7–9

Money Hungry

by Sharon G. Flake (Hyperion, 2001). Raspberry Hill is thirteen and knows what it's like to be homeless, and she swears she won't live on the streets again. Her endless schemes at earning money may get her some cash, but not enough to prevent her mother from packing their belongings in plastic bags, leaving the projects, and facing the fears and frustrations of life without a home once again. 188pp., grades 5–8

Pitch Black

by Youme Landowne and Anthony Horton (Cinco Puntos Press, 2008). A chance meeting on New York subway leads to a collaboration between a young white woman and a young African-American man. The graphic novel format perfectly illustrates the story about an abandoned child who lives in a shelter that is worse than the streets so he retreats into the depths of the subway tunnels to live and do his art. The book opens with these words: "Just cause you can't see don't mean ain't nothing here." 64pp., grades 6–12

Shifty

by Lynn E. Hazen (Tricycle Press, 2008). At age fifteen, Soli (nicknamed Shifty) has lived in many foster care settings and his current home with Martha is the best. Soli appreciates his foster mother's care for him and Sissy, a little girl finally coming out of her shell, and a baby they call Chance. Still, as much as Shifty tries to stay out of trouble, it keeps finding him. He tries to prove he can be responsible and part of a caring family. Includes a list of organizations dedicated to helping children in foster care. 188pp., young adult

DIGITAL CONTENT

Recommendation from the Field

The Road by Cormac McCarthy (Knopf, 2006). 256pp., grades 10–12

Sketches

by Eric Walters (Viking, 2008). Dana has to get away from home and joins a band of kids living on the streets. When she finds Sketches, a drop-in art center for homeless teens, she begins to resolve the issues of her past and breaks her silence to find the help she needs. 232pp., grades 8–10, mature themes

Soul Moon Soup

by Lindsay Lee Johnson (Front Street, 2002). In this prose-poem, Phoebe Rose, age eleven, describes life "in the hard poor middle of the city," where she and her mother sleep in shelters or doorways. When her dream of being an artist is torn away, no one notices; she becomes invisible. Only when she is sent to live in the country with her Gram does Phoebe learn, "When things come apart it's your chance to rearrange the pieces." 134pp., grades 7–10

Where I'd Like to Be

by Frances O'Roark Dowell (Simon & Schuster, 2003). After living in her share of foster homes, Maddie, age twelve, moves into the East Tennessee Children's Home. She finds an eclectic group of kids who join together to build a fort, a home of their own. As they fill this structure with their stories and dreams, Maddie wonders whether she will find a place to really call her home—or at least find people who feel like home. 232pp., grades 4–7

Worth

by A. LaFaye (Simon & Schuster, 2006). In this rich historical fiction novel, the orphan trains of the late 1800s come alive. The narrator, eleven-year-old Nate, crushes his leg in a farming accident. To help pick up the slack, his family brings in John Worth, an orphan from the orphan trains. Nate carries more pain from his father's rejection than he does from the farming accident. His resentment keeps him distant and he feels no sympathy for John who lost both parents in a fire. However, when the animosity between farmers, who need land for crops, and ranchers, who need land for cattle, proves dangerous, the two boys join forces. 160pp., grades 4–8

DIGITAL CONTENT

Interviews with Authors: The Story Behind the Story

In the companion digital content, you'll find interviews with authors Lindsay Lee Johnson (*Soul Moon Soup*) and Marion Hess Pomeranc (*The Can-Do Thanksgiving*) that tell the "story behind the story" of their books.

Chapter 12

Immigrants

When we escaped from Cuba, all we could carry was our education.

—Alicia Coro, educator

What causes a person to uproot and move to a new country, where language and cultural differences may seem insurmountable? History offers up many reasons: famine, political differences, financial hardships, war, revolutions, forced relocation, and slavery. Climate change has always been an impetus as weather patterns create droughts or floods. Of course, people have also immigrated for other, more positive reasons, too, such as a sense of adventure, a hope for better employment or a better education, a promise of a stronger economy, or simply the expectation of a better life waiting. In today's world, are reasons for immigration so different?

Probably not. Yet though the reasons may be the same, the ease of movement from place to place has caused unanticipated population shifts. All across the globe we see people bringing their cultures and backgrounds to take root on new soil. This alters the face of community, and brings challenges that need to be examined and addressed. Government has a role, as do everyday people. What needs to be considered so people share empathy and understanding rather than fear and trepidation?

Immigration means moving somewhere to settle—not taking a vacation, not passing through. This new place becomes home. Sometimes families who make such moves are separated from loved ones. They face isolation and the challenges of learning a new language while unraveling the mysteries of a foreign culture. Young people in particular may struggle with whether to identify with their culture of origin or to abandon it, even temporarily, in order to fit in with their peers.

Service learning offers opportunities for reaching across differences of language, experience, and culture to learn about these new neighbors and to create an inclusive, diverse community. Kids are naturally curious and want to learn. The challenge is to ensure that their inquisitive minds develop in ways that make them open and thoughtful about others' experiences. Populations will continue to move from place to place, by choice or necessity. How others are welcomed makes a world of difference.

Preparation: Getting Ready for Service Learning Involving Immigrants

 The following activities can be used to promote learning and skill development related to immigrants. These activities are easily adapted to different grade levels during investigation, preparation, and planning to help your students examine key issues through research, analyze community needs, and gain the knowledge they need to effectively contribute to the design of their service plan. They can often be integrated into reflection and demonstration as students can lead the activities with others to build awareness. Since literature is often an important part of preparation, you can find recommended titles on this theme in the Immigrants Bookshelf later in this chapter.

Activity: Bringing the World Home. Where in the world are people coming from? This information is the foundation of any immigrant-based service learning project. You can't help until you know who to help. Reviewing news articles and interviewing government officials gets you going. Conducting a survey is a good way to find out where people lived before coming to your city or town. The survey's target population could be other students, school faculty, or a specific group in the community, such as members of an adult education class. Decide how far back to research. For example, the class could agree to find out the last three places a family responding to the survey has lived. Students may also want to find out the year of each move and the reasons for moving. Remind students that responding to all of the survey questions should be optional for the person completing the survey.

Next, using both world and national maps, track the survey responses using pins or stickers and string to depict the immigration and any other moves visually. Help students understand the difference between moving within a country and moving between countries. Discuss what immigrants bring to their new home, including language, values, information, skills, ideas, culture, and resources. Identify any stereotypes students may have about immigrant groups in their community, then have speakers from those groups or from agencies that serve immigrant populations address and discuss misinformation and prejudices. Once your students have identified the immigrant groups in the community and have learned more about their cultures, it is much easier to identify ways to reach out and address genuine needs.

Activity: Who Helps? Community agencies that assist immigrant populations can help students learn more about the recent immigrants in the region, find out who helps them become acclimated, bridge potential language or cultural confusion, and identify needs that can be addressed by youth. The following activities are easily tailored to students' abilities, the timeframe for the project, and the course curriculum.

- To encourage students to start thinking about immigration issues, they can read one of the bookshelf titles in this category or have a book read aloud to them. In *My Name Is Yoon*, for example, a young girl changes her name to try and fit in to this new country. *Any Small Goodness* describes an immigrant boy in East Los Angeles, where daily life combines blessings and risk. *First Crossing: Stories About Teen Immigrants* contains short stories featuring teens who immigrated for a variety of reasons and met challenges at every turn. These books can generate conversation regarding the challenges facing young people and their families and what the young people could have done in these stories to mitigate the problems.

- Continuing education is often very important for adult immigrants, so they can learn a new

Find Out More About Immigrants

To learn more about these issues and to get ideas for service and action, visit these Web sites and organizations online:

U.S. Citizenship and Immigration Services (www.uscis.gov) provides information on naturalization eligibility, the process, forms, news, frequently asked questions, citizenship quizzes, study material, and the *Guide to Naturalization* publication.

Citizen and Immigration Canada (www.cic.gc.ca) offers online information on immigration, refugees, permanent residency, and citizenship and helpful downloadable documents.

The International Rescue Committee (www.rescue.org) is a voluntary agency providing assistance to refugees around the world, including the United States. Many

United States cities have local offices and information about the program's involvement.

Everyday Democracy (www.everyday-democracy.org) is dedicated to finding ways for all kinds of people to engage in dialogue and problem solving on critical social and political issues. Their free resource materials for middle and high school grades include a unit on immigration, called "Changing Faces, Changing Communities," that can lead to social action projects.

Schools of California Online Resources for Education (score.rims.k12.ca.us) evaluates, aligns, and annotates quality resources from the Web to the California History/Social Science Content Standards and curriculum. Search the immigration topic in the lessons for a wealth of resources for relating immigration issues to classroom learning.

language or other information that will help them adapt to and thrive in their new home. Resources for continued learning can include local and state government offices and the school district, as well as nonprofit agencies. Adult schools may have information about enrollment in classes teaching English as a second language (ESL). Students can find out from the school program coordinators what services are offered and if there are needs that can be met through youth involvement. Based on the needs, students can then identify worthwhile projects and collaborate with agencies to carry them out.

- Students can interview other students or adults who are immigrants to learn about their experiences and needs. Preparation for the interview process is important, and professionals who work with immigrant populations can provide extremely useful assistance. Some students who are immigrants themselves or who have relatives who are immigrants may also come forward to volunteer knowledge and guidance.

Interacting with people who are immigrants always offers a multitude of opportunities for exchange and reciprocity that leave everyone richer in knowledge and understanding. Working with people from another culture is not a one-way street with help flowing in a single direction. Again, just as when working with elders, make sure to look for or create activities that make these mutual benefits explicit for everyone involved.

Making Connections Across the Curriculum

Some service learning activities naturally lend themselves to interdisciplinary work and making connections across the curriculum. These connections strengthen and broaden student learning, helping them meet academic standards. More than likely, you'll be looking for these connections and ways to encourage them well before the students ever start working on service learning activities. As with the entire service learning process, it helps to remain flexible, because some connections can be spontaneously generated by the questions raised throughout and by the community needs identified by the students. To help you think about cross-curricular connections and where you can look for them, the curricular web for this chapter (page 172) gives examples of many different ways this theme can be used in different academic areas. (The service learning scenarios in the next section of the chapter also demonstrate various ways that this theme can be used across the curriculum.)

Service Learning Scenarios: Ideas for Action

Ready to take action? The service learning descriptions that follow have been successfully carried out by elementary, middle, or high school students in schools and with community organizations. Most of these scenarios and examples explicitly include some aspects of investigation, preparation and planning, action, reflection, and demonstration, and all have strong curricular connections. These scenarios can be a rich source of ideas for you to draw upon. Keep in mind that grade levels are provided as a reference; most scenarios can be adapted to suit younger or older students, and many are suitable for cross-age partnerships.

A Good Trade: Grade 2

When a teacher in Washington state began to teach origami to her class, she quickly realized that she needed help in guiding all of her students in this hands-on task. A colleague knew of Japanese exchange students attending a local community college through an exchange program. After a few phone calls, six exchange students had volunteered to help the teacher. The volunteers ended up helping nearly every day over a two-week period. They also brought in recent immigrants from Japan who worked with the students on the craft project and told stories about their experiences in Japan and moving to the United States. To reciprocate, the children invited the college students and recent immigrants for a special program and presentation. The children taught about important Americans, including men and women of diverse cultures and ethnic groups, who had made contributions to U.S. society. Each guest received a compilation of these student-written stories as a gift. The exchange students let the children know how much the interaction had helped them learn and practice their English skills.

Immigrants Across the Curriculum

English/Language Arts

- Read stories about the personal experiences of immigrating to a new country
- Study interview techniques and practice listening and note taking
- Create English vocabulary books for ESL programs

Social Studies/History

- Conduct interviews with immigrants of different ages from the same population and compare their experiences
- Research reasons people leave specific countries and compare how this has changed over recent decades
- Learn about and document the contributions of immigrants in your community in a range of areas—social, political, cultural, and artistic

Languages

- Find words in English that have their roots in the language being studied
- Prepare lessons to tutor immigrants in English language skills
- Translate the school handbook for immigrant populations

Theater, Music, & Visual Arts

- Create collaborative theater events with people from many countries sharing talents
- Listen to world music and invite musicians from other countries into the classroom
- Explore the influence of many cultures on styles of art and architecture

Immigrants

Math

- Compare the decimal system with the metric system used in many parts of the world
- Study and chart statistics reflecting the number of immigrants in your region, where they are coming from, and their reasons for moving
- Make easy-to-use guides to money conversion for new immigrants

Physical Education

- Learn about games and approaches to exercise from different cultures
- Research athletes who are immigrants or children of immigrants who have made and continue to make contributions to sports
- Create a multilingual guide to places in your region for outdoor exercise

Computer

- Create computer-generated lessons on colloquial expressions for teen immigrants
- Research ways the Internet is used for genealogy and country of origin research
- Study language translation programs that can assist students who are learning English

Science

- Research how indigenous gardening techniques have been influenced by immigrants who bring their methods and plants
- Discuss whether or not the food pyramid is an accurate shape to depict the eating, exercise, and nutrition practices of people from different countries
- Learn about folk traditions and remedies for health concerns used by immigrants from their country of origin

A Music Fest: Grade 3

Third-grade students in a Spanish immersion elementary school in Santa Monica, California, enjoyed learning the rhythms and songs of Latin American music. They performed at a senior center that drew primarily Spanish-speaking elder community members. The elders so appreciated the students' joy in music that they invited the students to come again, this time to be taught dancing by the older people. The younger students returned several times during the school year for singing, dancing, and, of course, cookies.

Refugee Youth Project: Grades 3–12

In Pennsylvania, a service learning collaboration that included the International Rescue Committee and the American Red Cross was formed to meet the needs of young refugees resettled from Africa and the former Yugoslavia. College students tutored refugee students from elementary, middle, and high schools after school. The refugee students then extended their own learning and experience by doing service projects on weekends. These opportunities had multiple benefits for all involved. By helping with community cleanups, working in food shelters, and creating murals depicting their international experience, the students came to know and build community. They learned about community resources, gained skills through volunteering, and became engaged in the civic life of their new country.

The Story Cloth Museum: Grade 4

Fourth-grade classes in central California read *The Whispering Cloth* as a way to become more familiar with Hmong culture and the growing Hmong population in their community. Two parents from Cambodia visited the class and brought Hmong story cloths. Students were fascinated with the artistry and story telling on the fabric. They developed a project to teach the community about Hmong culture by making their own story cloths. After engaging in research, students told some of their family stories through a combination of drawing on fabrics and sewing to give the pictures more depth. The students invited the community to see their museum of story cloths, including Hmong cloths on loan from local families. Serving as docents, the students explained their cultural studies and shared family histories. Much to the students' delight, a local library, a bank, and city government offices asked to display the museum pieces.

Kid-to-Kid Guidebooks: Grades 4–5

What contributions have immigrants made to the United States? How do we separate fact from fiction regarding immigration? With support and guidance from Children Helping Children, a New York City organization that mobilizes children of all ages toward volunteerism, students at P.S. #110 in Brooklyn and P.S. #20 in Queens developed knowledge and empathy with a practical outcome. Students wrote guidebooks to help immigrants feel welcome in their new country. Text and illustrations covered a range of New York City facts and topics other kids want to know about: What are favorite places to go, eat, and shop? What about sports teams? How do you get around this big city? What's fun for kids to do all year long? Writing, editing, proofreading—academic skills came together in a product helpful to organizations and to kids.

Immigration and Activism: Grade 6

In a dynamic example of service learning, a middle school teacher at César Chávez Public Charter School for Public Policy in Washington, D.C., wove the topic of immigration into a curricular unit on "Immigration and Activism: Taking Action for What We Believe." This unique experience required students to anonymously interview day laborers at Casa de Maryland, an organization that assists immigrants with a variety of services. Through these interviews, students were able to hear firsthand what the immigration experience is actually like, rather than simply read about it in a textbook. Students also interviewed representatives from organizations and government agencies, including people directly involved in setting federal policy, gathering knowledge on the topic from many perspectives. To follow up, students developed their own Web site to educate the Chávez community about this critical issue. The site features immigrant surveys and results with graphs and maps and presents interviews, personal narratives (which afforded students extensive skill development in creating memoirs), immigration vocabulary, and most importantly, information on how others can make a difference in their communities. They also created posters and a petition expressing their collective opinion and putting forth ideas for a solution to the immigration debate.

Oral History—Across the Decades: Grade 6

Using a U.S. Library of Congress collection of interviews and oral histories from the 1930s, students learned about the everyday life of ordinary people who were immigrants. With guidance from teachers, the students then began collecting oral histories from recent immigrants in their own communities. The steps included doing background research, identifying interview subjects, developing interview questions, scheduling and conducting the interviews, and supplementing them with selections of primary source material, including photographs from magazines and from some of the immigrants. Students then wrote papers to compare the experiences of immigrants across the decades. Copies of these comprehensive portfolios were given to the immigrants involved, to support agencies, and to school and local libraries.

Let's Talk: Grades 6–8

Learning English requires practice, practice, and more practice. At one middle school, students learning English were paired with English-speaking students for conversational practice during physical education classes. Both student groups received orientation on the project. The English-speakers worked with counselors and a language specialist to develop skills, such as listening, speaking more slowly, repeating phrases, and answering questions. The English-learners prepared by working with a counselor and developing a document that addressed stereotypes or possible put-downs that could come up in these relationships. Together, both groups of students created a written agreement of how they would work together to be mutually respectful. Then they participated in a getting acquainted activity to identify common interests and topics to talk about, though much of the talking centered on the P.E. class work. As an unexpected benefit, some of the English-learners coached their partners in sports skills!

Neighborhood Resource Project: Grades 7–8

A middle school in New York has students from Cuba, Jamaica, Puerto Rico, Honduras, Mexico, Nicaragua, and Haiti. Many of them have been identified as being at risk, and often their families aren't familiar with the services available through government agencies and other providers. To remedy this, the students collaborated with a local agency to provide the neighborhood population with information regarding available services, including health care, after-school activities, drug prevention programs, adult literacy classes, and language and career training. Based on information acquired from field trips to local government meetings, civic organizations, and guest speakers, the students published a directory of services. The students met several educational objectives: basic awareness of social problems and their solutions, an in-depth study of government, computer literacy, knowledge of the immigrant experience, work skills, and cultural awareness.

> *!Sí se puede¡*
> Yes, it can be done!
> —*César E. Chávez, social activist*

In Honor of New Citizens: Grades 7–8

After participating in a two-week simulation about immigrants entering this country through Ellis Island, a middle school social studies class in Portland, Maine, wanted to do more. They knew their community was a resettlement area for refugees from around the world. To learn more, they met with staff with Immigration and Naturalization Services (INS), and an idea emerged. The students made a proposal to the INS asking to host a swearing-in ceremony for new citizens at their school. Students found out the countries of origin of the 32 people being sworn in and researched the culture, foods, art, and social and political histories of those countries. They reached out to the community for food donations (including many ethnic treats) and made room decorations. They also arranged for the educational television channel to record and air the event. On the day of the ceremony, they greeted the guests and interviewed the new citizens, later compiling their stories (with permission) into books with smiling family photographs. Many of the families wrote letters thanking the students for a most meaningful and memorable event. Still, the students were not finished—they had found another need to fill. They created "welcome kits" for the children of the immigrant families that included cartoon-style maps of the area, places to go for entertainment and sports, lists of after-school and weekend activities, a guide to youth expressions, and a small journal and pen.

ESL Tutors: Grade 9

In Minnesota, several ninth-grade social studies classes spent one class period every two weeks throughout the academic year tutoring new immigrants in English and other basic skills. These freshmen linked their experiences to what they were learning about different cultures and current events. Unexpectedly, the teacher noticed that the students' writing skills improved as they began to pay more attention to sentence structure and communicating clearly.

Beginning with Earthquakes: Grades 9–10

A high school English-as-a-second-language class in Los Angeles completed an in-depth study of earthquakes. Where to take their knowledge? To a traditional science class. The ESL students developed interactive lessons; each agreed to lead a small-group discussion. The lessons were successful on many levels: The ESL students became more confident in their English skills, students who often kept to their own cultural group became acquainted with others, and the science students agreed to continue the exchange by leading an interactive lesson in return. Although the project was led by a student teacher who was only with the class for a limited time, this reciprocal arrangement continued for the remainder of the school year.

A Cup of Knowledge: Grades 9–11

Enterprising high school students from around the world cooked up language skills as they served coffee. A nonprofit organization north of Los Angeles created a coffee shop, "A Cup of Knowledge/*Taza de Conocimiento*," to connect ESL students with their community. Students in ESL classes plus additional students identified by school counselors worked with representatives from the nonprofit on planning the coffee house, including design and marketing. The students suggested ways to make the coffee house more enticing for a teen crowd and along the way learned entrepreneurial and food service skills. The students improved language skills through free classes and workshops they offered for younger students. The older teens also offered bilingual story hours, quilt-making classes, and art classes in the coffee shop to

attract families and their children as regular customers. To promote these offerings, students created flyers for community bulletin boards and to send to neighborhood newspapers.

Exploring "Mango Street": Grades 9–12

At Abraham Clark High School in Roselle, New Jersey, ESL students combined language arts, civics, consumer science, and career exploration during a three-week unit of study, using literature as a springboard. After reading Sandra Cisneros's *The House on Mango Street,* they assisted in separating, categorizing, and packing donated goods at a local food bank. Academic markers were met throughout as they used this well-known American novel to explore universal themes that reveal the immigrant experience. Students studied the effect of poverty on individual health and well-being and became aware of the amount of food donated and distributed to people in need in northern New Jersey. They explored issues facing immigrants and examined cultural identity questions, including traditional gender roles and responsibilities. Through their interactions at the food bank, students learned about different positions necessary to run an organization and the skills required for employment. They viewed a film that reinforced class discussions and assisted in developing language skills, empathy, and a sense of civic responsibility. Integrated into daily lesson plans were journal writing, vocabulary, graphic organizers, rubrics, and sketched visualizations of metaphors found in the book.

Honoring Chávez Through Stories: Grades 9–12

"Where did you come from?" "How was your life before you came here?" "What has changed now that you live in Chicago?" Students from Chicago high schools honored César Chávez Service Learning Month by conducting extensive interviews with immigrants preparing for their citizenship exams. Students then created transcripts for radio broadcast on a local station. The stories they learned and reported took students beyond what can be learned in textbooks. The interactions helped students replace stereotypes with accurate information, understand motivation factors rooted in caring for family and working long hours in multiple jobs to make ends meet, and connect back to their own families.

Welcome Buddies: Grades 9–12

New kid in school? Welcome Buddies are there to greet you. Young people designed, improved, and continue to implement this ongoing project at their Los Angeles high school, which registers many immigrant students each semester. Pairs of students drawn from world history and language classes meet, greet, and assist young people coming into their school. Orientation programs are held every few months; special mixers and other activities help students become acclimated and stay involved with positive social and academic activities. "Welcome Buddy" programs can also help students find their way around campus, supply a buddy to have lunch with, and provide homework helpers.

A Large Window to Immigration: Grades 11–12

"Windows to History" at Drury High in North Adams, Massachusetts, focuses on educating students about their community through researching local history related to immigration. The U.S. history students conducted research with primary sources to develop Web sites with primary source documents, interviews, and artifacts with their accompanying narratives. The Web sites now provide the North Adams community with a digital museum of local history. They also provide an avenue for the community to submit stories and archives that will allow North Adams local history to be even more accessible. The class partnered with the local historical society and the public library. The students developed and met historical thinking benchmarks for primary source analysis, connecting local events to a national theme, and generating a chronological overview of a specific region, while covering subject matter on the Massachusetts Frameworks. The students were also able to develop technology skills and gain greater appreciation for their community and how people from many parts of the world continue to make significant contributions.

Helping to Address Challenges: Grades 10–11

A high school in Hawaii with a large number of immigrants recognized the challenges that many students faced attending a new school and living in a new country. High school classes partnered with a local immigration center and became knowledgeable about the services offered and the potential difficulties immigrants in the community could encounter. Students combined this new information with skills learned at school to assist the center in updating the brochures given to new immigrants. This project met writing, civics, and diversity standards.

The Immigration Experience—Seeing, Helping, and Telling: Grade 11

To understand and learn more about the experience of immigrants in Hawaii and across the United States, eleventh-grade students at the Punahou School in Honolulu read *The Joy Luck Club*, a book exploring family and immigration experiences of four women from China and their daughters. They considered critical questions: What forces "push" people away from their native land? What forces "pull" people towards the United States? What challenges face immigrants upon arrival? Does the reality of life in the United States match the American Dream and the values espoused in American society, such as freedom, equality, and justice? On what do people base their identity, and what struggles does that cause in immigrant families? To support Project SHINE—a national service learning initiative (Students Helping in the Naturalization of Elders)—groups of students designed posters for the local Chinese Community Action Coalition (CCAC). The posters helped recruit tutoring volunteers and potential clients who wanted to become naturalized American citizens. For reflection, students wrote an essay that combined a moment from their own family's immigration history with lessons learned about the posters. More than 20 posters were showcased at the national SHINE conference (www.projectshine.org).

Oral History—An Exchange in Spanish: Grade 11

To foster improved community relations and to emphasize the value of being literate in a second language, students in an advanced Spanish class adopted an adult literacy class for recent immigrants. During four visits to the class, held at the local community center, students interviewed the immigrants in Spanish to create written histories of their immigration and life experiences. Using computers at school, students wrote the histories in Spanish, adding photographs and other graphics to produce a book. Copies were presented to the adults at a final gathering. The book was meaningful reading material for the new immigrants and provided a way for students to improve their language skills while acquiring knowledge found outside of their textbooks.

A World View: Grades 11–12

As part of a World Studies class, students in Chicago examined immigration issues. To further students' understanding of the problems facing immigrants, the teacher collaborated with a community organization to develop a service learning plan. The first step was to lead students through team-building activities. Next, guest speakers discussed local issues related to immigration: the problems of work conditions for day laborers and immigrant documentation, specifically referencing a federal initiative that enabled documented immigrants to help family members who were not documented. The students discussed their options and ideas, and decided to work on the documentation issue. With training from lawyers specializing in immigration issues, the students hosted a day to begin the documentation process of immigrants. Two hundred local residents attended and received assistance from students and legal experts. The teacher continually linked the experiences with classroom learning and guided the students in reflection.

Language in Action: Grades 11–12

High school advanced language students put their skills to use as "cultural aides." After developing lists of ideas, students individually or in pairs developed a plan that would assist community members. Ideas included helping prepare a bilingual brochure for families on how to access local resources, acting as a guide for back-to-school night, helping with health aid programs, translating materials for local agencies, maintaining bilingual information on the school's Web site, and translating school correspondence sent home to parents. Once this program was in place, language teachers saw skill levels rise, and classroom discussion became enriched as students brought real-life problems to solve into the classroom.

Civics with a Purpose: Grade 12

A high school civics class established a valuable partnership with a local refugee center, resulting in benefits for all involved. The students applied their classroom knowledge to coach new immigrants who were studying for their citizenship tests. Students came to value their own citizenship as they learned that people sometimes put their lives at risk to move to their new country. Students also provided childcare during classes and study groups.

> Reading makes immigrants of us all. It takes us away from home, but more important, it finds homes for us everywhere.
>
> —Hazel Rochman, author

The Immigrants Bookshelf

The books on the Immigrants Bookshelf (pages 178–179) give us the opportunity to walk, if only for a while, in the shoes of another person. For young people who are immigrants, the books may ease the telling of their own life stories. For others, understanding may encourage empathy and comradeship. To help you find books appropriate to what the students are learning and the action being taken, the book chart classifies the titles according to several topic areas: learning from the past, the story of many, focus on one story, and fitting in.

In general, the bookshelf features:

- An annotated bibliography arranged and alphabetized by title according to the general categories of nonfiction (N), picture books (P), and fiction (F). For nonfiction and fiction, length and recommended grade levels are included. The entries in the picture book category do not include suggested grade levels, since they can be successfully used with all ages.

- A chart organized by topic and category to help you find books relevant to particular projects.

- Recommendations from service learning colleagues and experts that include a book summary and ideas for service learning connections. (The number of recommended books varies in each bookshelf.)

- *Please note:* additional titles for this category are listed in the digital content; some of these were out of print at the time of publication but still worth finding.

Nonfiction: Immigrants

Breaking Through: Sequel to The Circuit
by Francisco Jiménez (Houghton Mifflin, 2001). These stories continue the struggles of the Jiménez family through separation, poverty, prejudice, and hope. Each episode reveals the tenacity and fortitude brought by hard work and "the generous people

Immigrants Bookshelf Topics

Topics	Books	Category
Learning from the Past These stories, drawn from the not-so-distant past, shed light on the experience of immigrants and reveal their similarities to today's immigrants.	*The Clay Marble* *Dragonwings* (see digital content) *Esperanza Rising* *The Whispering Cloth: A Refugee's Story*	F F F P
The Story of Many These books offer an overview of the issue of immigration, with all of its political, economic, and personal implications.	*Denied, Detained, Deported: Stories from the Dark Side of American Immigration* *First Crossing: Stories About Teen Immigrants* *Forty-Cent Tip: Stories of New York Immigrant Workers* *The Middle of Everywhere: The World's Refugees Come to Our Town*	N F N N
Focus on One Story From the perspective of one cultural group, what is the story that moves people from one place to another to find a new home?	*The Bonesetter's Daughter* *Breaking Through: Sequel to The Circuit* *The Circuit: Stories from the Life of a Migrant Child* *Dancing with Diadziu* (see Elders Bookshelf—digital content) *Dear Whiskers* (see Literacy Bookshelf—digital content) *Four Feet, Two Sandals* *The Grapes of Wrath* *The Importance of Wings* *Libertad* *A Movie in My Pillow/Una película en mi almohada* *My Diary from Here to There/Mi diario de aquí hasta allá* *My Name Is Yoon* *Reaching Out* *The Revealers* (see Safe and Strong Communities Bookshelf—digital content) *The Skirt* (see digital content) *The Summer My Father Was Ten* *Tangled Threads: A Hmong Girl's Story* *Too Young for Yiddish* *Xóchitl and the Flowers/Xóchitl, la Niña de las Flores*	(see page 106) N N P F P (see page 167) F F P P P N F F (see page 142) F (see page 104) (see page 142)

Page references are given for books that can be found in the bookshelf lists of other chapters.
(GN) These books are graphic novels.

Immigrant Bookshelf Topics (continued)

Topics	Books	Category
Fitting In Books in this category show the challenges experienced by immigrants—coping with a new culture that may clash with family traditions; experiencing loneliness; and struggling for acceptance.	*Any Small Goodness*	F
	The Arrival	F (GN)
	The Gold-Threaded Dress	F
	Happy Birthday Mr. Kang	P
	The Have a Good Day Cafe	P
	A New Life	F
	No English	P
	One Green Apple	P
	Shadow of the Dragon (see Safe and Strong Communities Bookshelf—digital content)	F
	A Step from Heaven	F
	The Ugly Vegetables (see Gardening Bookshelf—digital content)	P
	Uncle Rain Cloud	P

Page references are given for books that can be found in the bookshelf lists of other chapters.

(GN) These books are graphic novels.

who commit themselves to making a difference in the lives of children and young adults." The family members come alive in Francisco's recounting of his journey toward adulthood. 200pp., young adult

The Circuit: Stories from the Life of a Migrant Child
by Francisco Jiménez (University of New Mexico Press, 1997). This autobiography starts with the author as a young boy living in a Mexican village in the late 1940s, who then travels with his family as they enter California illegally to find work. The family moves continuously from picking cotton to topping carrots, from one labor camp to the next, from one school to another. They remain close despite backbreaking work and poverty. These compelling short stories intertwine and paint an intricate picture of the life of migrant *campesinos*. 134pp., young adult

Denied, Detained, Deported: Stories from the Dark Side of American Immigration
by Ann Bausum (National Geographic Children's Books, 2009). These stark and powerful stories of people seeking freedom and safe haven and receiving denial and denigration will resonate with students. Among the informative stories are those of Jewish families escaping the Holocaust on a boat denied from docking in port after port, Chinese and Mexican laborers welcomed for exploitation and then rejected, and the detention of Japanese Americans that exposes racism harbored within the political system. Current issues and a most relevant topic make this a book to spark discussions and action. 112pp., grades 6–12

Forty-Cent Tip: Stories of New York Immigrant Workers
by The Students of Three New York International High Schools (Next Generation Press, 2006). Sixty-seven short stories written by public school students and teachers tell about friends, relatives, and neighbors who immigrated to New York City to work. These narratives and accompanying pictures poignantly relate the hardships and hopes of immigrants and demonstrate the sensitivity and insight of the young authors who tell their stories. 72pp., grades 6 and up

Reaching Out
by Francisco Jiménez (Houghton Mifflin, 2008). In this fictionalized autobiography, the author enters Santa Clara University as the first member of his Mexican-American migrant family to attend college. The transition has countless challenges, yet his family and friends help guide him to mentor others and eventually become a college professor. This candid portrait sheds light on those who are the first in their family to attend college today. 200pp., young adult

The Middle of Everywhere:
The World's Refugees Come to Our Town
by Mary Pipher (Harcourt, 2002). Liem's dad had been a prisoner of war in Vietnam. Two teens lived in northern Bosnia during the war. Two sisters, Shireen and Meena, arrived with their family from Pakistan. From Sierra Leone, Kosovo, Macedonia, from across the globe, refugees arrive in Lincoln, Nebraska, their new home. Their stories enlighten us about the world and about how Americans are perceived by others. 390pp., grades 9 and up

Picture Books: Immigrants

Four Feet, Two Sandals

by Karen Lynn Williams and Khadra Mohammed (Eerdmans Books for Young Readers, 2007). When Lina finds a sandal in the truck bearing donated clothing, she is elated. But she immediately discovers that another girl has already taken the matching sandal. Though initially they each go their separate ways, in the days that follow the pair of shoes brings their owners together. This is the story of the development of one friendship in a refugee camp in Pakistan. The book paints a picture of two of the 20 million refugees worldwide, most of whom are children like Lina and Feroza who lose their parents to violence and war.

Happy Birthday Mr. Kang

by Susan L. Roth (National Geographic Society, 2001). Mr. Kang paints poems, reads the *New York Times*, and cares for his hua mei bird as his grandfather did in China. On Sunday, Mr. Kang carries his bird in a bamboo cage to Sara Delano Roosevelt Park in Manhattan, joining other Chinese immigrants with their birds. When his seven-year-old grandson questions whether "a free man should keep a caged bird," Mr. Kang opens the bamboo door. Will the hua mei fly away?

The Have a Good Day Cafe

by Frances Park and Ginger Park (Lee & Low, 2005). A Korean family struggles in their business selling food from a cart in a park. Everyone sells hot dogs and sodas. It's only when Grandma has arrived to live with Mike and his parents that she brings a new idea: selling the food that is their tradition! Soon people line up for *bibim bap, chajang myunm,* and *kalbi!*

No English

by Jacqueline Jules (Mitten Press, 2007). When Diane sees her new desk mate Blanca drawing during spelling time, she is quick to raise her hand and tell the teacher. But when another teacher comes in and announces that she will be teaching Blanca English, Diane realizes she has made a horrible mistake. She and her classmates find respectful ways to communicate with Blanca as language barriers vanish.

A Movie in My Pillow/Una película en mi almohada

by Jorge Argueta (Children's Book Press, 2001). Young Jorge moves to San Francisco from his beloved El Salvador, bringing with him sights, sounds, and smells of his native rural home. He also carries the sorrow of war and of leaving loved ones. To this is added the confusion and joy of reuniting with family in his new urban home. Through Jorge Argueta's poetry and accompanying artwork by Elizabeth Gómez, each story comes alive. In English and Spanish.

My Diary from Here to There/Mi diario de aquí hasta allá

by Amada Irma Pérez (Children's Book Press, 2002). Amada writes in her diary, "I overheard Mamá and Papá whispering . . . about leaving our little house in Juárez, Mexico, where we've lived our whole lives, and moving to Los Angeles. . . . Am I the only one scared to leave? What if we're not allowed to speak Spanish? What if I can't learn English?" Young Amada learns she has the strength to survive the exciting and painful move. Through her family and her diary, Amada finds a new home. In English and Spanish, based on the author's experience.

My Name Is Yoon

by Helen Recorvits (Farrar Straus Giroux, 2003). Yoon's name means "Shining Wisdom." When written in Korean, her name looks happy, but the shapes seem lonely when written in English. Yoon decides to try different names—*cat, bird,* even *cupcake.* Only as she finds her place in her new country does she become Yoon again.

One Green Apple

by Eve Bunting (Clarion Books, 2006). On her second day in this new school, riding in a hay wagon and picking and processing apples with the rest of her new class, recent immigrant Farah has heightened sensibilities. Everything is fresh and new—even if some actions toward her are unkind. Though Farah cannot yet communicate in English, friendly, helpful classmates and a common purpose allow her to be part of a rich community.

Uncle Rain Cloud

by Tony Johnston (Charlesbridge, 2001). Carlos delights in the stories his uncle, Tio Tomás, tells him of Mexico and the tongue-twister gods, *los dioses trabalenguas.* Sometimes, though, Tomás is stormy, having difficulty adjusting to his life in Los Angeles and his frustration with English. Carlos has his own struggles in third grade. As they forge a partnership, each teaching the other, change comes more easily.

The Whispering Cloth: A Refugee's Story

by Pegi Deitz Shea (Boyds Mills Press, 1995). Little Mai watches the Hmong women in the refugee camp in Thailand as they stitch stories onto cloth. Traders buy the brightly colored *pa'ndau.* Mai's grandmother shows her how to stitch the border, but only Mai can find the story for her cloth. Mai's cloth whispers the story of her escape, life in the camp, and dreams for a bright future—her cloth is not for sale!

Fiction: Immigrants

Any Small Goodness

by Tony Johnston (Scholastic, 2001). Moving from Mexico to Los Angeles with a little English in his pocket, eleven-year-old Arturo Rodriguez struggles to make sense of his world. As his father says, "In life there is *bueno* and *malo.* If you do not find enough good, you must yourself create it." Arturo's journey includes reclaiming his heritage, valuing his teachers and mentors, rescuing the family cat, and living where "what you love is always at risk." His "retaliation" is heartwarming. A glossary translates the Spanish vocabulary used. 128pp., grades 4–8

The Arrival

by Shaun Tan (Arthur A. Levine Books, 2007). This wordless graphic novel captures the displacement and awe with which immigrants respond to their new surroundings. It depicts the journey of one man to a new country, threatened by dark shapes that cast shadows on his family's life. The only writing is in an invented alphabet, which creates the sensation immigrants must feel when they encounter a strange new language and way of life. 123pp., young adult

The Clay Marble

by Minfong Ho (Farrar Straus Giroux, 1991). After fleeing their war-torn Cambodian village, twelve-year-old Dara and her family create makeshift dwellings in refugee camps on the Thai-Cambodian border. The terror is inescapable, as are the calamities and tragedies they face in daily life. Separated from her loved ones, Dara discovers the courage and confidence to find her family. 163pp., grades 5–8

DIGITAL CONTENT

Recommendation from the Field

Dragonwings by Lawrence Yep (HarperTrophy, 1975). 336pp., grades 5–9

Esperanza Rising

by Pan Muñoz Ryan (Scholastic, 2000). Esperanza lives in luxury on her father's ranch in Mexico and assumes that her lifestyle of fancy dresses and servants will last forever. A tragedy on the eve of her birthday in 1930 shatters all she knows. She and her mother escape to California to become migrant farm workers. Esperanza is ill prepared for hard labor and the financial struggles of the Great Depression, but her mother's illness causes her to rise above oppressive circumstances. 262pp., young adult

First Crossing: Stories About Teen Immigrants

edited by Donald R. Gallo (Candlewick Press, 2007). These ten moving and fast-paced short stories are written by award-winning young adult authors and told through the eyes of the teens. Fourteen-year-old Marco hides next to a car engine to enter the United States from Mexico. Ameen struggles for a fair chance to play football quarterback in New Mexico. A Korean girl cannot "fit" with her adopted American family. Real-life characters represent Mexican, Venezuelan, Kazakh, Chinese, Romanian, Palestinian, Swedish, Korean, Haitian, and Cambodian cultures. They share the struggle all teens have for self-identity and how to relate to friends, parents, and school.

These kids have the added struggle of communicating in a new language, dealing with ignorance and prejudice, and maintaining cultural roots. "About the Author" follows each story. 224pp., young adult

The Gold-Threaded Dress

by Carolyn Marsden (Candlewick Press, 2002). In America, Oy's teacher renames her "Olivia." Having just arrived from Thailand, Oy is unaccustomed to many of the behaviors she encounters in school, from being left out of games to being teased. When the other children learn about her traditional silk dress, they taunt her by promising to be her friend if only she will bring the dress to school. Will Oy betray her family to fit in? 73pp., grades 3–5

The Importance of Wings

by Robin Friedman (Charlesbridge, 2009). Roxanne lives with her father and sister in New York City while her mother still resides in Israel. She struggles to fit in as an American teenager—but her idea of what it means to be American and how to fit in changes with the arrival of another Israeli girl in town. 176pp., grades 4–6

Libertad

by Alma Fullerton (Fitzhenry & Whiteside, 2008). When their mother dies, Libertad and Julie must leave their home in the Guatemala City Dump. These brothers bravely begin a dangerous adventure to find their father in the United States. This travel journal tells about the people they meet as they walk thousands of miles in hope of a better life. A tribute to perseverance, courage, and hope. 224pp., grades 6–9

A New Life

by Rukhsana Khan (Groundwood Books, 2009). Move from Pakistan all the way to Canada? For Kadija (in grade three) and her older brother Hamza (in grade five), this new home requires many adjustments. There are kids bullying on the playground, and English sounds like gibberish, but there is also a fountain with plenty of water to quench a thirst and a library filled with books. The day-to-day life unfolds with realistic descriptions of what a family goes through, from adapting to school to their father driving a cab for two years awaiting the approval of his teaching certificate. An appreciation for what is made available in this new home permeates the story. 64pp., grades 4–6

DIGITAL CONTENT

Recommendation from the Field

The Skirt by Gary Soto (Delacorte Press, 1992). 74pp., grades 4–5

A Step from Heaven

by An Na (Front Street, 2001). Moving from Korea to California is supposed to bring Young Park's family closer to heaven. Instead, learning English, financial hardships, and her father's rage and abuse cause painful difficulties. Each chapter adds to a poignant portrait of a young girl from age four to eighteen striving to turn her dream of finding heaven on earth into a reality. 156pp., young adult

Tangled Threads: A Hmong Girl's Story

by Pegi Deitz Shea (Clarion, 2003). After spending ten years in a refugee camp in Thailand, Mai Yang travels to Rhode Island with her grandmother to join the only living relatives—aunts, uncles, and cousins who had gone five years before. The cultural differences are exacerbated by her rebellious cousins, while Mai uses the threads of the traditional *pa'ndau* cloth to help her stay connected to her Hmong heritage. 236pp., grades 4–8

DIGITAL CONTENT

**Interviews with Authors:
The Story Behind the Story**

In the companion digital content, you'll find interviews with authors Francisco Jiménez (*The Circuit, Breaking Through, La Mariposa,* and *Reaching Out)* and Tony Johnston *(Any Small Goodness)* that tells the "story behind the story" of their books.

Chapter 13

Literacy

When I look back, I am so impressed again with the life-giving power of literature. If I were a young person today, trying to gain a sense of myself in the world, I would do that again by reading, just as I did when I was young.

—*Maya Angelou, poet*

Reading unlocks doors to new worlds. Words on a page can provide knowledge and opportunity, excitement and adventure, humor and tragedy. For many, learning to read comes easily; for others and for many reasons reading is a struggle fraught with frustration and embarrassment.

Service learning provides many opportunities to assist people having difficulty with reading. Tutoring and mentoring activities are most common; young people can also make books, perform to create enthusiasm for reading, and help with general language development when the reader's first language is not English.

Preparing for literacy service learning opportunities, especially for tutoring, involves understanding struggling readers' emotions and recognizing how much hard work reading can require of them. Works listed in the Literacy Bookshelf such as *La Mariposa, Dear Whiskers,* and *Thank You, Mr. Falker* can provide insight.

The bookshelf also includes works such as *The Year of Miss Agnes, A Bus of Our Own, That Book Woman,* and *Indian School: Teaching the White Man's Way* that tell about people whose reading difficulties or access to schools arose from social and cultural disadvantages rather than reading disabilities or language differences. Books such as *Nasreen's Secret School: A True Story from Afghanistan* remind us that the opportunity—as well as the ability—to read is closely linked to the rights to life, liberty, and the pursuit of happiness in modern society.

Preparation: Getting Ready for Service Learning Involving Literacy

The following activities can be used to promote learning and skill development related to literacy. These activities are easily adapted to different grade levels during investigation, preparation, and planning to help your students examine key issues through research, analyze community needs, and gain the knowledge they need to effectively contribute to the design of their service plan. They can often be integrated into reflection and demonstration as students can lead the activities with others to build awareness. Since literature is often an important part of preparation, you can find recommended titles on this theme in the Literacy Bookshelf later in this chapter.

Activity: Cross-Age Tutoring in Reading Skills. Elevate tutoring programs from a casual experience to high-level service learning. Here are some tips to prepare student tutors before they begin and to support continued preparation and skill review for ongoing tutoring relationships.

- Discuss the challenges some students have in learning. Ask students to think of their own challenges. This can be discussed in small groups or written in journals with feedback from the teacher.

- Use fiction and nonfiction from the Literacy Bookshelf to build knowledge and empathy.

- Invite a reading specialist to talk with the class to review the specific needs of the children who will be tutored.

- Ask students to bring in some of their favorite children's books from home or from the library. Discuss what makes a story engaging. Practice reading aloud to each other in pairs or small groups.

- Have tutors get to know their tutees by using the Personal Inventory form (see page 51). The tutors can pair up and practice using the form and the interview process. Discuss ways this can be helpful in getting to know the tutee and identifying high-interest books.

- In pairs or small groups, ask the tutors to design kinesthetic experiences that could help students learn the alphabet, punctuation, or any other writing skill. For example, making letters out of tactile materials or magnets, having students trace over letters with their fingers, or use their bodies to make the shapes of letters. (Simple stretches before a tutoring session can help by removing the "squirmy" factor in learning.)

- Ask students to consider all the reasons why listening skills are essential for the reader and learner. Have students think of ways to reinforce listening—for example, by reading a passage to the tutee and having the child summarize.

- Brainstorm with the tutors ways that quotes might be used with their tutees. Useful quotes are brief, convey an important message, and call for analyzing the meaning of a very short piece of writing or interpreting a metaphor. Some quotes relate directly to the tutoring experience: "No matter what accomplishments you make, somebody helps you" (Wilma Rudolph, athlete). Another metaphorical quote extols the value of reading: "A book is like a garden carried in the pocket" (Chinese proverb). Another removes the pressure of always "getting it right": "If you can't make a mistake, you can't make anything" (Marva N. Collins, educator). Find more quotes throughout this book and look at Quotable Quotes on page 72.

- Since reflection is an important part of the service learning process, suggest that students use reflection with their tutees. For example, the tutor can have the tutee reflect on such ideas as "Today I learned . . ." and "What I want to remember is . . ." Responses can be written down by the tutor and reviewed in the next session to reinforce lessons and skills learned.

- Tutors can involve their tutees in *doing* service learning. Tutees can make alphabet books to demonstrate their skills, write stories or poetry, or create other compilations. Copies can be given to the class or library or exchanged with other students for continued skill development. Many other service learning possibilities exist that often can be linked back to the students' original inventory of interests, skills, and talents.

Activity: A Right or a Privilege? Students generally attend school without considering this question: Is education a right or a privilege? Approximately 134 million children in the world ages seven to eighteen have never been to school,[*] and an estimated 218 million children are engaged in labor that threatens or prohibits their education.[**] Students can develop research questions to investigate both the history of education and the current struggles to learn for people in many parts of the world. What historical events have made education accessible to the masses? Slavery, women's rights, and child labor laws are part of this story. Where in the world are students now deprived of education because of war, famine, forced child labor, or other factors? In Malawi, for example, as well as other African nations, students can only attend classes if they can afford classroom supplies. In times of war schools close and in refugee camps there may be no schools. In Afghanistan, setting up schools for girls places one's life at risk.

The next step is using this new knowledge and awareness to determine ways to take action. Immigrants locally may need support in order to take full advantage of available opportunities. For example, students could provide free childcare during language classes.

---

[*] Gordon et al, *Child Poverty in the Developing World*. Bristol, England: Policy Press, 2003.

[**] *The End of Child Labour—Within Reach*, report to the International Labour Conference, 95th Session 2006.

Advocacy for children in other nations can be accomplished through many international organizations, such as Oxfam (www.oxfamammerica.org), Amnesty International (www.amnestyusa.org), and Peace Corps Kids World (www.peacecorps.gov/kids). Collections of school supplies or books may also help.

Find Out More About Literacy

To learn more about these issues and to get ideas for service and action, visit these Web sites and organizations online:

The **In Our Village** book and movement (www.inourvillage.org) was created to help young people see the daily lives of other children across the globe and has led to the In Our Global Village international literacy project. All are welcome to view the Web sites, download the other "village" books, and create their own.

The National Service Knowledge Network (www.nationalserviceresources.org), a service of the Corporation for National and Community Service, offers information and many publications to help enhance any service learning experience, including "Reading Helpers," a manual for tutors.

The International Labour Organization (www.ilo.org) has a virtual classroom on child labor with resources for elementary and high school students and teachers. The site includes information on what kids are doing to end child labor and enable all kids to attend schools.

Making Connections Across the Curriculum

Some service learning activities naturally lend themselves to interdisciplinary work and making connections across the curriculum. These connections strengthen and broaden student learning, helping them meet academic standards. More than likely, you'll be looking for these connections and ways to encourage them well before the students ever start working on service learning activities. As with the entire service learning process, it helps to remain flexible, because some connections can be spontaneously generated by the questions raised throughout and by the community needs identified by the students. To help you think about cross-curricular connections and where you can look for them, the curricular web for this chapter (page 186) gives examples of many different ways this theme can be used in different academic areas. (The service learning scenarios in the next section of the chapter also demonstrate various ways that this theme can be used across the curriculum.)

Service Learning Scenarios: Ideas for Action

Ready to take action? The service learning descriptions that follow have been successfully carried out by elementary, middle, or high school students in schools and with community organizations. Most of these scenarios and examples explicitly include some aspects of investigation, preparation and planning, action, reflection, and demonstration, and all have strong curricular connections. These scenarios can be a rich source of ideas for you to draw upon. Keep in mind that grade levels are provided as a reference; most scenarios can be adapted to suit younger or older students, and many are suitable for cross-age partnerships.

Everything You Need to Know About Kindergarten: Kindergarten

Think of the big difference between kindergartners on their very first day of school and on the last day of the school year. Kindergarten teachers in Los Angeles harnessed that growth and transformation into a creative and valued service learning activity. In early spring, the soon-to-be first graders identify what they have learned: how to sit in a circle, where to put their lunches, how to take care of library books, where to recycle paper, and so on. They use their knowledge to produce a book about their kindergarten year. Students work in pairs to create one page of the book on a selected theme. After drawing illustrations, the students dictate the words to an adult. All work is done in black ink for easy duplication. As parents register their children for the next year's kindergarten, the family receives a copy of "All About Kindergarten." On the first day of school, one parent reported, "My daughter slept with her kindergarten book all summer, it was her security for the transition." The idea

Literacy Across the Curriculum

English/Language Arts

- Discuss: What is your favorite book and why?
- Study stories and practice storytelling techniques, including those from other cultures
- Prepare annotated bibliographies of recommended books for peers

Social Studies/History

- Create and "attend" a classroom environment from the past, e.g., the early 1900s
- Study the Indian Schools established in 1879 by the federal government and its impact on tribal culture then and now
- Learn about pending current legislation that would impact your school and education

Languages

- Learn about education in the countries of the language being studied, and compare to your own
- Create lessons to familiarize younger children with this language and culture
- Identify idioms and slang expressions that are hard to translate into the language being studied, and find similar kinds of expressions in the language being studied

Theater, Music, & Visual Arts

- Write skits that promote reading as an adventure
- Find and learn contemporary or popular songs that promote learning and education
- Find quotes in books, online, or elsewhere about the wonders of books and reading, then create posters

Literacy

Math

- Research literacy rates for your state and compare with national statistics
- Prepare "math in a box" kits of basic math concepts with directions and games
- Discuss: What does it mean to be "math literate"? How has this changed with calculators and computers?

Physical Education

- Discuss: How does physical activity help children learn?
- Design an activity to teach the alphabet by having students forms the letters with their bodies either individually or in groups
- Create an annotated list of books about sports or athletes to share with younger children

Computer

- Access the Internet for illiteracy data and local resources and programs
- Make a list of computer terms and meanings in a picture book format
- Research places in the community that need computers for kids, like shelters or community centers, and seek donations from businesses

Science

- Study about learning differences, variations of learning styles, and learning disabilities
- Prepare science lessons for young children that incorporate various learning styles
- Help younger students record science experiments

spread around the country and the globe. A Missouri class made a splendid book with each student writing their information. Since they used inventive spelling, a typed "translation" also appeared on the page. These students felt so proud about being authors!

Postman Platypus: Grades K–1

At All Saints Anglican School on the Gold Coast of Queensland, Australia, five- to-six-year-old students participated in "Postman Platypus." Each child contributed an original story, most often about themselves—their lives, their families. These stories were compiled into three different books that Postman Platypus delivered to a school in a different place and country: Tanzania; Papua, New Guinea; and one Aboriginal community in Wadeye, Australia. The recipient classes each compiled original stories about their own lives, again delivered by this amazing platypus! The results: This reciprocal literacy experience opened the eyes to how children live in the world. The stories become a teaching point, since they all fit into the curriculum. And as they learn about the world, children at All Saints ask: "Why do these children have to walk two miles to fetch water? Why don't they turn on the tap?" This leads to vital lessons of similarities, differences, and the world stage. A great book to integrate: *A Life Like Mine: How Children Live Around the World* (Social Change Bookshelf—digital content).

A Broad Approach: Grades K–8

An independent school in Minnesota took a broad approach to promote literacy and service learning. All students read books about service to inspire discussions, ideas, and class projects. For example, some fifth-grade students tutored beginning readers once a month at a nearby public school while others shared book selections with elder friends at a residential facility. At the middle school, teens selected and read poetry with second graders to stimulate conversations about making wise choices. Story analysis, discussion and reflection were well-integrated into this school-wide effort.

Collections: Grade 1 (with Grade 6 Helpers)

First graders focus on literacy as they sponsor an all-school new and "gently used" book drive to support libraries. Counting skills come in to play, as well as writing, since each student writes a book review of one book he or she is donating. With the help of

middle school students, the children sort the books into groups according to reading level. The books are personally delivered by the children.

Original Books for the Community: Grades 1–5

So many original books are written by students, but where do they go? Usually home, and that's it. Students at a school in Washington state make two copies of each book (or more if the book is a class collaboration), so one copy can be contributed to a place that needs more books: a library, children's center, after-school program, homeless shelter, hospital, emergency room, or free health clinic. Students learn about the community as they select a place for their books to go and often deliver the books themselves and read them aloud to younger children. Some children have added multiple languages to produce bi- and even tri-lingual books that have a broader community reach.

Books on Tape: Grade 2

Books on tape are welcome in many places. Second graders in a Chicago suburb discovered this after taping a choral reading for the Junior Blind organization. Next, they made tapes to donate to emergency waiting rooms, hospitals, and a ward for premature infants, who seemed to thrive while listening to the lovely voices of children. Recording original stories also gave students an incentive to improve their writing skills.

Idioms in Pairs: Grade 2

Two schools, two different socioeconomic groups, two languages, and grade two children: a perfect partnership. Students from The Center for Early Education and Gardner Elementary met in West Hollywood, California, for cultural, recreational, and academic interaction which led to a service learning activity. The process began when one of the schools hosted a Russian storytelling troupe. A second-grade class invited the predominantly Russian-born second-grade students from a nearby school to participate. After social interaction (and lunch), teachers from both schools led activities on idioms, which are very difficult for students learning English as a second language to grasp. Working in pairs, students took an idiom, such as "Don't let the cat out of the bag," and discussed its interpretation and meaning. The students also drew two pictures to illustrate; for example, for "Don't let the cat out of the bag," one picture showed a cat peeking out of a sack, and one showed a child saying "Shh!" The pictures were compiled into a workbook for use in these and other neighboring schools.

My Librarian Is a Bus: Grade 2

A class of students at Oakwood Elementary School in North Hollywood, California, was inspired to action by the book *My Librarian Is a Camel* that shows stunning photographs of books arriving in remote villages by donkey, elephant, wheelbarrow, and camel—and by bus. Using the book for research, the class contacted the mobile bus librarian in Pakistan and found out they need preschool books in English. The kids went to work notifying other classes about how important books are everywhere in the world. Once they had collected the books, a big question followed: How do we get them to Pakistan? They contacted Pakistan's Embassy and found their contact was more than pleased to deliver the books, free of charge. Later, a Pakistani diplomat visited the school to express appreciation and share career information to inspire diplomats of the future.

Turn Off the TV! Grades 3–5

In a multi-age classroom that included grades three through five, the children used a chart to keep track of how much television they each watched in one week's time. For two TV programs, they counted any violent images they saw on the shows or commercials. The next week they recorded how much time they played or read books outside of school. A huge class chart consolidated the data and students compared the amounts. Using information from the TV-Turn Off Network, the teacher presented information about how violent images impact children and about the "couch potato" syndrome—how inactivity affects children's weight and health. Students decided to educate the rest of the school. They made presentations to other classrooms along with posters and signs announcing "Turn Off the TV Week." Many students in the school pledged to exchange television for books for an entire week, culminating in a read aloud and book exchange to keep the pages turning, and the television turned off.

I must say that I find television very educational. The minute somebody turns it on, I go to the library and read a book.

—*Groucho Marx, actor*

Especially for New Parents: Grade 4

An elementary teacher in Maine asked her students, "Do you enjoy having your parent or a teacher read you a story?" The response was an overwhelming "Yes!" Students eagerly described what they liked about story times. Later, teachers discussed in a staff meeting the finding that parents in their community didn't spend much time reading to their children. They decided to invite students to address this issue. Children began gift-wrapping original books and writing letters explaining "why it's important to read to your child—and why I like someone to read to me." With assistance from a local community organization, the wrapped books were donated to the local county hospital and given to each new parent as a "welcome baby" gift.

Tutor Buddies Build Community: Grade 4

Entering fourth grade brings a special privilege at one elementary school in Mount Vernon, Washington. Every fourth grader, regardless of skill level, is partnered with a younger student. These "tutor buddies" meet four times per week, twenty minutes each time, and work on the younger children's reading skills. On the fifth day of the week, the tutors continue their training and work on development of their own skills. The school atmosphere has been transformed by these relationships. Every student is valued as having something to offer. Older children have greater empathy for the role of teacher. Younger children look up to their mentors as role models. Service learning is woven into the fabric of this school.

Annual Community Read! Grades 4–6

At Jefferson Elementary in Charleston, Illinois, teachers wondered: How can students learn to serve in their community while increasing their literature skills? The answer: A student-led community read. Each year the Service Learning Committee of students chooses a novel that reflects the theme of service and selflessness. The first year's choice: *Edwina Victorious* (page 225). All students experience the text as a read aloud in the classrooms of Jefferson Elementary. Teachers engage their students in text discussions, prompting high level thinking and questioning. Once the novel is read, the committee—consisting of one student from each class in the school—begins to roll out the excitement throughout the community. They prepare the distribution of 300 to 500 copies of the book purchased by the school with the message: "Read and Pass It On!" As they deliver the books to more than thirty locations, students learn about careers all over their city. The books have response cards inside to survey community needs and collect ideas for how Jefferson students can improve Charleston for everyone. The students also promote their project through brochures, posters, school board presentations, an all-school assembly, and features in the local newspaper and TV stations. Finally, the entire school sets out to address the needs requested. The results? Students read more and with a purpose!

A Kids' Library in Vietnam: Grades 5–11

A librarian and teacher at Wheeler Elementary in Oahu, Chun traveled to Hoi An, Vietnam, and met kids who wanted to learn but didn't have any books. As a librarian, she couldn't imagine what it was like to lack these books. So along with another librarian, she applied to several charity foundations and received enough grant money to open a small public library. The Hoi An library was born. What if young people ran the library, like the kids who come from the town's orphanage, the street center, and the soccer team? Today, these young librarians, ages ten to sixteen, maintain the book collection and teach younger children how to care for the books. They also lead one-to-one reading activities using different storytelling methods like puppet shows.

Through this library, kids find out they can take care of themselves and others. They run the library themselves. The library has provided the people of Hoi An with their first opportunity to take home free resources that can be shared and studied. The library even has a computer with Internet access.

> This is a good environment to open my mind. It's good to improve knowledge, improve my speaking skills and reading skills, to help me know more about the culture of many countries of the world.
>
> —*Vo, age 14*

Math Support: Grade 6

Literacy extends to math as well. In one school, sixth graders willingly gave up their usual lunch-time activities to tutor their peers in math. The tutors took extra time to learn how to break down a skill into manageable steps and to teach it effectively. Math tutoring became a sought-after program.

Women Count! Grades 6–8

Middle school students developed math literacy by showing that "women count" in the world of math—in the past, the present, and the future. At the Mary Lyon School in Boston, Massachusetts, students read books and wrote short biographies about women in history who have made contributions in math. Next, the students interviewed women in their school and community and wrote essays about how these role models use math every day—as professionals, homemakers, parents, and teachers. Students added their own ideas about their futures and how math would be part of reaching their ambitions and dreams. Equipped with the knowledge they acquired, students developed math lessons and "math success kits" to inspire and motivate fourth graders. To demonstrate their accomplishments, the middle school students created a virtual math museum on a computer to help others learn about an important life equation: math + women = women count!

Kids for Computer Literacy: Grades 6–8

The rural community of Kansas, Oklahoma, had no public library to provide access to computers, and many families did not have computers at home. What could middle school kids do to help? They decided to open their school's computer lab on Tuesday evenings and Saturday mornings for instruction and assistance. To prepare, the students practiced creating and leading computer lessons, and learned how to use the résumé templates on the computer. After surveying parents and community members to find out their interests, they also located Web sites that would provide information the community was interested in.

Giving a Head Start with Reading: Grades 6–8

Middle school students in the rural community of London, Kentucky, wanted to write books. They immersed themselves in children's literature, exploring the nuances and writing styles of their favorite books. In further preparation, a communication specialist visited the students and talked about writing short stories. Students took their creative ideas and applied them for a specific audience—preschool children. They used computers and other forms of technology to organize and produce their books. Finally, children from a local Head Start program visited the middle school library, and met the "big kids," who read to them and presented them with a classroom full of original picture books.

In Our Village: Grades 6–12

In a world of digital technology and designer coffee, the 5,000 residents of Kambi ya Simba, Tanzania, illuminate the night with lanterns and drink from streams and pumps that often carry illness. And yet, equipped with digital cameras and tape recorders, and with assistance from the U.S.-based nonprofit What Kids Can Do, 350 students at Awet Secondary School documented daily life in their village. They held cameras and tape recorders for the first time. They reflected on their work saying: "It stretched our imagination in so many ways. Before this, we had never seen a book with photographs. Of the larger world, we know only what our teachers have told us." Their book, *In Our Village* (see page 192) has been read by over 30,000 students around the world. As a result of their book sales, students have received scholarships to continue their education.

In Our Global Village: Grades K–12

Reading the book *In Our Village* (described previously) inspired the author of *this* book to act. In the book's preface, Barbara Cervone writes of the student authors she worked with: "On our parting, they told me this: 'It astounds us—and we remain unconvinced—that anyone outside our village would care about our lives and our challenges.'" This notion compelled me to collaborate with Barbara and launch the In Our Global Village

project, an international book writing experience based on the original. Over twenty-five books have been written to date in eight countries. To write a book, young people must take initiative and decide what to share about their local community. They compose questions, conduct interviews, take photographs, and compile wonderful books that are available on the project's Web site: www.inourvillage.org. The books comprising this "village" have been created by classes across the United States and in Estonia, India, South Africa, and Vietnam. In writing these books, students develop local literacy while contributing to global literacy.

Free Quality Tax Preparation: Grades 9–12

The Volunteer Income Tax Assistance Site (VITA) at Santa Barbara High School has prepared about 600 tax returns for low income individual and families each year. All tax returns are prepared free of charge and all student volunteers are certified by the IRS. VITA provides students with valuable experience and training, while saving the community large sums of money. For over fifteen years, students have run the operation. Usually, accountants prepare taxpayers' returns for at least $200. The Los Angeles branch of the IRS called the program "the best practice model to be emulated for quality and utility." After they graduate high school, some students start VITA at their university.

Dependable Tutors: Grades 9–11

As part of a high school service class, students daily went to a local elementary school for one period as tutors for younger students. The high school students had been taught tutoring techniques by a local community college instructor to prepare for the experience. At the end of the semester, they produced a unique reflection piece to present to others—teachers, parents, community members, and peers. Teachers at the elementary school provided regular feedback on the high school students' performance, and skill development was ongoing. Students also learned about dependability. One student wrote: "When I didn't show up on Tuesday, I thought it wouldn't be a big deal. On Thursday, I came in as if everything was normal, and Sara, a little girl I always read to, wouldn't talk to me. Finally, after about twenty minutes, she climbed on my lap with tears in her eyes. 'Where were you? I missed you!' I was speechless. I didn't know she was counting on me."

Romeo, Romeo! Grade 10

In love with Shakespeare? Tenth-grade English students in Alabama discovered an unexpected passion for the great bard, so they wanted to share their excitement with younger students. They interviewed upper elementary teachers to find out if this would have value. Based on the responses and what they discovered about learning styles, the sophomores employed two different strategies. One group performed short versions of *A Midsummer Night's Dream* in modern language. Another group made "Shakespeare's Tales" story books. The younger students were delighted with their introduction to Shakespeare and began reading *Twelfth Night* as a class.

A Hero's Journey: Grades 11 and 12

For a British literature course, students in South Carolina went on their own "hero's journey" while reading *Beowulf*. Each student found a way to be heroic in the community by providing a response to an authenticated need to an individual or organization. The students documented their service experiences in language comparable to that used in the epic poem. The culmination of the semester was a video presentation made by several students set to music. Recipients of the service were invited to the presentation and learned how much the students had gained from the experience.

Education for All—in Afghanistan: Young Adult

A young girl's family fled the violence in Afghanistan to settle temporarily in Pakistan. As refugees they faced many challenges, however, the daughters were permitted to attend school. In 1994, at age fourteen, Sadiqa returned to her home village and amazed the villagers with stories of her education. During that time, the ruling Taliban made it nearly impossible for girls to be educated. Since 2001, the restrictions have eased somewhat, but the situation remains volatile. In 2003 Sadiqa opened her first Afghani girls' school, the Oruj Learning Center. Now, with four schools, Oruj supports 1,200 girls seeking an education.

> When I got my library card, that was when my life began.
>
> —*Rita Mae Brown, author*

School Connections: Grade 11 with primary and university students

At the University of Western Sydney in Australia, the Community Action Support initiative involves pre-service teachers heading to remote Tennant Creek in Northern Territory to work with Aboriginal communities. The pre-service teachers mentor year eleven high school students during a community studies course. These year eleven students are guided to be effective literacy mentors for primary school students. The program is also intended to motivate these high school students to go to university and perhaps return as teachers to their communities, where there is a severe shortage of teachers from Aboriginal backgrounds. After the five-week practicum, the established relationships continue through online mentoring with video links set up for regular communication between the university students, the aboriginal communities, and the high school students.

The Literacy Bookshelf

The ability to read is one part of literacy, and some of the books on the Literacy Bookshelf (pages 193–194) deal with issues related to this ability. Other stories tell of people yearning for an education, and others describe appreciation of books and reading. To help you find books relevant to your particular projects, the book chart classifies the titles according to several topic areas: seeking an education, learning to read, and appreciation of books and reading.

In general, the bookshelf features:

- An annotated bibliography arranged and alphabetized by title according to the general categories of nonfiction (N), picture books (P), and fiction (F). For nonfiction and fiction, length and recommended grade levels are included. The entries in the picture book category do not include suggested grade levels, since they can be successfully used with all ages.

- A chart organized by topic and category to help you find books relevant to particular projects.

- Recommendations from service learning colleagues and experts, which include a book summary and ideas for service learning connections.

(The number of recommended books varies in each bookshelf.)

- *Please note:* additional titles for this category are listed in the digital content; some of these were out of print at the time of publication but still worth finding.

Nonfiction: Literacy

The Forbidden Schoolhouse: The True and Dramatic Story of Prudence Crandall and Her Students

by Suzanne Jurmain (Houghton Mifflin, 2005). This story of courage in the pursuit of justice began when a black woman asked the director of The Canterbury Female Boarding School, Prudence Crandall, if she could attend her classes. When Prudence responded, "Yes," the white students abandoned the school. Prudence reopened her school with the purpose of educating young black women. Regardless of threats, arson, boycotts, arrests, and trials, Miss Crandall and her students persisted, helped by her family and the famous abolitionist, Reverend William Lloyd Garrison, until a frightening attack on the school one night caused it to close. 160pp., grades 5–12

How Lincoln Learned to Read: Twelve Great Americans and the Educations that Made Them

by Daniel Wolff (Bloomsbury, 2009). How has education mattered in the lives of twelve influential people? Read about Ben Franklin finding "his own way to what he needed to know" and becoming a champion of schooling. Learn about Belle, born in 1797, whose "main school would be slavery." Follow the story of Helen Keller who wrote in her autobiography, "Knowledge is love and light and vision." Learn how Elvis attended school in "the poorest white neighborhood in town [with] electricity, indoor plumbing, and heating: 'a shared source of pride and joy.'" And for Lincoln, just read the book! 345pp., grades 10–12

Indian School: Teaching the White Man's Way

by Michael L. Cooper (Clarion, 1999). In 1879, eighty-four Sioux boys and girls were forced to leave their tribal homes to attend the Carlisle Indian School. This was the first institution opened by the federal government for the education of Native American children, intending to "civilize" the Indian children and teach them the "white man's way." While a few children succeeded in this setting, for the majority it was an isolating and painful experience in acculturation. 103pp., grades 5–10

In Our Village: Kambi ya Simba through the Eyes of Its Youth

by Students of Awet Secondary School, edited by Barbara Cervone (Next Generation Press, 2006). Equipped with digital cameras and tape recorders, students recorded their daily lives in a remote village in Tanzania. As we read these brief detailed chapters, drawn from essays by 350 students and interviews with villagers, our sense of global literacy is increased. In a world where education is far from being uniform and in a place without books, these young authors' achievement is astonishing. 64 pp., all ages

My Librarian Is a Camel: How Books Are Brought to Children Around the World

by Margriet Ruurs (Boyds Mills Press, 2005). From elephants, donkeys, and camels, to buses, boats, and trucks, this book shows us all the ways that dedicated people bring books to kids who might be hard pressed to find a local library within traveling distance. Photographs, maps, and narrative make this text come to life! 31pp., grades 1–12

My School in the Rain Forest: How Children Attend School Around the World

by Margriet Ruurs (Boyds Mills Press, 2009). Read about a school that floats on a lake, one that is high up in the Himalayas, and another that takes place via Web cam. Travel to Afghanistan to see girls attend a school hidden behind a wall. See a school run by volunteers in a jungle in India. A fascinating way to study geography. 32pp., grades 3–6

DIGITAL CONTENT

Recommendation from the Field

The Narrative of the Life of Frederick Douglass by Frederick Douglass (Oxford University Press, 1999, original publication 1845). 192pp., all ages

A School Like Mine: A Unique Celebration of Schools Around the World

by Penny Smith and Zahavit Shalev (DK Publishing, 2008). Images of vivacious children from all over the world accompany facts about the active lives of forty-one students and the schools they attend. This book serves as a reminder that education must be available everywhere, that equity in education needs to be a priority, and that the dreams and aspirations of those who pursue education are more similar than we might imagine. 78pp., all ages

You Can't Read This: Forbidden Books, Lost Writing, Mistranslations, and Codes

by Val Ross (Tundra Books, 2006). These eighteen thrilling stories tell about bold and persistent struggles of individuals, scholars, believers, and transgressors to engage in writing and reading in civilizations across the globe throughout history. These fascinating tales teach readers about the adversity surrounding an activity we often take for granted, as they tell us about the important times and places in which each story occurs. 152pp., grades 7–10

Literacy Bookshelf Topics

Topics	Books	Category
Seeking an Education When social inequities exist, education is usually withheld from some part of the population. These books contain stories of people's struggles simply to be in a place where they can learn, to get to a school, to create a school to be in.	*The Absolutely True Diary of a Part-Time Indian*	F
	Breaking Through	(see page 177)
	A Bus of Our Own *	P
	The Circuit	(see page 179)
	Extra Credit	F
	The Forbidden Schoolhouse: The True and Dramatic Story of Prudence Crandall and Her Students	N
	Goin' Someplace Special	P
	Howard Thurman's Great Hope	P
	How I Learned Geography	P
	Indian School: Teaching the White Man's Way	N
	In Our Village: Kambi ya Simba through the Eyes of Its Youth	N
	Linda Brown, You Are Not Alone: The Brown v. Board of Education Decision (see Social Change Bookshelf—digital content)	N
	The Lost Boys of Natinga: A School for Sudan's Young Need to Go to School: Voices of the Rugmark Children (see Hunger, Homelessness and Poverty Bookshelf—digital content)	N
	Miss Little's Gift	P
	My School in the Rain Forest: How Children Attend School Around the World	N
	Nasreen's Secret School: A True Story from Afghanistan	F
	A School Like Mine: A Unique Celebration of Schools Around the World	N
	Sequoyah: The Cherokee Man Who Gave His People Writing *	P
	The Strength of Saints *	F
	The Year of Miss Agnes	F
Learning to Read Learning to read is not a "one size fits all" proposition. It can be a challenging process for some young people and adults. Language barriers, embarrassment, and lack of resources can be stumbling blocks; community support can make all the difference.	*Dear Whiskers (see digital content)*	F
	Flight	F
	The Hard Times Jar	P
	How Lincoln Learned to Read	N
	La Mariposa	P
	Mr. George Baker	P
	My Life as a Book	F
	The Narrative of the Life of Frederick Douglass (see digital content)	N
	Thank You, Mr. Falker	P
	That Book Woman	P

Page references are given for books that can be found in the bookshelf lists of other chapters.

* These books include examples of young people in service-providing roles.

Literacy Bookshelf Topics (continued)

Topics	Books	Category
Appreciation of Books and Reading Some people go to great lengths to have books in hand. Appreciation, joy, pleasure, excitement—all to be found within the covers of books and in the libraries where books live.	Amadi's Snowman	P
	A Book	P
	The Book Thief	F
	Fahrenheit 451 (see digital content)	F
	Glass Slipper, Gold Sandal: A Worldwide Cinderella	P
	I Hate to Read	P
	Josias, Hold the Book	P
	The Librarian of Basra: A True Story from Iraq	P
	The Library Card (see digital content)	F
	My Librarian Is a Camel: How Books Are Brought to Children Around the World	N
	Nonsense!	P
	Our Library *	P
	Too Young for Yiddish	(see page 104)
	You Can't Read This: Forbidden Books, Lost Writing, Mistranslations, and Codes	N

Page references are given for books that can be found in the bookshelf lists of other chapters.

* These books include examples of young people in service-providing roles.

Picture Books: Literacy

Amadi's Snowman

by Katia Novet Saint-Lot (Tilbury House, 2008). Being a businessman is all that matters to young Nigerian, Amadi. So why learn to read? When he finds an older boy reading a book about a snowman at the market he is stunned. "What's that?" he asks. When he learns about a thing called snow that falls from the sky to cover everything, suddenly reading may have meaning and purpose and actually *help* a businessman! A cultural excursion with lovely illustrations and a clear message.

A Book

by Mordicai Gerstein (Roaring Brook Press, 2009). Laugh your way through this wonderful topsy-turvy story telling of a young girl who lives inside a book trying to find *her* story. It sparks the writer in all of us!

A Bus of Our Own

by Freddi Williams Evans (Albert Whitman, 2001). Mabel Jean wants to attend school, a five-mile walk from home. She tries to find a way for the black children to have a school bus like the white children have. With support from family and friends, she succeeds. Based on real events in 1949.

Glass Slipper, Gold Sandal: A Worldwide Cinderella

by Paul Fleischman (Henry Holt and Company, 2007). This retelling of one of the world's most famous fairytales intertwines the eighteen global versions of the Cinderella story, from Mexico to Japan.

Goin' Someplace Special

by Patricia McKissack (Simon & Schuster, 2001). Tricia Ann is on her way to someplace special in the segregated Nashville, Tennessee, of the 1950s. After riding in the "colored section" of the bus, nearly sitting on a "for whites only" park bench, and suffering hurtful words of discrimination, she arrives at the public library, where the sign says, "All Are Welcome."

The Hard Times Jar

by Ethel Footman Smothers (Farrar Straus Giroux, 2003). Although young Emma Turner loves books, she has none at home. The money earned by her family of migrant workers goes strictly for necessities. So Emma works and saves her money until her plans are interrupted: she must attend school! There she finds books, but these cannot be taken home. Will Emma be able to follow the rules?

Howard Thurman's Great Hope

by Kai Jackson Issa (Lee & Low Books, 2008). Born in Daytona, Florida, in 1899, Howard held tight to the memory of his father's pride that he was smart, literate, and would be the first in the family to go to college. His was a nearly impossible dream, given segregation and the fact that Howard's school for "negroes" only went up to seventh grade. But when his principal offered to tutor him and he got a perfect score on his graduation exam, Howard's future was set—a scholarship, college, and on to being a preacher and civil rights leader.

How I Learned Geography

by Uri Shulevitz (Farrar, Straus & Giroux, 2008). During World War II, the author's home was bombed and his family had to move. Living in poverty, instead of bread one evening, the father brings home a huge map. The colors and shapes enliven the family's bleak home and transport the young boy out of the desperation of his hunger.

I Hate to Read

by Rita Marshall and Etienne Delessert (Creative Editions, 1992). Victor Dickens hates to read. But when a book's characters start to emerge all around him, he realizes that he does not want them to disappear. Soon he cannot put the book down! See also: *I Still Hate to Read* (2007).

Josias, Hold the Book

by Jennifer Riesmeyer Elvgren (Boyds Mills Press, 2006). Josias is one of four children in his Haitian family. His responsibility: the family garden. His friends keep pressing him to attend school, but he insists he is too busy tending the garden, especially since the beans are having trouble coming up this year. But soon he realizes that books may provide the necessary answers to his problem.

La Mariposa

by Francisco Jiménez (Houghton Mifflin, 1998). Francisco sits in first grade without understanding a word in this English-only school. His desire to learn begins to center on the caterpillar in the jar next to his desk: How does it turn into a butterfly? How long will it take? Through determination and imagination, Francisco overcomes his confusion and isolation and teaches others about tolerance and the love of learning.

The Librarian of Basra: A True Story from Iraq

by Jeanette Winter (Harcourt, 2005). Alia Muhammad Baker is an actual librarian living in Basra, Iraq. When rumors of war began to spread, she asked the government to help her move the books to a safe location. When they refused, she took matters into her own hands, storing the books with the help of her neighbors wherever she could find room—and in the nick of time. She still waits for a time when she can safely rebuild her library and exhibit this vast collection of ancient and modern texts.

Miss Little's Gift

by Douglas Wood (Candlewick Press, 2009). Based on his own experience as a child before the condition known as Attention Deficit Hyperactivity Disorder (ADHD) was diagnosed, the author tells the story of a young boy who can hardly sit still to read. As the youngest student in Miss Little's class, young Douglas found the help he needed, the patience to guide him through reading *The Little Island*, and the inspiration to become a lifelong reader and author.

Mr. George Baker

by Amy Hest (Candlewick Press, 2004). Mr. Baker is 100 years old, a famous drummer, and he cannot read. And so every morning he and his young pal Harry wait for the bus. And when the bus rolls up, they go to school to do the hard work of making all those letters come together, like the beat of Mr. Baker's drum.

Nonsense!

by Sally Kahler Phillips (Random House, 2006). This book shows us that when we learn new words, we gain new tools for thinking about the world and all the things we can do in it.

Our Library

by Eve Bunting (Clarion Books, 2008). When devotees of a local library learn that it will close, they read their way to a solution and manage to save this important community center.

Sequoyah: The Cherokee Man Who Gave His People Writing

by James Rumford (Houghton Mifflin Books, 2004). This is the story of how a magnificent tree got its name and how an extraordinary man developed a writing system. Sequoyah was a metalworker and physically handicapped. And though he never held a high position in his tribe and was not able to maneuver in the world as others did, he preserved his native Cherokee language with a written form still in use today. Written in both English and Cherokee.

Thank You, Mr. Falker

by Patricia Polacco (Philomel, 1998). At first, Trisha loves school, but her difficulty reading makes her feel stupid. Finally, in fifth grade, a teacher helps her overcome her problem. The rest of her odyssey is a learning adventure, and she grows up to write books for children. This semi-autobiographical tale inspires learners, teachers, and tutors!

That Book Woman

by Heather Henson (Atheneum, 2008). This captivating book was inspired by the actual Pack Horse Librarians known as "book women" who traveled through Appalachia beginning in the 1930s, bringing books to remote communities. We are introduced to Cal who is "no scholar-boy." But "that book woman" somehow stirs Cal's curiosity to finally open a book. What used to be "chicken scratch" to Cal turns into words, and Cal turns into a reader.

Fiction: Literacy

The Absolutely True Diary of a Part-Time Indian

by Sherman Alexie (Little, Brown & Co., 2007). Alexie teams up with cartoonist and illustrator Ellen Forney in telling the story of a young teenager, Junior, who is tired of getting bullied and wants a better education for himself. So he switches from his school on the Indian reservation to an all white school twenty-two miles away. Narrated from the boy's perspective, this is a witty and moving chronicle of Junior's efforts to fit in and cope with the hardships at home. 288pp., grades 7–10

The Book Thief

by Markus Zusak (Knopf, 2007). A unique telling of the story of World War II centering on the life of Liesel Meminger, who we meet at age nine, a girl with a passion for books. We follow her journey from being left by her mother in foster care with her father's acquaintance through her adjustment, and the relationships that follow with a boy Rudy, a Jewish refugee Max, the mayor's reclusive wife who entices her to visit her astounding library. The travails of war, the necessity to join a Hitler's youth group, the separation from her beloved foster father when he goes to fight, all weave together with exceptional writing to provide this unique look at war and intricate relationships. 576pp., young adult

Extra Credit

by Andrew Clements (Simon & Schuster, 2009). Abby Carson may be held back unless she can improve her grades. For extra credit, she chooses to exchange letters with a pen pal in Afghanistan and finds that words sent across an ocean build an unexpected friendship, deep understanding, and surprising commonalities. 192pp., grades 4–7

DIGITAL CONTENT

Recommendations from the Field

Fahrenheit 451 by Ray Bradbury (Simon & Schuster, 1953/1993). 190pp., young adult

The Library Card by Jerry Spinelli (Scholastic, 1996). 148pp., grades 5–8

Flight

by Elizabeth Stow Ellison (Holiday House, 2008). Twelve-year-old Samantha has great loyalty to her older brother Evan, a high school freshman gifted in athletics and art, who frequently gets into trouble at school. With his parents always on his case, will Samantha be able to help Evan enter a local art contest? And he needs help even with the forms because he can't read. Set in 1982, this compelling story has a deep secret—family illiteracy and not only Evan's. Confronting the truth and family loyalty are at the core of this gripping story. 245pp., grades 5–7

My Life as a Book

by Janet Tashjian (Henry Holt, 2010). Derek wants to enjoy summer and escape from the diabolical summer reading list that threatens to make his life miserable. What he does read is a newspaper article about a mysterious drowning that seems to involve *him* when he was a baby. Along the way Derek illustrates his vocabulary words with amusing images. This technique helps him demystify the hard words and makes reading fun. Filled with action, humor, a heartfelt resolution, and plenty of drawings by the author's teenage son. 211pp., grades 4–6

Nasreen's Secret School: A True Story from Afghanistan

by Jeanette Winter (Simon and Schuster, 2009). When her parents are taken by the Taliban, Nasreen stops talking. Her grandmother enrolls her in a secret school for girls, hoping it will help her heal. With caring teachers, classmates, and books, Nasreen finds her voice. Based on a true story. 40pp., grades 2–5

The Strength of Saints

by Alexandria LaFaye (Simon & Schuster, 2002). Harper, Louisiana, 1936. Fourteen-year-old Nissa Bergen has a mind and will of her own. As the librarian in a small town with narrow ideas about integration, she has created "separate-but-equal" libraries. Still, she is plagued with a conscience that wants to unite the community. Doing what is right may not be easy, but Nissa's independent spirit and convictions triumph. This third book about Nissa easily stands on its own. 183pp., grades 6–10

The Year of Miss Agnes

by Kirkpatrick Hill (Aladdin, 2000). A new teacher arrives in a remote Alaskan town. Frederika, "Fred" for short, age ten, doubts that Miss Agnes will last in this community that smells of fish. But the one-room schoolhouse comes alive as never before with the creative spirit of a dynamic teacher, who reaches out and values every child, including Bokko, Fred's twelve-year-old deaf sister. 113pp., grades 4–8

DIGITAL CONTENT

Interviews with Authors: The Story Behind the Story

In the companion digital content, you'll find interviews with Janet Tashjian (*The Gospel According to Larry, Vote for Larry,* and *My Life as a Book*); Jake Tashjian, Janet's son and illustrator of *My Life as a Book;* and Ann Whitehead Nagda *(Dear Whiskers).* The interviews tell the "story behind the story" of these books.

Chapter 14

Safe and Strong Communities

Generosity is the first step toward peace.
—*Buddhist saying*

In today's world, the idea of feeling and being safe is paramount in our communities. On school playgrounds, children wonder how to react to bullying and to the temptation to bully others. Young people wrestle with peer pressure and worry about exclusion. Gang activity and other acts of violence create fear and feelings of helplessness. Acts of terrorism and war know no national boundaries. Service learning provides an educational strategy for sorting through these challenging and complex issues. Literature and the process of service learning help students examine new questions and develop sensitivity to people in places they may never see. This can help them determine ways to participate in constructive actions.

Whether responding to an incident on a playground, in a neighborhood, or in a war zone, examining issues related to safety affords the opportunity to examine the concept of community. What is community? Is community within walking distance or can community be global? Although the term is common, the actual meaning can be difficult to grasp and define. Each person brings a different understanding based on individual and collective experience. One perspective comes from looking at the history of the term. The word *community* has roots reaching back to the Indo-European bases *mei*, meaning "change" or "exchange," and *kom*, meaning "with," which combined to produce the word *kommein*: "shared by all."* We might define *community*, then, as a shared change or exchange. This definition illustrates community as dynamic, a concept that can be influenced—in this case, by service learning.

---

* Peter M. Senge, Art Kleiner, Charlotte Roberts, Richard B. Ross, and Bryan J. Smith in *The Fifth Discipline Fieldbook* (New York: Doubleday, 1994).

> To be alive, to have freedom to build communities, are privileges not to be taken lightly.
>
> —*Ngoan Le, Chicago Department of Human Services*

Preparation: Getting Ready for Service Learning Involving Safe and Strong Communities

 The following activities can be used to promote learning and skill development related to safe and strong communities. These activities are easily adapted to different grade levels during investigation, preparation, and planning to help your students research key issues, analyze community needs, and gain the knowledge they need to effectively contribute to the design of their service plan. They can often be integrated into the reflection and demonstration stages also, as students can lead the activities with others to build awareness. Since literature is often an important part of preparation, you can find recommended titles on this theme in the Safe and Strong Communities Bookshelf later in this chapter.

Activity: Draw Community. To make the idea of community more concrete, have students present the idea visually. Provide lengths of butcher paper and plenty of markers. Invite students to be absolutely silent. Then give the assignment with just two words: "draw community." This silence helps maintain the integrity of each student's concept of community, encourages them to collaborate differently, and strengthens the reflection that follows this exercise. Refrain from providing any further instructions or clarification of the task. Students may all work on the same paper or in groups of at least four students around smaller sheets as they draw what community looks like to them. Following five to ten minutes of art, have students discuss their drawings and observations. Did the students work individually or collaborate? How did the silence affect the process? Were they aware of what others drew, and did that influence them? What is most apparent in their drawings—people, buildings, or animals? Is something missing? Does the art reflect the best of the community or the challenges? What would they add to improve their community, and how could this be done? Once students have experienced this activity, they often enjoy leading it with other students or adult groups followed by student-led discussions, all to illuminate the concept of community.

Activity: A Look at Conflict and Community Building. Exploring the nature of conflict can be valuable in examining issues of community safety. Ask a group of people whether conflict is positive or negative, and the majority will probably respond "negative." However, the Latin root of conflict—*confligere*—means "to strike together." This implied friction is absolutely necessary for moving forward and motivating change. Perhaps the personal and collective skills key to resolving conflicts that inevitably occur are more important than the conflicts themselves. Use these ideas to help you explore the nature and importance of conflict with your students.

In class, read aloud any picture book or fictionalized story from the Safe and Strong Communities Bookshelf, and examine the storyline for conflict. Where is it? What is the dilemma facing the characters? At any point pause the story and ask, "What would you do?" Have students write the next part of the book. Delve into conflict as the compelling element in all forms of storytelling, including literature, television, film, and song lyrics. Encourage students to be specific and explicit, even creating a "timeline for change" that shows the evolution of a character or an event. Next, have your students identify what characters in the books do to build community. What ideas do your students have about safety needs, for repairing conflict, and for promoting positive social interaction? How do they think older students could be role models

for younger children in promoting healthy, thoughtful behaviors? What shared experiences do they think bring community members together?

Compare the fictionalized examination of conflict and community with news stories that cover our day-to-day lives. What is similar to how real people address issues of community change? How do media report distant conflicts that shape others' lives and perhaps touch our own?

All of these questions can help you and your students lay the groundwork for a range of different kinds of service experiences that promote and build safe and strong communities.

Find Out More About Safe and Strong Communities

To learn more about these issues and to get ideas for service and action, visit these Web sites and organizations online:

Teens, Crime, and the Community (www.ncpc.org, under "Programs") is a program of the National Crime Prevention Council and Street Law and includes anti-violence curriculum, information on anti-violence training opportunities, and prevention tips to help combat violent crimes among teens.

Educators for Social Responsibility (ESR) (www.esrnational.org) helps educators create safe, caring, respectful, and productive learning environments. Their Online Teacher Center includes resources on conflict resolution issues ranging from national security to peacemaking and violence prevention in the classroom.

The National Association of S.A.V.E. (Students Against Violence Everywhere) (www.nationalsave.org) is a student-driven organization encouraging young people to learn about alternatives to violence and practice what they learn through school and community service projects. Their Web site includes a back-to-school safety guide and a list of warning signs for schools at risk of increased student violence.

Making Connections Across the Curriculum

Some service learning activities naturally lend themselves to interdisciplinary work and making connections across the curriculum. These connections strengthen and broaden student learning, helping them meet academic standards. More than likely, you'll be looking for these connections and ways to encourage them well before the students ever start working on service learning activities. As with the entire service learning process, it helps to remain flexible, because some connections can be spontaneously generated by the questions raised throughout and by the community needs identified by the students. To help you think about cross-curricular connections and where you can look for them, the curricular web for this chapter (page 200) gives examples of many different ways this theme can be used in different academic areas. (The examples in the next section also demonstrate various ways that this theme can be used across the curriculum.)

It is better to be part of a great whole than to be the whole of a small part.

—*Frederick Douglass, abolitionist*

Service Learning Scenarios: Ideas for Action

Ready to take action? The service learning descriptions that follow have been successfully carried out by elementary, middle, or high school students in schools and with community organizations. Most of these scenarios and examples explicitly include some aspects of investigation, preparation and planning, action, reflection, and demonstration, and all have strong curricular connections. These scenarios can be a rich source of ideas for you to draw upon. Keep in mind that grade levels are provided as a reference; most scenarios can be adapted to suit younger or older students, and many are suitable for cross-age partnerships.

Peace Keepers Everywhere: Grades K–5

An elementary school administration decided to educate children about ways to reduce bullying and teasing. With faculty and student council agreement, educators from a local nonprofit organization led workshops and trainings on conflict resolution and peer mediation for teachers. Parent information sessions were held and an article was published in the back-to-school newsletter about the new campaign. Education on conflict resolution was carried out in all classrooms. To augment student skills and involvement, eighty children in the third through fifth grades attended workshops to become "peace keepers" and peer mediators on the playground and school buses. They did such an effective job that they became a theater troop performing plays about nonviolence and replacing bullying with friendship at schools in their area.

Six Billion Paths to Peace: Grades K–12

Students at the Blake School in Minnesota were introduced to the Six Billion Paths to Peace initiative at an all-school assembly. Continuing conversations occurred as students grew inspired to take their ideas further. The initiative impacted different subject areas and grade levels in the daily teaching and learning at the school. Students initiated and engaged in various service learning experiences with mutual benefit for their immediate and international neighbors. While this response is ongoing, examples of impact were seen by the end of the first year:

- Ten students individually designed service projects that grew from their strengths and talents. One made a calendar for every classroom in the school, while another played the violin during weekly visits to an elders center.

- Students and teachers collaborated to create a Diversity Week at the high school and held a "1,400 Paths to Peace" challenge.

- After learning about local and international hunger issues, students donated milking cows to an orphanage in Kenya, packed dry meal ingredients to be shipped overseas, and made sandwiches and fleece blankets for local shelters.

- A Six Billion Paths to Peace camp was designed for summer months.

Safe and Strong Communities Across the Curriculum

English/Language Arts

- Write stories or skits that feature characters being bullied or teased and the ways they deal with it
- Make a library display of books that teach about friendship
- Read and write narratives of everyday people who make community building a priority

Social Studies/History

- Meet representatives from local historical societies to learn about their roles in building strong communities
- Research about hate crimes and the organizations that intervene
- Follow current events that demonstrate efforts by governments and grassroots organizations to resolve international turmoil; compare strategies and results

Languages

- Research the symbols used for public safety in different countries
- Learn how to say words related to peace in many languages
- Make multilingual posters that promote peace and peer conflict resolution

Theater, Music, & Visual Arts

- Create and perform skits that illustrate peer mediation skills and problem solving in settings where conflicts often occur, such as during lunch, on the school bus, or on the playground
- Research the origin of and perform songs from different countries about peace
- Find political cartoons that use images to comment about issues related to crime, violence, bullying, or conflict on the world stage, then create original cartoons

Safe and Strong Communities

Math

- Research and create a report on local crime statistics
- Monitor the rate of discipline referrals before and after peer mediation or conflict resolution programs are instituted
- Survey students to find out how often they are teased, bullied, and pressured to conform with peers; tabulate and report statistics

Physical Education

- Play noncompetitive games and invent new ones
- Learn strategies for responding in risky situations; be certain to make examples age-appropriate
- Mentor younger children in sports as a means of community building

Computer

- Using the Internet, read about global peace-building events as reported by newspapers in different countries or by different organizations; compare findings
- Research student-created Web sites that discuss safety issues such as gun safety, peace forums, and anti-bullying campaigns
- Brainstorm how computers can build community, i.e., newsfeeds, email lists, message boards, Web sites, or blogs to discuss community issues and events

Science

- Study "happiness theories": that people who use their skills and talents on behalf of others experience greater joy
- Examine the short- and long-term impact war has on natural resources
- Research stories of community building through environmental activities such as beach clean-ups, community gardens, and student-led recycling campaigns

Reaching Out Across the Globe: Grades K–12

Students in schools across the United States have found ways to reach across the globe to war-torn countries and places that have been devastated by natural disasters. They have:

- Made health kits for people who have had to leave their homes because of war. The kits, which can be distributed by relief agencies such as the Red Cross, contain a towel, a toothbrush, and soap.

- Made T-shirts to sell at community fairs to raise money for the Heifer Project. The Heifer Project buys cows, sheep, and chickens for families around the world.

- Collected canned goods for earthquake victims.

- Participated in a bike-a-thon to raise money for Bikes Not Bombs, which is a group that collects old bikes, fixes them, and gives them to people in other countries who cannot afford them.

- Collected used eyeglasses for "The Gift of Sight," a Lions Clubs program that repairs and gives eyeglasses to people in other countries. On Halloween, this program sponsors Sight Night. Children leave signs on their neighbors' doors in late October to let them know that they will be collecting eyeglasses. Then, on Halloween night, they pick up the glasses as they trick-or-treat. Collected eyeglasses are cleaned, repaired, and hand-delivered during optical and medical missions to developing countries.

A Community Finds Heroes: Grades 1–5

As a response to events of September 11, 2001, elementary school children in West Hollywood, California, were invited by their city council to contribute art and poetry based on several themes: "Wishes for the World," "We Give Thanks," and "Our Heroes." Age-appropriate discussion allowed students to share thoughts and feelings and to ask questions of adults. The students' artwork and words were displayed in City Hall. After reviewing the heroes identified by students, teachers and after-school-program specialists scheduled visits to bring these people face-to-face with the kids through field visits. In pairs (a male and female in each set), students interviewed doctors and sheriffs. Firefighters received first-grade visitors at the fire station, and a third-grade class met farmers at the local farmer's market. Students conducted thorough interviews with their heroes and published a series of books, with words and art: *Our Heroes*.

Slow Down—You Move Too Fast! Grade 3

Third-grade students in Wisconsin observed that the speed limit in front of their school was too high and decided to do something about it. They partnered with local police to record the speeds of the cars going by and created a graph showing how fast cars were going. Next, they held a car wash and surveyed adults regarding the speed in front of the school. Finally, they prepared a presentation for the city council requesting that the council immediately lower the speed limit in front of the school. When the students delivered the presentation, the council members were so impressed that they suspended the rules and voted to lower the speed limit that night. The result? A lower speed limit in front of the school and a safer place for the children.

Spreading the Ideas of Conflict Resolution: Grades 4 and 5

In an annual event sponsored by a city government in California, elementary students at two schools meet to celebrate their peer mediation programs. The Conflict Wizards and Peace Patrol groups begin with getting-acquainted activities and then role-play common situations they encounter on the playgrounds, such as disagreements over game rules. The groups then create a spiral-bound book together. Previous titles written by the students include *The ABCs of Peer Mediation*, *Poems for Peace*, and *Creating Safe Schools for Kids*. These books are distributed to every local school and library and made available to community agencies. As a "thank you" to the students for their dedication, the city awards certificates of merit and presents each young person with a copy of Barbara Lewis's *Kids with Courage: True Stories About Young People Making a Difference*.

You must be the change you wish to see in the world.

—Mahatma Gandhi, statesman

Documenting Stories of War and Peace: Grades 4–12

Social studies and government teachers have used the parable *Feathers and Fools* to examine issues of combat and coexistence, when teaching about war and conflict. The students drew parallels between the book and the specific dilemmas faced in historical or current events. From this launch pad, students have interviewed war veterans, as well as people who did not serve in the military but felt the impact of war at home. They have asked, for example, questions about how living through times of war has affected how these people have lived in times of peace. Stories have been compiled into books, presented at community gatherings, posted on the Web, used to create a "living museum," and used as the basis for dramatic presentations.

Building Friendships: Grade 6

A sixth-grade English/social studies teacher asked students to write about their earliest experiences of friendship or bullying. Through discussion, the class concluded that elementary children often struggle with both—how to maintain and build strong friendships and how to stand up to bullying behaviors. They identified third grade as a place where they could have an impact and wrote letters to the third-grade classes in a nearby elementary school to verify the need. The project: to lead interactive lessons that model friendship. Using the book *How Humans Make Friends,* the middle school students developed skits and scenarios, which they presented to the younger kids, and made posters, which they left in the classrooms. The students visited three classes weekly for three weeks. Feedback from the third-grade teachers in between visits made the reflection sessions instructive and improved the project and experience for everyone involved.

Creekwood Middle School World War I Model: Grades 6–8

Capturing the stories of elders took on great significance for the student body at Creekwood Middle School in Humble, Texas. After a teacher brought in the news story of Frank Buckles, the last surviving United States veteran of World War I, then age 108, the entire school became involved. With participation of the photographer who had interviewed and taken portraits of the last twelve U.S. veterans of this war, students became invested in knowing the general history of the war and also about the particular experiences of these individuals. A school-wide experience of engagement ended with a community teach-in reaching over 1,000 people. The sixth through eighth graders presented what they learned from the display of the aforementioned photographs, first-person accounts of the twelve remarkable veterans, and the displays of artifacts and stories gathered from their families. The students led a rally to support Frank Buckles's dream of creating a World War I monument in Washington, D.C., and raised money. A representative of the group flew to Virginia to present Frank a check for $12,000 for this cause.

Community History, Community Pride: Grades 6–12

In Albion Central School District in upstate New York, students work to build a strong local community that takes pride in and embraces its past. Students:

- Developed and led a ghost walk telling about famous residents from the past that were connected to local historic buildings and important events; over 600 community members attended.

- Designed a kiosk in the center of town spotlighting architecturally significant buildings in the village square that are listed in the National Register of Historic Places.

- Created brochures for the historic Mount Albion Cemetery that highlight famous men and women of Mount Albion and list the meanings of various gravestone symbols found throughout the cemetery.

- Designed a stone monument in honor of sixty-two black pioneers of Orleans County.

- Developed an interpretive panel of the Cobblestone Museum as well as activity books highlighting the museum's history for visitors.

- Erected "Welcome to Albion, Where History Lives" wooden signs at the entrance to the village district.

- Assisted a community organization with a campaign titled "This Place Matters" sponsored by the National Trust for Historic Preservation, spotlighting many buildings and structures of historic significance in the community.

A Symposium for Peace: Grades 6–12

Bringing students and community together offers an opportunity for learning, community building, and collaborative action. Following the attacks on September 11, 2001, adults and students in St. Cloud, Minnesota, designed a symposium that allowed them to spend time together examining issues of mutual concern. Topics included religious tolerance, dispute resolution, teen suicide, and local refugee programs. Students invited agency representatives to visit classes, and agencies asked young people to participate in community forums and planning meetings.

Teen Violence: Grades 7 and 10

Seventh-grade students read *Give a Boy a Gun* as part of their English studies. As the students discussed the multiple points of view represented in the story, they asked questions about real instances of youth violence in their region. With their teacher, they designed a course of study to learn about the issue. Their studies included collecting articles on teen violence from the Internet and inviting a local reporter to their classroom for a discussion of responsible journalism. Based on what they had learned, they developed an educational evening for parents and other students. They read selections from *Give a Boy a Gun* and discussed ways to maintain ongoing mutually respectful parent-child communication. Later, they documented the resulting recommendations in an article for their school newspaper, which included "Tips on Talking with Your Teen."

A high school teacher who learned of the seventh graders' project adapted the process in her tenth-grade class using the book *Big Mouth and Ugly Girl*. The high school students discussed the challenges of breaking down cliques and reaching out to students known as "loners" or just "different." They initiated a "Mix-It-Up Day" in which some students agreed to have lunch with randomly assigned people and then to meet with their lunch partners once a week for three weeks. During the second semester, the project was repeated with twice as many students. Later, students even encouraged a similar project for improved teacher-to-teacher interaction. Comments during reflection showed an increase in tolerance and appreciation that extended even to students and faculty who had not taken part.

Oral Histories on Violence: Grade 9

After conducting a community needs survey in their study skills class, students in San Francisco chose to study violence. They conducted research on one of the four types of violence—hate crimes, relationship violence, gang violence, and police brutality. Students read biographies, fiction, a play, newspaper articles, and expository text. They formed a coalition with local organizations and planned a community conference to raise issues and have discussions about violence. Also, after conducting a practice interview with a former teacher who had been the victim of police brutality, students conducted interviews with people who had perpetrated or been the target of violence. Their compilation of these people's stories, *I Have Been Strong: Oral Histories on Violence*, has been given to many local agencies and schools.

Transforming the "Bully": Grades 9 and 10

High school students in the Youth Explorers Program in central California worked with local law enforcement to reach out to younger children. They selected *Toestomper and the Caterpillars* as the ideal book for their Friendship Campaign. Students created posters highlighting the key points of the story. At after-school programs, the Explorers held the kids' attention with the humorous story and dramatic effects and led small group discussions about friendship and transforming the "bully" in all of us.

The Campaign for "Truth": Grades 9–12

Creativity hit a peak when Florida high school students were given a voice in developing "Truth," an antismoking social marketing campaign using tobacco settlement funds. Their candid approach and youthful appeal has reduced smoking by teens in Florida, and now their public service announcements have hit the national airwaves. On the other side of the United States in Hawaii, students used theater to discourage smoking. They conducted pre- and post-tests with their young audiences to find out the impact of their original performances. The results: Similar to their Florida peers, the teens' dramatic efforts have been more effective in making an impact than adult-initiated forms of prevention.

Rock Out on Tolerance: Grades 11 and 12

High school students in Florida used popular culture to send an important message to their peers about tolerance. Tapping their collective creative talents, students wrote an original song addressing three relevant issues of prejudice: race, physical differences, and sexism. Through their campus media center, the students learned the skills necessary to create a rock video that would illustrate the drama of discrimination and cause viewers to think about their personal behavior.

How wonderful it is that no one need wait a single moment before starting to change the world.

—Anne Frank, diarist

The Safe and Strong Communities Bookshelf

The Safe and Strong Communities Bookshelf (pages 205–207) covers a broad spectrum of topics. To help you find books relevant to your particular projects, the book chart classifies titles according to several topic areas: personal confidence and safety, bullying, conflict resolution, local violence, hate crimes, our world today, preserving history, and community building.

In general, the bookshelf features:

- An annotated bibliography arranged and alphabetized by title according to the general categories of nonfiction (N), picture books (P), and fiction (F). For nonfiction and fiction, length and recommended grade levels are included. The entries in the picture book category do not include suggested grade levels, since they can be successfully used with all ages.

- A chart organized by topic and category to help you find books relevant to particular projects.

- Recommendations from service learning colleagues and experts that include a book summary and ideas for service learning connections. (The number of recommended books varies in each bookshelf.)

- *Please note:* additional titles for this category are listed in the digital content; some of these were out of print at the time of publication but still worth finding.

Nonfiction: Safe and Strong Communities

Afghan Dreams: Young Voices of Afghanistan

by Tony O'Brien and Mike Sullivan (Bloomsbury Children's Books, 2008). Meet Rohul Ali, age fourteen, who already has worked as a car mechanic and is now employed at a bakery in Kabul. Meet Nasi, age thirteen, who works in the morning at the bazaar selling plastic boxes and studies in the afternoon. From diverse backgrounds and regions in Afghanistan, these children and others carry out their lives in the midst of war and do so with strength and hope. They each have dreams for their future—to be a teacher, a journalist, a midwife. Through their words and paired photographs, this book paints a rich landscape of both the beauty and sorrow of the people and their country. 80pp., grades 4–12

Alan's War: The Memories of G.I. Alan Cope

by Emmanuel Guibert (First Second, 2008). This graphic novel memoir tells one veteran's experience serving in World War II, the challenges and joys of life after war, and his glimpses into the lives of his comrades long after the war has come to an end. Most compelling is the beauty of this oral history. Alan died in 1999. This tribute is a must-read. 304pp., grades 9–12, mature themes

The Cat with the Yellow Star: Coming of Age in Terezin

by Susan Goldman Rubin with Ela Weissberger (Holiday House, 2006). Ela had to give up her childhood when her family was forced to live in Terezin, a Nazi concentration camp outside of Prague during World War II. In grim circumstances, other interned adults taught classes to make life more bearable. Ela studied art and music, and when *Brundibar*, a children's opera, was written and performed, she played the lead role of a cat. Her story of loss shows how her survival depended upon creativity, friendship, and love. The opera is still performed today as a tribute to the resistance. 40pp., grades 5–12

Children of War: Voices of Iraqi Refugees

by Deborah Ellis (Groundwood Books, 2009). By traveling to Jordan, author Deborah Ellis collected stories of the overlooked voices of Iraqi children refugees who have been displaced since the beginning of the war in 2003. She begins each account with a short and poignant introduction of the context and themes that the individual touches on—whether it's lack of health care or schooling, the difficulty of receiving services, and the tremendous interruption of lives caused by war. 144pp., grades 7–12

Safe and Strong Communities Bookshelf Topics

Topics	Books	Category
Personal Confidence and Safety Personal safety involves being confident about our skills and abilities and knowing how to take care of ourselves in a wide variety of situations at home, at school, and in the community.	*Drita: My Homegirl* *Handbook for Boys* *Holes* (see digital content) *The Kindness Quilt* *Know the Facts About Personal Safety* *Looking Like Me* *A Step from Heaven* *Trouble Talk*	F (see page 104) F P N P (see page 182) P
Bullying Inside every child who exhibits bullying behavior on the playground is a child who needs to be reached. These selections look at peer pressure, isolation, and being "different," as well as how to make friends.	*The Dunderheads* *Harry Potter and the Sorcerer's Stone* (see digital content) *Hey, Little Ant* *The Hundred Dresses* *Larger-Than-Life Lara* *The Liberation of Gabriel King* *The Misfits* *Our Friendship Rules* *Poison Ivy: 3 Bullies, 2 Boyfriends, 1 Trial* *Scat* * *Thank You, Mr. Falker* *Totally Joe*	N F P F F F F P F (see page 132) (see page 195) F
Conflict Resolution The best defense has nothing to do with hitting, kicking, or punching. Finding the tools of tolerance and peaceful resolution helps make communities safer.	*Define "Normal"* *Mole Music* *Playing War* *Siddhartha* (see digital content) *The Skirt* *The Summer My Father Was Ten*	F P P F (see page 181) (see page 142)
Local Violence Making sense of violence is always a challenge. Books offer a safe haven to investigate what happens in our communities and help us think about our choices.	*Any Small Goodness* *Bat 6* (see Social Change Bookshelf—digital content) *Give a Boy a Gun* *If You Come Softly* (see Social Change Bookshelf— digital content) *Jumper* *Romeo and Juliet* (see digital content)	(see page 180) F F F F F

Page references are given for books that can be found in the bookshelf lists of other chapters.

* These books include examples of young people in service-providing roles.

(GN) These books are graphic novels.

Safe and Strong Communities Bookshelf Topics (continued)

Topics	Books	Category
Hate Crimes Breaking the cycle of hate requires taking a firm stand. When we read about an individual willing to risk personal safety to protect others or about a community that bands together, we are encouraged to stand stronger.	*A Different Kind of Hero* (see Immigrants Bookshelf—digital content) *Passage to Freedom: The Sugihara Story* *When Plague Strikes: The Black Death, Smallpox, AIDS*	F (see page 224) (see page 81)
Our World Today Being informed about the challenges faced in other parts of the world develops knowledge and empathy. From Tibet to Ireland to Sudan to New York City, we can learn about others and become citizens of the world.	*Afghan Dreams: Young Voices of Afghanistan* *Behind the Mountains* (see Immigrants Bookshelf—digital content) *Bull Rider* *Children of War: Voices of Iraqi Refugees* *Clay Marble* *Duty Free* (see Social Change Bookshelf—digital content) *A Life Like Mine: How Children Live Around the World* * (see Social Change Bookshelf—digital content) *The Middle of Everywhere: The World's Refugees Come to Our Town* *Off to War: Voices of Soldiers' Children* *The Photographer* *Purple Heart* *Refresh, Refresh* *Shooting the Moon* *Silent Music: A Story of Baghdad* *Stand Up for Your Rights* * (see Social Change Bookshelf—digital content) *Sunrise Over Fallujah* *The Things They Carried* (see digital content) *Three Wishes: Palestinian and Israeli Children Speak* *Wanting Mor*	N F F N (see page 181) F N (see page 179) N (see page 227) F F (GN) F P N F (GN) F N F
Preserving History We learn through history to gain knowledge, to hold and carry forward the people and their story, and to make more effective choices for our future.	*Alan's War* *The Cat with the Yellow Star: Coming of Age in Terezin* *Cracker! The Best Dog in Vietnam* *The Donkey of Gallipoli: A True Story of Courage in World War I* *The Grand Mosque of Paris: A Story of How Muslims Rescued Jews During the Holocaust* *The House* *Mr. Williams* *One Thousand Tracings: Healing the Wounds of World War II*	N (GN) N F P N P (see page 104) P

Page references are given for books that can be found in the bookshelf lists of other chapters.

* These books include examples of young people in service-providing roles.

(GN) These books are graphic novels.

Safe and Strong Communities Bookshelf Topics (continued)

Topics	Books	Category
Community Building Coming together to build a diverse and thriving community is a memorable experience. Books in this category offer models to examine and stories to emulate.	14 Cows for America	P
	Albert the Fix-It Man	P
	A Child's Garden: A Story of Hope	P
	Seedfolks *	(see page 142)
	Somebody Loves You, Mr. Hatch	(see page 104)
	Something Beautiful * (see Social Change Bookshelf— digital content)	P
	The Story Blanket *	P
	Wartville Wizard	(see page 131)

Page references are given for books that can be found in the bookshelf lists of other chapters.

* These books include examples of young people in service-providing roles.

(GN) These books are graphic novels.

The Grand Mosque of Paris: A Story of How Muslims Rescued Jews During the Holocaust

by Karen Gray Ruelle and Deborah Durland DeSaix (Holiday House, 2009). This little known story shows the bravery of the people of the Grand Mosque and the resistance staged by the Kabyles that protected many Jews and brought them to safe places of refuge. Compiled through extensive research with survivors. 40pp., grades 4–12

Know the Facts About Personal Safety

by Judith Anderson (Rosen Central, 2009). What are the risks faced by teens these days? Each chapter examines a theme teens can relate to—safety at home and away, peer pressure, bullying, cell phones, and Internet use. Includes facts, sample scenarios, and tips for staying safe. 48pp., grades 5–8

Off to War: Voices of Soldiers' Children

by Deborah Ellis (Groundwood Books, 2008). A life in the military separates families. This collection of interviews with children from Canada and the United States whose parents serve in the military creates a vivid portrait, acknowledging their day-to-day experiences, fears, and concerns. An estimated 1.2 million children living in the United States have a parent in the military; a lesser number in Canada. These stories acknowledge the diverse families who make significant sacrifices, and the toll service takes on soldiers and their children. 176pp., grades 4–12

Three Wishes Palestinian and Israeli Children Speak

by Deborah Ellis (Groundwood Books, 2004). Deborah Ellis's book provides the reader with first-hand accounts from children who have lived in the Israeli/Palestinian conflict since the Intifada began in the year 2000. Each story begins with a brief historical introduction, allowing the reader to understand each child's perspective and the depth of the conflict. Photographs add to the stories of personal life and continued struggles. By alternating each story, one Palestinian and one Israeli, the author encourages the reader to listen to both sides. When this book was published, 429 children had died in the conflict; their names are listed. 106pp., grades 5–12

Picture Books: Safe and Strong Communities

14 Cows for America

by Carmen Aga Deedy (Peachtree Publishers, 2009). When a Masai man returns to his homeland after being in New York City on 9/11, he describes to his people what took place. While the elders offer their blessing, the community wants to offer something more. They invite a diplomat from the United States to their village and give him fourteen cows. To the Masai, "the cow is life." They give this gift "because there is no nation so powerful it cannot be wounded, not a people so small they cannot offer mighty comfort." Based on a true story.

Albert the Fix-It Man

by Janet Lord (Peachtree, 2008). Albert fixes anything for the people in his community—a clock, a cup, a truck. But what happens when Albert needs some fixing up? His neighbors know exactly how to lend a hand.

A Child's Garden: A Story of Hope

by Michael Foreman (Candlewick Press, 2009). This is the beautiful story of a boy who nurtures life in one corner of his demolished town by caring for a plant until it blooms into a garden. His persistence is contagious, and, despite the destruction, the children living near him on either side of a barbed-wire fence bring color and human connection back into their world.

The Donkey of Gallipoli:
A True Story of Courage in World War I

by Mark Greenwood (Candlewick Press, 2008). This is the true tale of a boy who leaves his home in England to work in Australia. When given the opportunity to enlist in the army to fight in World War I, Jack jumps at the chance to serve his country, and hopefully earn a ticket back home. Instead, he trains in Egypt and fights in the battlefields of Gallipoli, Turkey. There, he heroically saves over 300 people in twenty-four days by leading wounded men back to camp on a donkey he finds one day. Though he never returns home, Jack is well remembered since his brother was among those whose life he rescued.

The Dunderheads

by Paul Fleischman (Candlewick Press, 2009). What if the teacher were a bully? And what if the teacher confiscated a boy's cat that was to be a gift for his mom? Could the class of students that the teacher—Miss Breakbone—calls "mind-wandering, doodling, dozing, don't-knowing dunderheads" use their unique skills and talents to rescue the cat and save the day?

Hey, Little Ant

by Phillip and Hannah Hoose (Tricycle Press, 1998). In this song-turned-book, a boy is about to stomp on an ant when the ant speaks up: "Please, oh please, do not squish me." In the dialogue between boy and ant that follows, the boy wrestles with his conscience, peer pressure, and the logic of this teeny creature. Sheet music for the song is included.

The House

by J. Patrick Lewis (Creative Editions, 2009). Built in 1656 when the Plague ravaged the community, this house has generations of stories to tell and to show. Intricate pictures that show how the house and its residents changed over hundreds of years are partnered with short quatrains—words that encourage readers to imagine the life inside. Oh, if walls could only talk! In The House, they do.

The Kindness Quilt

by Nancy Elizabeth Wallace (Marshal Cavendish Children, 2007). When Minna and her classmates read a story about kindness, they decide they want to do acts of kindness, too. They draw pictures representing acts they have done and bring them to school. Soon their classroom wall becomes a quilt and a lesson in collaborative learning, transforming ideas into action, and communicating the pleasure that comes with kindness.

Looking Like Me

by Walter Dean Myers and Christopher Myers (EgmontUSA, 2009). With a hip-hop beat this father-son duo capture the essence of a boy celebrating his identity as son, brother, runner, friend, and so on—the list appears endless, just as it should.

Mole Music

by David McPhail (Henry Holt, 1999). Though Mole digs tunnels by day, he has begun to feel that there is something missing in his life. After hearing beautiful music on television, he "wants to make beautiful music, too." With much practice, he learns to play, and his violin echoes through the night. He imagines his music reaching into people's hearts, dissolving anger, and "changing the world." Without knowing it, he does change the world.

One Thousand Tracings:
Healing the Wounds of World War II

by Lita Judge (Hyperion Books for Children, 2007). A young girl and her mother help families starving in Germany after World War II by collecting canned food, soap, and shoes. This story reminds us that the hardship of war doesn't end with the cessation of violence, and that there are many ways to help others, even if they live across an ocean.

Our Friendship Rules

by Peggy Moss and Dee Dee Tardif (Tilbury House, 2007). When a new "popular" girl shows up at school, Alexandra is so intrigued by the prospect of her friendship that she betrays her best friend. She quickly comes to regret her mistake when she sees the pain she caused someone she loves so much. Alexandra tells and illustrates her own story about her enduring friendship and the power of forgiveness.

Playing War

by Kathy Beckwith (Tilbury House, 2005). When a group of friends are feeling too lethargic in the summer heat to play basketball, they decide to play war . . . until one friend, Sameer, tells them his story of real war.

Silent Music: A Story of Baghdad

by James Rumford (Roaring Brook Press, 2008). A boy in modern-day Baghdad loves to engage life's rhythms, whether on the soccer field, on the dance floor, or on the page. When his city is under fire he remembers a great ancient calligrapher who fled to a high tower to write his way through an attack on the city some 800 years ago. Similarly, Ali struggles with composing words and their power to reflect and affect the world around him.

The Story Blanket

by Ferida Wolff and Harriet May Savitz (Peachtree, 2008). All the children gather to listen to Babba Zarrah's stories on her beautiful woolen blanket. Then Babba's blanket begins to get smaller and smaller—what is happening? Could it have to do with the scarf the postman needed, the socks for a child, or the mittens for a schoolmaster?

Trouble Talk

by Trudy Ludwig (Tricycle Press, 2008). Here is a look at the dynamics that occur when a rumor is spread, one person talks about another, and some kids get excluded. Relationships of young girls are explored when one has a "really big mouth" and other girls keep getting hurt. Includes author's note, questions for discussion, and resources.

Fiction: Safe and Strong Communities

Bull Rider

by Suzanne Morgan Williams (Margaret K. McElderry Books, 2009). Cam is not interested in the family sport of bull riding—that is, until his brother comes back from Iraq transformed from a brain injury. Cam puts away his skateboard and with fierce determination enters a bull-riding contest with a hefty prize to provide money for his brother's future. 241pp., grades 6–9

Cracker! The Best Dog in Vietnam

by Cynthia Kadohata (Aladdin Paperbacks, 2007). Here is the story of an unlikely pairing: a young anxious soldier newly deployed in Vietnam and a heroic German shepherd who sniffs out enemy weaponry and soldiers. With crisp dialogue that places the reader right alongside the characters, this book shows the difficult path home from war. 312pp., grades 6–9

Define "Normal"

by Julie Anne Peters (Little, Brown, 2000). When she agrees to meet with Jasmine as a peer counselor at their middle school, Antonia, an overachiever, never dreams this "punker" girl with the black lipstick and pierced eyebrow will help her with a serious family problem and become a valued friend. 196pp., grades 6–8

Drita: My Homegirl

by Jenny Lombard (Scholastic, 2006). This story is told from the perspectives of two girls: Drita, who recently moved to New York City from Kosovo, and popular, commanding, not-always-sensitive Maxie, who is in Drita's class at school. When Maxie's welcome of Drita is not to the teacher's liking, Maxie is assigned a project to develop empathy . . . and the project is Drita. Each girl learns the importance of staying open-minded to friendship, even if it's unexpected. 135pp., grades 3–5

Give a Boy a Gun

by Todd Strasser (Simon & Schuster, 2000). After two years of constant harassment and beatings from school jocks, two boys storm a school dance equipped with guns to take their revenge. This book gives voice to the many sides of the school violence issue—school counselors, parents, teachers, and the troubled kids. Along with providing numerous facts about violence in America, the book insists that we consider whether this tragedy could have been prevented and what we can do now. 208pp., grades 7–12

DIGITAL CONTENT

Recommendations from the Field

Harry Potter and the Sorcerer's Stone by J.K. Rowling (Scholastic, 1998). 309pp., grades 4–12

Holes by Louis Sachar (Farrar, Straus and Giroux, 1998). 233pp., young adult

---

Jumper

by Rita Williams-Garcia (Harper, 2009). Trina, a happy-go-lucky young artist, walks between Dominique and her friends at school one day and is oblivious that she has caused a problem. For Dominique this is an insult and she attacks Trina on the spot. Leticia sees this happen, but will she get involved? A powerful account of teen girl violence. 168pp., young adult.

Larger-Than-Life Lara

by Dandi Daley MacKall (Dutton, 2006). Lara is large, and as the new girl in school, she is teased, ridiculed, and overlooked for a lead in the school play that she deserves. Treated as an outcast by students and teachers, Lara stands strong with her smiles and spontaneous original poetry. However, when a mean trick is played on her at the school play, her classmates and teachers realize too late how their behavior drives Lara and her family to move away. This is a vivid depiction of how bullying harms the entire community. Lara's classmate, Laney, narrates the story in first person using writing skills learned in class. 151pp., grades 3–5

The Liberation of Gabriel King

by K.L. Going (G.E. Putnam's Sons, 2005). Frita and Gabriel share fears and adventures that deal with issues of race, bullying, friendship, and courage in the summer of 1976. In small town Georgia, two very different friends consider the dangers of entering fifth grade and growing up in a town full of social and racial tension. 153pp., grades 4–7

The Misfits

by James Howe (Antheneum, 2002). Four students who do not "fit in" at their middle school create a third party for student council elections: the No-Name Party. These good friends laugh together, openly discuss their upsets, and talk about important issues. This "Gang of Five" (they say "five" to keep others off guard) enters the challenging world of adolescent popularity, politics, love, and loss and, on the way, change their school forever. 274pp., grades 4–7

Poison Ivy: 3 Bullies, 2 Boyfriends, 1 Trial

by Amy Goldman Koss (Roaring Brook Press, 2006). When American Government teacher Ms. Gold asks for topics to litigate, no one offers suggestions. However, Ivy's angry written lament on the insistent bullying that three popular girls in her class have put her through for years provides Ms. Gold the perfect subject. Told in amusing narratives by eight students who play different roles in the trial and their social environment, these perspectives show how the surface is often more complicated than imagined, and that events are often more predictable than one would hope. 176pp., grades 6–9

Purple Heart

by Patricia McCormick (HarperCollins, 2009) The complexity of war becomes vivid after Matt tries to reconstruct what happened in the alley on a day in Baghdad. Slowly his memory rebuilds the incident when he suffered a head trauma and a kid, Ali, who had seemed more of a mascot than a threat, was shot and killed. The notion of "guilt" and "innocence" become intertwined and harder and harder to understand. 199pp., young adult

Refresh, Refresh

by Danican Novgorodoff (FirstSecond, 2009). This graphic novel chronicles the dilemma faced by three high school students whose fathers are serving in Iraq. As they move toward graduation, two plan to join the military and one intends to go to college. They spend their time playing, fighting, going to parties, hunting, chasing girls, and sneaking into bars—but their fathers' absence is continually felt. 138pp., grades 9–12, mature themes

DIGITAL CONTENT

Recommendations from the Field

Romeo and Juliet by William Shakespeare (Cambridge University Press, 1999/1595). 224pp., young adult

Siddhartha by Hermann Hesse (Bantam, 1982/1992). 152pp., young adult

Shooting the Moon

by Frances O'Roark Dowell (Atheneum, 2008). Twelve-year-old Jamie Dexter is excited when her brother joins the army and ships out to Vietnam. Instead of letters, Jamie receives rolls of film from the front lines that her brother entrusts only to her to develop. With these images, Jamie sees through her brother's eyes the hardship of war and its mystique is replaced with real bullets and irretrievable loss. Based on the author's memories of growing up on a military base, this story becomes vivid through Jamie's time spent in the recreation center and all the characters who come alive on the page. An excellent read for any service learning projects related to photography. 163pp., grades 5–8

Sunrise Over Fallujah

by Walter Dean Myers (Scholastic, 2008). Robin "Birdy" Perry is a long way from his Harlem home as a young soldier taking part in Operation Iraqi Freedom. As a member of Civilian Affairs, he and his squadron are supposed to secure the Fallujah area through successful interactions with the Iraqi people. The problem is discerning the good guys from the bad, and coming to terms with the harrowing experiences of war and loss. Through the caring relationships built with others in his unit, Birdy grows in ways unimagined and replaces "winning" and "losing" with finding the things worth living for. 290pp., grades 7–12

DIGITAL CONTENT

Recommendation from the Field

The Things They Carried by Tim O'Brien (McClelland & Stewart, 1990). 256pp., young adult

Totally Joe

by James Howe (Ginee Seo Books, 2005). This sequel to *The Misfits* begins as the student election for class officers ends, and we see what transpires with No Name-Calling Day. However, this is Joe's narrative, written in response to an assignment to write his autobiographic ABCs, with each story having a life's lesson. In the "V" chapter for "Victim No Longer," Joe exposes how bullying is affecting him and others and the time has come to stop it once and for all. 208pp., grades 6–9

Wanting Mor

by Rukhsana Khan (Groundwood Books, 2009). Jameela aches for her *mor*, the Pusto word for mother, who has died of illness during the war in Afghanistan in 2001. When her father remarries, her stepmother first mistreats Jameela and then convinces Jameela's father to abandon his child in the marketplace of Kabul. The girl finds kind people who help her and is placed in an orphanage where she is able to attend school and have surgery to repair her cleft lip. When she meets her father and his family again, she has grown into a person of strength. Based on a true incident. Includes a glossary of Pusto words used throughout. 190pp., grades 5–9

DIGITAL CONTENT

Interviews with Authors: The Story Behind the Story

In the companion digital content, you'll find author interviews with Sharleen Collicott (*Toestomper and the Caterpillars*), Phillip Hoose (*Hey, Little Ant; We Were There, Too!; Claudette Colvin; The Race to Save the Lord God Bird;* and *It's Our World, Too!*), James Howe (*The Misfits, Totally Joe, Pinky and Rex and the Bully,* and *The Drop Dead Inn*), and Jerry Spinelli (*Stargirl, Wringer, Maniac Magee,* and *The Library Card*) that tell the "story behind the story" of their books.

Chapter 15

Social Change: Issues and Action

If we have learned one thing from our past, it is that to live through dramatic events is not enough; one has to share them and transform them into acts of conscience.

—Elie Wiesel, author and Holocaust survivor

Social change brings a requisite call to action. Change requires awareness, movement, and momentum. The need for social change is frequently rooted in intolerance. This intolerance can be focused on issues of race or ethnicity, religion, sex, poverty, sexual orientation, physical ability, or immigration status among others. Simple ignorance or stereotypes can bloom into prejudice, discrimination, or even hate crimes. In all of its many facets, intolerance is something to recognize, discuss, and finally, address. Classroom discussion can open minds and eyes alike, however this is just the beginning. As educators, we must make a concerted effort to replace prejudices and stereotypes with accurate information, opportunities for understanding, and mutual appreciation.

The need for change often results in social and political action. The action can involve raising community awareness through letters to the editor, making public service announcements online or on local cable television, and participating in the actual democratic process by speaking at city council meetings or writing letters to Congress. Students have been involved in establishing a much-needed community youth center, working for inclusion in government advisory committees, and speaking out against unjust actions such as slavery in the Sudan. Social change can be local *and* global in its scope and ambition.

Social change can also be key to achieving real depth in service learning by compelling students to investigate public policy, question the world around them, extend their practice into new areas, and encourage peers to become active in the civic process. Delving into social change, however, may take time to achieve, and curriculum requirements may push

you to move on to the next lesson or activity, leaving opportunities behind.

You may also find yourself working with students who are unaware, disengaged, apathetic, or even angry because they feel powerless: "We're just kids. What can we do?" Some students are reluctant. They're told, "You need to give back to the community," yet they don't believe that they've received much from their community or think that whatever they have to offer the community doesn't want. Civic engagement and democratic processes also may not seem real to students whose only opportunity to participate in "government" are school elections that frequently promote popularity over ideas of substance.

The good news is that service learning can be sequenced so that students hand off an issue of public policy to the next civics class to further a cause. There are numerous examples of disenfranchised kids who find connection with teachers or youth group leaders who listen to their concerns, honor their voice, and assist in opening doors so an idea can have a chance. Leaders have learned to mitigate these challenges and develop the capacity for patience, resilience, and perseverance, which are integral aspects of youth participation. Social change *is* occurring through service learning.

Your students will find themselves questioning a variety of assumptions as they learn about social change issues. Do people have equal access to vote? Is life in a new country always better for immigrants than the one they left behind? How does economic status impact recreational, educational, and employment opportunities? Why do the most vulnerable in our societies—children and elders—often face exploitation? These questions encourage your students to look at familiar issues in new ways. These questions also require teaching strategies that promote in-depth examination and use varied technologies that excite and enliven kids.

As students learn about their world—the issues, the problems, the people and programs helping to create social change—they begin to find their own place as social activists. This is as true for reluctant students as it is for enthusiastic ones. Young people of all ages want their beliefs and actions to have value and relevance, and they will respond when offered a challenge, even when it comes with hard work and struggle. Often they are surprised at what can be accomplished with their collective efforts and determined minds and hearts.

> Until the great mass of the people shall be filled with the sense of responsibility for each other's welfare, social justice can never be attained.
>
> —*Helen Keller, author*

Preparation: Getting Ready for Service Learning Involving Social Change

The following activities can be used to promote learning and skill development related to social change. These activities are easily adapted to different grade levels during investigation, preparation, and planning to help your students examine key issues through research, analyze community needs, and gain the knowledge they need to effectively contribute to the design of their service plan. They can often be integrated into reflection and demonstration as students can lead the activities with others to build awareness. Since literature is often an important part of preparation, you can find recommended titles on this theme in the Social Change: Issues and Action Bookshelf later in this chapter.

Activity: Vocabulary That Matters. Prejudice, stereotype, discrimination, tolerance—these are influences that shape our ideas and actions. What do they mean? Even young children can learn these words and

concepts, and recognize the behaviors that promote positive ways of interacting with others or stop the negative ways. The following activities can encourage students to think about their beliefs and local social issues, and develop the capacity to initiate plans that promote communication and tolerance both within the school and the larger community.

- **A Look at Prejudice.** Students can examine and discuss the roots of the word, *pre* and *judge*. How does prejudice happen? How do we learn attitudes about others? Students can discuss the quote, "You can't judge a book by its cover," and then identify the various "covers" or categories they use to judge people. Examples of these "covers" can include: size, race, language ability, athleticism, religion, sexual orientation, and wealth.

- **Recognizing Stereotypes.** Examine the term *stereotype* beginning with the roots of the word. A stereotype can be defined as an oversimplified generalization about a particular group, race, or sex, which usually carries derogatory implications. Using different forms of media, including Web pages, television programs, print advertisements, and children's books, students can learn to recognize stereotypes. Create a simple checklist for students to identify tokenism, inaccurate information, favoritism, or ridicule.

- **Discrimination Happens.** Students can look at historical examples of discrimination, particularly with young people. Have students write a list of words or short phrases that describe a time they felt discriminated against as a young person. Then turn these into collaborative class poetry, short paragraphs, creative nonfiction stories, or essays. Beginning with their own experiences can lead into next examining discrimination against others—ethnic groups, elders, people in poverty, and so on.

- **Teaching Tolerance.** Ask each student to think of a time he or she felt "different." Students often think of wearing glasses, speaking a different language from others, being unable to hit a baseball, or feeling left out of a social gathering. Younger children can share these stories and talk about ways to increase respect and understanding for the experiences of others. Older students can draw an image that represents their experience at the top of a page. Underneath, students can make two columns placing "respecting others" and "knowledge and understanding" at the top of each. In the respective column, students articulate their thoughts and feelings that emanate under that heading. From these activities, ask students to consider, "What is tolerance?" How can we respect, learn about, and appreciate others who are both similar to and different from us?

Activity: Social Commentary. Where do we find social commentary in today's media? And how do people get their ideas and opinions into the public arena? These are important questions for students to address as they prepare to work for social change. There are many different kinds of media that students can explore and learn to use. Consider these options:

- **Fact or Opinion?** Compare two newspaper articles on a similar topic—a standard news story and an editorial. Have students find as many similarities and differences as possible, and then create a chart of do's and don'ts for each category. They can continue their research by reading books that clarify the differences, or having a speaker visit the class. A high school newspaper editor can be an ideal visitor for an elementary or middle school class, or contact your local newspaper.

- **Dear Editor.** Select several letters to the editor for your students to review. Have the students form small groups and give one letter to each group. What is different about this form of writing in comparison to a news article or editorial? Ask each group to write their own sample letter to the editor that conveys an idea, an emotion, or both.

- **Political Cartoons.** Find several political cartoons on different subjects. Depending on the age of the students, have them identify how this medium uses humor or satire to tell a point of view. Are there consistent themes or symbols that appear? (For example, donkeys to represent the Democratic Party and elephants to represent the Republican Party.) Why are the cartoonists

choosing those symbols? Show several to convey the variety of approaches used by these artists.

- **PSAs.** Public service announcements (PSAs) inform people about a variety of issues, including voter registration, eliminating discrimination, gun safety, and the hazards of cigarette smoking. Students can research how PSAs are used on radio, television, the Internet, and even in movie theaters to educate and inform. If media facilities are available through the school or community, students can apply what they've learned to create social marketing campaigns that can make a considerable impact. Children as young as second graders have used PSAs as a vehicle to educate the community about important issues, to raise awareness and take social action, and to invite participation from the community at large.

Making Connections Across the Curriculum

Some service learning activities naturally lend themselves to interdisciplinary work and making connections across the curriculum. These connections strengthen and broaden student learning, helping them meet academic standards. More than likely, you'll be looking for these connections and ways to encourage them well before the students ever start working on service learning activities. As with the entire service learning process, it helps to remain flexible, because some connections can be spontaneously generated by the questions raised throughout and by the community needs identified by the students. To help you think about cross-curricular connections and where you can look for them, the curricular web for this chapter (page 214) gives examples of many different ways this theme can be used in different academic areas. (The service learning scenarios in the next section of the chapter also demonstrate various ways that this theme can be used across the curriculum.)

Social Change Across the Curriculum

English/Language Arts

- Read a biography about a person who has worked for social change
- Compare newspaper editorials to learn about methods and styles used to persuade public opinion
- Discuss and write an essay on how young people experience stereotyping and prejudice

Social Studies/History

- Study how each branch of government directly impacts the life of your community
- Read about César Chávez and his movement; find out about current migrant worker issues
- Learn how voting rights were gained by suffragettes, the civil rights movement, and the events after South Africa's apartheid era

Languages

- Create public service videos in different languages about the school, local government, or helpful organizations; distribute through local agencies and cable access
- Learn about opportunities to serve in other countries, including the Peace Corps
- Study the needs of refugees in the United States, including the challenges of language and prejudice

Theater, Music, & Visual Arts

- Adapt a piece of literature about social change for a reader's theater performance
- Find out how folk music has been used to communicate social and political messages, inspiring people to learn and to take action
- Examine murals as artistic and cultural methods of expressing public opinion; include graffiti art in the research

Social Change

Math

- Create a public opinion poll regarding an issue of concern in the community; survey, tabulate, and report student responses
- Write about famous mathematicians and the impact of their work on society
- Examine the cost and benefits of fund-raising events that aid the community; develop ideas for cost-cutting measures and efficient record-keeping methods

Physical Education

- Study how Title IX became landmark legislation that bans sex discrimination in schools, and especially how this impacts school athletics
- Research playground safety information and visit a public playground; document needed changes and make recommendations to the appropriate local government agencies
- Research how physical challenges such as walk-a-thons and bike rallies engage the community and also benefit social causes

Computer

- Survey local community agencies such as shelters, meals-on-wheels, or immigrant centers to find out how students can help with computer technology needs
- Create a database of agencies that need student volunteers and a database of ideas and student skills that community agencies can access
- Do Internet research on careers in public service; create a Web page with links to service agencies and organizations throughout your community

Science

- Find out how funding of global initiatives has affected the fight against disease and the movement toward global health and stabilization in developing countries
- Research community needs of people in low-income housing for safety equipment such as smoke alarms or emergency kits
- Learn about the connection between science and public relations by researching how social marketing campaigns are used to educate communities about health related problems such as potable water

Service Learning Scenarios: Ideas for Action

Ready to take action? The service learning descriptions that follow have been successfully carried out by elementary, middle, or high school students in schools and with community organizations. Most of these scenarios and examples explicitly include some aspects of investigation, preparation and planning, action, reflection, and demonstration, and all have strong curricular connections. These scenarios can be a rich source of ideas for you to draw upon. Keep in mind that grade levels are provided as a reference; most scenarios can be adapted to suit younger or older students, and many are suitable for cross-age partnerships.

Young Advocates: Preschool

At the Pacific Oaks Preschool in Pasadena, California, when handed a "flesh-colored" adhesive bandage for a cut, a student remarked, "That's not the color of *my* skin!" This comment led to an impromptu classroom survey. Each child took a turn to see if the bandage matched her or his skin color. Within this classroom's diverse population, ten percent more or less matched, forty percent of the children came close, but fifty percent definitely didn't match. After discussing how melanin contributed to the color of their skin and reading books that featured children of all skin colors, the kids decided to write the bandage company and report their results. They also suggested that the company find a new term to describe the product. The company responded with a thank-you letter and another box of "flesh-colored" bandages. Still, the seeds of activism had been planted.

> Pick battles big enough to matter, small enough to win.
>
> —*Jonathan Kozol, author*

Kids That Type: Grade 1

After hearing the book *Click, Clack, Moo: Cows That Type* read aloud by their teacher, first-grade students decided they wanted to be "Kids That Type." They decided to look for improvements needed in their surroundings and to write letters to start things changing for the better. They walked around their school and found several areas on the playground in disrepair. They met with the principal to learn about getting the playground fixed and found out that three requests had already been submitted to the district office. The children composed a letter and visited other first-grade

---

Find Out More About Social Change

To learn more about these issues and to get ideas for service and action, visit these Web sites and organizations online:

Randomkid (www.randomkid.org), founded by a "kid," works to harness the giving power and ingenuity of kids and teens. They educate, mobilize, unify, and empower young people across the world to directly impact a broad spectrum of local, national, and global needs.

Tolerance.org (www.tolerance.org), a Web project of the Southern Poverty Law Center, promotes and supports anti-bias activism in every venue of American life and includes information and resources for teachers, parents, and children on fighting hate and promoting tolerance. Be sure to check out "Mix It Up at Lunch Day."

At the Web site for **Amnesty International** (www.amnestyusa.org) students can learn about and participate in human rights advocacy efforts.

Do Something (www.dosomething.org) is an organization that helps young people get involved in their communities by identifying the issues they care about and creating projects that turn ideas into action.

What Kids Can Do (www.whatkidscando.org) promotes myriad ways young people across the world respond to local and global concerns with determination and creativity. The Web site also invites students to share their service learning stories, with a focus on giving a voice to marginalized youth.

classes, read their letter aloud, and asked for signatures from their peers. The mailed letter was signed by over one hundred children. The repair was made within three weeks. For the "Kids That Type," this would be the first of many letters.

Helping Children in Shelters: Grade 3

An elementary student saw a television newscast about children living in shelters because they had been victims of domestic violence. The student initiated a discussion of the issue in class, and fellow students wanted to learn more and find ways to help. A social service worker showed the class an age-appropriate video and answered questions. The class generated a range of options for helping and presented their ideas to other classrooms at various grade levels. The students collected needed materials for children living in shelters, including backpacks with school supplies, journals and pens, and current magazines. Letter writing to local businesses assisted in skill development and yielded a substantial quantity of donated goods. Students also discussed showing respect to peers living in a variety of settings, including shelters.

Making the Census Count: Grade 4

Fourth graders attending Sullivan School in North Adams, Massachusetts, studied the importance of the federal census and the impact on the area if people do not complete and return the forms. Students learned from city officials about the history of poor returns and how this affects federal funding for local needs. The census count also determines how many people can represent that state in the House of Representatives. Plus, all information is aggregated; personal information is never revealed. Armed with this information, the students designed and executed a public service campaign to educate the community about the importance of participating in the census. They created a billboard, brochures, radio and television public service announcements, and editorials for the local paper. Their advocacy work culminated with an informational night to help community members fill out the census forms.

Fair Trade and Philanthropy: Grade 4

Fourth graders at the Casady School in Oklahoma City, Oklahoma, learned about fair trade chocolate from World Neighbors, a local nonprofit that embraces self-reliance and leadership in remote villages across the globe. The children sold chocolate and taught high school students and faculty about fair trade principles. Proceeds of the sales went to student-selected nonprofits in percentages that students determined after learning about and analyzing the mission, vision, and purpose of each agency.

Identifying a Female State Hero: Grades 4 and 5

While preparing for a visit to their state capitol, fourth graders at New Canaan Country School in Connecticut learned about the state flowers, state song, and state flag. When the time came to tour the capitol building, they found a huge statue of a male "state hero" in the rotunda. The students wondered, "Is there a female state hero?" This observation redirected their course of study. Step by step, the students demonstrated their capabilities as they defined what heroes are and what actions are heroic, researched appropriate female role models from their state, and debated their selection. After learning how a bill becomes a law, they found a state legislator willing to introduce a bill that named their designee, Prudence Crandall, as the Connecticut state heroine because of her stand against prejudice. In spite of the students' informed presentation to the legislature, their bill failed. The kids regrouped. As fifth graders, they created a play about their hero's life and toured the state to gather signatures from the populace in support of their new bill. The second time around, the bill passed. Then, fourth-grade students from Ellen P. Hubbard School in Bristol, Connecticut, raised considerable funds to help pay for the statue of Prudence Crandall in the state capitol.

Creating a Web of Opportunity: Grade 6

Middle school students in computer classes found their talents valued. Local nonprofit organizations were in dire straits. Some were being bombarded with more requests than they could handle for youth volunteer opportunities; others were not contacted at all. The need: building kid-friendly, information-rich Web pages for the organizations so young people could learn about specific issues and base their involvement on social concern. At first, students thought they could create dozens of Web pages in a flash. Instead they discovered they had to slow down to learn enough about the issues to create meaningful connections. In the process, the students shared knowledge about the agencies in their English and social studies classes, which led to other service learning activities. Several students began to volunteer their computer skills after school to help with agency needs. The students also made presentations to high school humanities classes, where service learning was part of the curriculum. Feedback from the agencies was extremely positive, and many other agencies wanted to sign on.

Unity Week: Grades 6–8

"We had been studying about the civil rights movement in social studies, and we decided to create a day of school unity. But once we began listing our ideas, the day grew into a week's worth of activities, and we needed more help. Every social studies class in the entire school took part!" The eighth-grade students in this social studies class were surprised their idea had such impact on students, teachers, parents, and the community, when everyone helped turn possibilities into plans. The students wanted to create events that would stimulate ongoing conversation and a veritable buzz of excitement. English classes assigned students to read *Bone by Bone by Bone, The Circuit,* or *Jakeman* for discussions and writings on social inequalities and racism in society. Sixth-grade social studies classes used *Through My Eyes,* while seventh- and eighth-grade classes read and discussed selections from *Remember Little Rock: The Time, the People, the Stories.* Students delivered famous speeches, and choirs sang about peace and harmony at lunch rallies. Every social studies class had guest speakers from community agencies who led workshops on local issues of tolerance related to immigrants, people with special needs, and racial issues. During "Unity Tonight," students and teachers performed music and slam poetry for the invited community members. On the last day of the week, the students who had initiated Unity Week led reflection sessions in every social studies class. In addition to finding out what was learned, they asked, "What ongoing activities can we establish at school to continue building unity and community?"

A Bus Display on Courage: Grades 6–8

Claudette Colvin's courageous act as a teenager in 1955 aboard a Montgomery city bus contributed significantly to ending segregation on U.S. transportation. The "Understanding Courage" project engaged today's teens in telling her story—on the city buses of Portland, Maine. King Middle School students and the school librarian read and discussed *Claudette Colvin: Twice Toward Justice.* Maine College of Art's art education students guided the discussions into artistic expression, and the middle school students created an art panel series to be displayed on city buses, reflecting the words and acts of courage in the book.

Student Building Planners: Grades 6–10

Students in a university course on facility planning and management worked with the local school district to identify a school in need of remodeling, additions, or new facilities. They surveyed the buildings and grounds; interviewed students, faculty, and administrators; and researched the history of the school and buildings. Then they worked to redesign existing areas they considered to be misused, as well as to design additional space for present or future needs. Middle and high school students became actively engaged in the process, attending university classes, offering feedback and ideas, and preparing drawings and presenting them to the college students, school administrators, and parents. The process allowed students, who are often neglected in the creation of schools and other public places, to become involved, learn community organizing methods, and make decisions.

Dreams of a Youth Center: Grades 6–12

In 2001, middle school students in Baltimore, Maryland, realized kids need a place to go after school to keep them off the streets. They came up with an ambitious plan: to purchase and renovate a house to serve as a neighborhood youth center. With teacher support, these "Youth Dreamers" took action. Through letter and grant writing and phone campaigns, students raised over $600,000 from government, nonprofit, and corporate sources. They worked with a pro bono architect and general contractor to design and construct the house. The students now have their youth center, and in May 2009, they held their house warming. After completing an application and interview, teens at the center guide younger members through tutoring, classes, and recreation. The Youth Dreamers continue to generate service ideas, write grants, run fund-raisers, design and evaluate programs, manage an annual auction, volunteer at a free health clinic, and partner with adults to teach classes. Check out their Web site: www.youthdreamers.org.

A Mural to Honor Social Change: Grade 7

In San Francisco, California, the Horace Mann Middle School humanities class wanted to make a mural on an outside school wall. They had been reading biographies and wished to represent their favorite people in the books they had read. But then a student suggested finding *real* people in the community to honor and the other students decided this was perfect. To find their subjects, they created a public service announcement for the local radio station and wrote a story for the neighborhood newspaper asking for nominations. They selected eight people that represented the community's diversity and had made a variety of different community contributions. Students conducted interviews, made sketches of their honorees, and, with the help of local artists, completed a ten-foot mural. The students also wrote a booklet of stories about their accomplishments and how they selected their mural subjects. The cover of the booklet is the mural.

Voter Education: Grades 7–8

To make an impact on voters in the 2000 elections, students in Chicago planned two approaches. First, they developed a voter education guide highlighting the presidential candidates. Then the students researched the candidates and the issues to develop the informational guide, which was distributed to students, parents, and community residents. The second approach was helping register new voters at their school by advertising to parents and unregistered voters in their community. The students teamed up with community organizations to make the registration drive a success. Teachers reported that students followed the election closely and had a true investment in the process. For follow-up, students worked with the high school to make sure each eighteen-year-old received a birthday card with a voter registration form inside. Next, students hope to examine school government election procedures and transform "popularity" elections into elections involving substance and issues.

A Site to Behold: Grades 9–11

Was there really a sacred Native American site on the University High School campus in Los Angeles? The rumor had been floating around for years, but finally an American history class decided to study the history of their school site and find out whether the story was myth or reality. Students discovered that in fact a stream on the school's site had been important to the indigenous people in the area. In collaboration with local Native American groups, students restored the area. Overcoming hurdles involving the school board and the city took time and skill. The process was eventually handed to the next year's class, so more students became invested in the process. The day the area was permanently restored and opened to the public was a festive community celebration bringing together people of diverse cultures and ages.

Sharing Nonviolence Lessons: Grades 9–12

In Providence, Rhode Island, teens teach about nonviolent social change. Their peer education program, TITAN (Teens Informing Teens About Nonviolence), provides knowledge and skills young people need to do the community organizing they want to do. The guiding principle: to create positive individual, community, and social change. This partnership between teens, adults, and the community provides leadership training enabling young people to then lead and manage community outreach and educational programs. The teens write grants, meet with city and state officials, and raise funds to support their work. The process includes learning the history of social justice movements in America, replacing myths with accurate information. For example, learning that Rosa Parks was an accomplished community leader before she refused to give up her seat on the Montgomery bus showed the teens what can occur through collective decision-making, willed risk, and coordinated action. This has energized and inspired them to acquire these skills. TITAN leaders focus on educating middle school students, because research shows that is the critical age we need to begin passing on lessons of nonviolence and encouraging academic excellence.

Acting Out: Grades 9–12

Community education is a major focus for drama students at a magnet high school for the arts. Students devote several hours per week to developing plays to perform for children. The plays have a variety of themes related to important community topics identified through surveys and community feedback: diversity and tolerance, fire safety, and school violence. Students are sharing their methods through a documentary describing the how-to's of using theater as a vehicle for service learning.

Each time a person stands up for an ideal, or acts to improve the lot of others, or strikes out against injustice, he sends forth a tiny ripple of hope, and crossing each other from a million different centers of energy and daring, these ripples build a current that can sweep down the mightiest walls of oppression and resistance.

—*Robert F. Kennedy, former U.S. Senator and Attorney General*

Speaking Out for Funding: Grades 11–12

School cutbacks have meant a loss of many teachers and activities, such as music programs, shop classes, and physical education. What are kids to do? In communities already hard hit with economic woes, some students have decided to speak out. A group of seventeen students from across Ohio testified before the state's House Primary and Secondary Education Committee in support of a bill that would fund regular public schools before providing funding for charters and private school voucher programs. The teens spoke for all their peers and addressed the needs of the poorer Ohio school districts. Students learned that even if you can't vote, you can have still a voice. They learned that students have a great deal to contribute toward school reform and they deserve to know what is really going on inside the school buildings.

A School Out of Balance: Grade 12

High school seniors wanted to draw attention to what they believed to be educational inequities at Santa Monica High School in southern California. After investigating issues of racial discrimination on their campus, they made a proposal to the school administration to plan and lead a one-day summit to address these issues and begin a plan to make significant changes. The event brought together students, parents, faculty, administration, the district superintendent, community college administrators, and community members. The program began with testimonials from African-American and Latino students regarding bias on the part of counselors and teachers. Next, a local education policy expert presented a study of inequities within the school district based on race and

socioeconomic background. Finally, in small groups, participants discussed the findings and proposed recommendations and follow-up plans, to be compiled, summarized, and published by the student leadership group. Additional meetings were scheduled to factor this information into the plans for restructuring the high school into smaller learning communities.

The Social Change: Issues and Action Bookshelf

The Social Change: Issues and Action Bookshelf (pages 220–221) is an annotated bibliography of works covering a broad spectrum of topics, from individual issues to community building. To help you find books relevant to your particular service learning idea, the book chart classifies the titles according to several topic areas: historical perspectives, our world today, planning for action, prejudice and discrimination, and working for change.

In general, the bookshelf features:

- An annotated bibliography arranged and alphabetized by title according to the general categories of nonfiction (N), picture books (P), and fiction (F). For nonfiction and fiction, length and recommended grade levels are included. The entries in the picture book category do not include suggested grade levels, since they can be successfully used with all ages.

- A chart organized by topic and category to help you find books relevant to particular projects.

- Recommendations from service learning colleagues and experts, which include a book summary and ideas for service learning connections. (The number of recommended books varies in each bookshelf.)

- *Please note:* additional titles for this category are listed in the digital content; some of these were out of print at the time of publication but still worth finding.

I recognize no rights but human rights—I know nothing of men's rights and women's rights.

—*Angelina E. Grimké, suffragette*

Social Change: Issues and Action Bookshelf Topics

Topics	Books	Category
Historical Perspectives The past is a rich source of information and examples of action undertaken by individuals and groups working for the benefit of many. Their stories influence our own.	*1968* *Alive in the Killing Fields: Surviving the Khmer Rouge Genocide* *Belva Lockwood: Equal Rights Pioneer* *The Breadwinner Trilogy* *Crossing Bok Chitto: A Choctaw Tale of Friendship and Freedom* *Democracy* *Draw What You See: A Child's Drawings from Theresienstadt/ Terezín* *Fire from the Rock* * *Journey of Dreams* *My Mother, the Cheerleader* *Passage to Freedom: The Sugihara Story* * *Remember Little Rock: The Time, the People, the Stories* *The Rock and the River* *See How They Run: Campaign Dreams, Election Schemes, and the Race to the White House* *We Were There, Too! Young People in U.S. History* *	N N N F P N N F F F P N F N N
Our World Today What realities in our world do we need to know about? The interconnectedness of our societies and our common humanity urge us to become knowledgeable in order to create mutually respectful social change.	*Chanda's Wars* *Every Human Has Rights: What You Need to Know About Your Human Rights* *If the World Were a Village* *A School Like Mine: How Children Learn Around the World** (see digital content) *Slavery Today* *Sold* *We Are All Born Free: The Universal Declaration of Human Rights in Pictures*	F P P N N F P
Planning for Action Are you ready for action? These books can help with the key stage of preparation. Information, planning tools, and ideas are waiting.	*The Kid's Guide to Service Projects: Over 500 Service Ideas for Young People Who Want to Make a Difference* * *The Little Engine That Could* (see digital content)	N P
Prejudice and Discrimination These books delve into such topics as prejudice, stereotypes, discrimination, and racial intolerance. The stories also tell us about strength of spirit, character, and resolve to overcome injustice.	*Across the Alley* *Animal Farm* (see digital content) *Bifocal* * *Bone by Bone by Bone* *First Crossing: Stories about Teen Immigrants* *The Goat Lady* * *The House on Mango Street* (see digital content) *I Am a Taxi*	P F F F (see page 181) P F F

Page references are given for books that can be found in the bookshelf lists of other chapters.

* These books include examples of young people in service-providing roles.

(GN) These books are graphic novels.

Social Change: Issues and Action Bookshelf Topics (continued)

Topics	Books	Category
Prejudice and Discrimination (continued)	*Shine, Coconut Moon*	F
	Six Million Paper Clips: The Making of a Children's Holocaust Memorial * (see Safe and Strong Communities Bookshelf—digital content)	N
	Smoky Nights (see Safe and Strong Communities Bookshelf—digital content)	P
	Taking a Stand Against Racism	N
	To Kill a Mockingbird (see digital content)	F
	Also see titles on the Immigrants Bookshelf	
Working for Change The path of social change is a long, well-traveled road, and these examples guide us and remind us of what we can accomplish.	*After Gandhi: One Hundred Years of Nonviolent Resistance* *	N
	Akira to Zoltán: Twenty-Six Men Who Changed the World *	N
	Brundibar *	F
	The Carpet Boy's Gift *	P
	Claudette Colvin: Twice Toward Justice *	N
	Close Encounters of a Third-World Kind *	F
	Delivering Justice: W.W. Law and the Fight for Civil Rights	P
	Edwina Victorious *	F
	The Gospel According to Larry *	F
	Healing Our World: Inside Doctors Without Borders *	N
	Hitch *	F
	I Could Do That! Esther Morris Gets Women the Vote *	P
	In the Time of the Butterflies * (see digital content)	F
	Jakeman *	F
	The Juvie Three	F
	Knitting Nell * (see digital content)	P
	Listen to the Wind *	P
	One Hen: How One Small Loan Made a Big Difference *	P
	Peeled *	F
	The Photographer	F (GN)
	Sacred Leaf *	F
	¡Sí, Se Puede!/Yes, We Can! Janitor Strike in L.A. *	P
	Summer Wheels * (see Safe and Strong Communities Bookshelf—digital content)	P
	That's Not Fair! Emma Tenayuca's Struggle for Justice/¡No Es Justo! La lucha de Emma Tenayuca por la justicia	P
	Three Cups of Tea: One Man's Journey to Change the World . . . One Child at a Time *	N
	Wangari Trees of Peace: A True Story About Africa *	P
	We Are One: The Story of Bayard Rustin *	N
	We Need to Go to School: Voices of the Rugmark Children *	N

Page references are given for books that can be found in the bookshelf lists of other chapters.

* These books include examples of young people in service-providing roles.

(GN) These books are graphic novels.

Nonfiction: Social Change

1968

by Michael T. Kaufman (Roaring Brook Press, 2009). Poignant headlines and memorable photographs help recall the year 1968. The climate is evoked in this exploration of ten settings and events that made this year one of the most noteworthy in recent history. 148pp., young adult

After Gandhi: One Hundred Years of Nonviolent Resistance

by Anne Ibley O'Brien and Perry Edmond O'Brien (Charlesbridge, 2009). From 1908 to 2003, key moments of activism occurred through the tireless work of courageous individuals. Read about each of them in this book, for the inspiration we all need to promote nonviolent social change. In addition to well-known heroes like Dr. Martin Luther King Jr., come to know Thich Nhat Hanh's work for Vietnam, Charles Perkins's commitment to the Aboriginal Rights Movement, and Aung San Suu Kyi's struggle for democracy in Myanmar. The author also has a chapter reflecting on "The Future of Nonviolence." Important words are included, along with many memorable quotes. 181pp., grades 4–12

Akira to Zoltán: Twenty-Six Men Who Changed the World

by Cynthia Chin-Lee (Charlesbridge, 2008). Colorful collage-style portraits accompany short descriptions of and quotes by the twenty-six men profiled in this book. These are men from around the world who many children may not recognize and who have accomplished feats that influenced their worlds. 32pp., grades 3–6 (See also: Amelia to Zora: Twenty-Six Women Who Changed the World.)

Alive in the Killing Fields:
Surviving the Khmer Rouge Genocide

by Nawuth Keat with Martha E. Kendall (National Geographic, 2009). At age nine, Nawuth experienced the violence of the Khmer Rouge as his mother, two siblings, aunt, and uncle were brutally murdered in his presence. This narration, accompanied by photographs, brings us into this nightmare and leads us through his journey of survival. 112pp., grades 6–9

Belva Lockwood: Equal Rights Pioneer

by Jill Norgreen (Twenty-First Century Books, 2009). Belva Lockwood was a woman all but lost to history. She became a lawyer at a time when women were rarely admitted to law school. She was the first woman to bring a case before the United States Supreme Court and the second woman to run for president—all before women even had the right to vote. Throughout her life she fought for social justice for women and all underrepresented people. 100pp., young adult

Claudette Colvin: Twice Toward Justice

by Philip Hoose (Farrar Straus Giroux, 2009). At age 15, Claudette Colvin refused to relinquish her seat on the bus to a white passenger. At that moment she became part of the civil rights movement. Later that year Rosa Parks was seen as the "face" of the protest that followed, while Claudette participated as a plaintiff in the court case that eventually integrated Montgomery's buses. An exceptional portrait placed into the events of the times. 144pp., young adult

Democracy

by James Laxer (Groundwood Books, 2006). Part of the Groundwork Guides series, this book explores the development of democracy from ancient to modern times and provides readers with an overview of developing democracies today. 144pp., young adult

Draw What You See: A Child's
Drawings from Theresienstadt/Terezín

by Helga Weissova (Wallstein Verlag, 2008). This book is a collection of the vivid illustrations that Helga Weissova drew as a child at the Terezín concentration camp. This was the "model" concentration camp set up by the Nazis for visits from the Red Cross to show how "well" Jewish people were being treated. Helga's father told his daughter: "Draw what you see." And she did. Her drawings provide the historical account we have today that otherwise would not exist. At times amusing and at times wrenching, these illustrations are accompanied by descriptions in three languages—German, Czech, and English—providing a glimpse into the everyday reality of the prisoners from the singular perspective of a child. 168pp., grades 6–12

Healing Our World: Inside Doctors Without Borders

by David Morley (Fitzhenry & Whiteside, 2007). Former executive director of the Canadian section of Doctors Without Borders, Morley adeptly represents the organization, whose mission is to help create a humanitarian world. In an engaging format, we learn the facts (e.g., two billion of the world's people live without safe sanitation facilities), we read about the daily contributions of volunteers from many professional backgrounds (offering great career exposure for teens), and we learn what they do in emergencies such as earthquakes and bombings. The final chapter is about hope. 121pp., young adult

The Kid's Guide to Service Projects: Over 500
Service Ideas for Young People Who Want to
Make a Difference (Updated 2nd Edition)

by Barbara Lewis (Free Spirit Publishing, 2009). Ideas for both simple and large-scale service projects for young people who want to make a difference. Newly revised and updated with tips on using the Internet in service. 160pp., grades 4–12

Remember Little Rock: The Time, The People, The Stories

by Paul Robert Walker (National Geographic, 2009). This gripping narrative of the integration of Little Rock's Central High School in 1957 interweaves first-person accounts and historical narrative to remind us of the bravery and hardship at the core of our flourishing interracial society. 61pp., grades 5–8

See How They Run: Campaign Dreams, Election Schemes, and the Race to the White House

by Susan E. Goodman and Elwood H. Smith (Bloomsbury Children's Books, 2008). This fun cartoon guide explores the laws and strategies behind the American electoral process by introducing young readers to historical events, anecdotes, and the men (thus far) who managed to make it to the highest office in the land. 96pp., grades 4–6

Slavery Today

by Kevin Bales and Becky Cornell (Groundwood Books, 2008). Part of the Groundwork Guides series, this important introduction to modern slavery reminds us that the malignant abuse of human life is not a thing of the past. The book includes statistical data, timelines, and a brief history to help us contextualize and understand how this institution continues to thrive and what we can do to finally put its overdue end. 141pp., young adult

Taking a Stand Against Racism

by Cath Senker (Rosen Publishing, 2010). This book presents a historical perspective on racism that helps readers understand why it's directed toward different groups because of culture, background, and religion. Systemic reasons for racism make it clear why it will require diligent work and much time to overcome this insidious aspect of our societies. 48pp., grades 6–9

Three Cups of Tea: One Man's Journey to Change the World . . . One Child at a Time

by Sarah Thomson (adapter), Greg Mortenson, and David Oliver Relin (Puffin, 2009). This teen version of the adult best seller *Three Cups of Tea* details Mortenson's journey to a Pakistani village where he ultimately helps build schools. His transformation and contributions are highlighted through text and photographs. 240pp., young adult

We Are One: The Story of Bayard Rustin

by Larry Dane Brimmer (Calkins Creek, 2007). Bayard Rustin, child of a Quaker mother and father born a slave, grew up in a family always supporting causes of freedom and justice. This book tells of Bayard's extraordinary life of protest: he was one of the first blacks to sit at "white-only" lunch counters; he conducted freedom rides before they had a name; he was a teacher to Martin Luther King Jr.; and he organized the March for Jobs and Freedom, one of the most legendary, effective protests ever to gather in Washington, D.C. Though a story of bold, persistent action for change, the book also exposes the terror of the times: lynchings, segregation, and rampant hate and fear. With photos and lyrics of songs Bayard often used to end speeches, this book gives context to the legends of Rosa Parks and Martin Luther King Jr., and voice to a vision of peace that changed America. 48pp., grades 6–12

We Need to Go to School: Voices of the Rugmark Children

by Tanya Roberts-Davis (Groundwood Books, 2001). At age sixteen, the author traveled to Nepal to live with children who had spent years in forced labor in carpet factories. Now in Rugmark rehabilitation centers attending school, these children tell their stories through oral accounts, poetry, and pictures. Opportunities to become active in working to end child labor are included, along with other resources, a glossary, and an overview of Nepal. 48pp., grades 5–12

We Were There, Too! Young People in U.S. History

by Phillip Hoose (Farrar Straus Giroux, 2001). What role have young people played in American history? How have they made their mark, their contribution? In this comprehensive collection of stories and photographs, we see that young people, from the boys who sailed with Columbus to the young activists of today, have been a significant force in history. An indispensable reference for any American history-related class and an inspiring book to read. 264pp., grades 4–12

Picture Books: Social Change

Across the Alley

by Richard Michelson (G.P Putnam's Sons, 2006). Young neighbors exchange lessons across an alleyway after bedtime. When the Jewish boy discovers that he is better at baseball than violin, and the African-American boy realizes that he is better at violin than baseball, they take their talents into their respective communities, proving that stereotypes don't always play out.

The Carpet Boy's Gift

by Pegi Deitz Shea (Tilbury House, 2003). Nadeem works in a carpet factory in Pakistan. He is not paid and working conditions in the factory are dismal. One day he receives a piece of paper from a boy named Iqbal telling him there is a law against child slave labor in Pakistan. Iqbal hands him a pen, igniting Nadeem's desire to go to school. The character of Iqbal is based on the life of a former child slave laborer who, at age twelve, infiltrated factories to inform young workers of their rights. Despite international praise for his efforts, upon returning home from an international tour, he was tragically assassinated at twelve years old. Still, his courage inspired children and workers to pursue the change that he lived and died for. This book provides resources for educators and readers who want to change this devastating situation.

Crossing Bok Chitto: A Choctaw Tale of Friendship and Freedom

by Tim Tingle (Cinco Puntos Press, 2006). This is the moving tale of the accidental and risky bond that develops and matures between a slave of African descent and a Choctaw girl in the American South.

Delivering Justice: W.W. Law and the Fight for Civil Rights

by Jim Haskins (Candlewick Press, 2005). This is the true story of one man who served his country by fighting for justice in the civil rights movement and as postal worker. It reminds readers that many individuals strove for justice as a part of a daily commitment within their everyday duties.

Every Human Has Rights: What You Need to Know About Your Human Rights

by National Geographic (National Geographic Society, 2008). This picture book interprets the Universal Declaration of Human Rights for a young audience by integrating the poetry of young adults, images of the citizens from all over the world whom the declaration affects and a translation of each of the document's rights into language that is accessible and relevant to young people.

The Goat Lady

by Jane Brigoli (Tilbury Press, 2008). Noelie, an elder French Canadian woman, appears to live a disheveled life according to the townspeople. However, when a young neighbor assists Noelie with her goats, the girl realizes Noelie's generous spirit for helping others. The girl asks her mother to paint pictures of her new friend. This art exhibit, showcased in the community by this book's author, transforms perception and guides the community to recognize and honor Noelie for her good work. Based on a true story in Dartmouth, Massachusetts.

I Could Do That! Esther Morris Gets Women the Vote

by Linda Arms White (Farrar, Straus and Giroux, 2005). One of the untold stories of the women's suffrage movement, this book tells the true tale of Esther Morris, who knew that she could do just about anything that anyone else could do. So when her family moved to Wyoming, she held tea parties and lobbied legislatures to ensure that she would be able to cast her ballot on Election Day. Through her efforts, Wyoming became the first state in the union to allow women to vote.

If the World Were a Village

by David J. Smith and Shelagh Armstrong (A&C Black, 2003). Imagine the world were a village populated by one hundred people: nine speak English, twenty-five have televisions, seventeen cannot read, and so on. When drawn to a more comprehensible scale, the world becomes a place we can understand and strive to change. Evidence shows that although wealth and food are not equally distributed, there are resources enough to feed everyone on our planet.

DIGITAL CONTENT

Recommendations from the Field

Knitting Nell by Julie Jerslid Roth (Houghton Mifflin, 2006).

The Little Engine That Could by Watty Piper (Grosset and Dunlap, 1930/1978).

Listen to the Wind

by Greg Mortenson (Dial, 2009). This is the children's version of the story told in the book *Three Cups of Tea*. It shows the value of learning about other cultures and the steps taken to build mutual respect and educational opportunities for others while informing about Pakistani culture. Collage art plus photos and scrapbook images entice the reader.

One Hen: How One Small Loan Made a Big Difference

by Katie Smith Milway (Kids Can Press, 2008). One loan equals one hen. One hen equals eggs for the family and eggs to sell. Money earned equals more hens and jobs for others. This is about Kojo, who lives in a small town in Ghana, and the process of microloans is bringing new opportunities to communities across the globe. The afterword introduces us to the real Kojo, who now has a community microlending program to assist others. Also includes information about the history of microfinancing and what you can do to help.

Passage to Freedom: The Sugihara Story

by Ken Mochizuki (Lee & Low, 1997). In 1940, five-year-old Hiroki Sugihara, the son of the Japanese consul in Lithuania, saw hundreds of Jewish refugees from Poland ask in desperation if consul Sugihara would write visas for them to escape the Nazi threat. When the Japanese government denied Sugihara's request to issue visas, the Sugihara family decided to do what they could to save thousands of lives, even if it placed their own lives at risk.

¡Si, Se Puede!/Yes, We Can! Janitor Strike in L.A.

by Diana Cohn (Cinco Puentas Press, 2003). Carlitos, a young boy, is proud of his mother who works long hours for low pay as a janitor. In April 2000, when 8,000 janitors in Los Angeles put down their mops and brooms and went on strike, his mother is among the leaders. Carlitos wants to help and he does: he joins with other children to make posters and join the marchers. The book includes an essay by author Luis J. Rodriguez, whose father was also a janitor. The inside of the dust jacket is an informative poster that explains about the role of labor unions and strikes. In English and Spanish.

That's Not Fair! Emma Tenayuca's Struggle for Justice/¡No Es Justo! La lucha de Emma Tenayuca por la justicia
(Wings Press, 2008). Follow Emma Tenayuca beginning in her childhood as she became aware of the roots of injustice and grew to a young woman who organized Mexican American laborers to protest for higher wages. In English and Spanish.

Wangari Trees of Peace: A True Story About Africa
by Jeanette Winter (Harcourt, 2008). After growing up in rural Kenya, Wangari Maathai, founded the Green Belt Movement, a sustained grassroots collaborative that has improved her country's economy and individual and collective well-being. A true story, inspiring and important for our times.

We Are All Born Free: The Universal Declaration of Human Rights in Pictures
by Amnesty International (Frances Lincoln Children's Books & Amnesty International, 2008). This iteration of the Universal Declaration of Human Rights brings the thirty articles to life in pictures. Drawn by artists from all over the world, varying in setting and style, the combination reflects the diversity of lives impacted by this crucial, life-affirming document.

Fiction: Social Change

DIGITAL CONTENT

Recommendation from the Field

Animal Farm by George Orwell (Prentice Hall, 1946). 140pp., young adult

Bifocal
by Deborah Ellis and Eric Walters (Fitzhenry & Whiteside, 2007). A lunchtime raid at a city high school results in a student being arrested as a terrorist. Jay, a junior football player, observes the commotion from a secret place on the roof with the football captain. He sees Haroon handcuffed and dragged out to the police car because he is also a "brown" student in the same room with the suspect. In alternating chapters, Jay and Haroon question their identities and examine personal loyalties in athletics, race, religion, school, and family. When they finally meet, both have developed a sense of agency about their everyday actions. 273pp., grades 9–12

Bone by Bone by Bone
by Tony Johnston (Roaring Brook Press, 2007). The year is 1950, in small town Tennessee. In this exquisitely written book, we follow young David, whose father has instilled in him a fascination with the human body with the intention of him one day becoming a doctor like he is. But then David's brotherly friendship with a black boy, Malcolm, comes up against his

father's racism and the Ku Klux Klan placing Malcolm's life at risk. 184pp., young adult

The Breadwinner Trilogy
by Deborah Ellis (Groundwood Books, 2009). This trilogy combines three connected stories. *The Breadwinner* begins in Afghanistan with eleven-year-old Parvana dressing as a soldier to find food for her family. *Parvana's Journey* continues after Parvana's father dies and now, as a thirteen-year-old refugee, she seeks to find her other family members. *Mud City* shifts the focus to fourteen-year-old Shauzia who hopes to leave Pakistan for France and a new life. These compelling stories provide insights about survival and hope. 520pp., young adult

Brundibar
by Tony Kushner and Maurice Sendak (Hyperion, 2003). Aninku and Pepicek discover their mother is sick and rush into town for milk. They see a hurdy-gurdy grinder, Brundibar, and decide to perform for money as he does, all to purchase the milk. But Brundibar tyrannizes all who sing in town and the brother and sister feel defeated. Then, with the help of three talking animals and 300 helpful school kids, they chase Brundibar away. This book is based on a Czech opera for children performed fifty-five times by the children of Terezín, the Nazi concentration camp. 56pp., grades K–2

Chanda's Wars
by Allan Stratton (HarperCollins, 2008). In this sequel to *Chanda's Secrets*, Chanda must find her siblings who were abducted to serve in the children's army in Africa. This contemporary, frightening issue still looms large in today's news and is vivid in this powerful story of the destructive nature of war and how it tears apart families while placing young people in adult roles. Chanda's strength and tenacity give us a character to remember. 400pp., young adult

Close Encounters of a Third-World Kind
by Jennifer Stewart (Holiday House, 2004). Annie is not looking forward to the two-month family stay in Nepal, where her father will work with a medical team. But then her summer improves dramatically when she makes a friend and begins volunteering at the local health clinic. This book gives a close look at what living in a "foreign" culture looks and feels like. Also, while humor and a lighthearted feeling accompanies the story, the author paints a vivid picture of the challenges facing many in the community, such as Annie's friend's family, where there are six girls, and a single pregnant mother. A compelling, memorable story. 149pp., grades 3–6

Edwina Victorious
by Susan Bonners (Farrar Straus Giroux, 2000). Mayor Granger has been repairing a playground, transforming a vacant lot, and planning a long needed make-over of the zoo, all inspired by letters received from ninety-year-old community activist

Edwina Osgood. However, the letters are actually written by young Edwina Osgood posing as her namesake great-aunt! What happens when the truth is revealed? 131pp., grades 3–6

Fire from the Rock

by Sharon M. Draper (Speak, 2007). This historical fiction novel brings to life the racial struggles of 1957 in Little Rock, Arkansas. As a top student, Sylvia is initially thrilled when asked to be one of the first black students to attend Central High School, but this soon turns into fear and trepidation. Integration could bring isolation, loneliness, and a risk of personal harm. This story takes the civil rights struggle to the personal level and leaves readers asking themselves: What would I do in her shoes? 240pp., young adult

The Gospel According to Larry

by Janet Tashjian (Henry Holt, 2001). Lonely seventeen-year-old Josh is a teenager with a passion for learning and for becoming his best friend Beth's boyfriend. He also wants to make a difference in the world. But when his blog (under the pseudonym of "Larry") criticizing consumer culture becomes bigger than expected, his anonymity becomes a choice that consumes him. His blog postings lead to clubs, rock festivals, a chance to be on TV, and a huge family mess. Will Josh's true identity finally be revealed? Will he "get the girl"? Will his blog have an effect on consumerism? A must-read to find out. 227pp., grades 7–12

Hitch

by Jeanette Ingold (Harcourt, 2005). Moss Trawnley doesn't like his options. Work is scarce during the Great Depression, and he wants to break the pattern of being jobless and homeless like his alcoholic father. At age seventeen, a new opportunity arises: joining President Roosevelt's Civilian Conservation Corps—a guarantee of food and shelter and bit of salary in exchange for hard work. Many things surprise him about the experience: the good friends he makes, his development as a leader, and his ability to care for others and face his future. 272pp., grades 7–10

DIGITAL CONTENT

Recommendation from the Field

The House on Mango Street by Sandra Cisneros (Vintage Books, 1991). 110pp., young adult

I Am a Taxi

by Deborah Ellis (Groundwood Books, 2006). Set in Bolivia, this story chronicles the unique life of a twelve-year-old boy who lives with his mom in a women's prison. The novel traces the adventures of Diego both inside prison and in the world

outside, trying to do what little he can for his family wrongly accused of growing cocaine. His attempts to aid his family result in him unwittingly joining the drug trade, which he must find a way to escape. 208pp., grades 5–8

DIGITAL CONTENT

Recommendation from the Field

In the Time of the Butterflies by Julia Alvarez (Plume Books, 1994). 325pp., grades 9–12

Jakeman

by Deborah Ellis (Fitzhenry & Whiteside, 2007). Jake and his older sister, Shoshona, sneak out of their foster care residence to take a long bus ride with other children for a brief visit with their incarcerated mothers on Mother's Day. Though not seen as a good student, Jake is a skilled cartoonist whose barbed wire superhero "Jakeman" represents his own resilience and determination. A true superhero adventure ensues, as these kids, who have been failed by the social system, insist their voices be heard. Every chapter ends with Jake's letters to the Governor pleading that his mother be pardoned. Grippingly real and filled with human touches, humor, and memorable characters. 201pp., grades 6–12

Journey of Dreams

by Marge Pellegrino (Frances Lincoln, 2009). This is Tomasa's story of how her family escaped the Guatemalan army's "scorched earth" campaign. Her mother and older brother already left, and now Tomasa and her younger brother and sister must stay close to Papa and his hopeful stories as they bravely travel across borders on a perilous journey to the United States. 250pp., grades 6–9

The Juvie Three

by Gordon Korman (Hyperion, 2008). Douglas Healy sets up an experimental halfway house for three juvenile delinquents: Gecko, Terence, and Arjay. Getting out of their detention centers is a great opportunity for them, even if school, therapy, and community service are part of the equation. But when an accident leaves Douglas hospitalized with amnesia, the three teens have to decide between right and wrong. Determined to be model citizens, getting a second (third and fourth) chance requires more work and determination than they ever expected. 249pp., young adult

My Mother, the Cheerleader

by Robert Sharenow (Harper, 2007). Thirteen-year-old Louise lives with her eccentric mother in their boarding house in the ninth ward of New Orleans. What could happen in her neighborhood? Not much, she thought. Then desegregation arrives and Louise is pulled out of school. Her mother joins the Cheerleaders—white women who stand by the entrance of William Frantz Elementary School each morning to taunt and threaten an African-American girl named Ruby Bridges on her way to class. When a man arrives from the city and takes an interest in both Louise and her mother, everything suddenly becomes so right and so wrong at the same time. As Louise's world transforms, so does ours in this stunning young adult novel. 289pp., grades 6–12

Peeled

by Joan Bauer (Penguin, 2008). Doing what is right is not always easy. Hildy Biddle and the Banesville High staff at *The Core*, the school newspaper, are striving to be great reporters by telling the truth and taking small steps that make a moral struggle worth standing up for. Can a high school paper bring a small town together? Can students hold their ground opposite affluent developers and political savvy officials and a principal who may shut down the paper? 247pp., grades 6–10

The Photographer

by Emmanuel Guibert, Didier Lefèvre, and Frédéric Lemercier (First Second, 2009). This beautiful graphic novel follows photographer Didier Lefèvre as he records his work with Doctors Without Borders in Afghanistan starting in 1986. The novel interlaces photographs with a graphic narrative of his encounter with this other culture and its important history—a history he was ignorant of at the time and which remains crucially relevant to the geopolitical landscape today. 267pp., grades 9–12

The Rock and the River

by Kekla Magoon (Aladdin, 2009). The year is 1968. Fourteen-year old Sam can hardly stand the mounting tension between his nonviolence-preaching father and his older brother who has joined a new group in Chicago called the Black Panthers. Sam breaks his father's rules and trust as he steps into a world where people want to avoid violence but are willing to cross the line if necessary. A powerful portrait of a split community willing to come together for justice. 289pp., grades 7–12

Sacred Leaf

by Deborah Ellis (Groundwood Books, 2007). In this sequel to *I Am a Taxi*, Diego has been taken in by the Ricardos, a family of coca farmers. Diego's short-lived comfort ends when the Bolivian government takes the harvest of coca leaves with the intention of destroying the crop. For centuries, native people of Bolivia have used the sacred coca plant for tea and medicine, but now coca is turned into cocaine and smuggled into North America. Diego joins the farmers in a massive protest, torn between his newfound loyalty to the Ricardos and his desire to return to his own family. 206pp., grades 6–12

Shine, Coconut Moon

by Neesha Meminger (Margaret K. McElderry Books, 2009). Seventeen-year-old Samar, a.k.a. Sam, has a full life with school, friends, and a cute boyfriend. Then 9/11 happens, and her mother's brother appears, bringing an Indian heritage that her mother has intentionally kept under wraps. Is Sam really a "coconut"—brown on the outside but white on the inside? Why hasn't she spent any time with her grandparents or other relatives? How can she live in two worlds when her roots are foreign to her? While her uncle is taunted with "Go back home, Osama," can Sam find *her* way back home? 253pp., grades 7–10

Sold

by Patricia McCormick (Hyperion, 2006). At age thirteen, Lakshmi knows what she wants: earn enough money to buy her mother a tin roof for their house and to marry the boy Krishna to whom she has been promised. But life changes dramatically after her stepfather sells her into prostitution. Thinking she is going to the city to work as a maid, Lakshmi travels to and finally escapes from Calcutta's red light district. This novel paints a vivid picture of the sex trade in India. 265pp., young adult

---

DIGITAL CONTENT

Recommendation from the Field

To Kill a Mockingbird by Harper Lee (Warner, 1961/1988). 288pp., young adult

Interviews with Authors: The Story Behind the Story

In the companion digital content, you'll find interviews with authors Deborah Ellis *(I Am a Taxi, Sacred Leaf, and Jakeman),* Sonia Levitin *(Dream Freedom),* and Diana Cohn *(¡Sí, Se Puede!/Yes, We Can!)* that tell the "story behind the story" of their books.

Chapter 16

Special Needs and Disabilities

What a thrill to find out I only see things, perceive things, and receive things differently from others, and that is okay. It is my normal. . . . It is simply for us anyway, a different way of life, one as rich and rewarding as anyone else's, in our own special way.

—*Liane Holliday Willey, Ed.D., author (speaking about having Asperger's syndrome)*

The population of children with special needs and disabilities is growing, and chances are you have at least one young person with special needs—or perhaps several—in your classroom or group. This chapter looks both at how to design service learning plans that address the actual needs of people with disabilities or special needs and at how *everyone* in your classroom or group can participate in and benefit from service learning. Young people with special needs or challenges can take part in service learning and make valuable contributions, regardless of whether you are teaching an inclusive class or one specifically for students with special needs; this is true for any theme, including the ones in this chapter. Service learning experiences involving special needs and disabilities can take a number of different forms: students can lobby for better access for the disabled in the community, donate time and resources to agencies that work with populations with special needs, or work directly with peers with special needs.

A "special need" can be defined as anything that requires care or intervention outside of the norm; it can take the form of a disability, however this is not always the case. Some special needs are fairly visible—using a wheelchair or communicating with sign language. Others are "invisible"—attention deficit hyperactivity disorder or autism. Often the latter are harder to identify for teachers and peers and can be more challenging for young people to understand. Information is available in many forms to teach both educators and students about special needs issues and to help them cultivate mutually respectful relationships with students and people with special needs in the community. As all students learn more about each other, differences become less significant and similarities become more important. Supportive adults can foster increased understanding by providing accurate information, raising awareness, and encouraging open day-to-day interactions.

Be not afraid of growing slowly; be afraid only of standing still.

—*Chinese proverb*

Preparation: Getting Ready for Service Learning Involving Special Needs and Disabilities

The following activities can be used to promote learning and skill development related to special needs and disabilities. These activities are easily adapted to different grade levels during investigation, preparation, and planning to help your students examine key issues through research, analyze community needs, and gain the knowledge they need to effectively contribute to the design of their service plan. They can often be integrated into reflection and demonstration as students can lead the activities with others to build awareness. Since literature is often an important part of preparation, you can find recommended titles on this theme in the Special Needs and Disabilities Bookshelf later in this chapter.

Activity: Understanding Dis-Ability. This activity explores the idea of differences, challenges, and disability. Start by writing the word *ability* on the board, and ask the students to share their abilities. This usually results in a broad array of different abilities, from playing football to drawing to "I can stand on my head." When students are asked, "What does the word *ability* mean?" the answer usually is "something that a person does well." Ask students to think about the talents of people they know well: "Are they all the same?"

Now add the prefix *dis* to the front of *ability*, and ask your students for a definition. Most often, they will say "something someone cannot do well." This comes from a common societal perception and from turning the word "ability" into a negative, with *ability* meaning "can do" and *disability* meaning "cannot do." Have your students take a closer look; is this really true?

For example, a blind person can't see, so the question you can pose is, "Can a blind person learn to read?" Students usually know that blind people can learn to read using Braille. So blind people can learn to read, but they may have to learn in a different way and the task may be more challenging because of the disability. *Disability*, then means something that a person can do but may do differently or may have more difficulty doing. Can a deaf person learn to speak? Can a person in a wheelchair play basketball? Yes—but with differences.

Attitudes are the real disability.

—*Anonymous*

Activity: What About a Peanut? It may seem simple, but a peanut can be a useful and delicious tool to introduce and discuss the elements of special needs and disabilities. Provide each participant with peanuts still in the shell. Pose the question: "What makes these peanuts similar, and what makes them different?" Write the answers on a two-column chart with the word *peanut* at the top of the chart, *similar* over one column, and *different* over the other. Characteristics could include:

- Similar: basic shape, all have the same thing inside, most people like them.

- Different: appearances and shapes vary, uses vary.

Now cross out the word *peanut*, leaving the letter *p*, and write the word *people*. Review the chart to examine how people are alike and different. Most of the characteristics listed will still apply, and new ones can be added. This chart can become quite detailed and cover a wall or two. Include emotions, attitudes, likes, and dislikes in addition to physical attributes.

**Find Out More About
Special Needs and Disabilities**

To learn more about these issues and to get ideas for service and action, visit these Web sites and organizations online:

Austism Speaks (www.autismspeaks.org) is the nation's largest autism science and advocacy organization, dedicated to funding research into the causes, prevention, treatments, and a cure for autism; increasing awareness of autism spectrum disorders; and advocating for the needs of individuals with autism and their families.

The National Service Inclusion Project (www.serviceandinclusion.org) is a training and technical assistance project to increase the participation of people with disabilities in community service.

Special Olympics (www.specialolympics.org) provides year-round sports training and athletic competition for more than 2.5 million children and adults with intellectual disabilities in more than 180 countries.

Best Buddies International (www.bestbuddies.org) is an organization dedicated to enhancing the lives of people with intellectual and developmental disabilities by providing opportunities for one-to-one friendships and integrated employment, with programs specifically designed for middle and high schools; also includes an "e-buddies" program accessible at www.ebuddies.org.

Project Linus (www.projectlinus.org) is a volunteer nonprofit organization providing a sense of security, warmth, and comfort to children who are seriously ill, traumatized, or otherwise in need through the gifts of new, homemade, washable blankets and afghans, created by volunteer blanketeers.

Special Needs and Disabilities Across the Curriculum

English/Language Arts

- Build vocabulary by learning the current and respectful terms used to describe specific disabilities
- Create child-friendly informational materials for a local community organization, agency or outreach program serving a community with special needs
- Invite someone who reads Braille to talk about how they learned it; compare to the process of learning to read for sighted students; what are the similarities? Differences?

Social Studies/History

- Discuss: If money weren't a concern, how could the community be made truly accessible for everyone?
- Study about people with special needs who have been local, national, or international leaders
- Research the Americans with Disabilities Act (1990) and the impact of this and more current legislation

Languages

- Research the laws that impact people with disabilities in the countries that use the language you're learning
- Have a conversation using only picture symbols
- Compare the sign language systems of various countries

Theater, Music, & Visual Arts

- Create a theater performance showing people of all abilities as contributing participants in the community
- Identify music that has repetition and easy rhythms to teach children with developmental disabilities
- Work on art projects with younger students in a special needs class and create an art display for the community

Special Needs and Disabilities

Math

- Create activities that could be used in math centers for children who need practice identifying shapes, counting, or sorting
- Make a bulletin board of numbers or geometric shapes with each item offering a different tactile experience
- Find out and chart the national statistics on disabilities

Physical Education

- Research athletes with disabilities who succeed in sports like skiing, biking, mountaineering, and skydiving
- Prepare dance lessons for students with special needs
- Play basketball in wheelchairs or "beep baseball" where players are blindfolded and have assistance

Computer

- Learn how technology has been adapted to help people with special needs and disabilities be independent
- Compare Web sites that teach American Sign Language (ASL); select the one that's easiest to use and promote it within the school
- Using the Web, research careers related to working with people with disabilities

Science

- Assess an outdoor habitat or nature trail for accessibility
- Learn how the human neurological system is affected by different special needs conditions
- Select a special need and learn about recent scientific research that benefits people who have it

Making Connections Across the Curriculum

Some service learning activities naturally lend themselves to interdisciplinary work and making connections across the curriculum. These connections strengthen and broaden student learning, helping them meet academic standards. More than likely, you'll be looking for these connections and ways to encourage them well before the students ever start working on service learning activities. As with the entire service learning process, it helps to remain flexible, because some connections can be spontaneously generated by the questions raised throughout and by the community needs identified by the students. To help you think about cross-curricular connections and where you can look for them, the curricular web for this chapter (page 230) gives examples of many different ways this theme can be used in different academic areas. (The service learning scenarios in the next section of the chapter also demonstrate various ways that this theme can be used across the curriculum.)

Service Learning Scenarios: Ideas for Action

Ready to take action? The service learning descriptions that follow have been successfully carried out by elementary, middle, or high school students in schools and with community organizations. Most of these scenarios and examples explicitly include some aspects of investigation, preparation and planning, action, reflection, and demonstration, and all have strong curricular connections. These scenarios can be a rich source of ideas for you to draw upon. Keep in mind that grade levels are provided as a reference; most scenarios can be adapted to suit younger or older students, and many are suitable for cross-age partnerships.

Being Good Neighbors: Grades K–8

Young students with autism at Giant Steps of St. Louis, Missouri, created and then delivered valentines to residents at a senior residential facility next door to the school. In spring, peers from the general population of the school helped their peers with autism paint ceramic pots and plant them. With parents and teachers, the students hand-delivered the pots to the

seniors. The following weekend, parents and siblings of the students with special needs joined with some of the active seniors to plant an outdoor garden at the residence in a courtyard area in desperate need of sprucing up. A teacher commented, "When the parents stood back and watched their kids planting alongside the elderly, some of them started to cry. This was the first time their child had done service for others. Once the children were comfortable in the seniors' residence, they began helping on the inside. They prepped the dining room for lunch, delivered mail and newspapers, and led armchair exercises. Every single parent asked when they could do this again. And the kids were delighted. Anyone who started out skeptical ended up as an advocate of service learning for all kids."

> The best and most beautiful things in the world cannot be seen or even touched. They must be felt with the heart.
>
> —Helen Keller, author

Increasing Access at School: Grades 2–10

Can students improve access for people with disabilities on their school campuses? Second graders were able to create parking for people with disabilities where there had been none at their school. Seventh graders worked with a shop teacher to build a portable ramp for access to a previously inaccessible entrance. And tenth-grade students, concerned about the lack of physical accessibility in school buildings, worked with a local agency to survey the entire campus. A proposal for change was sent to the school board.

Kids and Canines: Grades 3–5

In Tampa, Florida, students who have been identified as being emotionally disturbed take part in an ongoing program by spending two sessions learning about service dogs, their handlers, and their prospective owners. The students also learn about pet care and responsibilities that come with owning a dog. Once a week, an elementary student, a service dog, and a handler visit a nearby nursing home. The interactions help the students develop social skills, empathy, and community awareness through interactions. Preparing for and carrying out basic conversations has given the students more confidence. And the elders enjoy meeting the children and being with the animals.

We'll Bring the Farm to You! Grades 3–5

In the rural community of Walker, Louisiana, educating young people about the history and process of farming has great value. As part of a sustainable agricultural lesson, special education students at South Walker Elementary developed a vegetable garden to share with prekindergarten and kindergarten classes. They incubated eggs in their classroom and assisted four other classes to do the same. The students also shared newborn goats with several kindergarten and preK classes. And for career connections, the students met with a veterinarian to discuss caring for goats and learn about the profession. Later, they learned and demonstrated bread making using whey left over from making goat cheese. All of these farm-related activities developed dynamic cross-age partnerships with the older kids teaching the younger ones about healthy living and food groups. This naturally led to the special education students reading to their "little friends," with notable feedback: a twenty-eight percent increase in reading fluency scores on a standardized reading fluency test. With service learning, these students who were used to being on the receiving end of assistance had opportunities to take care of others. They also had to face fears when reading in front of others, take full responsibility for a garden and chicks, and present their finished products. From the beginning, these students took initiative to actively plan, make decisions, and implement their program.

Swim Buddies: Grades 4–5

In an Anderson, Indiana, elementary school, every fourth- and fifth-grade student learned the skills and knowledge necessary to be an effective and responsible one-on-one swimming instructor for a preschool child with special needs. The upper elementary students all received training in water safety and basic childcare. Classroom integration continued as disability awareness and sensitivity training was woven into reading, health, computer skills, and civics. Youth voice and choice were evident as the swim buddies found additional ways to interact with the preschool students. They assisted during lunch and recess, and planned additional special events to enjoy their new reciprocal relationships.

Learning About Independent Living: Grades 7–8

Fifteen seventh- and eighth-grade students in Herrin, Illinois, participated in an after-school program at a center for independent living, serving people who have special needs. Students learned about the problems and adaptations made so people with disabilities can live independently. They learned about Braille and the computers adapted for this use, and studied American Sign Language. They saw firsthand how people move in wheelchairs or with canine assistance. Twice a month students provided assistance to people who are blind, deaf, and/or otherwise physically challenged. In reflection, students recognized how their ideas about people living with disabilities changed as they grew to be friends and advocates.

Setting the Course for Service: Grade 8

After attending a service learning workshop, an eighth-grade accelerated math student at the Academy for Academics and Arts in Huntsville, Alabama, found a way to apply conceptual mathematics to meet authentic community needs. After interviewing special needs teachers, the school nurse, the librarian, the art teacher, and researching scholarly journals, he used geometry to design an indoor obstacle course for the school's special education students to encourage sensory development. He also interviewed a city planner of a special needs playground and researched trade catalogs. He used math to calculate materials and supplies, presenting a proposed budget to the school administration. Along the way, he found out about fascinating careers: city planner, special needs advocate, and architect.

Family Helpers: Grades 9–11

After a series of workshops to become familiar with the role of in-home assistance for children with special needs, high school students visited homes identified by their partner agency. Students always worked in pairs. Most often, the activity involved playing with a developmentally disabled child whose learning benefits from additional stimulation and interaction. Students had regular meetings with the sponsoring agency for reflection, role playing, and further training.

Getting Physical: Grades 9–12

A squad of cheerleaders took their pep and enthusiasm into a class with teens who have Down syndrome. With teacher guidance and regularly scheduled visits, they taught a series of exercises that grew, over time, to be more complex. In addition to stretches and aerobics, they taught popular dance steps.

Job Coaching Mentally Challenged Peers: Grades 9–12

Leadership and Career Exploration students in a Panama City, Florida, high school provide mentoring for their mentally challenged peers as they prepare to enter the job market. Over the course of the high school years, these students volunteer together for ninety minutes a day in childcare programs, hospitals, humane societies, school and public libraries, rescue missions, teen court, and other community organizations. The mentoring students develop the work and monitor the program. The process begins in ninth grade, when special education students are placed in jobs on the high school campus to learn basic job skills and practices. With their mentors, they work the switchboard, file, make copies, and work in the library. For the next three years, at second period, 120 students on three buses leave campus for ninety minutes; on board is one job mentor for every three special education students. Tenth graders work primarily at childcare centers, and eleventh- and twelfth-grade placements are individualized for student interests and skill levels. Once the special education students can do the jobs independently, the mainstream students take on additional tasks to help the agencies. Recruiting job mentors is never a problem; this is a popular and well-received program.

No act of kindness, no matter how small, is ever wasted.

—Aesop

Trolley Activists: Grades 9–12

The Trolley Project in Panama City, Florida, was a natural outgrowth of the job coaching program described in the preceding scenario. Through observation, class discussion, and reflection, students came to understand that some people want to work but can't because of a lack of confidence, an impairment, difficulty finding employment, or lack of knowledge about how to place themselves in the workforce. Transportation can also be a deciding factor. For example, many community members with special needs use the city's downtown trolley as a primary form of transportation for getting to work, the public library, the senior center, or the technical college. The trolley was also used by many older people who could no longer drive. When the students learned that the downtown trolley, supported by transportation disability funds, would be shut down and the money used elsewhere, they were outraged and began to speak out. In collaboration with other interested groups, they convinced city administrators to keep the trolley running. Students also spoke to groups of older people about how use the trolley to take outings with their grandchildren. They volunteered to teach senior citizens and students with special needs how to use the trolley. A student-written coloring book that was distributed showed sights to see on the trolley and gave ideas for picnic locations. Almost every day, a school group goes out on the trolley.

School Clubs: Grades 9–12

In many New York high schools, students with and without disabilities meet weekly to share their commonalities and differences. In addition to sharing lunchtime and large group activities, they form pairs or trios and choose a school activity or service project to do together. All students receive orientation and have reflection sessions to ensure that relationships are mutually beneficial and to answer questions as they arise.

The Special Needs and Disabilities Bookshelf

The Special Needs and Disabilities Bookshelf (page 235) provides information that will help students to more ably provide service or serve alongside special needs peers. To help you find books relevant to your particular projects, the book chart classifies the titles according to these topic areas: learning about special needs, and interaction and peer relationships.

In general, the bookshelf features:

- An annotated bibliography arranged and alphabetized by title according to the general categories of nonfiction (N), picture books (P), and fiction (F). For nonfiction and fiction, length and recommended grade levels are included.

The entries in the picture book category do not include suggested grade levels, since they can be successfully used with all ages.

- A chart organized by topic and category to help you find books relevant to particular projects.

- Recommendations from service learning colleagues and experts which include a book summary and ideas for service learning connections. (The number of recommended books varies in each bookshelf.)

- *Please note:* additional titles for this category are listed in the digital content; some of these were out of print at the time of publication but still worth finding.

Nonfiction:
Special Needs and Disabilities

All Kinds of Friends, Even Green!
by Ellen B. Senisi (Woodbine, 2002). "I am lucky because I have so many friends," says Moses, a seven-year-old born with spina bifida and sacral agenesis. In his full inclusion classroom, Moses ponders his assignment to write about friends. Should he write about Jimmy, who shares secrets, or Jocelyn, who also sits in a wheelchair? Moses picks a "green" friend who has "something inside her the same as me." 32pp., grades K–4

The Black Book of Colors
by Menena Cottin (Groundwood Books, 2008). This truly is a black book and helps a sighted person empathize with a person with limited or no sight. The raised line black drawings on black paper must be felt to be "seen." Words and Braille accompany the facing page. Originally published in Mexico, this book is a brilliant treasure. 24 pp., grades K–8

Can You Hear a Rainbow?
The Story of a Deaf Boy Named Chris
by Jamee Riggio Heelan (Peachtree, 2002). Chris, a deaf boy, explains how he uses American Sign Language, hearing aids, and his other senses to communicate. Through a mix of photographs and art, we see Chris playing soccer, attending school, enjoying friends, and performing in a play. 29pp., grades K–5

Keep Your Ear on the Ball
by Genevieve Petrillo (Tilbury House, 2007). When Davey enters his elementary school class, all the kids are impressed with how easily he gets around and how engaged he is at school, considering that he is blind. Playing kickball remains difficult, however, until the class finds a creative way to include him without playing *for* him. The book is based on the true story of a boy who grew up to be an exceptional man. 32 pp., grades 3–6

Seeing Beyond Sight: Photographs by Blind Teenagers
by Tony Deifell (Chronicle Books, 2007). These photographs show skill involving composition and use of light—and all are taken by blind teens. The book includes a description of their Sound Shadows program, detailing the process and showing how the creative process extends beyond many boundaries. 152pp., grades 5–12

Picture Books:
Special Needs and Disabilities

The Deaf Musicians
by Pete Seeger and Paul DuBois Jacobs (G.P. Putnam's Sons, 2006). When a great jazz musician, Lee, loses his hearing, he thinks his music career is over. But then he meets another former musician when he goes to learn sign language. On the subway ride to and from school, the two friends begin playing the music they love with their hands. Eventually, they not only form a band, they also find an audience, and Lee realizes that music is a powerful language of unity.

The Printer
by Myron Uhlberg (Peachtree, 2003). "As a boy, my father learned to speak with his hands. As a man, he learned to turn lead-type letters into words and sentences. My father loved being a printer." The narrator tells of his deaf father's work and heroism in the printing plant where a daily newspaper was produced. Ignored by hearing coworkers, his father faced a terrible situation when a fire erupted in the noisy pressroom. How would he tell of the danger when they could not hear him? The author's note tells the story of his deaf father and why he became a printer.

The Treasure on Gold Street/El tesoro de la Calle Oro
by Lee Merrill Byrd (Cinco Puentas Press, 2003). This is a story about a real person named Isabel, who has an intellectual disability, and many of the people who live in her neighborhood. A young girl named Hannah is Isabel's good friend. Hannah likes the fact that Isabel is a grown-up who doesn't criticize and is never in a hurry. On Isabel's birthday, everyone on her street recognizes her as a true neighborhood treasure. English and Spanish text.

Fiction: Special Needs and Disabilities

Accidents of Nature
by Harriet McBryde Johnson (Henry Holt and Company, 2006). Jean has cerebral palsy, but she has always attended a "normal" school and insists that she is the same as everyone else. However, attending summer camp for kids with disabilities, she discovers a community of "crips" that she never knew existed. She also forms friendships that change how she thinks of herself and others, discovering similarities in the ways they are different. 273 pp., young adult

Special Needs and Disabilities Bookshelf Topics

Topics	Books	Category
Learning About Special Needs As we learn more about special needs, we respond more appropriately and effectively. These books increase knowledge and heighten sensitivity about different kinds of special needs.	*All Kinds of Friends, Even Green!*	N
	The Black Book of Colors	N
	The Boy Who Ate Stars	F
	Can You Hear a Rainbow? The Story of a Deaf Boy Named Chris	N
	The Cay (see Elders Bookshelf—digital content)	F
	The Curious Incident of the Dog in the Night-Time	F
	Owning It: Stories About Teens with Disabilities	F
	The Printer	P
	Seeing Beyond Sight: Photographs by Blind Teenagers	N
	Singing Hands	F
Interaction and Peer Relationships Common interactions include: neighbors spending time together, relationships between siblings, friendships at school, and challenges being met and resolved. Reading about these dynamics can assist both in learning about specific disabilities and in recognizing the possibility of forming successful relationships.	*Accidents of Nature*	F
	A Corner of the Universe	F
	The Deaf Musicians	P
	Jerk California	F
	Keep Your Ear on the Ball	N
	Of Mice and Men (see digital content)	F
	Rules	F
	Stoner and Spaz	F
	The Treasure on Gold Street/El tesoro de la Calle Oro	P

Page references are given for books that can be found in the bookshelf lists of other chapters.

The Boy Who Ate Stars

by Kochka, translated by Sarah Adams (Simon & Schuster, 2002). When Lucy and her parents move into their new home in Paris, there is so much noise coming from the apartment upstairs that Lucy's father goes up to see what is going on. The next day Lucy, a curious girl with a voracious appetite for language, goes upstairs to see for herself and meets Matthew. Matthew, she soon learns, has autism. But the dictionary's definition of the word fails to resonate with her increasingly intimate interactions with Matthew, and she realizes that often words and labels fail to capture the richness of human experience. 107 pp., grades 4–9

A Corner of the Universe

by Ann M. Martin (Scholastic, 2002). It is the summer of 1960, and Hattie relishes summer days and her upcoming twelfth birthday. But this summer turns her upside down as she meets her Uncle Adam, whom no one has told her about. Hattie sees herself in this developmentally delayed young man, who opens her heart and causes her to defy her parents and grandparents. 191pp., young adult

The Curious Incident of the Dog in the Night-Time

by Mark Haddon (Vintage Contemporaries, 2003). Movingly and ingeniously written, this story is told from the perspective of a teenager with autism caught in the whirlwind of the moral and emotional unsteadiness of an adult world. After being blamed for killing a neighbor's dog and being told "don't get involved," he plays detective to find out, like any curious teen. The truth, and how he uncovers it, stuns everyone involved. A popular book for an all-school read. 226 pp., young adult

Jerk California

by Jonathan Friesen (Penguin Group, 2008). Sam has Tourette's syndrome. This is an engaging story about Sam's social and physical teenage life. His muscle jumping and blurting out leads to isolation and loneliness. In spite of bullying and ostracism, Sam becomes close friends with beautiful Naomi. Sam offers Naomi support as they take a trip to California where they both find the courage to build a positive life. This captivating adventure story highlights the misconceptions about Tourette's syndrome and Sam's courage as he learns to live a healthy, full life. 327 pp., grades 8–12

DIGITAL CONTENT

Recommendation from the Field

Of Mice and Men by John Steinbeck (Penguin, 1937/1994). 137pp., young adult

---

Owning It: Stories About Teens with Disabilities

edited by Donald Gallo (Candlewick Press, 2008). Edited by a leading expert on teen literature, this is a collection of short stories written from the perspective of kids who have disabilities. Stories explore the lives of teens who suffer from various mental and physical disabilities, such as alcohol addiction, migraines, blindness, and brain damage. They remind us that disabilities aren't always obvious, and regardless of how identifiable they may be, it takes strength to live with them on a daily basis—on the part of the individuals and their friends and families. 215 pp., grades 7–12

Rules

by Cynthia Lord (Scholastic, 2006). This summer Catherine anticipates how a new next-door neighbor will become her best friend. But while waiting for her brother, David, at his physical therapist's office, she instead makes a different and unexpected new friend who has a special need. Struggling with her feelings of frustration toward David and defending him no matter what, Catherine learns that you can have very normal feelings for extraordinary people, and that sometimes doing a courageous thing does not feel courageous at all—it just feels right. 200pp., grades 6–9

Singing Hands

by Delia Ray (Clarion Books, 2006). Based on her mother's stories and experiences, the author imaginatively re-creates the life of a young, defiant girl in Alabama, 1948. Gussie and her two sisters are hearing, but their parents are deaf. Through Gussie's adventures we witness the compelling experience of a life split between two worlds and a girl unsure of how to live in either. 224pp., grades 5–8

Stoner and Spaz

by Ron Koertge (Candlewick, 2002). At age sixteen, Ben, who has cerebral palsy, has no parents, no friends, and no life outside school and the movies. An unexpected friendship with drugged-out Colleen places him in risky situations that have him making choices for the first time about relationships, engaging in an adolescent world, and letting people know what he has to offer as a thoughtful, humorous, and creative person. 169pp., young adult, mature themes

---

DIGITAL CONTENT

Interviews with Authors: The Story Behind the Story

In the companion digital content, you'll find interviews with authors Ellen Senisi (*Just Kids: Visiting a Class for Children with Special Needs* and *All Kinds of Friends, Even Green!*) and Cynthia Lord (*Rules*) that tell the "story behind the story" of their books.

Part Three

A Culture of Service

Chapter 17

Creating a Culture of Service

Why a Culture of Service Learning?

 While service learning may begin in a single classroom, the increasing value of this pedagogy often leads to a school- and district-wide initiative. In the early days, we thought service learning could be accomplished by adding a small project to whatever kids were studying. Or by stopping academics to "make a difference." Teachers and students from other academic areas or grades became interested and involved perhaps by lending a helping hand, providing information, giving advice, or otherwise joining by directly connecting their content areas to the service. Students from art classes would make posters, or a computer class would design and create brochures for a campaign on recycling. A math class might generate statistics for a civics or science effort. Or what started in one fifth-grade class naturally extended into a beneficial all-school service learning process.

This still occurs; the influence of one successful educator can be transformative. However, now we know more, and we know better. Service learning is a powerful teaching strategy that creates an environment conducive to developing transferable skills and knowledge, high engagement, and relevance that gives meaning and purpose to school—for teachers as well as students. Teachers continually tell me that their students go far beyond class requirements with service learning. When they care about the subject matter and have authenticated a need, students discover intrinsic motivation. And that is the key.

DIGITAL CONTENT

Voices from the Field: Legacy Projects

"As a middle school student, Holly LaCount witnessed her grandmother's losing battle with cancer. Not one to sit idly by, Holly sought to make a difference for others facing cancer. When registering for classes at Eureka High, she found a class that would give her a chance to take action. Holly selected the service learning elective 'Seeking Solutions' EAST Lab. In this class, Holly would combine her passion for horses with her desire to serve others to create the 'Ride for Life,' benefiting the American Cancer Society."
—*Ron Perry, Facilitator, Seeking Solutions EAST Lab, Eureka High School, Eureka, California*

Read the complete essay in the companion digital content.

Recently in the United States, service learning initiatives have come from a variety of directions. State departments of education, school superintendents, and district leadership understand and recognize the merits of service learning and school, district, and statewide plans are emerging to create and expand a culture of service tied to academics. Similarly for teachers, service learning exposure can occur in university within general courses and teacher education programs, where it is woven into numerous classes from education psychology to grade-level and subject-specific courses. Nonprofit organizations also invest significant staff time in studying how service learning can best improve the delivery of programs to young people. These efforts are supported by national education organizations that weave service learning into professional development experiences—from keynotes to all-day pre-conference sessions to workshops.

Service learning also thrives outside the United States. Overseas and American International Schools value service learning. International Baccalaureate programs have service learning and community service interwoven in their approach. Argentina has deep roots for service learning; Spain includes seventh-grade civic engagement studies; Roots & Shoots—a global youth initiative of the Jane Goodall Institute—has youth involvement in hundreds of countries; Liberia is developing service learning initiatives for youth achievement and community development; England has a long-standing civic engagement movement, and so on.

In all these contexts, service learning improves the underlying culture and addresses critical needs of the youth while actually improving the current delivery system for education; this is an imperative . . . and a very large topic! This chapter explores the concept of a "culture of service" and seeks to enliven conversations for you and other stakeholders who value youth success and want to improve how education occurs in the daily lives of our communities.

Connecting Service Learning to School Priorities

During my earliest days developing what grew into a comprehensive approach to service learning, I met individually with thirty high school principals in the Los Angeles Unified School District to interest them in adopting this approach. I quickly discovered that their agendas were full and the idea of "one more initiative" would result in polite discourse at best. Instead of launching into an onslaught about service learning, I simply asked, "What are your priorities?" This led the conversation toward investigating how service learning could help this school community meet the imperatives of the day, and looking at system-wide improvements and school reform. Implementation of high-quality service learning helps create the conditions for students to do better academically, which is always part of a school's priorities. Service learning can also lead to meeting other school priorities such as student retention and better community relations. Research has shown that service learning promotes resilience, empowerment, pro-social behaviors, motivation for learning, and student engagement—all mediators of academic success.

Years after my initial meeting with those thirty principals, a Los Angeles School District administrator asked if I would develop a curriculum to assist students' transition from elementary school (fifth grade) to middle school (sixth grade). As part of a summer transition program, students identified as being weak in math would have a daily two-hour remedial math program and then two hours daily of this "service learning." Quickly, the conversation became about how service learning is always in the context of content: students lacking math skills typically could use assistance with a range of literacy skills and social and emotional development—and these could best be delivered using service learning as a key methodology. Meeting the needs of these students with service as part of the pedagogy led to the program expanding to the transition from middle school to high school as well.

Service learning can be seen as an essential component of a healthy school community, with value added in targeted outcomes. Its practice adheres to the business of education—growing academically and socially adept youth who can participate in a rich civic and personal life. Promoting and instilling this practice as part of the school culture makes perfect sense.

Determine Your Priorities

What are the priorities in your school, district, or community organization? Include voices from diverse stakeholders, especially young people.

- Examine the mission statement of your school or organization. How can service learning help deliver the ideas?

- List your short- and long-term mandates. Brainstorm ways service learning can be a critical approach to advancing and meeting these.

- Find out what other groups have done to advance similar priorities.

While research will continue to reveal vital information about service learning, keep in mind that service learning has already been shown to improve academics, increase attendance; develop leadership, character, and social-emotional traits; and generate appreciation for the school community.

DIGITAL CONTENT

Voices from the Field: Mission and Coordination

"Create a school service mission statement. As an example, The Blake School Service Learning mission statement is: 'Through service learning at The Blake School, students gain a better understanding of themselves, the world in which they live, and the opportunity and responsibility they have to improve both. Service learning experiences at Blake often grow out of student interests and remain strongly tethered both to curriculum and to many communities. Reflection deepens the understanding students gain through these experiences. As a result of engagement in service learning while at Blake, students develop lifelong habits of heart, mind, and action that lead to lives as responsible world citizens. Fostering student development in this area is central to the mission of the school.'"

—*Nan Peterson, Service Learning Director, The Blake School, Minneapolis, Minnesota*

Read the complete essay in the companion digital content.

Literacy, School Climate, and Character Development

While traveling the globe, three priorities emerge as critical for educators today. First, achieving high-level literacy skills gives youth the requisite abilities to achieve while improving test scores and accountability. Second, we know safe schools mean kids arrive knowing adults will provide the care needed for them to learn, while eliminating outside threats and mitigating bullying and harassment behaviors inside the building. And third, every young person can internalize behaviors that lead to manifesting caring, thoughtfulness, and productivity, while building internal social and emotional foundations and qualities of character. How can service learning be an answer to questions regarding literacy, safety, and personal development?

Literacy: Form and Function

When asked to define literacy, the most common response is: the ability to read, write, and comprehend. Add fluency—another essential element that makes these skills almost second nature—and one might think the picture is complete. This is, however, only the *form* of literacy. When we neglect literacy's *function*, students often wonder why they need to work so hard to acquire these skills. The function of literacy requires the ability to apply the form of literacy with purpose and intent toward successful participation in society. This includes:

- **civic literacy**—the ability to participate and contribute to the dynamics of a class, neighborhood, or community, and may lead to interaction with government, organizations, and businesses to improve quality of life

- **social literacy**—the ability to differentiate appropriate behaviors for a variety of settings and populations

- **cultural literacy**—the ability to have tolerance and understanding of similar and different behaviors and attitudes drawn from a variety of backgrounds and lifestyles

- **any other "literacy"** that matches interest and assists personal growth and constructive participation, such as music literacy, sports literacy, financial literacy, media literacy, environmental literacy, and so on

Literacy functions rely on knowledge of history, science, literature, math, arts, technology, and other content areas. Enabling students to use knowledge in varied situations becomes the educator's challenge. Through well-delivered and guided service learning experiences and related activities and lessons, students strengthen form and function. Applying prior and acquired knowledge and skills through service learning creates an explicit and deliberate arena for students to experience the relationship between "real life" and what is often perceived as "strictly academics." The relevance of school and the connection between subjects becomes apparent. "Why am I learning this?" is replaced with, "I get it!"

DIGITAL CONTENT

Voices from the Field: Urban Service Learning

"At a recent student leadership meeting in Chicago, the discussion turned to the current state of the economy. The facilitator asked: 'Are you seeing the impact of the economy on anyone in your community?' One student nodded her head vigorously and responded, 'I have seen so many houses foreclosed and boarded up in the last couple of months. I know a lot of people who have lost their homes.' In Chicago, 85 percent of public school students qualify for free and reduced-cost lunch. This means their families were living at the margins of society even before the serious downturn in the community. So the question about the economy should really have been stated differently: 'Has the economy further exacerbated the situation for anyone you know?' The social issues that students in urban areas across the country address through service learning have direct and immediate impact on their lives and the lives of people they know personally."
—*Jon Schmidt, Service Learning Manager, Chicago Public Schools, Chicago, Illinois*

Read the complete essay in the companion digital content.

Transferable Skills

While the actual service performed may involve reducing our carbon footprint or documenting events in a town's history, the transferable skills developed through the process are of paramount importance. Consider this list and the intrinsic benefit gained from internalizing these skills and being able to access them in any learning situation. These foundation incremental skills can be deliberately woven into the Five Stages of Service Learning, enabling students to:

- ask questions

- listen and retain

- be observant

- identify similarities and differences

- recognize diverse perspectives

- work independently, with partners, and in groups

- identify and apply skills and talents

- acquire assistance as needed

- be resourceful
- gather and manage information
- summarize
- take notes
- effectively solve problems
- test hypotheses
- follow through with reasonable steps

Explicit inclusion of these and other such skills dramatically deepens the service learning experience and applies to all populations of students. Rather than assuming students have these competencies, service learning affords opportunities to develop skills in deliberate and explicit ways as students ask questions to investigate community needs, develop step-by-step plans, construct persuasive arguments, and role-play how to ask for help when a challenge arises. The results are students who can "read" the world around them and know how to apply their skills toward learning and life.

The Use of Quotations and Books

Consider also the potential for literacy skill development in the use of quotes that are placed throughout this book. Through frequent exposure to a range of inspiring and thought-provoking quotes, students come to appreciate the importance and power of words. These bite-size pieces of literature expose students to symbolic representation, interpretation, analysis, parts of speech, similes and metaphors, well-selected vocabulary, and a succinct manner of communicating a message. Using quotes with students may also:

- reinforce memory and retention through repetition of brief, easily remembered sentences
- convey how few words can communicate big messages
- validate prior thoughts or feelings by reading well-known quotes by others
- introduce words of wisdom or cultural ideas handed down through generations, often perceived as universal truths
- elevate awareness of how words can be uplifting
- generate ideas for using words or quotes for the benefit of others

Of course literacy also implies the core ability to engage and relate to text, whether words, numbers, or other symbols. You probably have already read chapter 3 of this book, and noted the bookshelf sections of every thematic chapter. Placing books in the hands of children and young adults that answer their questions, meet their personal interests, generate curiosity, and ultimately lead them to participate in a form of social activism is an essential part of service learning. Finding compelling books is reason enough to read again and again and again.

School Climate

To establish an improved school climate and culture with safety for all at the core requires some form of change. This requires an interpretation of "change" as favorable, quite different from a school setting where the mere mention of change by the principal at a staff meeting causes eyes to roll and deep sighs. In the article "How We Learn,"* professor Alison Gopnick describes two key principles that influence meaningful learning: role models and guided discovery. Establishing role models who demonstrate positive change, and creating an atmosphere where all participants can discover firsthand the benefits of change, can lead to a successful school culture. Moving toward constructive change with willing participants school-wide leads to a learning environment where the entire community thrives.

Holding to this concept, teachers must become agents of change for students to become change agents. When this is done in overt ways, students discover what change looks like and can then choose to adopt favorable behaviors to change internally and externally. For example, when a teacher changes toward a more democratic classroom by inviting students to determine the course of an otherwise predetermined service learning experience, this captures students' attention.

Seeing Through the Lens of Change

What would be required of teachers to add the lens of change to how students view subjects being studied? What would be the value in this perspective? If we seek strategies to model change, we can look directly at

---

* *New York Times Education Supplement,* January 16, 2005.

content and skills being taught. Every curricular area is ripe with examples of change. Becoming familiar with the concept of change and recognizing change as part of life assists students with changes they experience daily. Students apply their developing knowledge of change toward academic skills as they track character changes in literature, chemical changes in science, and develop a timeline of changes throughout history and current events.

Service learning as a process may be the epitome of change. As described in Part One of this book, youth examine needs and create action plans. They make change happen—and in the process, they grow and transform. As one teacher said in a workshop, "They change the world, and the world changes them."

Through service learning, students become change agents in their own school, intent on creating a safe, healthy environment for every student and adult member of the community. School can be considered an initial laboratory for applying skills and competencies. When students can see the daily benefits of their actions, they develop the requisite abilities to then step outside into their environs (and beyond) and accomplish more.

The theme of change can continue to connect with academics as students track how the kids in foster care change in the novel *Jakeman*, or how the perspective of war changes when a spontaneous ceasefire occurs on Christmas between soldiers during World War I in the nonfiction book *Truce*. Studying the role of nonprofit organizations in social studies, whether in first or tenth grade, enable young people to see how communities change through collaboration. Looking at our oceans and waterways through the lens of change—how they once were, how they are now—can help students wade through the science lessons and come up with action plans. With a solid foundation built from improving their school setting, students can then step out into the larger world.

Examples of Student Initiative

Following are some examples of student initiative that I have culled from various schools in recent years.

About Our School—Students produce a video to welcome new students. This video can highlight the value of every school member—from custodial staff to clerical staff to teachers, administrators, and students—creating mutually respectful relationships throughout the school.

Elementary Tutoring—Every fourth grader tutors a first, second, or third grader in reading for twenty minutes a day, four days a week, and reviews tutoring skills on the fifth day. Multiage relationships thrive as mutual respect grows.

No Name-Calling Week and *Mix It Up Day*—These two exemplary national initiatives enable students to adopt pro-social behaviors and craft opportunities for learning about others.

Homework Tips—Homework skills help students succeed in academics and build confidence. Students compare homework strategies and initiate a school-wide campaign led by students of diverse abilities. They create sets of study tip bookmarks and other collectibles with the theme: "Make Homework a Slam Dunk." They also lead homework workshops and write study guides.

Welcome Buddies—Students identify the struggles of new classmates during the school year and design a plan to continually support them through teams of buddies made up of members of various social groups.

Peace Garden—Students need a place to go for thoughtful conversation and reflection: a peace garden. Blending art and design, science, history, and English, students can create a butterfly garden with benches made of recycled wood and "plant" quotes and book passages among the flowers.

Character Development

At its most basic level, perhaps service learning is about raising student awareness of how their words can transform into ideas and then into action. Then, words matter deeply, whether used by students or by the adults in their lives. This concept has been introduced in Quotable Quotes (page 72) and permeates as a message throughout this book. Words come alive with meaning and purpose in service learning, leading to pro-social choices and internalized actions. The aim is to influence behavior for the good of the individual, and for this behavior to be extended into the community. Such personalization and transference adds purpose and meaning to education.

DIGITAL CONTENT

Voices from the Field: Character and Service

"In the era of school accountability focused almost entirely on test scores, how does a school district know if it is meeting its mission of educating the whole child? The mission of the Albion Central School District is 'Achievement, Character, Success for Life.' It is the belief of the Albion community, many of whom were involved in crafting our mission, that the development of the character of our young people is equally as important as helping them to reach their potential academically. The instructional methodology that provides the most integrated, comprehensive, and public demonstration of character development is service learning. It is through fruitful collaborative partnerships in the community that our students, as budding citizens, become visible in the community as they tackle very real problems."
—*Ada Grabowski, Superintendent, Albion Central School District, Albion, New York*

Read the complete essay in the companion digital content.

As students become aware of their talents and skills (see Personal Inventory on page 51) and apply these toward meaningful acts of service, they recognize a level of significance and value that deepens their sense of self. At a workshop I led, a teacher commented, "My students only think about themselves." That sounded developmentally correct to me! Children and adolescents need to determine who they are and their place in the world. This begins with self-awareness: knowledge of one's self in place and time, and what happens as a result of thoughts, feelings, and actions.

What occurs through service learning that may be different from other teaching pedagogies is this: By generating ideas and activities—for example,

participating in National No Name-Calling Week and reducing bullying within their school—students realize they have a sphere of influence that reaches the parameters of their campus. And when students design and develop a food drive campaign that results in the local food bank having ample supplies through the summer, they recognize that their influence extends into the community. Likewise, with the "In Our Global Village" project, when students in a remote village in Tanzania write a book about their community and inspire students in over ten countries to write books in an international youth-to-youth exchange of knowledge about diverse cultures, each young participant's sphere of influence extends beyond boundary of city, country, and even continent. Service learning strengthens character and social and emotional presence by validating opportunities for authentic learning; these opportunities, in turn, provide reflections of self.

Intrinsic versus Extrinsic Rewards

Can all this be accomplished when competition is part of this service learning equation? Compare a competitive classroom environment with one valuing collaboration, connections, and supporting self and others—all markers for social and emotional growth and stability. The more collaborative environment places greater importance on opportunities for intrinsic knowledge and growth than on extrinsic rewards. The dilemma between extrinsic and intrinsic rewards appears when students do something "good" and expect a prize. This instills a pattern. In the case of a canned food drive, if designed as a competition where the class that brings in the most cans wins a pizza party, what is first and foremost in the students' minds? Winning. Likewise, in school situations where children are rewarded with prizes for being "caught" doing something kind or good for others, there is a risk that they will consistently desire to be *seen* doing these acts and thus rewarded, rather than behaving out of a genuine generosity they might otherwise naturally experience.

A teacher in Albion, New York, guided her fifth-grade students in transforming a penny collection for children with leukemia into an authentic service learning experience. The students studied about cancer through online resources, by interviewing doctors and family members impacted, and by reading the novel *Bluish* (see page 154). The class worked in small groups making presentations to every other class in the school, elevating the experience from simply placing coins into a container, to developing authentic skills and pertinent knowledge. The receiving agency was impressed and notified the teacher that this class had done so well they had won (can you guess?)—a pizza party! The teacher excitedly announced this outcome to the class expecting delight, and instead a student remarked, "We didn't do this for a pizza party. Can we donate the cost of the pizza to the cause?" The verdict was unanimous among all the students. When the teacher called the agency representative to pass on this message, the response was, "Can I at least send a box of candy?"

No pizza, no candy; kids may understand this concept better than adults. Young people have been known to express disdain for what they see as disregard for the real reason they contribute their hard work, dedication, and time to a cause. Like teachers who entered education to make a difference in the lives of kids, kids give their hearts and minds in service to make a difference and exercise their influence for the common good. Rather than breed competition, we can develop intrinsic knowledge and reflective insight—where *competence* and *confidence* go hand in hand.

Growing Service Learning at Your School

Schoolwide interest and participation can draw an entire community into a continuing ethos of service. Service learning by its very nature is conducive to collaboration and building community. As you incorporate service learning successfully into your classroom or organization, spreading the word and involving your colleagues can happen naturally. Perhaps the cultivation of a service learning culture at your school is part of a formal effort on the part of the school's administration, the district, or leaders in your organization. If you have had successes with service learning in your classroom, you may have even been drafted to coordinate and educate your colleagues, or to take part

in an ongoing conversation to build upon an existing foundation.

Whether you are a service learning coordinator for a school, district, region, or organization, or a teacher or youth worker seeking to expand the practice, much of the material in this guide can help you do this effectively. Many of the exercises included here, such as brainstorming and cross-curricular collaborations, lend themselves to working with other teachers and administrators. These interactions can be the beginning of a culture of service learning at your school or organization. Peer-led discussions and workshops—that may be integrated into faculty or staff meetings and professional learning communities—can build upon these initial collaborations.

Regardless of the impetus, the more people are involved in service learning, the more people benefit. Deliberate service learning impacts the culture of an entire school. Young people can become more empowered, aware, invested, and emotionally engaged with their schoolwork. As teachers develop and refine their service learning practices, they become increasingly able to help their students meet academic requirements, develop and sustain community partnerships, and encourage student leadership and initiative. The community becomes aware of the valuable role students play in caring for people and places. Sound idealistic? It's actually realistic. Over time and with collaboration and good work, service and learning can weave into the fabric of the extended school community and the lives of its members.

This chapter is designed to help you use its information, strategies, and select forms with your stakeholders. These materials will help you create collegial buy-in into implementing and expanding service learning, by helping others see benefits for students in *their* classrooms, *their* school, *their* community. Well-informed stakeholders—administrators, other faculty, school support teams (from office to custodial), parents, and community members—offer tremendous resources, whether acting as role models or participants. When everyone contributes to creating a culture of service, everyone benefits.

Voices from the Field: Collaboration

"The true success of the educational system consists of forming citizens that can improve society, and not just their own résumé. To improve society, the educational centre (primary, secondary, university) must collaborate actively with the social agents in the community: NGOs, town or city council, the neighborhood's social and educational organizations, foundations, and so on. It should replace a culture of working in isolation with a network-driven approach, and service learning affords the educational centre many opportunities for doing so. Service learning is not just an educational methodology; it is also a tool for community development and cohesion. It is both educational and social, in that requires the collaboration of all the actors involved.
—*Roser Batlle, Centre Promotor Aprenentatge Servei (Service Learning Center of Catalonia), Barcelona, Spain*

Read the complete essay in the companion digital content.

Resources for Creating a Culture of Service

This chapter includes the following resources to communicate the concept of quality service learning in professional development workshops and in-service sessions:

- **Adapting Previous Forms**—Suggestions for adapting forms presented in prior chapters of this book.

- **Activities and Using New Forms**—Additional ways to engage teachers and promote buy-in to the concept and practice of service learning.

- **Small (and Large) Learning Communities**—Open-ended questions to use in various groups, including professional learning communities, to examine and advance service learning practice and pedagogy.

- **Voices from the Field**—Throughout this chapter, you have read excerpts from essays contributed by colleagues accomplished in service learning who offer their expertise along with ideas and suggestions. Complete essays from these contributors are found in this book's companion digital content.

These tools will enable you to share your knowledge and experiences productively with your colleagues, collaborators, and community. Creating a culture of service at your school or organization requires concentrated effort, yet rewards are tremendous and ongoing—handed from student to student, teacher tocolleague, teacher to parent, and school to community.

Voices from the Field: Building Sustainable Partnerships

"Schools can facilitate a successful partnership with frequent and explicit communication:

- Present to the partner a clear and easy-to-understand definition of service learning. How is it different from community service?

- Share your learning intentions with the partner, introducing proposed academic content and standards in jargon-free terminology. What expertise does the partner have that can benefit student learning?

- Learn about the mission of the organization or agency, and how the proposed plans will meet that mission. What does the community partner expect from the student service?

- Introduce the concept of *youth voice*, explaining its importance to student engagement. How will the partner accommodate youth leadership within the student service experience?

- Think '*win-win.*' What assessment measures will be used to demonstrate how both learning objectives and community needs are met?"

—*Susan A. Abravanel, Vice President of Education, Youth Service America*

Read the complete essay in the companion digital content.

How to Create and Build a Culture of Service: Adapting Previous Forms

The first two chapters of this guide are rich sources of material that you can use to explain the principles and practices of service learning to your colleagues and others involved in the process. Forms in chapter 2 that may be particularly helpful from the book include: Establishing Curricular Connections: Points of Entry, K–12 Service Learning Standards for Quality Practice, The Five Stages of Service Learning, Personal Inventory, Gathering Information About a Community Need, and Planning for Service Learning. These can be used in staff development sessions, and even divided into mini-workshops for faculty meetings. Following is a discussion of each form and how it may be used in creating a culture of service.

DIGITAL CONTENT

Voices from the Field: Youth Empowerment

"If your students are motivated and passionate, they will lead the way to creating a culture of service. At the beginning of each semester in our district, youth empowerment training is conducted by students who have been in the service learning program for at least one year and/or have met the criteria to become a student empowerment trainer. Key district and community members are invited to attend the youth empowerment training. The leadership training 'sessions' are written by students."

—*Evelyn Robinson, Service Learning Program Specialist, Lake School District, Tavares, Florida*

Read the complete essay in the companion digital content.

Establishing Curricular Connections (page 47) presents five points of departure that can be used as the basis for initiating service learning. The form details sample ideas and literature resources. In staff development or teacher education settings, discuss each point of departure. Consider which approach is appropriate or preferred for a particular classroom or grade level, academic program, or teaching style. In small groups, teachers can develop sample ideas for each point of departure based on the examples provided. Selecting a schoolwide point of departure can be helpful in unifying the staff if the process incorporates genuine youth voice, especially through investigation of a community need. Consider the food drive transformation referenced in chapter 1 on page 18.

K–12 Service Learning Standards for Quality Practice (page 47) describes the eight essential elements of service learning. In a service learning workshop or teacher education class, discuss these questions: How do these essential aspects enhance the learning process in general? How do they affect the service provided? How do they complement one another?

The Five Stages of Service Learning (page 47) outlines the service learning process that students follow: investigation, preparation and planning, action, reflection, and demonstration. During teacher workshops or in teacher education classes, discuss these questions: How do investigation, preparation and planning, action, reflection, and demonstration maximize the potential for meaningful learning and service? How is each stage consistent with other effective teaching methods and theories?

Focus on the Investigation stage of service learning by leading teachers through a **Personal Inventory** process (page 51). When students do this activity, they complete a Getting Ready for Personal Inventory process (pages 50–51) and then conduct face-to-face interviews with a partner, writing down what they learn from asking questions. With teachers I vary the format and ask them to find a partner from a different table and take two minutes to discover this person's interests by asking questions. Then I gather their responses and create a list on chart paper. Next, I ask them to find a new partner and repeat, this time finding out about the person's skills and talents. Again, I gather and list the responses. Finally, we discuss what they learned from the experience and how knowing these things about their students is valuable, whether or not they even do service learning! The process is enjoyable, improves social skills, and moves us all beyond first impressions to more intimate knowledge. The information gathered is critical to student participation in a dynamic learning environment and of paramount value when planning and actualizing service learning.

Next, have teachers "workshop" the **Gathering Information About a Community Need** activity (page 51). More and more I find this to be important to help resolve the difficulties students have in conducting research. Lead teachers through the exact activity as described on the form. This has been an "Aha!" moment for many teachers in my workshops and conference presentations. The intent is to help students form a common language for research that carries them from elementary through high school, and even on into college and careers.

Teachers use the **Planning for Service Learning** form (page 50) in designing and planning service learning activities and identifying collaborative opportunities. The example forms in the book and in the digital content are helpful models of what service learning can look like with different topic themes, in different geographic areas, and with students of different ages and abilities. As such they can be used to explain and demonstrate the process of service learning to your colleagues and various other audiences—administrators, parents, potential community partners, and students. In a workshop setting, I request an idea for a service learning experience from a participant. Using the form on my computer with a projector allows me to fill in the spaces as we brainstorm ideas. Participants see this is a nonlinear tool to collect and map out suggestions,

demonstrating service learning as a team sport. Then teachers form cross-curricular clusters or small groups based on grade level or department, and begin using the form to think through their own lessons, while leaving ample room for youth voice and choice.

Thirty-nine examples of completed Planning for Service Learning forms are in the digital content—an elementary, middle, and high school example for every thematic chapter in this book. This form is also used by student teachers in creating samples of service learning activities that can be reviewed in methodology classes and implemented during student teaching assignments.

How to Get Started Creating a Culture of Service: Activities and Using New Forms

Talking about service learning is a good way to start engaging your colleagues in the process. There are a number of different topics you can address over the course of several meetings or workshops.

Activity: Create a Definition of Service Learning for Your School or Group

What's the first way you can start a lively discussion about service learning? Create a collaborative definition of service learning that fits your school, youth group, or organization. Involve every person in this activity as you also model an engaging teaching strategy adaptable for every classroom.

At a meeting or an in-service:

1. Begin by describing several examples of service learning from your school or region that make explicit connections to curricula, or by using appropriate examples from this book. When possible, select examples that illustrate different entry points, use photos (a picture is worth a thousand words), and show literature connections. Keep each example brief yet powerful.

2. Then, present the challenge. Break participants into small groups and give them four minutes to write their own definitions of service learning in ten words or less. Have them write their definitions on paper or, even better, distribute chart paper and markers. This allows for visual representation along with written.

3. Each group presents their definition. If chart paper is used, post them on the wall.

4. Look for key words and concepts that emerge. Most often, each small group adds a different aspect to the big picture of what service learning is all about. Encourage discussion of any ideas or aspects that are missing.

5. Afterward consolidate the results into a working definition and distribute copies to everyone who attended.

Revisit this definition in several months, after your colleagues have experience with service learning in their classes or groups. What would they change? What in this definition proved most true to their experiences? Encourage participants to do this activity with young people to help them understand the value of service learning. Did their students make interesting suggestions about what they think service learning means?

Comparing and sharing the different perspectives may be revealing and may help to create an increasingly dynamic definition for your school or group.

Activity: Linking to the Curriculum

Take time to highlight curriculum connections through the use of the blank document Across the Curriculum (in digital content). While there are thirteen completed forms in the book, one in each thematic chapter, using this blank form allows teachers to discover for themselves the rich landscape of academic possibilities with service learning.

Provide copies for all teachers and ask them to form small groups. Once they're in working groups, select one of these options for procedure:

- If the school or group has an overarching theme such as "environment," write this at the top of the form and have each group select a sub-theme of the environment such as water, pollution, recycling, or climate change, and write this in the center.

- If teachers have copies of this book, have them look at the contents and select one theme from Part Two, and then close the book. Fill in this theme at the top of the form and add an optional sub-theme in the center, or simply repeat the main theme as the sub-theme.

- If you have a school-wide community service effort you'd like to transform into service learning, hand out the form with the top line and sub-theme already completed. For example, "Food Drive Across the Curriculum" at the top, and "Poverty and Hunger" in the center.

Each group works as a team. Explain they are coming up with *learning* connections now, and the service ideas will come later. Allow about four to five minutes for them to fill out the form. Then ask what they have learned about service learning in this process. Request that some ideas be shared. Then, if copies of this book are available, have groups look at one of the thirteen completed forms related to their topic for more ideas. At the conclusion, ask if people found at least one idea they could do. Keep in mind this form, like all the forms in this book, is adaptable and subjects can be added or changed to fit your school community.

Activity:
Identifying the Benefits of Service Learning

What are the benefits of service learning? Once participants have a sense of what service learning looks like and the key components, divide them into four small groups, assigning each group a category: students, teachers, schools, or community. Ask the question, "In a school where service learning is used as an effective teaching method, what are the benefits to your category?" Allow time for groups to compile a list of benefits. Have each group present the top three items on their list, and invite others to contribute ideas. Compile the items into a master list of benefits for use during future discussions about what is already in place and what could be done to further manifest desired benefits during the service learning process. Were the benefits realized? Did unexpected benefits emerge for certain groups?

Form: Benefits of Service Learning (page 252)

This handout is provided at the end of this chapter for reference. Keep in mind this list will grow and change depending on the populace and practice being done. You can also use this form, along with other material suggested in this section, to explain and support service learning in presentations to others who may become vested in the process, such as parents, administrators, community members, and school board members.

**Activity: Clarifying Roles for
Success with Service Learning**

As a well-traveled observer of service learning
implementation, I began to notice teachers doing far
more than their students in the process. Rather than
teach the requisite skills, teachers step in and do the job
themselves, wanting perfect timely outcomes rather than
what can be authentic and sometimes "messy" when
done by students. The true value of service learning is
in the students' *doing*: learning what they need to know
(both skills and information), testing their ideas and
theories, and reflecting on what happened.

Teachers serve as vital guides.

Form: Clarifying Roles for Success with Service
Learning (page 252)

This document guides this conversation with teachers
who want to advance their service learning practice.
Teachers complete the form in pairs or groups. Invite
them to think of one specific service learning experience
and write at the top the percentage that was truly done
by them and what was truly done by the students. Then
underneath, ask them to write the percentage they
want to aim for. Allow for talking and thinking time
about how to make this transformation. Share ideas.
Have teachers who excel at different aspects lead mini-
workshops on improving the service learning process.
Remember, service learning is a team sport for teachers
as well as students.

Small (and Large) Learning Communities

Consider holding a series of discussions on a variety
of related topics that draw in different groups integral
to successful service learning. Administrators, teachers
or group leaders, school or organization support staff,
parents, community organizations, and of course students, all play significant roles in creating a culture of
service. The more viewpoints that are represented, the
greater the likelihood for success. Collaboration is what
establishes a solid foundation. Invite all participants to
discuss the topics on the following forms, included as
reproducible forms at the end of this chapter:

- Building Foundations for Service Learning (page 252)

- Establishing Curricular Connections (page 253)

- Increasing Youth Voice and Choice (page 253)

- Encouraging Teachers to Be Involved (page 253)

- Parent Involvement in Service Learning (page 253)

- Establishing Authentic Community Partnerships (page 254)

Use these forms in groups to stimulate conversation, planning, and action toward a systemic approach
to integrating service learning into the culture of your
school or organization. Use them in large or small
group settings and with different groups of collaborators. Each form includes questions for discussion and
key areas to explore. Adapt them as needed. Additional
topics for discussion will most likely emerge.

Finally, you will find forms that will be helpful reference handouts for initial discussions and workshops
on service learning. Descriptions of these follow.

Service Learning: Knowing the Terms (page 254).
This form provides definitions of the terms *volunteer*,
community service, and *service learning*. Use these definitions in meetings or workshops to discuss what the
terms mean in your school or organization. Discuss
how the terms connect with school priorities such as
students' personal and academic development.

A Brief Step-by-Step Guide to Service Learning (page 254). The steps detailed on this form provide a service learning sequence to follow, which is especially helpful for teachers new to service learning and students acting as peer or classroom leaders. A poster showing this outline can provide a useful visual aid for discussion and reference.

Form: Service Learning Vocabulary (page 254). This form can be a helpful reference to think about how service learning expands a developing vocabulary. Teachers in grades K–12 can use the ideas and word list to enhance critical thinking skills and language development.

DIGITAL CONTENT

Voices from the Field:
A Local Service Learning Association

"What do teachers need to advance service learning? Time to meet together. Time for collective education about service learning, collegial stories, support, ideas, and resources to build effective and lasting school integration. The Educators Consortium for Service Learning (ECSL) was founded by administrators, teachers, and parent activists who deeply agree that service learning advances youth development and academic success. They also recognize that through association, concepts can be taught, ideas exchanged, motivation inspired, and everyone improves. Now, over sixteen years later, the evidence is in: this original cadre has made a lasting impact."
—*Cathryn Berger Kaye and Donna Ritter,*
The Association for Service Learning Education,
Los Angeles, California

Read the complete essay in the companion digital content.

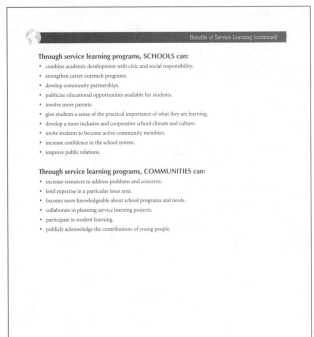

Benefits of Service Learning

Who benefits from service learning? Students, teachers, the school population as a whole, and the community benefit from well-designed service learning programs. Benefits vary depending on program design and what occurs through preparation, implementation, reflection, and demonstration. These lists have been compiled by school and community stakeholders based on their service learning experiences. While research continues to examine the benefits of service learning, presently service learning is known to promote resilience, empowerment, prosocial behaviors, motivation for learning, and engagement. These are mediators of academic success and help create the conditions for students to do better academically.

Through service learning programs, STUDENTS may:

- increase motivation and desire to learn.
- develop responsibility, think critically, make decisions, and solve problems.
- improve academic knowledge and performance, including writing and communication skills.
- cultivate self-perception.
- develop ability to work well with others.
- experience reciprocity.
- replace stereotypes with respect for others.
- interact with adults who have different roles in society.
- be exposed to career options including those in public service.
- become more knowledgeable about their community and the resources available for themselves and their families.
- experience civic responsibility.
- begin to develop a lifelong commitment to public service and to learning.

Through service learning programs, TEACHERS may:

- observe students' enthusiasm for learning.
- improve communication and understanding among students.
- increase the relevancy of education for students.
- develop curriculum through collaboration with other teachers and community partners.
- learn about many different community organizations and how they serve the populace.
- identify resources to enhance educational opportunities for students.
- bring the classroom and community together.
- feel inspired professionally and personally.
- participate in professional development and become mentors for other teachers.

Through service learning programs, SCHOOLS can:

- combine academic development with civic and social responsibility.
- strengthen career outreach programs.
- develop community partnerships.
- publicize educational opportunities available for students.
- involve more parents.
- give students a sense of the practical importance of what they are learning.
- develop a more inclusive and cooperative school climate and culture.
- invite students to become active community members.
- increase confidence in the school system.
- improve public relations.

Through service learning programs, COMMUNITIES can:

- increase resources to address problems and concerns.
- lend expertise in a particular issue area.
- become more knowledgeable about school programs and needs.
- collaborate in planning service learning projects.
- participate in student learning.
- publicly acknowledge the contributions of young people.

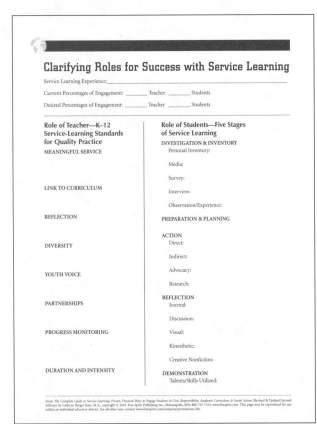

Clarifying Roles for Success with Service Learning

Service Learning Experience: _____

Current Percentages of Engagement: _____ Teacher _____ Students

Desired Percentages of Engagement: _____ Teacher _____ Students

Role of Teacher—K–12 Service-Learning Standards for Quality Practice

MEANINGFUL SERVICE

LINK TO CURRICULUM

REFLECTION

DIVERSITY

YOUTH VOICE

PARTNERSHIPS

PROGRESS MONITORING

DURATION AND INTENSITY

Role of Students—Five Stages of Service Learning

INVESTIGATION & INVENTORY
Personal Inventory:

Media:

Survey:

Interview:

Observation/Experience:

PREPARATION & PLANNING

ACTION
Direct:

Indirect:

Advocacy:

Research:

REFLECTION
Journal:

Discussion:

Visual:

Kinesthetic:

Creative Nonfiction:

DEMONSTRATION
Talents/Skills Utilized:

Building Foundations for Service Learning

Consider:

- What elements within a school contribute to establishing a culture of service?
- What steps do we need to take to move in this direction?

Discuss:

- understanding and visibility of service learning already in place.
- clear roles and responsibilities for all involved, including students, school administrators, faculty, support staff, community partners, parents, agencies, and government.
- leadership from within each group of participants.
- expectation of challenges.
- experienced teachers as coaches for new faculty.
- inclusion of service learning in school and district mission statements.
- flexibility in school schedules to allow for service learning opportunities.
- unequivocal expression of support from principal and other school leaders.

See digital content for full-size reproducible pages.

Establishing Curricular Connections

Consider:

- Are we letting community service pass for service learning?
- What steps do we need to take to move toward well-integrated service learning?

Discuss:

- teacher preparation and staff development opportunities for service learning.
- allowing for both community service and service learning where appropriate for students.
- collaboration in which teachers help, encourage, and challenge each other.
- classroom activities that demonstrate high-quality practices.
- expectation that every student will be able to have service learning experiences.
- resources to support practices, including transportation, books, materials, mailings, phone calls, supplies, grant-writing assistance, and so forth.
- establishing formal links between service and standards.
- making service part of grade and formal course assessment.

Increasing Youth Voice and Choice

Consider:

- How are young people given opportunities to make real choices and what opportunities do they have to express and act on thoughtful choices?
- What practices are already in place, and what will advance us to the next level?

Discuss:

- establishing a service learning vocabulary with students.
- developing authentic ways for students to be creative, have input, make decisions, solve problems, help design service activities based on preparation, and participate in project evaluation.
- developing an age-appropriate sequence for service learning.
- enabling students to experience success and failure—removing the "safety net" of adult intervention.
- encouraging intrinsic value over extrinsic rewards.
- listening to students and creating forums for their concerns, questions, and ideas.
- allowing experienced students to help their teacher and other teachers plan and implement projects.

Encouraging Teachers to Be Involved

Consider:

- How can teachers "buy in" and develop an engagement with service learning?
- Are opportunities available for teacher leadership and professional advancement?

Discuss:

- teacher in-service opportunities.
- collaboration options for making teacher-to-teacher connections.
- hiring teachers with service learning experience or interest, and providing learning opportunities and teacher mentors for new hires.
- regularly including service learning in discussions at staff meetings.
- establishing new school-wide service learning opportunities annually.
- resolving challenges involving transportation and out-of-pocket expenses.
- creating a library of service learning literature and resource materials.
- establishing college connections for professional learning and partnerships to advance implementation.

Parent Involvement in Service Learning

Consider:

- How can parents become advocates for and partners in service learning at school?
- Can parents help instill the value or idea of service within the family?

Discuss:

- keeping parents informed.
- finding meaningful roles for parents.
- preparing parents for their roles through workshops.
- creating a system run by parent volunteers to inform others about opportunities for family service.
- establishing parent service learning liaisons for grade levels or departments.
- designing activities that require students to work with parents and vice versa, such as collecting oral histories and learning about other cultures.

Note: The term *parent* as used here applies to any significant adult in a child's life.

See digital content for full-size reproducible pages.

Establishing Authentic Community Partnerships

Consider:

- How are valued, sustainable, and reciprocal partnerships built?
- What agencies, organizations, or individuals are or could be proponents of service learning?

Discuss:

- coming to understand "community" as a dynamic exchange between people.
- allowing for change and flexibility in partnerships.
- facilitating a process in which schools and organizations/agencies can learn about each other.
- identifying government partners.
- involving youth in community outreach.
- documenting partnerships.
- finding the intersection of interests between the school and community organizations.

Service Learning: Knowing the Terms

Service to others takes many forms and has many names and connotations. In a school context, examining different types of service helps clarify and define service learning as a teaching method.

Volunteer: One who contributes time without pay.

Community service: Helping the community by choice or through court requirement; may or may not be associated with academics, curriculum, or reflection.

Service learning: A teaching method that:

- enables students to learn and apply academic, social, and personal skills to improve the community, continue individual growth, and develop a lifelong ethic of service.
- focuses on both the service and the learning.
- is appropriate for all students and all curricular areas.
- encourages cross-curricular integration.
- helps foster civic responbility.
- provides students with structured time to reflect on the service experience.

A Brief Step-by-Step Guide to Service Learning

Step One: *Points of Entry*
Select your method for getting started and making curricular connections, beginning with an existing program or activity, content and skills, a theme or unit of study, a student-identified need, or a community-identified need.

Step Two: *Review the K–12 Service-Learning Standards for Quality Practice*
Familiarize yourself with these eight recommended categories that support best practices for service learning. Referring to this list will give you reminders for what will provide the greatest impact for both learning and civic participation.

Step Three: *Map Out Your Plans*
Identify your curricular objectives. Write out your specific ideas for curricula, community contacts, literature, and each stage (of the five stages) of service learning.

Step Four: *Clarify Partnerships*
Make contacts with any collaborators—teachers, parents, community members, agency representatives, or others—who will participate. Discuss and clarify specific roles and responsibilities for all involved.

Step Five: *Review Plans and Gather Resources*
Review your plans. Gather needed resources, such as books, newspaper articles, Web sites, and reference materials from partner agencies. Schedule any visits, guest speakers, or field trips. Note that these are good tasks for students to take on as they gain skills and experience.

Step Six: *Begin the Process of Service Learning in Action*
Initiate the process of investigation, preparation and planning, action, reflection, and demonstration. Encourage youth voice and choice as you move through the service learning process. Be flexible! Service learning works best when students are able to see their own ideas in action. Continue to look for opportunities for reflection.

Step Seven: *Assess the Service Learning Experience*
Once the demonstration and the closing reflection have been completed, review and assess the learning accomplished, the impact of the service, the planning process, the reciprocal benefits for all involved, and ways to improve for next time. Debrief with all partners.

Service Learning Vocabulary

During service learning, students develop or deepen their understanding of many terms. Some will be new and will add to their growing vocabularies. Here are some of the terms students are likely to encounter:

caring	implementation
helping	reflection
community	collaboration
respect	demonstration
need	documentation
purpose	outcomes
plan	interdependence
action	responsibility
skills	feedback
talents	commitment
interests	service
teamwork	civic participation
change	advocacy
resources	research
proposal	flexibility
contingency plan	reciprocity
preparation	

Discuss the words in class to enhance students' critical thinking skills. Use books and stories to broaden students' thinking and to generate discussion of these terms and concepts. Consider these ideas as well:

- Post a "word of the week" on a bulletin board.
- Use quotes containing the words to inspire thoughts about service and community involvement.
- Incorporate the words in writing assignments or dramatic activities.
- Keep an eye out for the words in news articles.
- Have students write about service learning for a school paper and include some of the terms.
- Ask students to develop a list of words that their peers will need to learn as they start working toward a more comprehensive service learning program; students can create a dictionary with definitions as a service to the school community.

See digital content for full-size reproducible pages.

An Author's Reflection

One evening around bedtime, when my daughters were much younger, my eldest asked, "When am I going to have adventures like you?" I turned that question around in my mind for some time, realizing that, like all young people, Ariel longed for the opportunity to extend herself into experiences unknown. In *Identity: A Novel*, author Milos Kundera defines *adventure* as a way to embrace the world. What a beautiful image, and one I hold for our children as they maneuver through our educational systems, weaving their own patterns of learning and understanding.

With service learning as an integral part of school life, young people have a greater likelihood of achieving a sense of self through experience. The mystery of "Why am I learning this subject?" is replaced with engagement. Studies that once seemed fragmented become interconnected. Learning occurs in the classroom *and* also in the nature preserve, senior center, and food bank. Young people interact with their community, whether by taking a short walk to read to preschoolers at a Head Start program or by extending their voices across the globe as advocates for children who are forced laborers. Wait for adventure? Just enter the world of service learning.

While action is essential, reflection remains a key aspect of service learning. What does reflection look like? In the book *Something Beautiful*, a young girl seeks what is beautiful in a neighborhood filled with trash, where people sleep in doorways and the word "Die" is painted on her front door. She asks her neighbors, "What is beautiful?" and finds a variety of responses: new shoes, a baby, a ripe red apple, a rock carried in a pocket for decades. She sits on her front stoop in reflection, looking at the trash and the graffiti. In this pause, she considers her ideas and her potential for making "something beautiful." Then she stands up, gets the supplies she needs, and scrubs the word "Die" right off her front door. In a society filled with busyness, finding time for reflection can seem like a chore. Reflection, however, actually gives us a way to sink knee-deep into experience and discover what is waiting to be revealed.

Author E. L. Konigsburg draws upon an age-old adage to teach about reflection. In her book *The Mixed-Up Files of Mrs. Basil E. Frankweiler*, two children run away from home and spend several adventurous nights hiding out in the Metropolitan Museum of Art. As their escapade ends, they meet eccentric Mrs. Frankweiler and ask her about the value of learning something new each day. This question has personal resonance as I treasure the memory of my mother's voice—joining the choir of mothers across the globe—asking me every day after school, "What did you learn today?" The question, of course, implies that learning every day is expected. This makes Mrs. Frankweiler's response all the more surprising when she disagrees, stating that, "You should also have days when you allow what is already in you to swell up inside of you until it touches everything. And you can feel it inside you. If you never take time out to let that happen, then you just accumulate facts, and they begin to rattle around inside you. You can make noise with them, but never really feel anything with them. It's hollow."*

Within service learning lies the balance: the dynamic of combining learning and action with thoughtful integration. A deep sense of purpose is here to be found, along with self-discovery, knowledge, the joy of collaboration, and the ability to apply our best efforts toward improving our planetary home.

Enjoy the journey—both the adventure and the reflection.

---

* From *The Mixed-Up Files of Mrs. Basil E. Frankweiler* (35th Anniversary edition) by E. L. Konigsburg, Simon & Schuster, p.153.

Resources

These organizations and agencies have made significant contributions to the expanding field of service learning through ongoing research and the development of outstanding materials and information.

ABCD Books

13108 Warren Avenue
Los Angeles, CA 90066
(310) 397-0070
www.abcdbooks.org

ABCD Books is author Cathryn Berger Kaye's Web portal for books, resources, and curriculum. Find articles to download, new publications, and information on scheduling Cathryn to speak at your conference, school or district, university, or organization on a variety of custom-designed themes. Check often to see special institutes being offered and find out when Cathryn is scheduled to come to your region.

America's Promise Alliance

1110 Vermont Avenue NW, Suite 900
Washington, DC 20005
(202) 657-0600
www.americaspromise.org

With more than 400 national partners, America's Promise Alliance is devoted to improving the lives of young people. The partners' collaborative work assists young people by promoting and providing resources for service learning and career exploration among middle school students as a strategy to increase high school graduation rates.

EarthEcho International

2101 L Street NW, Suite 800
Washington, DC 20037
(202) 350-3190
www.earthecho.org

EarthEcho International is a nonprofit organization whose mission is to empower youth to take action that protects and restores our water planet. EarthEcho International engages youth to effect global change by meeting local needs, helping them to understand the very real connections between community priorities and today's critical ocean and fresh water and related issues. This organization was founded by siblings Philippe and Alexandra Cousteau in honor of their father Philippe Cousteau Sr., famous son of the legendary explorer Jacques Yves Cousteau.

GenerationOn

281 Park Avenue South, 6th Floor
New York, NY 10010
(917) 746-8182
www.generationon.org

GenerationOn, a merger between New York's Children for Children and Points of Light Institute, brings together the world's largest network of volunteer action centers to offer K–12 service learning curricula, training and technical assistance, and resources to support service learning for teachers, families, and kids.

KIDS Consortium

1300 Old County Road
Waldoboro, ME 04572
(207) 620-8272
www.kidsconsortium.org

KIDS (Kids Involved Doing Service-Learning) Consortium is a nonprofit organization preparing young people to be active, responsible citizens by supporting educators, organizations, and youth in best practices for service learning. KIDS offers professional development, free Web site resources, and publications.

National Center for Learning and Civic Engagement

Education Commission of the States
700 Broadway, #810
Denver, CO 80203
(303) 299-3608
www.ecs.org/nclc

The National Center for Learning and Citizenship at the Education Commission of the States assists education leaders to promote, support, and reward citizenship education and service learning as essential components of America's education system. NCLC identifies and analyzes policies and practices that support effective service learning and citizenship education; disseminates analyses of best practices and policy trends; and convenes national, state, and local meetings to share information about service learning and citizenship education.

National Dropout Prevention Center

Clemson University
209 Martin Street
Clemson, SC 29631
(864) 656-2599
www.dropoutprevention.org

In their work to prevent student dropout, the National Dropout Prevention Center stresses the connection between service learning and student retention through its publications, videos, conferences, and workshops. The center also provides independent evaluations of service learning efforts.

National Service-Learning Clearinghouse

National Youth Leadership Council
1667 Snelling Avenue North, D300
Saint Paul, MN 55108
(651) 631-3672
gsn.nylc.org/clearinghouse

At this Web site, users can find materials for all grade levels, submit questions, find examples, and access documents about service learning. The Clearinghouse supports service learning in grades K–12, higher education, community-based initiatives, tribal programs, and programs for the general public.

National Youth Leadership Council

1667 Snelling Avenue North, Suite D300
St. Paul, MN 55108
(651) 631-3672
www.nylc.org

NYLC provides service learning training and produces publications, videos, and other resources for educators, youth, and other adults involved in service learning. Contact them for information on the Generator School Network, the National Service-Learning Conference, National Youth Leadership Training, and the WalkAbout Service-Learning Program.

The Providers' Network

Compass Institute
4253 Cottonwood Place
Saint Paul, MN 55127
(651) 787-0409
www.slprovidersnetwork.org

The Providers' Network is a global social network designed to assist those offering service learning professional development opportunities to collaborate and transform K–12 education and communities. The site offers a home page for members, over forty interest groups, standards, and a professional development library.

RMC Research Corporation

633 17th Street, Suite 2100
Denver, CO 80202
1-800-922-3636
www.rmcdenver.com

The RMC Research Corporation offers evaluation, research, technical assistance, and professional development opportunities, as well as help linking service learning to state and national education initiatives.

Roots & Shoots, a Program of the Jane Goodall Institute

1595 Spring Hill Road, Suite 550
Vienna, VA 22182
(703) 682-9220
www.rootsandshoots.org

Roots & Shoots is a nonprofit founded in 1991 by Dr. Jane Goodall and a group of Tanzanian students. The Roots & Shoots program empowers youth to design and implement community-based service learning projects to create lasting, positive change for people, animals, and the environment. With tens of thousands of young people in more than 120 countries, the Roots & Shoots network branches out around the globe connecting young people of all ages who share a common desire to make the world a better place.

What Kids Can Do
PO Box 603252
Providence, RI 02906
(401) 247-7665
www.whatkidscando.org

Using the Internet, print, and broadcast media, the What Kids Can Do organization demonstrates the power of what young people marginalized by poverty, race, and language can accomplish when taken seriously and given the opportunities and support needed. WKCD views youth as knowledge creators and brings their stories, advice, and resources to international attention and vice versa. The organization documents the good work of others and also sponsors projects.

Youth Service America
1101 15th Street NW, Suite 200
Washington, DC 20005
(202) 296-2992
www.ysa.org

Youth Service America improves communities by increasing the number and the diversity of young people committed to a lifetime of service, learning, leadership, and achievement. Initiatives include public mobilization campaigns such as Global Youth Service Day and Semester of Service; funding and recognition through grants and awards geared toward youth, educators, and program partners; and resources and trainings. Sign up for weekly briefings and grant alerts on YSA's Web site.

Index

Page numbers followed by f indicate forms or reproducibles.

About the Author

Cathryn Berger Kaye, M.A., enjoys books, nature, theater, writing, cooking, and the world of service learning. As a classroom teacher, she worked with grades K–12 in rural, suburban, and urban settings. Cathryn held positions in nonprofit organizations with local and national outreach developing service learning programs throughout the country. Now, through CBK Associates, she travels internationally as a well-respected, inspiring, and engaging keynote speaker and workshop and professional development leader. She assists state departments of education, university faculty and teacher education students, International Baccalaureate programs, school districts, and classroom teachers and administrators, and has helped corporations advance their civic and service agenda. Her on-site presentations cover a variety of issues such as service learning, literacy, civic engagement, youth leadership, engaging and effective teaching methods, and improving school climate and culture.

As an author, Cathryn's publications include *A Kids' Guide to Hunger & Homelessness; A Kids' Guide to Helping Others Read & Succeed; A Kids' Guide to Protecting & Caring for Animals; A Kids' Guide to Climate Change & Global Warming; Going Blue: A Teen Guide to Saving Our Oceans, Lakes, Rivers, & Wetlands;* and *Make a Splash! A Kid's Guide to Protecting Our Oceans, Lakes, Rivers, & Wetlands.* She has developed a comprehensive curriculum, *Strategies for Success with Literacy: A Learning Curriculum that Serves,* integrating high-level literacy skills with social and emotional development and service learning. Cathryn's articles appear online and in magazines such as *Principal Leadership* and *Middle Ground,* and she has assisted in the production of several publications for the National Service-Learning Clearinghouse. She also writes fiction and nonfiction stories and books for children and adults.

While Cathy has lived in many places and enjoys traveling, she is glad to feel the ocean breezes at home in Los Angeles. Most of all, she adores her family—husband Barry and two daughters, Ariel and Devora—who inspire her daily.

More Great Books from Free Spirit

Going Blue
A Teen Guide to Saving Our Oceans, Lakes, Rivers, & Wetlands
by Cathryn Berger Kaye, M.A.

*160 pp., full-color, illust., PB, 6" x 9".
Ages 11 & up.*

Real Kids, Real Stories, Real Change
Courageous Actions Around the World
by Garth Sundem
foreword by Bethany Hamilton

176 pp., two-color, PB, 5¼" x 7½". Ages 9–13

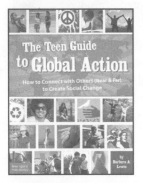

The Teen Guide to Global Action
How to Connect with Others (Near & Far) to Create Social Change
by Barbara A. Lewis

*144 pp., two-color, illust., PB, 7" x 9".
Ages 12 & up.*

Make a Splash!
A Kid's Guide to Protecting Our Oceans, Lakes, Rivers, & Wetlands
by Cathryn Berger Kaye, M.A.

*128 pp., full-color, photos, PB, 8" x 8".
Ages 8–12.*

The Kid's Guide to Service Projects
Over 500 Service Ideas for Young People Who Want to Make a Difference
(Updated 2nd Edition)
by Barbara A. Lewis

*160 pp., two-color, photos, PB, 6" x 9".
Ages 10 & up.*

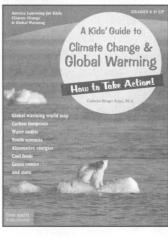

A Kids' Guide to Climate Change & Global Warming
How to Take Action!
by Cathryn Berger Kaye, M.A.

48 pp. Ages 10 & up.

A free download at www.freespirit.com
Other How to Take Action! series free downloads:

A Kids' Guide to Hunger & Homelessness
A Kids' Guide to Helping Others Read & Succeed
A Kids' Guide to Protecting & Caring for Animals

Join the Free Spirit Advisory Board

Teachers, Administrators, Librarians, Counselors, Youth Workers, and Social Workers
Help us create the resources you need to support the kids you serve.

In order to make our books and other products even more beneficial for children and teens, the Free Spirit Advisory Board provides valuable feedback on content, art, title concepts, and more. You can help us identify what educators need to help kids think for themselves, succeed in school and life, and make a difference in the world. Apply today! For more information, go to **www.freespirit.com/educators.**

> **Interested in purchasing multiple quantities and receiving volume discounts?**
> Contact edsales@freespirit.com or call 1.800.735.7323 and ask for Education Sales.
>
> **Many Free Spirit authors are available for speaking engagements, workshops, and keynotes.**
> Contact speakers@freespirit.com or call 1.800.735.7323.

For pricing information, to place an order, or to request a free catalog, contact:

Free Spirit Publishing Inc. • 6325 Sandburg Road • Suite 100 • Golden Valley, MN 55427-3674
toll-free 800.735.7323 • local 612.338.2068 • fax 612.337.5050 • help4kids@freespirit.com • www.freespirit.com